Data Rights Law 3.0

- Key Research Project of Key Laboratory of Big Data Strategy
- Key Research Project of Beijing Key Laboratory of Urban Science Research Based on Big Data
- Publishing Fund Project of the Think Tank Program of Beijing Cosmopolis Cultural Exchange Foundation

Data Rights Law 3.0

The Legislative Prospect

Key Laboratory of Big Data Strategy

Edited by Lian Yuming

社会科学文献出版社
SOCIAL SCIENCES ACADEMIC PRESS(CHINA)

PETER LANG
Oxford • Bern • Berlin • Bruxelles • New York • Wien

Bibliographic information published by Die Deutsche Bibliothek
Die Deutsche Bibliothek lists this publication in the Deutsche Nationalbibliografie; detailed bibliographic data is available on the Internet at http://dnb.ddb.de.

A catalogue record for this book is available at the British Library.

Library of Congress Control Number: 2021909767

A CIP catalog record for this book has been applied for at the Library of Congress.

Cover design: Brian Melville for Peter Lang

ISBN 978-1-80079-434-4 (print)
ISBN 978-1-80079-435-1 (ePDF)
ISBN 978-1-80079-436-8 (ePub)

Published by Peter Lang Ltd, International Academic Publishers,
52 St Giles, Oxford, OX1 3LU, United Kingdom
oxford@peterlang.com, www.peterlang.com

Academically supported by
The Research Center of Data Rights Law in China University of Political Science and Law

Specially supported by
The Research Base of Key Laboratory of Big Data Strategy in Zhejiang University
and
The Research Base of Key Laboratory of Big Data Strategy in China University of Political Science and Law

Institute Introduction

Key Laboratory of Big Data Strategy, established in April 2015, is an interdisciplinary, professional, international and open research platform co-founded by the Guiyang Municipal People's Government and Beijing Municipal Science and Technology Commission. It is a new-type, high-level think tank for the researches on Chinese big data development.

Relying on the Global City Development Corporation Council, Beijing (GDCC) and the Guiyang Innovation-Driven Development Strategy Research Institute (GDI), the Key Laboratory of Big Data Strategy established two research centers in Beijing and Guiyang, which set up five research bases, respectively: the research base in the China National Committee for Terms in Sciences and Technologies, the research base in Zhejiang University; the research base in China University of Political Science and Law, the research base of Shanghai Academy of Science and Technology; and the multilingual service research base in GTCOM. In Guizhou Province, three research platforms were approved and established, respectively, the Block Data Theory and Applicable Innovation Research Base, the Big Data Applicable Innovation Research Base for Urban Space Decision, and the Big Data Innovation in Culture Research Base. The "two centers, five research bases, and three research platforms" created a new research system and a regional collaborative innovation pattern.

In recent years, the Key Laboratory of Big Data Strategy has devoted itself to theoretical research of the new order of digital civilization, and published the "trilogy of digital civilization" successively, that is, *Block Data, Data Rights Law*, and *Sovereignty Blockchain*. Further, *Big Data Terminology*, compiled and published by the Key Laboratory of Big Data Strategy, has been recognized and recommended by the Chinese National Committee in terms of science and technologies and International Knowledge Center for Engineering Sciences and Technology under the Auspices of UNESCO.

Editor's Profile

Professor Lian Yuming
Doctor of Engineering
Member of the CPPCC National Committee
Vice Chairman of the Beijing Chaoyang District People's Political Consultative Conference
President of Global City Development Corporation Council, Beijing
Director of the Research Center of Data Rights Law in China University of Political Science and Law

Professor Lian Yuming is a renowned urban development expert in China. He is member of the Experts Consultative Committee for the People's Government of Beijing, chief expert in the Research Base of Beijing-Tianjin-Hebei Coordinated Development, as well as director of the Beijing Key Laboratory of Urban Science Research Based on Big Data. His research focuses mainly on urbanology, the science of decision-making, and sociology. His master works include a trilogy on new urbanism: *Awakening of the City, Strategy of the City, and Wisdom of the City*.

Professor Lian Yuming is also chief consultant to the CPC Guiyang Municipal Committee and Guiyang Municipal People's Government, president of Guiyang Innovation-Driven Development Strategy Research Institute and director of the Key Laboratory of Big Data Strategy. His representative publications include *Block Data*: *The Signal of the Arrival of Big Data Time*; *Block Data 2.0*: *Paradigm Revolution in the Era of Big Data*; *Block Data 3.0*: *Order Internet and Sovereignty Blockchain*; *Block Data 4.0*: *Activation Dataology in the Age of Artificial Intelligence*; *Block Data 5.0*: *Theories and Methods of Data Sociology*; *Data Rights Law 1.0*: *The Theoretical Basis* (published in simplified Chinese, English, French, German and traditional Chinese); *Data Rights Law 2.0*: *The System Construction* (published in simplified Chinese, English, and traditional Chinese);

Sovereignty Blockchain 1.0: Orderly Internet and Community with a Shared Future for Humanity; and *Blue Book of Big Data - Annual Report on Development of Big Data in China (No. 1–No. 4)*. He also edited and published *Big Data Terminology*, which is the first multilingual professional reference book to comprehensively and systematically study the standard terminology system of big data in the world.

Editorial Board

Translation Committee

Senior Translators	Li Zhangxian, Liu Yan
Translators	Li Zhangxian (Preface, Postscript, etc.)
	Liu Muqing, Liu Congying (Chapter 1)
	Guan Xiangying, Sun Baoling (Chapter 2)
	Zhang Xuecheng, Cheng Zhaoying (Chapter 3)
	Wei Xinghui, Zhou Yingzhen (Chapter 4)
	Zhang Weihua, Zhang Mingda (Chapter 5)
Translation Reviewers	Yue Ling, Xi Jinting

Contents

Tables

Editor's Foreword

Currently, a global pandemic intertwines with radical changes in the world, all unseen in a century, pushing for the transition from the old to the new world order. Just as the financial crisis of 2008 changed the world pattern, the current Covid-19 pandemic is accelerating changes in the world's economic pattern, interest pattern, security pattern and governance pattern formed in the industrial era over the last century. The year of 2020 may be a turning point for mankind, moving from an industrial society to a digital one. Previous societal changes have always triggered innovations in the legal world, and such innovations have now advanced ahead of time because of the global spread of Covid-19 and the transformation to a digital era. This new era requires a renewed enlightenment and space to develop a new society. It is exactly against this background that block data, data rights law, and sovereignty blockchain book series, as the "digital civilization trilogy" have been developed. Through years of hard work, the research paradigm of data rights law has made a leap from concept to theory and, thereafter, to rules; and this transformation has enabled us to acquire a new understanding and make new assessments of the development of the rule of law in the digital age.

First, a global data legal system has not yet been formed. The digital age has witnessed the loss of security control, misalignment of laws, immoral behaviors, ethical disorder, privacy compromise, and other risks that have become increasingly complex. In the context of digitalization, networking, and intelligent development, the traditional understanding and regulation of the digital world by force of law, the rule of law, and legal principles have encountered theoretical dilemmas and practical shortcomings that are difficult to deal with. This situation is closely related to the high complexity and uncertainty in the digital world, together with the development of the rule of law in the digital age, which is more challenging. The existing institutional supply cannot meet the increasing demands for data rights. Moreover, the global data legal system is far from being formed; data supervision has been absent for a long time, and there remains a lacuna in related laws. At the same time, the scale of global digital economy is constantly expanding, and the digital economy in China is entering a golden period of rapid development. A critical period has arrived for the formulation of a groundbreaking basic law for the digital age.

Second, data legislation is still behind what development requires. The use of data has become an important source of wealth, and the protection of data rights has become an important symbol of a digital society. From an objective point of view, global data legislation generally lags behind the development of the digital economy, the transformation towards a digital era, and the progress of this new digital society; and this is reflected more vividly in today's rapid technological development. For a long time, China has been a learner, an adaptor, and a follower of international data rules, showing limited ability to set agendas for the world in this regard. This does not match its role and status as a major country of the world stage. Therefore, it is necessary for us to carry out extensive and in-depth theoretical innovation and legislative exploration to expand the reserves of international data governance policies and the research of governance rules.

Third, data legislation is showing a clearer tendency toward decentralization. We are in an era when laws fall into various categories, and in every category new laws have been formulated or are being formulated, so the number of new laws is increasing. In fact, the world is moving toward an era of system integration, and the legal system is gradually transforming from classification to integration. In the digital age, we are faced with many complex problems, whose solution does not lie in specialized laws. Instead, the more complex the structural relationships are, the greater the need for a more systematic method to provide the solution. So far, the regulation of data protection is scattered in multiple branches of law, such as civil law, criminal law, economics law, and administrative law, which gives rise to issues such as legal repetition, fragmentation, inconsistency, and vacuum. The research of data rights law is accelerating the formation of a unique legal field, and the "fragmentation" of the data rights system urgently requires legislative cohesion so as to achieve a systematic and codified legal expression.

Fourth, experience can be drawn from foreign data legislations. Only by taking an international perspective, establishing a global mindset, and focusing on the world and the future, can we resolve the most forward-looking and complex issues in the digital era. Nowadays, more than 140 countries and international organizations around the world have enacted data protection laws, and dedicated legislation for data protection has become an international practice. With the rise of big data, blockchains, artificial intelligence and other technologies, many countries in the world have launched a new round of revising their data protection laws. In China, by way of contrast, the related theory and practice has sufficiently developed, but concrete systems still remain in their infancy. Therefore, we gathered more than 600 data compliance policies from around the world to develop the blueprint and translated foreign data legal documents to form the *Data Rights Law Translation Collection*, covering nearly 100 countries and international organizations and nearly twenty languages. Thereafter, we compared and analyzed relevant provisions to provide a theoretical basis and reference for China's ongoing legislation process in the digital field. We aim to bring the best of foreign experience into the formulation of the data rights law system with Chinese characteristics so that the Chinese system can be more inclusive, international, and farsighted.

Fifth, new branches of law are in the making. In recent years, computational law, digital law, intelligent law and other new branches of law have appeared one after another, forming a unique legal research field with data law at the core. The data rights law is a systematic integration of Chinese and western legal concepts for better global governance, and an institutional innovation against the background of a digital society. The aim of the data rights law is to analyze the influence of future social relations using existing legal systems and legal theories to find out the appropriate response, and further to construct a common rule system which keeps up with the times and adapts well to the global cyberspace governance. We call for the establishment of legal discipline, an academic system and a discourse system in the digital age under the guidance of data rights law, so as to promote the reform of the global governance system of the Internet and make a contribution to the construction of a community with a shared future for mankind.

Lian Yuming
Director of Key Laboratory of Big Data Strategy
Director of the Research Center of Data Rights Law in China
University of Political Science and Law
March 10, 2021

INTRODUCTION

What Kind of Data Rights Law Do We Need

Have you ever thought of an echo world, where everything is the same as in this current world? The movie *Redivider* tells us a fantastic story of the echo world. Today, such a fantasy is becoming a reality, and the development of digital technology is accelerating the migration of human beings from a physical space to a digital space. This grand immigration has already begun but many people are still totally out of it. Everything is changing too quickly, everything is scary, and everything is possible and attractive, too. We know very little about this world, but worry a lot. What can we do today if we are hoping for a better future? What decisions to make and what changes to push for? These are questions we need to ponder. The digital world is a common space for the development of mankind, and all countries share the obligation and responsibility to govern this digital world. Deepening mutual trust, creating collective governance, and improving the rules for the development of the digital world are important prerequisites for promoting the transformation of the global cyberspace governance system of networks, important choices for building a community with a shared future in cyberspace, and important guarantees for promoting sustainable development of the digital world.

I Data Rights Legislation: Three Balances

The balance between data protection and data utilization. Both data protection and utilization are important parts of the development of the digital industry. Traditional civil law attaches great importance to the protection of privacy when it comes to data and personal information, which is based on the principle that personal life should not be disturbed, and that data disclosure is controlled by the subject who should be respected to the maximum extent. As the application of digital technology deepens, the development of society relies more on the mining and use of data, and partial emphasis on data protection can no longer effectively meet the needs of social development.[1] Therefore, the first things to balance in the process of data rights legislation are data protection and data use; namely, how to regulate the collection, storage, and utilization of data (especially personal data) in the process of data mining, analyzing, and using, while effectively avoiding data leakage and abuse to ensure data security. To achieve such a balance, it is urgent that we build a dynamic equilibrium mechanism which encourages use and ensures effective protection.

The balance between the right to share and the right of privacy. The core of data rights is the right to share, which, as a system constructed based on the culture of altruism, deals with data sharing. The core of privacy is to realize unique personality interests through the control of the degree of openness to others. Data sharing and privacy protection in the digital age are in conflict in the fields of the self-determination of privacy, privacy in personal space, and information privacy, resulting from the game between public and private interests as well as the divergence between data property interests and personality interests in the new technological context. To maximize the value of data resources and strike a balance between the multiple interests involved, with the conflicts between the rights to share and the right of privacy, data rights legislation should follow some basic principles, such as the principle of public interest priority, the principle of derogation, the principle of proportionality, and the principle of equal protection. In addition, for data sharing, we aim to clarify its boundaries and limitations, set strict procedures thereto, strengthen supervision, and

1 See Zhu Xinli, and Zhou Xu Yang. 2018. "The Balance of Personal Data Utilization and Protection in the Era of Big Data – The Proposal of 'Resource Access Model'." *Journal of Zhejiang University (Humanities and Social Sciences Edition)*, 1st issue.

improve the liability and remedy mechanism of privacy infringement through specific legislation.

The balance between domestic law and international law. Domestic law and international law are parallel legal systems, the coordinated development of which is a basic requirement of contemporary international practice. We are not only against the erroneous tendency of denying generally accepted norms of international law by enacting domestic laws, but also object to negating national sovereignty through international law under the guise of human rights. Today, the world pattern is undergoing unprecedented changes and transformation, and mankind has entered a new era with numerous challenges and risks. In this regard, China provided the idea of a community with a shared future for mankind, which is a Chinese plan offered to people all over the world for the permanent and peaceful development of mankind. Under the guidance of this concept, international law can benefit from traditional Chinese culture and move from a perspective of conflict to of one of sharing in legislation. The theory of legal sharing is, instead of choosing one correct option from a number of conflicting laws, an approach that compares the laws of all countries involved and all related provisions from the perspective of substantial justice, according to the principle of proportionality so as to obtain the most reasonable and harmonious judgment. Based on innovations in science and technology, data rights law blazes new trails in the field of legal humanities; its core is to solve problems concerning the right to share. With altruism at the core, data rights law advocates the concept of legal sharing; reconstructs the discourse and value system of contemporary international law on the basis of the harmonious coexistence of the multiple cultures of all countries in the world; explores new ways to solve legal conflicts; and creates an international legal community with data rights at the core so as to push forward the building of a community with a shared future for mankind.

II Data Rights Legislation: Four Problems

The problem of subject. Who will take the responsibility for decisions on personal data? Who has the sovereign right to own, use, make a transaction, share, and process the data? How is the ownership of data to be protected? These problems need to be resolved in data rights legislation. Personal data, as the core part of the data used by enterprises, as well as a major area of security risks, is the focus of protection in data legislation and management in various countries. As the object of personal data, individuals have a status similar to the "owner" of their personal data and this status has been recognized by legislation, and their rights are also developing. For example, through *The General Data Protection Regulation* and other similar legal documents, the European Union has established a model of personal data rights that clearly includes the right to data portability, the right to know, the right to choose, the right to rectification, the right to erasure, the right to obtain freely, the right to claim, the right to be forgotten, and the right to revoke authorization. Conversely, personal data legislation in China is relatively scattered, and is mainly provided in the *Civil Code of the People's Republic of China.* Despite the two methods for the protection of personal data rights from the *Civil Code* – the right to claim in person and the right to claim in tort –many problems still exist in the legal remedy of personal data rights in the *Civil Code*, such as the blocked channels of civil compensation relief, the unclear liability undertaker in personal data infringement cases, the high cost of pursuing judicial relief for individual citizens, the long period of time required for the protection of legitimate rights and interests, the difficulty of providing evidence for victims, and the low cost of criminal acts against personal data, which leads to the repeated emergence of cases relating to infringement of personal data rights.

The problem of management. First, there are obvious defects in the current legislation of data rights in China, which is mainly reflected by the fact that there is no legal interpretation to define the legislation's specific object; the incomplete rights of the data subject; the question of whether legal persons and unincorporated organizations are entitled to proper subject rights; and imperfect rights, obligations, and legal responsibilities. Therefore, the number of cases of personal data infringements is increasing. And, due to the frequent occurrence of telecommunications fraud and malicious harassment brought about by personal data leakage, the personal and property rights of citizens are under great threat.

Second, there lacks relevant implementation rules in the judicial practice relating to data rights, which leads to vast discretionary power. Moreover, since there are no unified criteria for the determination of "serious circumstances" and "especially serious circumstances," the broad discretion of judges resulted in different judgments for similar cases in judicial practice.

Third, it is difficult to reach a balance between encouraging the development of relevant industries and effective supervision. The highly uncertain digital industry is always facing changes in terms of industrial paths, risk return, and market confidence, which challenges the traditional government supervision policy and the applicability of rules, and brings new problems to the goal and content of the governance of the industry.

The problem of technology. Technology is a key. It can open the door to heaven, and also that to hell. Which door it opens depends on the guidance and regulation of law: "We are in an area where technological developments are bringing about changes in human nature" (Xie Fang 2013).[2] The physical space and the digital space are merging, and digitalization will become the most important way of human existence. Science is about seeking truth while law is about seeking good. Truth-seeking itself cannot guarantee that its direction is correct. As the ancient saying goes, "They all regard that they were doing good according to the rules, but they did not know the true reason why they should do it." Only under the combined guidance of digital technology represented by blockchain and good law and governance represented by data rights can we move toward in the direction of the best for the development of mankind and ensure that science and technology does good. Wang Yangming, a great philosopher of the Ming Dynasty in ancient China, said that all men have a conscience.

2 Xiefang. 2013. "Science Fiction, Futurology and the Future Era." *Chinese Social Sciences Today*, January 25, A5.

Conscience is the ability that man is born with to distinguish between good and evil. Good is the ability and effort to achieve for yourself and others, to achieve for the world, and to bring more beauty, love, and light to the world. The proposal of technology for social good is based on the need of human beings for free living, development and liberation, and shows that science is rich in humanistic care and humanity is full of scientific wisdom, which means that people have a better understanding of the relationship between mankind and science and technology. "Technology is an ability and being good is an option." The jurisprudence culture of data rights law is about altruism and sharing, which in turn realizes the conscience of law and promotes technology for social good. Under the guidance of an altruistic and sharing culture, science and technology, and law will merge while being independent; be in harmony while remaining different with an appropriate level of tension between them. People will live in harmony with nature and society, and living and non-living beings will coexist in good coordination.

The problem of future. The history of human society, in the final analysis, is a history of connections. We are connected by traffic routes, communication links, the internet, and now data. These links constantly reconstruct social order. Throughout the legal history of the world, law has gone through stages of law for ethnic groups, law for city-states, national law, and international group law. With the development of digital technology, law is bound to enter this field. From the agricultural age to the industrial age, human laws have experienced thousands of years of accumulation and transition, but the digital age will not give us as much time to prepare for and adapt to it. While people enjoy the cyberspace for it breaks the boundaries of time and space in traditional society, some individuals also try to break the legal rules of traditional society by using digital technologies and the virtual space. Can we continue to use the traditional legal rules and how? How do we apply it effectively? Actually, all countries in the world have to reconstruct their legal rules. For the future, legal research should focus on the system of risk prevention, the system of legal subjects, and the system that can guarantee the freedom and equality of natural persons in the digital society. To construct these systems, we must face up to the interest balance and the value connections behind them. To this end, data rights law will be focused on the following questions: Will the changes of digital social relations bring about significant changes in legal relations? In what ways will these significant legal relations change? What major impacts will they have on the current provisions of legal relations? If existing social phenomena are only a seed, in order to make sure that it grows into what mankind needs it to become in the digital world, we must use digital rights law as shears to prune it, so that it will not grow rampantly to a state that will ultimately endanger the survival of mankind.

III Data Rights Legislation: Five Major Relationships

Basic positioning of data rights law in relation to other laws. For one thing, there is the relationship with the civil code. The civil code is a private law, which mainly regulates the personal relationships and property relationships between equal subjects. However, data rights law is a deep integration of public law and private law. On the one hand, it provides private law protection for data through the data rights system and the civil procedural mechanism based on it; on the other hand, by establishing special government regulatory agencies and formulating mandatory legal norms, imposing fines, and other administrative supervision means, it protects data in the way a public law provides protection. From this point of view, the data rights law and the civil law are not in a relationship of special law and general law, but two parallel laws with overlapping areas. For another thing, there is the relationship with cyber security law, data security law, and personal information protection law. From a functionalist point of view, data security law is the central law that embodies the holistic approach to national security in the digital sphere and focuses on the national security issues related to important data, while data rights law is based on data rights, focusing on data markets and resource allocation, data ownership confirmation and the corresponding powers and functions, open data and data sharing, data circulation and transaction, data security and compliance, and so on. As for network security law, the part of it that involves data will be gradually absorbed and replaced by data rights law and data security law, while the remaining part will focus instead on classified network security protection 2.0, critical infrastructure protection, and network security review systems. Therefore, data rights law is the basic law in the digital field; it, together with network security law, data security law, and personal information protection law, will build a holistic framework for data protection and data utilization.

Content of data rights: expansion vs. limitation. The right to privacy is prescribed in the *Civil Code of the People's Republic of China* as follows: "A natural person enjoys the right to privacy. No organization or individual may infringe upon the other's right to privacy by prying into, intruding upon, disclosing, or publicizing other's private matters." However, the *Civil Code* only defines personal information as "interest", not a "right," and provides that "A natural person's personal information is protected by law." Besides, the contents of the interest of personal information are limited to this: "A natural person may retrieve or make copies of his personal information... Where the person discovers that the information is incorrect, he has the right to raise an objection and request corrections or other necessary measures to be taken in a timely manner... Where a natural person discovers that an information processer has violated the provisions of laws or administrative regulations, or breached the agreement between both parties while processing his personal information, he has the right to request the information processor to delete it in a timely manner." In the case of *Ren Jiayu v. Baidu Co, Ltd*, the court held that the "right to be forgotten" does not exist in Chinese law and is unique to *The EU General Data Protection Regulation*. So why should we protect an individual's data rights? On the one hand, the violations of personal data rights such as a data black market, data leakage, and data abuse are serious. As Zang Tiewei, spokesman of the National People's Congress, pointed out, "The problems of random collection, illegal acquisition, excessive use, and illegal trading of personal information, and the use of these information to disturb the peaceful life of the people and endanger the lives, health, and property of the people are still very serious." On the other hand, digital rights are of great significance to the development of China's digital economy. If the digital economy is the "trunk" and "crown" of a tree, where we see clear advantages, then data rights will be the "roots" under the ground, invisible but playing an important role. Therefore, the construction of a digital rights system is particularly important. So we need to have in-depth and detailed debates to determine, in addition to the current rights of informed consent, consultation, reproduction, rectification, and erasure, whether we should add the right to be forgotten, the right of data portability, data property rights, and other kinds of rights. At the same time, the process of making provisions for existing data rights in current laws needs to be more systematic, targeted, and operable by adopting better legislative techniques.

Supervisory authorities: specialization vs. comprehensiveness. The EU *General Data Protection Regulation* requires that each member state shall provide for independent public authorities the responsibility for monitoring the application of the regulation, and grant these bodies investigative, corrective, authorization, and advisory powers. Besides which, it constructs a set of framework for an administrative relief system, under which each supervisory authority shall properly handle complaints lodged by a data subject. By way of contrast, the Federal Trade Commission, which is responsible for privacy protection enforcement, was established at the federal level; however, various industries in the United States still adopt a mode of classified regulation such as the US Consumer Financial Protection Bureau in the field of financial data, the US Department of Health and Human Services in the area of health care data, the US Department of Education in the field of educational data, and so on. So, should we set up an independent data regulatory agency for data rights law like the EU to solve the problem of scattered law enforcement caused by the failure to clearly define and divide the responsibilities of the government, enterprises, the capital market, and public institutions; or should we maintain the status quo and adopt a comprehensive governance model like the Federal Trade Commission and other agencies in the US? For the reason that data rights legislation objectively involves responsibilities of various fields and departments, and the threshold for law enforcement in financial, health care, and other specialized industries is high, establishing a new independent data regulatory body cannot actually solve the problem, but will weaken data supervision and law enforcement to a certain extent, and finally affect the implementation of national provisions. Therefore, it is suggested that the US model of data regulation be adopted. For example, the *Personal*

Information Protection Law of People's Republic of China (Draft) states that the national cyberspace authority shall play its coordinating role and be responsible for the overall coordination of the protection of personal information, while the national cyberspace authority and other departments concerned under the State Council shall, within the scope of their respective authorities, be responsible for the protection, supervision, and control of personal information.

Legal liability: strict or loose. "Legal responsibility, as a safeguard mechanism for the operation of the law, is an indispensable part of the rule of law" (Zhang Wenxian 2001, p. 101).[3] Except constitutional law, law for organization, law for authorization, and so on, there are basic provisions on legal liability in every country's legal system. For example, the *EU General Data Protection Regulation* not only provides administrative fines, which can be up to 20,000,000 euros or, in the case of undertaking, up to 4 percent of the total worldwide annual turnover in the preceding financial year, but also includes mandatory measures such as issuing warnings and reprimands. Stipulations on liability in data rights legislation is a process that seeks balance. Thus, it is necessary to have sufficient deterrent power, for example, by substantially increasing financial penalties; however, it should be noted that the criminal law cannot be applied at will, otherwise there will be a great threat to the development of the data industry. At the same time, strict legal responsibility must be concomitant with flexible enforcement of the law. For this, He Yuan, a Chinese professor, advocates that we should build an administrative compromise agreement system that takes the establishment of a data compliance mechanism as a condition for the application of this reconciliation procedure, introduce data compliance clauses into the agreement, timely announce the conclusion to interested parties, and set a specified test period to provide the enterprise with the opportunity to comply with the law.

Legal integration: the relationship between domestic law and international rules. International law, including public international law and private international law, is the sum of norms that have legal effect on

3 Zhang Wenxian. 2001. *On the Category of Law Philosophy*. Beijing: China University of Political Science & Law Press.

more than two countries, and prescribe the rights and obligations of the subjects. As a system of rules, international law covers most state activities. In contrast, domestic law is a general term for the internal legal system of a sovereign state. In modern times, international law and domestic law together constitute the complete legal system of human society. For data rights legislation, the future trend will be to seek common ground rather than to emphasize differences, and the importance of coordination and cooperation will be more prominent. To a certain extent, it can even be necessary for countries to transfer some of their judicial sovereignty so as to avoid situations where the divergent data rights laws and regulations in various countries evade legal boundaries. So, it has become inevitable that an international legal community be established. Considering that there exists a close relationship between laws and ideology, and values and national interests, the globalization of law needs not only the convergence of legal norms, but also that of culture and values. Thus, the international legal community needs to be constructed on the basis of a common value pursuit and belief in the rule of law. By reason that data is the most basic element in cyberspace, data rights become the most basic rights, and safeguarding national data sovereignty and protecting citizens' personal data rights should become a common rule. On this basis, it is probably not surprising that data rights law may become the common basic norm of global governance in cyberspace, aiming to guide, regulate, and restrain the behavior of each country in the legal governance of cyberspace, and to coordinate the rights and obligations of all countries in the management of cyberspace.

CHAPTER 1

Value Orientation of Data Rights Legislation

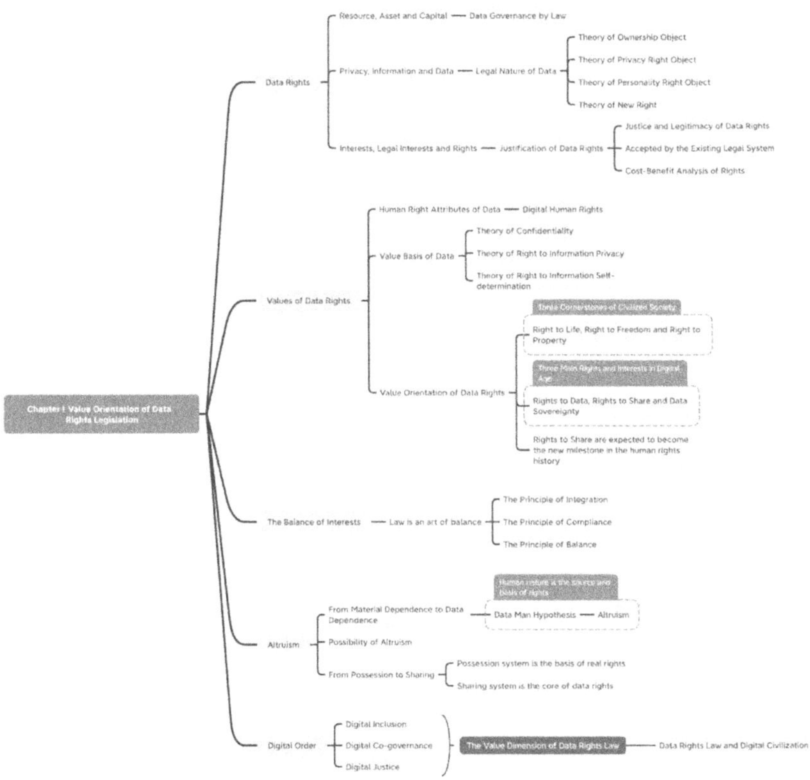

In today's world, human society is evolving toward networking, digitalization, and intelligent development, bringing unprecedented uncertainty to social, national, and global governance. With the global spread of the Covid-19 pandemic, our dependence on governance technology has been highlighted and intensified, and the question about how to promote the modernization of the digital governance system and governance capability involves many legal issues that urgently require legal research to respond to and explore. Uncertainty and certainty are the essential attributes of law. In most cases, uncertainty is a manifestation of neutrality. Only when uncertainty profoundly affects our cognition and practice, will it become a problem (Liu Zegang 2020, p. 49). Data rights law, as a scientific proposition, the theme of our times, and a legal research topic, is becoming our legal response to the digital age, our assessment of the general trend in the future development of technology, society and rule of law, and a legal interpretation of human civilization's march from an industrial to a digital society. Moreover, it is expected to be an innovative prescription for reforming the global cyberspace governance system and building a community with a shared future in cyberspace. Society keeps moving forward while legislation tends to lag behind. Laws are fixed, while legal principles are flexible. Only when fixed laws are interpreted with flexible legal principles can laws keep better up with the times. Therefore, to study the value orientation and conceptual pursuit of data rights is both necessary and urgent so as to improve the legal system of data rights. The primary issue in legislation is not the establishment of rules and legal systems, but the choice of a value orientation. Legislative activities are the process of setting rules and weighing values. Data rights legislation is no exception. Concerning data rights legislation, the core issue is the balance of interests; the basic orientation is altruistic sharing; and the purpose is to create a digital order.

Data Rights

The issue about the concept of data, i.e., whether it is a right or just an interest, is crucial to many other issues related to data, such as the definition of the legal nature of data, the scope of data protection, and the legal protection hierarchy. As Karl Marx put it, "Laws shall be based on society." The Second Industrial Revolution, especially the prosperity of journalism, gave birth to the concept of right to privacy. The Third Industrial Revolution, especially the development of computers, stimulated the need for personal information protection, and the drive of data technology and data economy prompted the emergence of digital human rights. Data empowerment is bound to happen. In this age of rights, empowerment by law seems to be the paradigm of legitimacy. Hence, data rights have naturally become the cornerstone of data rights law. "Legislation is the process of understanding and expressing interests. To balance among various interests, we will have to primarily establish the understanding and recognition of interests" (Guo Daohui 1997, p. 10).

Resource, Asset, and Capital

It is an inevitable trend in big data development that data is becoming a kind of resource, asset, and capital. "We are stepping into the era of data capital."[1] In general, the development of data value moves through three different stages. In the first stage, namely the data resource stage, data is a kind of resource that records and reflects the real world. In the second stage, which is called the data asset stage, data is regarded as not only a kind of resource, but also an asset which constitutes an important part of personal or corporate assets, and the basis for wealth creation. In the third stage, which is the data capital stage, data's characteristics as a resource and asset are further developed and data is transformed into capital through transactions and other circulation methods.

1 Guo Yike, director of the Institute of Data Science at Imperial College London, summarized the development of the data economy into four stages: "The day before yesterday" of data is the stage of data materials. In this stage, data was only a record and measurement of the physical world. "Yesterday" of data refers to the stage of data products. Data became a resource and product when it was used to provide services. Then a series of data products and services came into emergence. "Today" of data is the stage of data assets. People have realized that the definition of data ownership makes it an asset and the basis for generating wealth. Data has become an important part of personal total assets. "Tomorrow" of data is the stage of data capital. This stage is the era when data assets are connected to their value. Data assets realize their value through circulation and transactions, and eventually become capital.

Data as a resource. Preliminary processing transforms data from a "raw state" into a more advanced state where it can be collected and used. Different from the agricultural and industrial economy, the most distinctive feature of the data economy is that data is taken as a key factor of production. However, unlike the traditional factors of production such as labor, land, and capital, data is unique in that it is renewable, pollution-free, and infinite. Renewability means that data resources are produced by human beings instead of being obtained from nature, and processed data can afterwards become a new data resource. Being pollution-free means that data doesn't pollute the environment in the process of obtaining and using it. Infinity means that the data resource increases rather than decreases while it is used. The more often traditional resources are used, the less of them there will be, while the more data resources are used, the more data there will be.

Data as an asset. When data resource is combined with application scenarios, data will be endowed with practical value and undergo a qualitative change. With the development of digital economy, people have discovered that data is not just a kind of resource, but also carries the attribute of an asset. Assets are resources formed through a company's past business transactions, or various other matters, owned or controlled by the company, and expected to bring economic benefits to it. By definition, assets have three basic characteristics: actual existence, controllability, and economic identity. Actual existence indicates that assets must already exist, and things that haven't happened cannot be called assets. Controllability means that an enterprise owns the assets or has the right to control them. Economic identity means that assets are expected to bring economic benefits to the enterprise. Considering the above characteristics, data assets refer to data formed during the production, operation, and management activities of an enterprise, which can be possessed or controlled during the entire process of their application; this kind of data is also quantifiable and expected to bring economic benefits. The course of data's acquisition of these characteristics, and of being controllable, quantifiable, and realizable, reflects the value of the data, which is also the process of turning data into assets.

Data capitalization. It refers to the process of realizing the social allocation of data elements through data transactions and circulation. *The Rise of Data Capital*, jointly released by MIT Technology Review and Oracle, pointed out that data is now a form of capital, on the same level as financial capital in terms of generating new products and services. However, unlike capital in physical forms, data is non-rivalrous and non-fungible. Being non-rivalrous means that while physical capital cannot be used by multiple people at the same time, data capital can be used by an unlimited number of parties due to its reproducibility. Being non-fungible means that physical capital can be replaced, but data cannot. For instance, you can substitute one barrel for another, but a piece of data can't be substituted with another, because each piece of data carries different information and value. The process of data capitalization is the process of converting the value and use value of data assets into shares or capital contribution ratios, and turning them into capital through data transactions. In other words, the value of data as capital can only be fully reflected in the flow of data (Zhang Li 2019, pp. 6–8). This has caused major challenges in various circles, that is, the challenge of data property rights. Only when the issue of data property rights is clarified can data transactions acquire the premise and foundation of successful development.

The current wave of globalization is called hyper-globalization, which is different from what it was before the 1980s. Globalization from the end of World War II to the 1980s was based on the sovereign economic system, while the current wave features the global distribution of production factors. Worldwide, digital technology and the digital economy have become the focus of global competition. The digital revolution, and intelligent transformation, is bringing new changes to key production factors; digital resources such as data, algorithms, and computing power are becoming strategic factor resources. As the ancient saying goes, "If laws are adjusted to the time, there is good governance. If governance keeps up with the times, it will be highly effective." When data has become a production factor legislation must keep up with such a change and protect data just as it protects land, labor, capital, technology, and knowledge as production factors. Therefore, the legal positioning and legal protection of data as a production factor has become the most urgent issue at the moment; data objectively carries all the characteristics that production factors share in distribution, and individuals should be allocated corresponding rights to disposition, and the right to earnings in accordance with their data ownership. Our understanding of market-oriented allocation rules for this new production factor is still at an exploratory stage, and there are still many issues related to data in property rights, market allocation, balance of interests, and protection, which need to be explored urgently.

Privacy, Information, and Data

In 1968, the concept of "data protection" was put forward at the International Conference on Human Rights held by the United Nations, so the year 1968 became known as the first year of the "data revolution." Subsequently, the concept of personal data was adopted into the legislation of many countries. Academia generally believes that the *Data Protection Act* (*Hessisches Datenschutzgesetz*) enacted by the State of Hesse, Germany, in 1970 is the first dedicated personal data protection law in the world; the *Data Act* adopted by Sweden in 1973 is the first nationwide law in the world that protects personal data; and the *General Data Protection Regulation* (GDPR) of the European Union, implemented in 2018, is the most stringent data protection law ever. This legislative topic, which originated in the State of Hesse, has spread to many countries and regions around the world in less than fifty years. Beginning in the 1970s, the Organization for Economic Co-operation and Development (OECD), the Asia-Pacific Economic Cooperation (APEC), and the European Union (EU) have successively issued rules, guidelines, and regulations concerning the protection of personal information. Meanwhile, more than 140 countries and regions have enacted laws to protect personal information. However, there is not, as yet, any consensus on what exactly the term "personal data" refers to in legislation. In general, there are mainly three basic legal concepts: personal privacy, personal information, and personal data. The relationship among them is like a "Gordian Knot," intertwined and difficult to distinguish, and the person who unties the knot would "become the ruler of Asia." The use of these concepts in the legislature, judiciary, and academia, both at home and overseas, has shown a certain degree of confusion. Especially, academia has shown great arbitrariness in using them. Therefore, it is necessary to make a clear distinction between these similar concepts so as to determine respective litigation remedies, otherwise compliance costs will probably increase without knowing it.

Table 1. Definition of Privacy, Information, and Data in Major Countries and International Organizations

	Countries/ Organizations	Laws	Definition
Privacy	China	*Civil Code*	Privacy is the tranquility of the private life of a natural person, and the private space, private activities, and private information that s/he is unwilling to be known to others.
Information	China	*Civil Code*	Personal information is various information recorded electronically or in other forms that can identify a specific natural person separately or in combination with other information, including a natural person's name, date of birth, identity card number, biological recognition information, address, telephone number, email address, health information, and whereabouts information, among others. Private information in personal information shall be governed by the provisions on privacy rights; where there are no provisions, the provisions on the protection of personal information shall apply.
	Japan	*Act on the Protection of Personal Information (個人情報の保護に関する法律)*	Personal information in this Act means that information relating to a living individual whereby a specific individual can be identified.
	South Korea	*Act on Personal Information Protection of Public Agencies (공공기관 개인정보 보호법)*	Personal information means any personal identifiable information relating to a living individual, including symbol, words, voice, sound, and video, by which an individual can be identified in combination with other information such as the name and identification number. (It also includes the information which, even if it by itself does not identify a particular individual, may be easily combined with other information to identify a particular individual.)

(*continued*)

Table 1. Continued

	Countries/ Organizations	Laws	Definition
	Canada	*Personal Information Protection and Electronic Documents Act*	Personal information means information about an identifiable individual.
	Australia	*Privacy Act*	Personal information means information or an opinion (including information or an opinion which is part of the database) about an identified individual, or an individual who is reasonably identifiable: (a) whether the information or opinion is true or not; and (b) whether the information or opinion is recorded in a material form or not.
	India	*Personal Data Protection Bill*	Personal data means data about or relating to a natural person who is directly or indirectly identifiable, having regard to any characteristic, trait, attribute or any other feature of the identity of such a natural person, or any combination of such features, or any combination of such features with any other information.
Data	Brazil	*General Data Protection Law (Lei Geral de Proteção de Dados Pessoais)*	Personal data is any information that is related to an identified or identifiable individual.

	European Union	*General Data Protection Regulation*	Personal data means any information relating to an identified or identifiable natural person ("data subject"); an identifiable natural person is one who can be identified, directly or indirectly, in particular by reference to an identifier such as a name, an identification number, location data, an online identifier or to one or more factors specific to the physical, physiological, genetic, mental, economic, cultural or social identity of that natural person.
	Singapore	*Personal Data Protection Act*	Personal data means data, whether true or not, about an individual who can be identified: (a) from that data; or (b) from that data and other information to which the organization has or is likely to have access.
	UK	*Data Protection Act*	Personal data means any information relating to an identifiable living individual. By reference to personal data, an individual can be identified, or a data controller can get access to other information to identify an individual.
	France	*Act NO.78–17 of 6 January 1978 on Data Processing, Data Files and Individual Liberties*	Personal data means any information relating to a natural person that can be detailed or identified indirectly by reference to an identification number or any one or more personal factors.
	Germany	*Federal Data Protection Act*	Personal data is any information of privacy or specific state that is related to an identified or identifiable individual (data subject).
		Data Protection Act of the State of Hesse (Hessisches Datenschutzgesetz)	Personal data is the personal and factual information that is related to a specific or identifiable natural person (data subject).

Source: Compiled by the authors based on public information.

Relationship between personal information and privacy. Privacy protection emerged during the Second Industrial Revolution while personal information protection arrived in the Third Industrial Revolution. Between the two there is neither an inclusive nor an overlapping relationship. Moreover, they differ in connotation and extension, value foundation, protection principle, function and power systems, and tort liability. In terms of connotation and extension, the *Civil Code* of China recognizes the right to privacy as an independent personality right so as to establish direct protection for citizens' privacy rights and interests, and makes a clear distinction between privacy and personal information. First of all, it is clearly distinguished in the title of Chapter VI of Book Four Personality Rights that "rights to privacy" and "personal information protection" are two different concepts. Secondly, there is a precise definition of "privacy": Privacy refers to the undisturbed private life of a natural person and his private space, private activities, and private information that he does not want to be known to others.[2] This means that personal information may also contain private information that someone does not want to be known to others. Finally, the *Civil Code* further provides clear guidelines on how to apply laws to handle the relationship between "personal information" and "privacy" in practice, clarifying that "the provisions on the right to privacy, or, in the absence of which, the provisions on the protection of personal information, shall be applied to the private personal information." But it does not mean or cannot be simply understood that personal information contains privacy. Personal information focuses on identification,[3] while personal privacy puts

2 "Privacy is a human right" is rooted in Article 12 of Universal Declaration of Human Rights (UDHR) adopted by the United Nations in 1948: "No one shall be subjected to arbitrary interference with his privacy, family, home or correspondence, nor to attacks upon his honor and reputation. Everyone has the right to the protection of the law against such interference or attacks." This article is considered to be the direct basis for protection of personal rights to privacy, and it has been moved to Article 17 of International Covenant on Civil and Political Rights (ICCPR) as it is.

3 There is not a uniform definition of personal information in the legislation of international community, but "identifiability" of personal information is emphasized without exception (Paul M. Schwartz and Daniel J. Solove 2014). By observing

more emphasis on keeping it unknown to others (He Yuan 2020, p. 49). In terms of value foundation, privacy concerns the maintenance and protection of a peaceful private life, while personal information concerns the

Article 1034 of the *Civil Code* of China and Article 4 of the GDPR, it can be found that the definition of personal information in the *Civil Code* of China adopts the theory of indirect identification, which means that personal information refers to certain information which can be used by itself, or in combination with other information, to identify a natural person; the GDPR further differentiates between "identified" and "identifiable." The identification theory is the commonly accepted view of the international community, which provides that only certain information can be used to identify an individual will it be regarded as personal information. On this occasion only, the collection, processing, and use of it will then be considered as a manifestation of the infringement of personal rights to privacy. However, opinions of the subsequent personal information enumeration by countries are widely divergent. The GDPR, adopting the identification theory, lays down that personal information includes identifiers such as a name, an identification number, location data, and an online identifier, and one or more factors specific to the physical, physiological, genetic, mental, economic, cultural, or social identity of a natural person. Within the EU, the GDPR clearly defined names, identification numbers, and whereabouts as personal information, but it still requires a further explanation of other unmentioned elements to decide whether they can be regarded as personal information within the jurisdiction of the European Economic Area. In comparison, the *Civil Code* of China is more concrete than the EU's open-ended definition, regardless of the open-ended enumeration they share. However, if we compare China with countries and regions that adopt enumerative legislation; for example, *Standards for the Protection of Personal Information of Residents of the Commonwealth of Massachusetts*, personal information is clearly restricted to "name, social security number, driver's license number, financial account number and credit or debit card number," which may give rise to insufficient protection because some unlisted types of data can also be used to identify natural persons in combination with other information. Different from the legislative opinion in China is that the right to privacy, data, and personal information may come into existence simultaneously; "privacy and personal freedom" appeared more as a loose term without a clear definition in early European laws and regulations. For example, it is simply expressed as "the fundamental rights and freedoms of individuals, notably the right to privacy, with regard to the processing of personal data" in the 1995 *Directive*. The ambiguity in the definition of fundamental rights was not resolved until the emergence of the GDPR, replacing the relatively broad and unclear "right to privacy" with a "personal data protection right," laying a clear foundation for the EU's personal data protection law system.

balance of interests between information control and information flow. Different from "privacy," which is more of the private domain, "personal information" involves both protection and use, and requires reconciliation between private and public interests. Therefore, the protection of personal information in modern legislation is gradually separated from the right to privacy in the field of private rights, forming a relatively independent public law system (Zhou Hanhua 2020, pp. 53–4), and its legislative goal is also to achieve a balance between individual interests and the free flow of information. The GDPR of the European Union stated at the beginning, "This Regulation lays down rules relating to the protection of natural persons with regard to the processing of personal data and rules relating to the free movement of personal data." In terms of protection principles, personal information protection has its own unique principles, while privacy protection only focuses on information possession and confidentiality. In 1980, the OECD *Guidelines on the Protection of Privacy and Transborder Flows of Personal Data* provided several basic principles: the collection limitation principle, the data quality principle, the purpose specification principle, the use limitation principle, the security safeguards principle, the openness principle, the individual participation principle, and the accountability principle. Article 41 of the *Cybersecurity Law of the People's Republic of China* (hereinafter referred to as the "*Cybersecurity Law*") states that "[Network operators] collecting and using personal information shall abide by the principles of legality, propriety and necessity." In terms of the scope of power and function, the right to personal information has both positive and negative functions. The positive part includes the right to know, the right to correct, and the right to delete, which the right to privacy does not possess. In terms of infringement judgment, the liability of privacy infringement is based on the assumption that the right to privacy has been infringed, while that of the right to personal information is based on the violation of personal information protection rules. In terms of liability forms, infringement of rights to personal information leads not only to civil liability, but also often involves administrative and criminal liability (He Yuan 2020, p. 50).

Table 2. Categories of Personal Information in Legal Provisions in China

Sources	Categories
Paragraph 2 of Article 1034 of *Civil Code*	Including a natural person's name, date of birth, identity card number, biological recognition information, address, telephone number, e-mail address, health information, and whereabouts information.
Article 76 of *Cybersecurity Law*	Including but not limited to the natural person's name, date of birth, identity certificate number, biology-identified personal information, address, and telephone number.
Article 4 of *Provisions on Protection of Personal Information of Telecommunications and Internet Users*	Name, date of birth, identification number, address, telephone number, account number, passwords, and other information.
Article 12 of *Provisions of the Supreme People's Court on Several Issues concerning the Application of Law in the Trial of Cases involving Civil Disputes over Infringements upon Personal Rights and Interests through Information Networks*	Genetic information, medical history material, health inspection material, criminal records, household addresses, private activities and other personal information or personal privacy of natural persons.
Article 1 of *Interpretation of the Supreme People's Court and the Supreme People's Procuratorate on Several Issues concerning the Application of Law in the Handling of Criminal Cases of Infringing on Citizens' Personal Information*	Name, identification number, telecommunication contact methods, address, account password, property information, and whereabouts, among others.
Item 20 of *Minutes of the 2015 National Civil Trial Work Conference*	The Internet user's network authentication account and password, IP address, time online and offline, web browsing log, web address, keywords used in search engine, individual's name, occupation, family, marriage, fingerprints, audio, video, etc.

(*continued*)

Table 2. Continued

Sources	Categories
Article 3.1 of *Information Security Technology-Personal Information Security Specification*	Names, dates of birth, identification numbers, biometric information, addresses, telecommunication contact methods, communication records and contents, account passwords, property information, credit information, location data, accommodation information, health and physiological information, transaction data, etc.

Source: Compiled by the authors based on public information.

The relationship between personal information and data. Actually, not all data carries the value of information, and not all information is viewed as data. Information is the content reflected by data, while data is the presentation of information (Xie Yuanyang 2015, p. 98). In the cyber world, personal data and personal information overlap to a great extent. Generally, personal data is regarded as personal information. By rigorous logical thinking, the overlap between the two can only be described as "general" rather than "complete" (Zhou Sijia 2020, p. 90). A data right is not equivalent to an information right, because there are still differences between the two in the subject, object, nature, and content. In recent years, new interests and claims relating to data have mushroomed, and various parties of data rights and interests have called for changes in the legal system for data protection. The legal attribute of data, as the source of legal rights for data protection, plays an important role in all aspects of the design of the data protection system. Scholars in academia have brought forward divergent views on it, among which five theories have become mainstream, including "the theory of ownership object," "the theory of privacy right object," "the theory of personality right object," "the theory of property right object," and "the theory of a new right." With the advance of digitalization, networking, and intelligent development, more and more scholars advocate rights to data as an independent category of rights, which means that such rights, with both property interests and personal interests, are new rights that differ from personality rights and property rights. The theory of ownership object believes that personal data is a kind of property interest whose subject can be regarded as the owner and data can then be protected in the way that ownership is protected. According to the theory of privacy right object, personal data is considered to be a privacy interest. Infringement of personal data is essentially equivalent to the violation of privacy. Legislation of personal data protection should take the model of protection for rights to privacy, such as in the United States. The theory of personality right object believes that personal data doesn't fall into the category of privacy, and the personality interests it reflects are part of human dignity. Therefore, data rights can be treated as general personality rights whose protection should be done in the way that personality rights are protected, Germany being a typical case. Recently, some scholars have advocated establishing the independence of rights to data, which means that such rights, with both property interests and personal interests, are new rights that differ from personality rights and property rights, and the theory of a new right should be adopted to protect rights to data. In any case, it has become the consensus in academia that personal data carries both property interests and personality interests. Although the theory of ownership object plays an important role in protecting the property interests of personal data, it is obviously insufficient to protect personality interests; while the theory of privacy right object and the theory of personality right object are the opposite (Wang Dongsheng, 2019, p. 53). Therefore, in order to take the protection of both property interests and personality interests into account, we agree with the theory of a new right and hold that it is appropriate to regard personal data rights as a new set of rights. Nevertheless, whether data is an interest or a right is still a highly controversial issue.

Interests, Legal Interests, and Rights

Interests, legal interests,[4] and rights are part of the system of civil rights and interests can be transformed into one another under certain

4 Legal interests can be considered in a broad or a narrow sense. In a broad perspective, legal interests refers to all interests protected by law; rights are also included in legal interests. In a narrow sense, legal rights refers only to interests protected by law, which lie outside of rights.

conditions. Both legal interests and rights, carrying interest elements, are the means to realize an interest. Meanwhile, interests are the essence and cornerstone, as well as the starting point and objective of rights. The institutionalization of just interest is a legal right. Justice is the essential ingredient of a right and is the bridge between interest and right (Peng Chenxin 2004, p. 73). When it comes to quantity, interests are the largest, followed by legal benefits, then rights (Li Yan 2008, p. 73). In the *kissing right* case, the court held that "all rights must have a legal basis [...] interests are not equal to rights and don't always gain judicial relief. Looking at China's existing laws and administrative regulations, there is no kissing right mentioned in any of them. Therefore, a claim to a kissing right is legally groundless."[5]

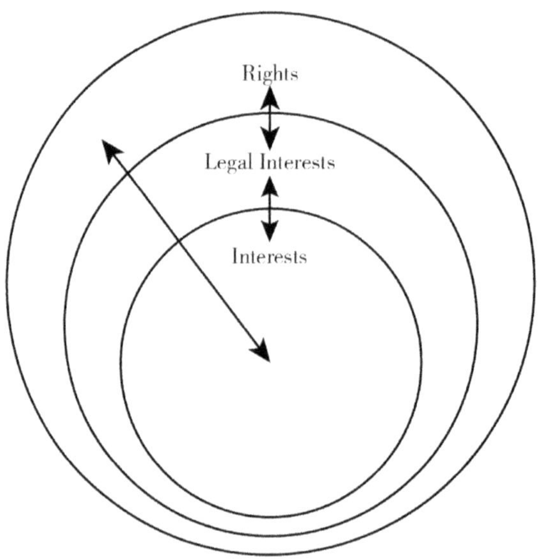

Figure 1. The Relationship among Interests, Legal Interests, and Rights (Li Yan 2008, p. 75)

5 See the No. 832 verdict (2001) of the People's Court of Guanghan City, Sichuan Province, over a compensation dispute over personal injuries suffered as the result of a car accident: Tao Liping v. Wu Xi.

Article 111 of *General Provisions of the Civil Law of the People's Republic of China* states: "The personal information of a natural person shall be protected by law." This is the first time that civil law in China has made an explicit stipulation of personal information protection (Table 3). Article 127 states: "Where any laws provide for the protection of data and network virtual property, such laws shall apply." For the first time, data is clearly included in the scope of civil rights protection, which is the official recognition of data as a legal right. Literally, this article seems to avoid the issue of data right forming, but since it is located in the chapter of "Civil Rights," a conclusion can still be drawn that data is an object of civil rights by analyzing the arrangement logic and exact content of this article. The *General Provisions of the Civil Law*, as the general guiding provisions, is inclusive and prudent regarding the issues to be discussed, such as the legal attributes, protection mode, and utilization modes of data. On the other hand, it is precisely these provisions that starts the formation of data rights legislation. *The Civil Code of the People's Republic of China* (hereinafter referred to as the "*Civil Code*") fully retains the concepts of privacy, personal information, and data in the *General Provisions of the Civil Law*. Actually, basic framework has been established for the coexistence of privacy, information, and rights to data, which provides a legislative basis for the subsequent separate regulations with detailed provisions about the protection of personal information, while leaving room for special legislation on data.

Table 3. Different Explanations of "Personal Information" in Article 111 of *General Provisions of the Civil Law*

Theories	Explanations
Theory of legal interests	*Illustrated General Principles of the Civil Law of the People's Republic of China* edited by Professor Wang Liming: This article simply stipulates that personal information shall be protected by law without such expression as "right to personal information," which indicates that *General Provisions of the Civil Law* doesn't consider personal information as a specific personality right. However, this article provides a legal basis for personal information protection of natural persons.
	Explanation and Application Guide of the General Rules of China's Civil Code edited by Professor Long Weiqiu and Liu Baoyu: The Second Review Draft took the issue of personal information into consideration. Nevertheless, in view of its complexity, personal information is not directly stipulated as a pure civil right, nor specifically a personality right. Instead, the Draft generally states that personal information shall be protected by law, which leaves space for future interpretation to balance the economic identity of personal information as an interest and support its relationship with the development of data economy.
Theory of close to personality right	*Commentary on General Principles of the Civil Code* edited by Professor Chen Su: Beyond right to privacy, the recognition of civil rights over personal information enjoyed by natural persons is, to a certain extent, confirmation of the right to personal information. This article does not directly stipulate that natural persons enjoy the right to personal information, but from the perspective of a natural person, it is indeed a provision for declaration and empowerment of their enjoyment of civil rights.
	Interpretation of General Provisions of the Civil Law of China by Professor Zhang Xinbao: According to the research by the Law Committee, the right to personal information is a significant right enjoyed by citizens in the modern information society. The clear personal information protection is of practical significance for protecting the human dignity of citizens, shielding citizens from illegal intrusion, and maintaining regular social order.

Table 3. Continued

Theories	Explanations
Theory of personality right	*Basic Points of General Provisions of the Civil Law and Case Analysis* by Professor Yang Lixin: This article defines the right to personal information enjoyed by natural persons and the obligation of obligors who shall not infringe such right.
Opinions of legislators	*Interpretation of General Provisions of the Civil Law of China* by Li Shishi: "This article defines the obligations of other parties to protect the personal information of natural persons." "Those who violate their personal information protection obligations shall bear civil liability, administrative liability and even criminal liability."
	Analysis on General Provisions of the Civil Law of China by Zhang Rongshun. The right to personal information is a significant right enjoyed by citizens in the modern information society. The clear protection of personal information is of practical significance for protecting the human dignity of citizens, shielding citizens from illegal intrusions, and maintaining regular social order.

Source: Compiled by the authors based on public information.

The world is currently entering the digital age and physical space and digital space are gradually being integrated. Digital technology, represented by the Internet, big data, the Internet of Things, blockchain, and artificial intelligence, has become the major symbol of this era. The life and survival of people are highly dependent on digital technology, and people's demand for a better life is broadly reflected in their demand for digital technology. According to the *Annual Report on China's Mobile Internet Development (2020)*, the number of mobile internet users in China had reached approximately 1.32 billion by the end of 2019, accounting for 32.17 percent of total global internet users. Data has become an important strategic resource and key production factor, involved in all aspects of a person's life from the cradle to the grave, and it has also become a new carrier and value expression of human rights in the new era. On June 12, 2020, United Nations Secretary-General, António Guterres, officially announced the long-awaited Roadmap for Digital Cooperation, whose overriding aim was to "connect, respect, and protect people in the digital age," and its main content includes "ensuring respect for human rights in the digital field."[6] This form of human right is undergoing a profound digital reshaping, and "digital human rights" have developed with the times.

On May 25, 2018, the *General Data Protection Regulation* of EU came into effect, of which Article 1 stipulates: "This Regulation protects fundamental rights and freedoms of natural persons and in particular their right to the protection of personal data," granting data subjects' personal data rights such as the right to know, the right to access, the right to rectification, the right to be forgotten, the right to restrict processing, the right to data portability, and the right to object. On May 25, 2020, data as a right first appeared in the *Work Report of the Supreme People's Court*.[7] On July 20, 2020, the Supreme People's Court and the National Development and Reform Commission jointly issued the *Opinions on Providing Judicial Services and Guarantees for Accelerating the Improvement of the Socialist Market Economic System in the New Era*, which requires that we "strengthen the protection of new rights and interests such as digital currency, network virtual property and data," and "strengthen the protection of data rights and personal information security."[8] On July 15, 2020, the *Shenzhen Special*

6 Guterres says: "The world is shifting from analog to digital technology at a faster pace than we could ever have predicted, and this creates both vast promise and some peril. The COVID pandemic has magnified many benefits and harms of the digital world. Technology is enabling the lifesaving work of healthcare providers, allowing businesses to operate remotely, educating our children and connecting us with friends and family. But we also have seen technology gravely misused. Hate speech, discrimination and abuse are on the march in digital spaces."

7 The *Work Report of the Supreme People's Court* delivered by Zhou Qiang at the Third Session of the Thirteenth National People's Congress clearly stated that to "strengthen the protection of data rights and personal information security, severely punish crimes that violate citizens' personal information such as data leakage and data reselling to support healthy development of digital economy," and "strengthening the judicial protection of data rights is conducive to the use of big data, the development of the digital economy, and the protection of citizens' personal privacy."

8 *The Opinions on Providing Judicial Services and Guarantees for Accelerating the Improvement of the Socialist Market Economic System in the New Era* notes that the protection of data rights and personal information security shall be

Economic Zone Data Regulations (Draft for Comment) was issued, in which "rights to data" were mentioned for the first time.[9] At present, there is no basic consensus on the correct construction of data. On the one hand, the diversity and complexity of data has resulted in a considerable tension between the requirements of right subjects and its fulfillment by right objects. On the other hand, data, as a new member of the rights family, has its own characteristics and its rights construction is distinct from other rights, which makes its analysis difficult. It is only when the value connotation of "justice" or "just" is maintained by rights will the interests, claims, qualifications, freedoms, and choices we regard as rights be protected by law (Fan Jinxue 2003). From Aristotle,

strengthened; the rules of the socialist market economy and the development practices of data-related industries shall be respected; data collection, use, and transactions and the resulting intellectual achievements shall be protected in accordance with the law; the legal system of data protection shall be improved; various disputes related to data shall be properly handled; and the in-depth integration of big data with other new technologies, new fields, and new business formats shall be promoted to serve the innovative development of data element market. It is also required to carry out the provisions relating to the protection of personal rights per the Book of Personality Rights of the Civil Code; improve the judicial protection mechanism for personal information rights and interests, such as the biological and social data of natural persons; understand the boundary between the development of information technology and the protection of personal information; and balance the relationship between personal information and the public interest.

9 The content about the rights appurtenant to data is one of the main innovations of the *Regulations*. First, these *Regulations* officially sets up rights to data. It was stipulated for the first time in the *Regulations* that rights to data are enjoyed by natural persons, legal persons, and unincorporated organizations in accordance with the Regulations and other laws and regulations. Rights to data refers to the specific data rights of independent decision, control, processing, earnings, and damage compensation in accordance with the law. Second, natural persons hold the rights to their personal data in accordance with the law. Third, public data is a new type of state-owned asset, where the rights are possessed by the state, which the Shenzhen Municipal Government exercises on its behalf. Fourth, entities of the data element market hold the rights to the data that is legally collected or generated by themselves.

who considered "righteousness" and "justice" as the core of collective rights and interests when expounding legal concepts in *Politics* to the Romans —maintaining justice by laws—and then to Hobbes who held out the theory of contract fairness, it can be said that the value connotation of "justice" runs throughout the history of rights development (Yan Lidong 2019, p. 65). There are three requirements from an interest to a right. First, the interest shall be just and legitimate, and second, it shall be accepted by the existing legal system, and, finally, there must be a cost-benefit analysis of rights. Specifically in the field of civil law, several questions should be answered before allocating protection to certain interests, by creating rights through statutory law or providing relief for the infringed ones. The first question is whether the interest is legal and whether it is necessary to be protected by law. Second, even if the answer to the first question is in the affirmative, it must then be considered whether this interest can be covered by the existing system of civil rights and interests. Finally, various conflicting values, especially the relationship between protecting the rights and interests and respecting the freedom of reasonable behavior should be balanced (Cheng Xiao 2019, p. 36).

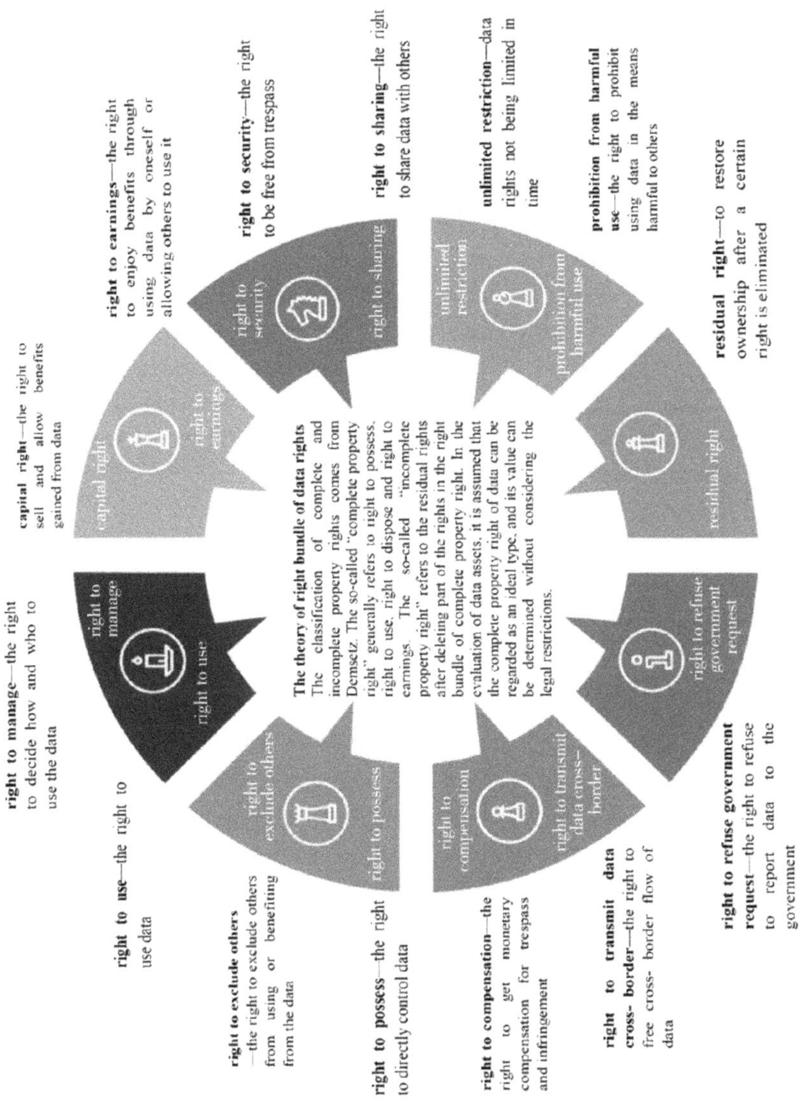

Figure 2 . Bundles of the Rights to Data (Deloitte and Ali Research 2019, p. 16)

Values of Data Rights

With social development and in-depth research, new connotations are gradually being accepted as human rights. The recognition of data rights as human rights has become a trend in the development of the constitutional laws of various countries, and a general tendency of all countries in the world is to institutionalize data rights as basic human rights, elevating ideal data rights to a legal level. Actually, a "right" itself is a question of value. Moreover, a right is the value orientation of a democratic society, and is closely related to other value goals of society, such as human rights, fairness, efficiency, freedom, and security. The same goes for data rights. Data rights are held out to be basic human rights, and are of great value for individuals, society, and the country. In-depth thinking about the value which should be embodied or realized by data rights helps to analyze the legitimacy and feasibility issues of data rights, and is conducive to the exploration of how to implement them as well.

Human Right Attributes of Data Rights

People-centeredness, as the soul of civilization's rule of law, should be given more emphasis when it comes to the construction of the rule of law in a digital society. Essentially, being people-centered means to regard human dignity, human freedom, and all-round human development as the ultimate goal of building the rule of law. General Secretary Xi Jinping transformed this notion into a political and legal proposition with contemporary and realistic characteristics. Moreover, President Xi put forward several relevant concepts such as "putting people first," "being people-oriented," and "upholding the dominant position of the people," which underlined that the construction of the rule of law shall "be for the people, rely on the people, benefit the people and protect the people" and, accordingly, clarified this proposition's legal essence and its new connotation for the times. As Professor Joel Trachtman said, cyberspace is moving from what is in effect a *res nullius* regime centered by "technology" to a system of property rights centered by "humans" (Trachtman 2013, p. 106). Although the operation of data activities depends on technology, the fundamental purpose of digital technology development is to meet the objective needs of the people and achieve the ultimate goal of being "people-oriented." After all, the digital society supported by data and algorithms is a society of human beings rather than things. Specifically, the construction of a people-oriented legal order in a digital society is to take people's rights as the foundation and consider the protection of digital human rights as the core.

Digital human rights are the embodiment of the basic rights of people's digital existence and development needs in a digital society. The claim of data rights is the need to strengthen the responsibilities and obligations of public authorities and platform companies to respect and protect digital human rights, to ensure that technology is for social good, to strengthen China's international influence in the rule of law, to seize the rule-making power in cyberspace, and to build the diversity of human civilization. International academia generally believes that the form of human rights worldwide has undergone three historical changes. The first, second, and third generations of the concept of human rights involve people, properties, things, and behavior in a physical sense, and there is barely any mention of concepts of information or data. As for the fourth-generation human rights system, human rights to safety, a clean environment, and data have become the major symbols, and among them digital human rights are the leading ones. There is no covering relationship between digital human rights and the first three generations of human rights, and digital human rights is not a negation of any of the first three generations of rights. Instead, it is a progressive expansion, transformation, and upgrading of the former three. These four generations of human rights together constitute the human rights system of the new era. Digital human rights provide a profound theoretical basis for human rights and human rights documents at different levels, such as international human rights conventions, regional human rights conventions, and domestic human rights policies in various countries, which all recognize digital human rights as basic human rights.

Table 4. The Comparison between the Four Generations of Human Rights

	The First-Generation Human Rights	The Second-Generation Human Rights	The Third-Generation Human Rights	The Fourth-Generation Human Rights (Digital Human Rights)
Backgrounds	It emerged in the 1789 French Revolution. The background of its birth was the anti-feudal and anti-authoritarian bourgeois revolution	It was proposed after the Russian October Revolution in the early twentieth century, whose background was the socialist revolution that opposed capital exploitation and eliminated the polarization between the rich and the poor.	It came into being during the liberation movement of colonies and oppressed people in the 1950s and 1960s. Behind its birth was the national revolution for national independence, national liberation and political democracy.	It was developed with the Fourth Technological Revolution represented by digital technology and the rapid economic and social changes. Behind its birth is an information revolution.
Claims	It includes the rights to life, personal liberty, freedom of religion, freedom of speech and the press, freedom of assembly and association, freedom of movement and residence, freedom from arbitrary detention, freedom of communications, and political rights such as the right to vote, and it especially stressed that the property rights shall not be violated.	It includes the right to labor and right to survival. Besides the rights claimed by first-generation human rights, it further proposed the rights to work, rest, healthcare, education, maintaining a moderate living standard, and laborers solidarity.	It includes rights to peace, development, environment, national self-determination, and human common heritage.	It includes, around data and information, the right to personal autonomy, the right to know, the right to express, the right to fair use, rights to privacy, and rights to property.

Highlights	It focuses on the maintenance of personal freedom in legal terms, opposing the state's improper interference with individual freedoms and rights in the name of political rights, and claiming that the state bears the obligation of negative inaction.	It requires that the state should build an appropriate social and economic environment to promote the realization of individual freedom, and it is stressed that the state should have an active obligation to the realization of human rights.	It focuses on solidarity and can be called "solidarity rights" with collective nature, aiming at self-determination and development of countries and nations.	It aims to eliminate the threats to human rights, including algorithm discrimination, digital divide, surveillance society, and algorithm hegemony, promote personal autonomy in a digital society, and strengthen the human rights protection of "digital humans."

Source: See Wang, Guanghui. 2015. *Human Rights Law*. Beijing: Tsinghua University Press; Qi, Yanping. 2015. *Evolution of the Ideology of Human Rights*. Ji'nan: Shandong University Press; Ma, Changshan. 2019. "The Fourth Generation of Human Rights and Its Guarantee under the Background of Intelligent Society." *China Legal Science*, 5th issue.

Digital human rights "take the relations of production and life in both physical and digital space as its social foundation, the human digital information facet and related rights and interests as its expression form, and the comprehensive development of people in a smart society as its core appeal" (Ma Changshan 2019, p. 16). The aim is to eliminate the threat to human rights, such as algorithmic discrimination, a surveillance society, data divide, and algorithmic hegemony. This will enhance the autonomy of people in the digital age and strengthen the protection of human rights for "digital humans." The connotation of digital human rights is very rich, "including 'the realization of human rights by digital technology,' 'the human rights in digital life or digital space,' 'the human rights standards of digital technology,' 'the legal basis of digital human rights,' and so on" (Zhang Wenxian 2019, p. 22). Digital human rights are produced in the context of a digital revolution, which is also an ideological emancipation and institutional innovation. However, digital human rights have subverted the production relations and life in the traditional industrial and commercial era through technological revolution rather than an armed struggle. In terms of connotative logic, digital human rights are different from the previous three generations of human rights. The first three generations of human rights, whether in economic protection, survival, development, or political participation basically share two common characteristics: first, claims are expressed based on the biological attributes of people; and second, digital human rights unfold within the logical framework of physical space. However, the revolution claim and objective development of digital human rights are neither an expansion of human rights in the traditional industrial and commercial era nor just an increase in the number and variety of rights, but a fundamental shift of human rights in the digital era. The development and reform of human rights at every stage will result in the upgrade and escalation of the core values of existing human rights. The second generation of human rights has surpassed the first generation toward a more substantive view of social, cultural, and economic rights. The third generation surpassed the second generation in that it moved to a view of collective rights focusing on survival and development. The same goes for digital human rights (Ma Changshan 2019, p. 18). Compared with traditional human rights, digital human rights are not the simple extension of traditional human rights, but an upgrade of the attributes of human rights by the smart society and the digital revolution. Facing a technological revolution with both opportunities and challenges, digital human rights shall effectively control the negative risks of digitalization, networking, and intelligent development; greatly transform the progress into improvement in people's capability of free development; and break through the biological boundaries of humans so as to get closer to the human value and dignity.

Value Basis of Data Rights

Theory of confidentiality. As the origin of the right to privacy, the confidentiality theory based on social relations was developed in Britain in the significant case, *Prince Albert v. Strange* in 1848,[10] whose judgment was based mainly on two grounds. First, a person shall be entitled to a state of privacy. Judge Bruce pointed out in his obiter dictum: "A man may employ himself in private in a manner very harmless; but which, if disclosed to society, might destroy the comfort of his life, and even his success in it."[11] Second, liability for the breach of trust. The judge held that the conduct of Strange in obtaining the copy from the person in the employment of the printer at Windsor "must be a breach of trust, confidence, or contract," and the person in the employment of the printer at Windsor was also "in violation of the confidence reposed in him." They "shall not make any information obtained during their work as an

10 In the case *Prince Albert v. Strange*, Queen Victoria and her consort Prince Albert made etchings from their family life, and a few were given to printers at Windsor for the purpose of printing off certain copies to distribute to members of royal family only. However, the publisher, William Strange, obtained one copy from the person in the employment of a printer at Windsor and made a catalogue of the etchings and printed fifty copies of it. Prince Albert then sued Strange and the High Court verdict prohibited Strange from printing and publishing the etchings (He Yuan 2020, p. 32).

11 See Prince Albert v. Strange, (1848) 41 Eng. Rep. 1171 (Ch.).

employee known to the public," otherwise such conduct shall be regulated by law.[12] In fact, in this common law jurisdiction there is a long history of protecting the personal information of natural persons from being disposed of by others, which is based on the confidentiality theory. This theory dates back to the Hippocratic Oath of more than 2,000 years ago and is basically reflected in the following two aspects in English law. One is the law of confidential relationships. Specifically, there are four elements of the law. First, evidentiary privileges. One party to a relationship was entitled to prohibiting the other party from revealing confidences in court or to the public. Second, confidential relations. Duties of nondisclosure attached to some special relationships emphasizing "trust," prohibiting one party from divulging the information of the other party to any unauthorized person on pain of liability. Third, blackmail law. What the blackmailer threatened to expose was not only actual crimes, but also infirmities, immoral conduct, or other things of personal privacy. Fourth, government records. The law demanded the government to protect the confidentiality of personal information that people supplied to the government. Besides the law of confidential relationships, the law of confidential communications also reflected the confidentiality theory in English law. Beyond protecting the exchange of information in professional and contractual relationships, the law also protected certain types of confidential communications between people in nearly all kinds of relationships. Communication information in the UK at that time generally included letters, literary expressions, and telegraph communications. Communicants were viewed as having a confidential relationship by British people. Therefore, British law prohibited either party from divulging their communications (Richards and Solove 2007, p. 123).

Theory of the right to information privacy. First, the theory of right was written by Warren and Brandeis. Like the confidentiality theory in Britain, the origin of Warren and Brandeis' theory is also the famous British precedent *Prince Albert v. Strange* and the obiter dictum attached to the judgment by Judge Bruce. However, they didn't take the

12 See Prince Albert v. Strange, (1848) 41 Eng. Rep. 1171 (Ch.).

confidentiality theory or explore the issue of privacy from the perspective of social relations. Instead, they took a different path and innovatively translated this case into one that is "protecting personal feelings from unnecessary disclosure and interruption." "The principle which protects personal writings and all other personal productions, not against theft and physical appropriations, but against publication in any form, is in reality not the principle of private property, but that of an inviolate personality" (Warren and Brandeis 1890, p. 205). Second, the theory of quartering method by Prosser. In 1960, the founder of privacy law in America, Professor Prosser, published *Privacy* in the *California Law Review*, summarizing privacy torts into four categories: intrusion upon the plaintiff's seclusion or solitude, or into his private affairs; public disclosure of embarrassing private facts about the plaintiff; publicity which places the plaintiff in a false light in the public eye; and appropriation, for the defendant's advantage, of the plaintiff's name or likeness (Prosser 1960, p. 389). This quartering method has profoundly affected the privacy legislation and judicature in the United States. However, with the increasing demands of social development, the traditional privacy theory in America, based on the quartering method, was gradually found to be insufficient to respond to and solve social problems in reality, because this method severely restricted the ability of the privacy law to resolve legal problems in the information age; this dilemma was mainly manifested in the limited scope of legal relief and the great difficulties in achieving that. Third, the theory of privacy control by Westin. In 1967, Westin, the founder of the privacy control theory in America, defined the "right to informational privacy" for the first time in his book *Privacy and Freedom*: "privacy is the claim of individuals [...] to determine for themselves when, how and to what extent information about them is communicated" (Westin 1967, p. 7). The U.S. Supreme Court has also demonstrated and strengthened Westin's theory by judicial precedent. In the case of *Griswold v. Connecticut* in 1965, the Supreme Court affirmed the "right to decisional privacy" and ruled that the legislation to prohibit contraception was invalid because a natural person has the right to freely decide his or her own affairs without government intervention. In the case of *Katz v. United States* in 1967, the "right to physical privacy" was established and the court ruled that the legal basis of government "surveillance" relied upon obtaining authorization by way of a writ, otherwise such surveillance would constitute a violation of the law. This is because a natural person has the right to privacy in their residence and other private places without government interference or intrusion. In the case of *Whalen v. Roe* in 1977, the "right to informational privacy" was systematically elaborated for the first time, when the court held that a natural person has the right to control their personal information. For the right to informational privacy, the theory of privacy control is crucial. With the advent of the digital age, data has become more and more important to individuals, society, and the country, and the privacy control theory has gradually transformed into the data control theory. In recent years, one of the core issues of data legislation that various states in the United States were coping with was represented by the *California Consumer Privacy Act* (CCPA). This is the legal basis for personal data control and processing, and the "consent mechanism" based on the theory of data control is key to this issue (He Yuan 2020, p. 36).

Theory of right to information self-determination. The "right to information self-determination" was first confirmed by the German Federal Constitutional Court in the case of "*Census*" in 1983. The court denied the legal force of the *Federal Census Act*, which involved the power to extensively collect personal information, and creatively raised the concept of "right to information self-determination" from the general clauses, such as Article 1.1 of "human dignity" and Article 2.1 of "general personality rights" in the *Basic Law of the Federal Republic of Germany* (Zhao Hong 2017, p. 149). The court then proposed the protection principles and the specific content of citizens' right to information self-determination: the "general personality rights" in Article 1.2 and Article 2.1 of the *Basic Law* contain the protection of personal data from unrestricted extraction, storage, use, and continued transmission in the context of modern data processing. This basic right has the function of securing the right of individuals to self-determine, and to prevent the disclosure or use of their personal data (Zhang Yuanquan 2009, p. 39). Through the interpretation of "general personality rights," the German Federal Constitutional Court explicitly put forward the concept of the "right to information self-determination," and outlined it as well. This right has the dual nature of constitutional law and private law, and its protection is the common mission of the constitution and private law. Even so, the German Federal Constitutional Court didn't absolutize this right. The "right to information self-determination is not unlimited. Individuals don't have any absolute or unlimited control over their own information." This is because "individuals develop their individuality in a social community. Therefore, even personal information is a reflection of social facts, rather than purely connected with individuals" (Zhao Hong 2017, p. 149). The right to information self-determination in Germany is one of the basic constitutional rights; "the theory of right to information self-determination" in Germany has broken through the confinement of American privacy law, extended its scope to "any identified (direct) or identifiable (indirectly) data of natural persons," and effectively responded to the need of information protection in the era of big data (Zhao Hong 2017, p. 152).

Value Positioning of Data Rights

According to Locke's natural right theory, everyone shall have the right to life, freedom, and property, which are the three cornerstones of a modern society. Data rights, adding new content and form to human rights, are independent and new human rights that need to be systematically protected through the comprehensive application of public law, private law, substantive law, and procedural law. Data rights are expected to become the fourth basic human right following the rights to life, property, and freedom. Data and data rights are the symbol of a digital society, and the development level of society depends on the extent to which data rights are used and protected. Data rights, as human rights in the digital living space, with data elements as the subject matter of rights, data interests as the object of rights, and data ownership, rights, utilization, and protection as the main content, are realized through digital technology and the digitalized rule of law. A data right is not just a simple right, but a collection of rights that contain the rights of different parties to the same object involving personality, privacy, property, and sovereignty.[13] Data rights include rights to data, rights to share, and data sovereignty, among which the right to share lies at its core. They aim to oppose digital hegemony, violence, and monopoly; eliminate and deal with human rights problems and challenges, such as digital divide, privacy violation, and algorithmic discrimination; and promote digital justice. Digital human rights guide digital technology to benefit mankind according to law, which is of great significance to human life and the construction of a digital order.

Data rights carry extremely rich legal values and jurisprudential connotations, which form a multi-layered, multi-faceted, and multi-dimensional system, and this system originated from the maintenance of data interests, and is capable of allocating the existing legal interests of data into the appropriate rights family. Moreover, the value of data rights lies in the social function and effect they play. In today's world data rights, as a rights bundle, contain abundant connotations of rights, and their powers and functions are constantly enriched and expanded. They are widely recognized and accepted by countries practicing the rule of law. On the one hand, data rights show the value of independence—the data legal interest of an independent individual is a reflection of self-consciousness and human freedom; data rights embody the value of dignity—they ensure the realization of data personality rights and data property rights through the realization of free will; and data rights uphold the value of freedom—they advocate the free flow of data and the freedom of data control. On the other hand, data rights realize the value of democracy—the realization of data rights is a reflection of data democracy diversification and the prerequisite for data autonomy; and data rights embody the value of order—the realization of data rights requires a balance between private and public rights and is a reflection of data ethics, corporate self-discipline, and industry heteronomy. We have reason to believe that, with constant improvement and effective protection, data rights should and will take its due position in the rule of

13 Article 37 of the *Cybersecurity Law* promulgated in 2016 clearly stipulates that important data should be stored within China, which clearly indicates sovereignty over data management by the state.

law in the future. For data rights, "their recognition by law as legal rights requires a precise definition to a certain extent, as well as detailed research to ascertain their unique inherent values. Data rights shouldn't just be used occasionally for some other legal purpose" (Stein and Shand 2004, p. 268).

Modern law was developed on the basis of the revival of Roman law, and one of its basic beliefs is that the value of law is simplistic, making people believe that the current legal order upholds one single value system. However, the development and changes made by the digital society have altered the landscape of legal values and require the coexistence of multiple values so as to achieve coordination and compatibility between different right claims and value orientations (Lv Zhongmei 2005, p. 61). This is exactly what data rights law sets out to do. Data rights law accommodates multiple values and keeps them compatible. This ensures its legitimacy and feasibility to a large extent and, moreover, provides insights as to how we are to correctly comprehend and handle the three relationships in data rights law. First, in the relationship between people and data, we are to ensure the realization of digital human rights. Second, in the relationship between individuals, we should promote digital inclusion. Third, in the relationship between citizens and the country, digital justice should be upheld. The recognition of data rights in legal systems is not only a must for the improvement of our legal systems, but also what is required for the fulfillment of the demands of society and the maintenance of social harmony and stability.

The Balance of Interests

Law is an art of balance. No law is neutral. Any law represents certain interest choices and value orientation. Since there are always interest conflicts, the balance between different interests becomes a fundamental issue. The choice of a stance reveals the intention of legislators or the objective functions of law and it may as well be deemed as the "soul of law." How we view interests is the premise by which to resolve problems of interests, and in the digital age this view can be rather complex as a reflection of the complicated reality. As there now tends to be multiple interest subjects, diverse interest demands, complex interest relations, and intensified interest conflicts, it is an important task for us to create a mechanism to balance data interests. The balance of interest conflicts is the core task in the regulation of interest relations in law. It should follow the principles of integration, compliance, and balance. As data is a public product, data rights are superior to the protection of data interests; personal data interests are superior to property data interests; and public interests are superior to private data interests.

The Principle of Integration

"The purpose is the creator of all laws" (Bodenheimer 2004, p. 114). The balance of interests in data rights legislation should be guided by the purpose; that is, to properly handle data relations. The immediate purposes are data protection and data utilization. In fact, "protection" means not only to keep from damage and avoid loss, but also to improve and increase. Therefore, data protection covers two aspects: One is that data interests shall not be damaged and the other is that data value continues to increase.

Data is a combination of the data subject's personal interests and public interests. The personality interests contained in data need to be protected through personal data rights. Data also reflects certain public interests when they circulate in society. The relation between personal interests and public interests will come into conflict to a certain extent. As a new element with both personality and property attributes, data collection and utilization is not a simple process of wealth gathering, but a process of balancing between personal interests and public interests. In addition to the data subject's own interests, data processing may also occur based on the public interest. Whether the public interest or the personal interest is the priority, the conflict of interests needs to be weighed to achieve the relative balance of interests. The direct manifestation of data interest conflicts can be roughly summarized as the conflict between the growing data protection needs and the growing data utilization needs, as well as the capacity to meet them or, more concisely, the conflict between personality interests and property interests. When balancing personality interests and property interests, we should not deliberately emphasize the set priorities as absolute, exclusive, and rigid arrangements. Instead, we should make efforts to resolve the separation between personal interests and property interests, promote the transformation from interest competition to cooperation, and advocate the realization of the principle of integration, which makes overall plans, takes all factors into consideration, and realizes a win-win situation.

Personality interests and property interests are in a relationship of homogeneity and symbiosis. Homogeneity refers to the conflict between those interests that originate from the tension between data privacy and data asset. Symbiosis means they both reflect the diversity of data value. Hereto, data rights legislation should adhere to the people-centered principle and attach importance to people's legitimate demands. Both personality interests and property interests are legitimate interests that should be protected by data rights law, and neither of them can be neglected; the conflict between them are non-antagonistic rather than antinomic, antagonistic in nature. According to Robert Alexy, conflicts between legitimate interests cannot be resolved through "exclusion," but only through "balance." By seeking balance, this can be regarded as the premise for the legitimacy and the basis of justification for resolving interest conflicts in the field of data rights law.

As data application scenarios get more refined, personal interests, commercial interests, social interests, and national interests carried by data tend to coexist in conflict in multiple dimensions. Based on their own capacity and value choices, countries adopt different interest balance models to build their own data protection systems for maximizing their own interests. For example, the European Union has established the personal data use model where data use is prohibited in principle and permitted when legally authorized data subjects are entitled to seven data rights, including the right to know, the right to access, the right to rectification, the right to erasure, the right to restriction of processing, the right to portability, and the right to refuse, see the *General Data Protection Regulation* (EU, 2016), so as to reshape the global data rule system through high-standard data protection. In the *Act on the Protection of Personal Information* (Japan, 2003), Japan does not reinforce the prior "informed consent" rule. It only stipulates that prior consent of users must be obtained for "personal information requiring attention," while the principle for general personal information is to limit abuse. The United States, relying on its powerful technological strength, strongly advocates free-market data utilization and encourages the personal data circulation mode where data use is permitted in principle and prohibited on condition. Taking the *California Consumer Privacy Act* as an example, it gives consideration to the protection of citizens' privacy on the basis of protecting extensive access to personal data. South Korea enacted the *Personal Information Protection Act* (South Korea, 2011), the *Credit Information Use and Protection Act* (South Korea, 2020), and the *Act on the Promotion of Information and Communications Network Utilization and Information Protection* (South Korea, 2020) to extend the scope of personal information that can be collected and used by individuals and enterprises, effectively easing the restrictions on data use and laying the foundation for the development of data-related industries.

The Principle of Compliance

The principle of compliance is that data subjects, data controllers, data processors, and other subjects of data rights law should not only abide by laws, regulations, rules, and regulatory policies, but also comply with relevant standards, governance principles, and ethical norms. Data controllers and data processors may face compliance risks, including legal sanctions, regulatory penalties, property losses, and reputation losses in the event of non-compliance.

The principle of compliance includes data legitimacy, data compliance, data governance, data ethics, and so on. Specifically, the data compliance system refers to the establishment and improvement of the data compliance governance process on the basis of identification, analysis, and evaluation of data compliance risks, so as to respond to and control data risks effectively. Though the system cannot prevent data controllers and data processors from violating laws and regulations, it can greatly reduce the risk of the violations. In some countries the data compliance system, established and effectively implemented by data controllers and data processors, can be used as a defense with which to diminish or exempt administrative, criminal or civil liabilities, which is likely to be accepted by the regulatory agencies or courts.

The premise and basis of the principle of compliance is the principle of legitimacy, consisting of the principle of conferral, the principle of transparency and openness, the principle of purpose limitation, the principle of accuracy, the principle of storage limitation, the principle of integrity and confidentiality, and the principle of accountability. The principle of conferral means that data subjects give their consent to the processing of their data based on one or more specific purposes. The principle of transparency and openness provides that data controllers and data processors shall process the subjects' data in a lawful and transparent manner. The principle of purpose restriction means they shall collect data for specified, express, and legitimate purposes, which will not be further processed in a manner that is incompatible with those purposes. The principle of accuracy is the obligation to ensure that the data is accurate and, where necessary, kept up to date—every reasonable step must be taken to ensure that personal data that is erroneous and contrary to the purposes of data processing is erased or rectified without delay. The principle of storage limitation provides that data that are not desensitized or anonymized should be stored for a time period no longer than is necessary for the purposes for which the personal data are processed. The principle of integrity and confidentiality provides that the subjects' data shall be kept in a manner that ensures appropriate security of that personal data, including protection against unauthorized or unlawful processing and against accidental loss, destruction, damage, or breach by using appropriate technical or organizational measures. Based on the above principles, data controllers and data processors are responsible for the legitimacy and compliance in data processing, and shall bear legal liability in respect of the same, such as compensation to the data subjects for the damage caused by a data breach, having been caused by their intention or negligence (He Yuan 2020, p. 12–16).

The Principle of Balance

Data interests are complex and an institutional arrangement should be established whereby multiple data interests are in a general balance. In other words, data protection is not an entitlement for individuals, but a code of conduct for balance between various interests. This is also the protection mode established at the beginning of personal data protection legislation in Europe, when the European Council formulated the *Convention for the Protection of Individuals with Regard to Automatic Processing of Personal Data* (hereinafter referred to as *Convention 108*).[14] The protection of personal data is regarded as the protection of individual rights. At the same time, the foundation and principles of legitimacy in personal data processing is used as the legal basis for personal data use (processing) rather than a single right of individual decision-making. At the time of amending *Convention 108* in 2012, when asked whether there should be a definition of right to data protection and privacy, experts held that there was "no need":

> [It] is useless to try to define privacy in the data protection convention. Because privacy is a set of interests with different expressions in different scenarios, and sometimes needs to be balanced with other interests. It is more appropriate to express it as a set of broad principles. There are other conventions (e.g. *Convention for the Protection of Human Rights and Fundamental Freedoms*) and precedents to interpret it. It is suitable to adopt a broad expression of privacy protection, so that different mechanisms can be used to protect. (Sylvia Kierkegaarda et al., 2011, pp. 223–31)

The purpose of the *General Data Protection Regulation* is to solve the problems of balance between personal data rights protection and data flow. Article 4 of *on the Protection of Natural Persons with Regard to the Processing of Personal Data and on the Free Movement of Such Data,*

14 Since the *Convention for the Protection of Individuals with regard to Automatic Processing of Personal Data* is numbered 108 in the European treaty series of the Council of Europe, it is conventionally called *Convention 108*, which is recognized as the most important international legal document on personal data protection.

and Repealing Directive 95/46/EC (General Data Protection Regulation) clearly states that personal data protection should not be regarded as a personal absolute right, that is,

> The processing of personal data should be designed to serve mankind. The right to the protection of personal data is not an absolute right; it must be considered in relation to its function in society and be balanced against other fundamental rights, in accordance with the principle of proportionality.[15]

Furthermore, Article 1, Paragraph 1 of the *General Data Protection Regulation* explicitly states "this regulation lays down rules relating to the protection of natural persons with regard to the processing of personal data and rules relating to the free movement of personal data"; Paragraph 3 emphasizes the importance of balance; that is, "the free movement of personal data within the Union shall be neither restricted nor prohibited for reasons connected with the protection of natural persons with regard to the processing of personal data."

According to the *Law of the People's Republic of China on the Prevention and Treatment of Infectious Diseases*, patients can isolated to prevent the spread of an epidemic. This is a case where the law gives priority to public interests; to be more specific, public powers may limit and deprive individual rights under exceptional circumstances. In the prevention and control of Covid-19, individual interests are protected in a comprehensive way when they converge with public interests, while individual interests of patients should be compromised when they conflict with public interests, which are not limited to the restrictions of freedom, but also include the transfer of data rights. On February 4, 2020, the *Circular on Personal Information Protection and Big Data Support for Joint Prevention and Control* issued by the Office of the Central Cyberspace Affairs Commission fully embodies the principle of balance. On the one hand, it strengthens personal

15 See Article 4 of the *Regulation (EU) 2016 /679 of the European Parliament and of the Council of 27 April 2016 on the protection of natural persons with regard to the processing of personal data and on the free movement of such data, repealing Directive 95 /46 /EC (General Data Protection Regulation).*

information protection in the joint prevention and control of the epidemic. For example, it stipulates that "any institutions or individuals except those authorized by the health authorities are not allowed to collect and use individuals' personal information without their consent, even for the purpose of epidemic control and disease treatment" [...] "it should be limited in principle to key populations" [...] "the use of individuals' information for purposes other than epidemic control and medical treatment is prohibited." On the other hand, it encourages the use of big data, including personal information, to support epidemic control. For example, on the basis of fully protecting personal information, it also encourages competent companies to analyze and predict the flow of key populations (including confirmed cases, suspects, and close contacts) using big data to support the joint prevention and control of the disease.

Public interests are important interests in the field of data protection. The realization of this protection requires the data protection system to promote and protect data collection, use, and circulation. In general, data value and interests are diversified, so the diversification of interests contained within the personal data determines that the use of personal data does not completely vest in the individual (Regan 1995). Personal data carries personal interests, social interests, and public interests, so the protection must be properly considered to realize these interests and their value (Gao Fuping 2019). Personal interests and public interests are interconnected and complementary. When necessary, individuals should transfer all or part of the rights contained within their personal data to ensure the realization of the public interest, which is not a complete denial of personal interests, but a reasonable proportionate derogation and tolerance. In fact, the aim of data rights protection is to limit data abuse on the basis of ensuring the reasonable social use of data and to keep data protection and the reasonable circulation of data in equilibrium. Public interests are of vital importance in modern society, especially for the rule of law. The principle of the public interest is a historical response to rights socialization, an inevitable requirement of an interconnected society, and a fundamental concept of a society ruled by law (Liang Shangshang 2016). The view on public interest is an inclusive view which advocates that neither private data interests nor public data welfare may expand without limit; instead, it advocates the balance and symbiosis between different interests under the premise of the limited priority of public interests, as well as the maintenance of moderate tension.[16] However, the concept of public interests is vague and uncertain in theoretical and judicial circles. Because of its abstract nature, an authorized concept has not yet been developed. That is why the public interest can be made void, weakened, and generalized in reality. Although China's constitution and civil law have established the basic principles of public interests, which have been widely used in judicial practice, there are still many problems waiting for theoretical clarification.

16 For example, Article 29 Paragraph 2 of the *Constitution of Japan* stipulates that "property rights shall be defined by law, in conformity with the public welfare." Article 10 Paragraph 2 of the *Constitution of the People's Republic of China* specifies that "the state may in the public interest take over land for its use in accordance with the law"; Article 13 Paragraph 3 states that "the state may, for the public interest, expropriate or take over private properly of citizens for public use, and pay compensation in accordance with the law." In short, the state may limit, derogate, or even deprive individual interests for the sake of public interest.

Table 5. Developing Stages of Views on Public Interest in Western Countries

Stage	Key Points
Holism view on public interest in ancient Greece and Rome	First, the public interests represented by the city-state interests are consistent with the personal interests of citizens; second, they are prior to the individual interests; third, they are the value standards to judge the legitimacy of the government. Clearly, this view has contained the core idea of the views on public interest in contemporary times, shaped the basic trend of the views on public interest in western countries, and exerted a wide and profound impact on future generations.
Theological view on the public interest in the Middle Ages	Adhere to the superiority of public interests. "The interests of society are greater and more sacred than those of individuals." Aquinas's view on public interests has taken a step forward; that is, it defines and studies the public interest at the spiritual level, which is beyond the material level and greatly enriches the content of public interests.
View on the public interest of social contract in modern times	In terms of the relationship between the law and the public interest, social contract theorists clearly proposed that legislation should be based on public interests, and public interests are the purpose of law. The greatest contribution of the view on public interest in this period is that its understanding of public interests is no longer limited as an abstract value judgment, but a specific social practice; in short, the principle of public interests has become a social construction principle.
Pluralistic views on the public interest in contemporary times	After the nineteenth century, social relations have become more complex, interests' contradictions have become more acute, and various thoughts of interests emerge constantly as follows. 1. The utilitarian view on public interest proposed by Bentham, Mill, etc., regards utilitarianism as a standard with which to measure the legitimacy of all behaviors, and regards personal interests as the basis of public interests and the only realistic interest. 2. The social-based view on public interest put forward by Keynes. 3. The individual-based, neoliberal view on public interest proposed by Rawls and Hayek emphasizes the priority of personal interests and denies the independent existence of public interests. 4. Communitarians hold that society is first; public good is better than individual good; the public interest comes before personal interests, therefore the pursuit of the public interest is the cardinal virtue of citizens.

Table 5. Continued

Stage	Key Points
	5. The new public managerialism puts forward some suggestions for the supply mechanism reform of public interests to meet the growing and diversified needs of public goods and public services, including changing the traditional single government supply mode, introducing the market competition mechanism, and encouraging the non-profit organizations to play a role. Generally speaking, views on the public interest in this period present a trend of diversified development, which is not only a theoretical response to social reality, but also deepens human cognition of public interests.

Source: See Gao, Zhihong. 2020. "The Connotation of the Contemporary Rule of Law in the View of Public Interest and Its Realization Path." *Tribune of Political Science and Law*, 2nd issue.

Altruism

As David Hume put it, "all the sciences have a relation, greater or less, to human nature and that however wide any of them may seem to run from it, they still return back by one passage or another" (Hume 1996, p. 6). The presuppositions of all human sciences are centered on humanity and focused on human nature. All systems are based on their different hypotheses of human nature, and they organize, lead, control, and stimulate people in different ways. In legal terms, "man" refers to the imagined or realistic image of man as depicted by the law. In recent years, Chinese and foreign scholars have been conducting more in-depth studies of man in legal terms, and the legal concept of man is turning from "man of status" to "man of equality and freedom" in the constitutional sense; from "abstract man" to "concrete man" in the realm of civil law; from "economic man" to "ecological man" in terms of environmental law; from "atomized man" to "socialized man" in terms of social law; and from "person of ethics" to "person of science" from the perspective of jurisprudence. Human beings are becoming "data man," which not only refers to the datamation of human beings, but also emphasizes that mankind has a highly developed digital civilization. Accordingly, man in legal terms is undergoing a transformation from "economic man" to "data man." The hypothesis of data man is a human nature presupposition of data rights law with altruism at its core. In the classic hypotheses of human nature, the economic man hypothesis highlights man's egoism; the social man hypothesis highlights man's non-economic sociality; while the data man hypothesis highlights man's altruism and sharing spirit. Data man pursues, creates, and realizes the value of data by following the basic principle of data value maximization. The data rights law system, which is based on the data man hypothesis, mainly aims to realize balance and coordination between the effective protection of data rights and making the best use of data. There is no doubt that data man cannot cover all aspects of man in data rights law. In fact, man has multiple images in modern law, and in the future data man will probably become a major facet of the image of man in law, while other facets of it will be merely modifications or supplements to it.

Data Man Hypothesis

In 1966, Cornelius Gallagher, a member of the U.S. House of Representatives, issued such a warning at the "federal data center" hearing:

> "Computerized people," in my opinion, refer to those who have been deprived of their independence and privacy. Relying on the standardization brought by the progress of science and technology, this kind of people's social status will be measured by computers, and they will lose their personal characteristics. Their life, their talent and even their ability to make money will be reduced to a tedious disk which has lost multiple possibilities that they used to have. (Regan 1995, p. 72)

"Computerized man" is not only a warning, but also a prophecy. In less than a decade this prophecy has almost become a reality. In 1973, the U.S.

Department of Health, Education and Welfare[17] published the *Records, Computers and the Rights of Citizens*, which contains many sad descriptions.[18] In 2004, the famous American privacy expert, Professor Daniel Solove, published a monograph called *The Digital Person: Technology and Privacy in the Information Age*, in which he directly described the crisis in the information age at the beginning:

> We are in the midst of an information revolution, and we are only beginning to understand its implications. The past few decades have witnessed a dramatic transformation in the way we shop, bank, and go about our daily business—changes that have resulted in an unprecedented proliferation of records and data. Small details that were once captured in dim memories or fading scraps of paper are now preserved forever in the digital minds of computers, in vast databases with fertile fields of personal data. Our wallets are stuffed with ATM cards, calling cards, frequent shopper cards, and credit cards—all of which can be used to record where we are and what we do. Every day, rivulets of information stream into electric brains to be sifted, sorted, rearranged, and combined in hundreds of different ways. Digital technology enables the preservation of the minutia of our everyday comings and goings, of our likes and dislikes, of who we are and what we own. It is ever more possible to create an electronic collage that covers much of a person's life—a life captured in records, a digital person composed in the collective computer networks of the world. (Solove 2006, p. 1)

Professor Solove's words probably sound very like reality in China today, though it has only been seventeen years from 2004 to 2020. A "digital China" has been in the making in front of the world at an unprecedented pace. Almost every detail of Chinese people's lives is permeated with

17 The predecessor to the U.S. Department of Health and Human Services.

18 Once upon a time, we always entrusted our personal information to people or institutions we trust face to face. This trust can be said to involve some symmetry and equivalence. Nowadays, individuals have to increasingly hand over personal information to a large number of unknown institutions for processing and use. As for who is using our personal information, we have no way to know, neither see nor touch, and even if we know who it is, we often get no response. Sometimes we don't even know that an institution still holds a record of information about ourselves. In most cases, we are kept in the dark; we cannot ask whether the information kept is accurate, or control that information from being spread, or prevent others from using it at will.

digitilization. Taking China's "four new inventions" as examples, China stays ahead in the digital economy represented by Alipay, bike sharing, and online shopping, while high-speed rail is now supported with more digital technology to improve its operational performance and service quality. We can now see the changes that digital technology has brought to our lives more clearly, comprehensively, and deeply. At this time, we also have to address the problems of "computerized people" and "digital people" that the American people have worried about for more than fifty years. Every person and everything in this world can be expressed with data; in other words, data will become the form of existence for all people and things, keeping records of the entire life of everyone—from the cradle to the grave. We are inextricably dependent on data, and this dependence arises at a time when we are not yet free from dependence on other things. And the image, connotation, and denotation of what we call "man" will change profoundly. "In the big data era, all social relationships can be represented with data in a world composed of data, and a person is the sum of related data" (Li Guojie 2014). All social relationships are in essence data relations closely bound up with privacy protection and the altruistic sharing of data, so the laws that regulate these relationships should also become "digitalized" laws. Meanwhile, human rights are undergoing a digitalization process. Accordingly, our approach to human rights should change, to be based on "data man." This makes it necessary to establish the new concept of digital human rights, construct corresponding human rights protection mechanisms, and provide necessary legal support for digital human rights (Ma Changshan 2019).

Data man is the new display of human nature in the big data era. History has proved that for each step human nature has moved forward, there has been an unprecedented impact on legislation and the value pursuit thereof. In the age of private law, man is the economic man in law. Then, social law came into being on the basis of reflections on the egoism of economic man[19] and the discovery of the sociality and altruism in human

19 Economists have gradually realized that the economic man hypothesis, which represents a model of definitional thinking, is facing severe challenges in our time of intelligence development and informatization and that it cannot explain the altruistic behaviors existing in reality, which directly proves the inadequacy of this

nature. It is undoubtedly a significant turn in the history of jurisprudence but it is not the last, because human nature will continue to evolve and improve with time. At present, global data security crises happen continuously. In this context, humankind again discovers that the social man hypothesis, among others, is no longer sufficient to resolve the conflicts between human and data and it is necessary to challenge and go beyond existing barriers and limitations through deeper reflections. Data man is what we came up with after such reflections; it is a new display of human nature in the big data era which takes altruism as its core:

> Human nature serves as the source and basis of rights and rights embody the requirements and nature of human beings. It is the rights based on human nature that are deep-rooted. Thus, the extent to which people understand human nature determines the extent to which people understand rights and are able to protect rights. (Tu Yongqian 2019)

Human nature is always marked with the characteristics of the times and, with time, human nature will inevitably drive the evolution and development of the value of the law. The change in human nature in the big data era, which is represented by the data man, will certainly bring about changes to the values of the law in terms security, sharing, and altruism in the end.

egoistic hypothesis. "We should frankly admit the limitations and incapability of the economic man hypothesis." We "don't have to deny but just have to go beyond the economic man" (Yang Chunxue 2005). From the perspective of economic philosophy, the doctrine of rational egoism is in a dilemma when it attempts to explain issues concerning contemporary economic behaviors and encounters challenges due to imbalance, information asymmetry and the frequent occurrence of uncertainties in the market economy of the twentieth century. In addition, it is just because human beings are not completely egoistic, and are full of altruistic feelings for relatives, friends, and even strangers, that mankind has survived, thrived, and created glorious civilizations. Human development would not have achieved what it has achieved today without the altruistic behaviors of people.

Possibility of Altruism

The word "altruism" was first proposed by Auguste Comte, a French philosopher and ethicist of the nineteenth century, who illustrated the rationality of altruism from the instinct and nature of humanity. "Just as there are rational requirements from people on thought, there are rational requirements on action, and altruism is one of them" (Nagel 1978, p. 3). The structure of relationships in this digital society determines that such a society is inherently decentralized, flat, and borderless, and that its basic spirits are openness, sharing, cooperation, and mutual benefit. That means that such a society and such an era are bound to be people-oriented with altruism as the core value. Huge cooperation surpluses give birth to an altruistic spirit, and altruism may lead people out of the prisoner's dilemma. Altruism enhances people's willingness to transfer and share data rights and, further, turns such transfers and sharing into actions with highly positive significance. In a certain sense, the data rights law plays the role of a midwife for altruism, helping nurture the altruistic spirit.

In the *Theory of Moral Sentiments*, Adam Smith clearly pointed out the altruistic nature of man at the very beginning, stating that:

> How selfish so ever man may be supposed, there are evidently some principles in his nature, which interest him in the fortunes of others, and render their happiness necessary to him, though he derives nothing from it, except the pleasure of seeing it. (Adam Smith 2015, p. 5)

Bacon also stated that, "there is, in man's nature, a secret inclination, and motion, towards love of others" (Francis Bacon 1983, p. 36). According to Abraham Maslow's hierarchy of needs, those who are at a lower tier in the hierarchy of needs tend to show egoistic behaviors, while the needs at higher tiers can only be satisfied through cooperation and sharing. A certain degree of altruism is, therefore, necessary for the satisfaction of such needs. "The higher people are in the hierarchy of needs, the more they will reveal the natural inclination to share" (Wang Tianen 2018). Thus, the higher the level of needs the more necessary altruism and sharing is for the satisfaction of such needs. Once the needs at the low tiers have been satisfied one will gradually move up the ladder to the level of self-actualization and, by then, there will be the chance and the possibility to resolve the conflicts and tensions that arise between egoism and altruism. Thus, when only the most basic material needs are pursued it is reasonable to seek the maximization of personal interests. However, once they move up the hierarchy of needs, egoism and altruism will no longer compete with each other. Instead, it will feel as if egoism has become part of altruism. As the division of labor becomes more refined and chains connect people more closely than ever, individuals' interests are actualized through the satisfaction of the needs of others, society, and the nation. If everyone pursues only the maximization of their personal interests and ignores the interests of others, mankind will find itself caught in the Hobbesian jungle. Mutual harm in society is in essence the result of the short-sightedness of excessive egoism and, if not regulated, it will evolve and lead to a mutual-harm society. By way of contrast, if everyone is willing to set aside their own interests for the benefit of others, a society of "all for one and one for all" will become possible.

According to Martin Nowak, a biologist at Harvard University, "co-operation is the architect of creativity throughout evolution, from cells to multicellular creatures to ant hills to villages to cities." When getting prepared for the new challenges of global governance, humankind must find new cooperation models, and altruism should be the basis of cooperation. As for countries, it is only when they cooperate with one another, observe the principle of data interests transfer, and seek common grounds or balance between the respective data interests of different countries and nations and the interests of a data community with a shared future for humankind, can it become possible for all stakeholders to maximize their data interests. History shows that as the human society progresses, humankind has gradually reduced elements of brutishness, greed, and selfishness, while altruism, inner law, and the idea of sharing has become the theme of life, leading mankind onto an altruism-based development path. The proposition of data rights law indicates that humankind has gained further understanding of the relationship between people and data. People have realized that they should make the best efforts to increase the data well-being of society based on the principle of transfer for the best interest of society on the whole. For society, it is righteous to create a system amplify the altruism in human nature, inspire the altruistic spirit, and build a more harmonious relationship between people and data.

From Possession to Sharing

The possession system is the basis of real rights, while a sharing system is the core of data rights. When designing the data rights system, we must take into consideration the altruism in human nature, do what we can to encourage the good in human nature, while oppressing the possibility of man doing evil things. Altruism is the human nature basis of data rights law, and is where the formulation and the implementation of data rights laws start and end. As the legal system governing the ownership, rights, use, and protection of data and the basic norm governing the data-related behaviors and maintaining data order, data rights law should aim to realize balance and coordination between the effective protection of data rights and making the best use of data so as to safeguard the public interest and public security while promoting the free flow and sharing of personal data. In this regard, citizens' transfer of data rights is, to a certain extent, crucial to the realization of balance and coordination between law-based protection and reasonable use of data. That is, data rights legislation is intended to promote the flow and use of data rather than to impose restrictions on data by spreading the dense net of justice.

As Gustav Radbruch once said:

> The concern of legal system was not about making people fix their eyes at all times like guards, but enabling them to occasionally and blithely look up at the bright stars, flowers, and trees in full bloom, as well as necessity of unconstraint and virtues. (Radbruch 2001, p. 9)

Altruism is the human nature basis and the human nature aspect of data rights law. This means that data rights law starts with altruism, conveys the requirements of altruism, takes altruism as its main content, and has sharing, which is the ultimate objective and value pursuit of altruism, and primarily aims at modeling and enhancing the altruism in man. Of course, this does not mean that the data rights law does not pursue other values, such as security, efficiency, and benefits, but the key is that these values should not take the place of altruism as an objective.

The traditional private law system was initially established on the scarcity of objects (mainly tangible objects), which led to the necessity of confirming rights and duties, resolving disputes by law, and made the rights-based resource allocation model a universally effective way in traditional society. It also forms the mutual dependence of objects and rights in law. The economic law based on scarcity provides that when the supply of goods increases, the cost of those goods will gradually decrease, which is the saturation law of industrial society. However, the principle of public reciprocity of data overturns that law, just as the popularization of fax machines and telephones increased the value of them, the value of the network comes from the sufficiency and popularization of data. In the data rights system, it is necessary to avoid the negative factors generated by many rights discourses, to get out of the fog of active protection of rights, and to establish the reciprocal social responsibility for data circulation. Advocating rights cannot be done at the expense of social responsibility. When uncontrolled rights go too far the demand for social responsibility may limit the unrestrained development of rights; when the law cannot respond to the needs and responsibilities of the real society, cultivating an altruistic social responsibility may be more realistic for data rights legislation. As a natural public good, data obeys the inherent principle of reciprocity and sharing. On this basis, the theory of data law should complete a transformation of its underlying way of thinking, that is, from scarcity-based law to abundance-based law, from the protection of private interests to the protection of public interests, and from the strengthening of data control to the modesty of data control, so as to establish "altruistic sharing" as the basic value orientation of data rights law (Mei Xiaying 2019).

Digital Order

Law is "the combination of order and justice" (Bodenheimer 2004, p. 332). It is the primary and conventional means to prevent, stop, and remedy disorder. The value of order and the value of justice are important criteria for evaluating "newborn" laws. Order ranks first in the value system of law and is the basic value that always accompanies legislation. In a sense legislation means order because law is formulated to establish and maintain order. One of the important goals of legislation is to achieve the "consistency, continuity and certainty" (Bodenheimer 2004, p. 234) for the whole of society. The rapid development of digital technology has brought fractures, uncertainties, and risks to the existing order, but at the same time it has injected strong momentum into the construction of a new order. Among the various risks, the most prominent is the failure of legal regulations; among the various challenges, the most serious is legal disorder. Law failure and legal disorder are mainly manifested as "governance deficit"; that is to say, the current governance system, rules, capacity, and technology can no longer effectively cope with the challenges in all aspects brought by digital technology, resulting in loss of control and disorder, and even endangering civil rights, social welfare, public order, national security, and world peace. "If one walks too fast, the soul will lag behind." This ancient saying of a nomadic tribe might as well be used to describe the current situation of humanity in the digital age, with hidden dangers and partial disorder. The traditional legal theory encounters problems when it is used to interpret the digital world and the corresponding methods of legal regulation are also faced with theoretical problems and practical shortcomings that are difficult to deal with in the current context. Therefore, it is both necessary and urgent to build legal order into our digital society to cope with the emergence of "governance deficits" in social governance, national governance, and global governance. To bring digital technology—dominated by data and algorithms—and its social influence into this legal framework, we urgently need to build a legal order for the digital society, featuring inclusion, digital co-governance, and digital justice. This is the top priority to crack the "governance deficit" of the digital society, and also the fundamental guarantee for the stable, long-term development of the digital economy.

Digital Inclusion

Inclusiveness is a symbol of modern civilization and a virtue of the modern rule of law. In a digital society what we need to establish and maintain is a legal order featuring digital inclusion. The openness, sharing, and altruism of data inevitably require that the digital social order is an order that respects differences and inclusiveness, an order in which data differences and conflicts can be resolved or eased on the basis of data jurisprudence and ethics, as well as an order supported by technological intelligence and legal rationality. In order to effectively cope with the constraints of social transformation brought by the development of digital technology, systematic, collaborative, and inclusive thinking about the rule of law can lead people to carefully consider issues such as mechanism, order, and governance capabilities, which can construct a more inclusive digital system of rule of law, while building a higher-level and higher-quality societal rule of law.

Handling the various dialectical relationships in a digital society with digital thinking and legal thinking: There are many balances of interests: dialectical relationships; value conflicts such as the relationships between data rights and data risks; data security and data development; data protection and data public benefits; data freedom and data supervision; data privacy and data sharing; and data property rights and data welfare. These incentives for data innovations and tolerance for data faults, as well as the structural contradictions between data supply and the data demand, the social contradictions between data protection and data utilization, the confrontational contradictions between data public rights and data private rights, and the competitive contradictions between strong countries and weak countries in data. They may exist for a long time and need to be carefully studied, reasonably regulated, and balanced in the process of law formulation and implementation so as to avoid attending to one thing and losing sight of another.

Learning from the achievements of foreign digital technology civilization systems in a more open, diversified, and comprehensive manner, objectively speaking, digital technology originated from developed countries in Europe and America. They encountered problems with digital technology and digital social governance earlier than, and more than, us; they also addressed legal regulations and ethical governance earlier than us. So, it is worth reflecting on their lessons and learning from their advanced practices. For example, the European Union enacted the *Directive 95/46/EC on Data Protection* in 1995 and the *General Data Protection Regulation* in 2016, which is the most systematic, elaborate, and stringent legislation in the history of data protection in the world. Nevertheless, the development of the data industry in the EU has been hindered by such stringent protection measures. In 2017, the German Bundestag enacted the *Act on Improving the Enforcement of Laws in Social Networks*, which defined "social network platforms," and included social network platforms like Facebook, Twitter, YouTube, and other similar for-profit platforms operating in Germany that shared arbitrary information with the public and users, and brought them within the scope of legal regulation. In addition, the Act clearly stipulated the responsibilities of internet platforms, governments (for regulation), and social network platforms (for content review and supervision). In the same year the *Road Traffic Law* of Germany was also revised, it set up legal norms for driverless vehicles, making clear the basic concepts of driverless cars, the rights and obligations and responsibilities of drivers, and laying the necessary legal foundation for the development of driverless cars. For another example, the *Principles of Human-centered Artificial Intelligence Society*, issued by Japan in 2018, clearly stipulated that the research and application of artificial intelligence should adhere to the social concepts of human dignity, pluralism, inclusiveness, and sustainability. Learning from the experience and lessons of the European Union, it also put forward a series of principles that should be followed, such as the principle of human-centeredness; the principle of education application; the principle of privacy protection; the principle of security protection; the principle of fair competition; the principle of fairness, accountability, and transparency;

and the principle of innovation. Hereto, the concepts, propositions, ideas, values, principles, rules, systems, mechanisms, formulation and implementation procedures, as well as the practical process of modification and improvement in the above legal documents are all worthy of study, research, and reference (Zhang Wenxian 2020).

Digital Co-governance

Co-governance lies at the center of good governance, hence a good digital legal order is derived from digital co-governance. The governance of the digital society is more complex than that of any other social form in that it requires not only mastery of digital technology, but also extensive social coverage for all digital citizens. That said, to resolve the "governance deficit," what we need to do is to bridge digital divergences, build a system for compatibility of diverse rules, create a co-governance structure for good governance with good laws, and establish a digital legal order centered on the co-governance of law and technology, law and ethics, and multiple parties. This is the inevitable choice for the building of a new legal order in the digital society.

Co-governance of law and technology. The purpose of the co-governance of law and technology is to promote the deep integration of institutional advantages and digital technology, as well as to give full play to the basic role of technology and the protective role of law, so that code-based regulation and legal regulation, algorithms and laws can be made complementary. Today, China not only has the institutional advantages of the socialist legal system with Chinese characteristics, but is a leader in digital technologies in fields such as e-commerce, the Internet, big data, cloud computing, the Internet of Things, blockchain, and artificial intelligence. Technology and systems, when deeply integrated, will form a new comprehensive advantage, which will inevitably produce huge governance efficiencies. In addition, China has launched its political and legal big data case-handling system; the world's first internet court, with the successive establishment of such courts in Hangzhou, Beijing, and Guangzhou, and smart systems for the political and legal authorities, courts, procuratorates, and public security organs all over the country. China Judgments Online has become one of the most influential online judicial document platform in the world. All of these show that the governance of China is about to make a great leap with the help of technological advantages. The co-governance of law and technology lies at the intersection of legal science and natural sciences, and joint efforts are required to guide technology for social good. As David Edmond Neuberger, the former President of the Supreme Court of the United Kingdom, said in a speech at the Royal Society:

> The rule of law is the cornerstone of a civilized society. As science continues to develop and explore in many fields, scientists should understand the relevant legal rules and the appropriate legal boundaries to guide their work. Besides, it is equally important that lawyers should be familiar with the development of science, and the law needs to keep up with the pace of the development of technology. (Neuberger 2020)

Co-governance of law and ethics. As President Xi Jinping once pointed out, "law is a written morality, and morality is the inner law." Morality is not only the root of law, but also the future of law. Law has never faced the challenges posed by the development of technology as it is today. We should pay close attention to frontier technology; actively respond to challenges; regulate possible risks; coordinate the development of law and technology, and law and ethics; and actively promote the transformation of law, the rule of law, and jurisprudence in response to the social transformation. In particular, with regard to the combination of ethics and jurisprudence, we need to examine and reflect on human relations and the digital order against the background of digital technology. This mainly includes two aspects: One is to re-examine the social subject.[20] The traditional legal

20 *The Development Plan of the New Generation Artificial Intelligence* issued by the State Council has specified the necessity of studying relevant legal issues and establishing an accountability system. It clearly took "establishing laws, regulations, ethical norms and policy system of artificial intelligence" as its strategic goal, and proposed "making laws, regulations and ethical norms that promote the development of artificial intelligence" is one of the safeguards to promote the healthy and rapid development of artificial intelligence. In addition, it particularly pointed out that it is necessary to actively participate in the global governance of artificial

system, especially the legal subject system has been, or is, facing unprecedented challenges.[21] In the future, human society is likely to be composed of

---

intelligence; promote research on major international common issues of artificial intelligence such as robot alienation and safety supervision; deepen international cooperation in laws, regulations, and international rules of artificial intelligence to jointly cope with global challenges; and optimize the allocation of innovative resources on a global scale. In terms of the specifications, standards, and regulatory methods of AI development, China shall be in line with international standards and participate in global dialogue. In addition, China shall prompt the research of laws and regulations related to artificial intelligence; clarify the relevant rights, obligations, and responsibilities of artificial intelligence; and focus on the study on legal status of artificial intelligence.

21 The data power and data relation in the digital age must be different from the legal theories and systems that take the assembly line in the nineteenth century and automation in the twentieth century as standard objects. In analyzing the significance of legal personality, Hoshino Echi, a Japanese jurist in civil law, stated that even beings, other than human beings, will be acknowledged if they are suitable for acting as subjects of rights and obligations in private law (Hoshino Echi 2004, p. 21). Israeli historian Yuval Noah Harari was of the opinion that "the law of the human race has come to recognize such an entity of intersubjectivity as a corporation or a nation and called it a 'legal person'. Toyota or Argentina has neither body nor mind, but both are bound by international law and can own land and money, and may become a plaintiff or defendant before the courts." (Yuval Noah Harari, trans. Lin Junhong 2017, p. 293). While a heated debate is going on in academic circles, the legislature has not been left behind. In 2017, the European Parliament's Committee on Legal Affairs proposed "creating a specific legal status for robots in the long run, so that at least the most sophisticated autonomous robots could be established as having the status of electronic persons responsible for making good any damage they may cause, and possibly applying electronic personality to cases where robots make autonomous decisions or otherwise interact with third parties independently" (European Parliament's Committee on Legal Affairs 2015. Report with Recommendations to the Commission on Civil Law Rules on Robotics, 2015/2103 (INL), <http://www.europarl.europa.eu/sides/ getDoc.do?pubRef=-//EP//NONSGML+REPORT+A8-2017-0005+0+ DOC+PDF+V0//EN>). Russia followed closely by proposing in Article 1 of the Grishin Law that robots be granted the legal status of "robot-agent" and stated that a robot-agent is supposed to possess independent property and assume liability for its own debts with such property and may receive and exercise civil rights and undertake civil obligations in its own name (Zhang Jianwen 2018).

natural persons, robots, and gene-edited people. Professor David Vladeck at the Law School of Georgetown University, United States, took the injury caused by unmanned robots as an example, and asked questions about how the law treats robots and how to bear the legal consequences of robots' actions. He believes that the legal status of robots is a problem that legislation has to face and said "with the development of intelligent robots, our constitution and laws may need to be revised or rewritten." The other aspect is to deal with issues such as reshaping the social structure in the risk society. Digital technology should take the realization of human interests as the ultimate goal, and embody respect for personality, the protection of human rights, and the elimination of risks. It is necessary to construct benign human relations and social orders based on digital technology, and establish the ethical norms and legal principles that the relevant subjects should follow in the process of digital technology development and application. Always bearing in mind the value of human beings, we should develop technology for social good.

Multi-party co-governance. Human society is moving from a binary world to a tertiary world. All mankind shares the same digital world, and human society is becoming a community with a shared future. The governance of the digital world is a complicated systematic project that requires both the soft constraints of ethics and the hard limits of laws, including an ethically oriented social norm system, an algorithm-based technological constraint system, and a legal-guaranteed risk prevention and control system. Digital governance should be built as a multi-level governance system with the participation and cooperation of multiple subjects, such as government agencies, industrial organizations, and the public, to form a co-governance structure and synergy for governance in the digital society. Through various measures, including ethical principles, technical standards, laws, and regulations, the development of digital technology will be brought within the auspices of the rule of law, and be good for humankind and society. The *Decision of the Fourth Plenary Session of the 19th CPC Central Committee* states that:

> It is necessary to strengthen and innovate social governance, improve the social governance system of party committee leadership, government responsibility, democratic consultation, social coordination, public participation, legal protection, and

> technological support, as well as build the community of social governance in which all people bear their responsibilities, do their duties as well as enjoy their rights and benefits.[22]

This constitutes an in-depth revelation that co-governance is part of the connotation of the "community of social governance" which represents the spirit of the times. In the digital world members of society are not opponents who fight fiercely for life, but teammates who will face future challenges together. Governments, internet companies, non-governmental organizations, and individuals must all fulfill their responsibilities. Everyone has a share in this; the community of social governance is, firstly, a community of practice and a community of responsibilities. Meanwhile everyone also enjoys their rights and benefits, demonstrating that the community is also a community of interests, a community of values, a community of rights, and a community with a shared future. That all people bear their responsibilities is the essence, that all people fulfill their duties is the premise, and that all people enjoy their rights and benefits is the result. This is consistent with the principles of collaboration, participation, and common interests for social governance.

Digital Justice

Fairness and justice are part of the basic values of a modern society and an important yardstick for measuring social progress. As Rawls said, "Justice is the primary value of social system, as truth is the primary value of ideological system." (Rawls 1988, p. 3). Fairness and justice are not only inherent requirements of law, they are also the soul and life of judicial practices. Human society is entering the digital age, exploitative relationships in this era are reflected in the social inequality caused by the "digital divide" and social injustice caused by the "digital deficit." Consequently,

22 See the Decision of the Fourth Plenary Session of the 19th CPC Central Committee.

the common goal of all humankind in the future will be "to change this unjust world determined by transnational digital capital that exploits global digital laborers into a new world of fairness and justice without exploitation and oppression through digital workers' concrete actions" (Zhou Yanyun and Yan Xiurong 2016, p. 267).

Ethan Katsh is the founder of the global digital justice theory and a leading figure in online dispute resolution (ODR). He and Orna Rabinovich-Einy put forward the theory of digital justice in the cyber world for the first time in *Digital Justice: Technology and Internet of Disputes*, pointing out that the theory of digital justice will gradually replace the traditional theory of justice and become the principle and criterion of the digital world. The theory of digital justice has epoch-making significance. For it is not just a milestone in the study of justice theory, it provides instructions and codes to guide us in the future, as well as understanding and mastering it. As Lord Briggs said:

> Traditional courts are the result of the industrial age, while online courts are the product of the internet era; traditional courts will inevitably decline, and online courts will rise. Achieving the goal of establishing online courts is worth the time, money and effort, because online courts will be the most revolutionary and subversive courts in this era and will change the way for courts to produce justice and the way for parties to achieve justice. (Lord Justice Briggs 2017, p. 49)

In the digital age, equality, freedom, democracy, law, order, and justice will all be redefined.

Since Aristotle, the kind of results that accord with justice through a certain process is the core issue of justice theory. There are many differences between digital justice theory and traditional justice theory, which are mainly manifested in three aspects. First, the digital justice theory is a kind of theory on justice formed in a digital society, in which laws and social rules need to be redefined and our view on justice needs to be reshaped. Second, the digital justice theory is a "bottom-up" justice theory. Digital technology has undoubtedly undertaken the mission of digital revolution and reshaped the idea of justice, which has a profound impact on ODR and internet justice. For example, an ODR mechanism that diverts cases can improve the efficiency and greatly reduce the cost of dispute resolution;

in the meantime, it fundamentally changes the court-centered justice realization path. Third, digital justice is a dynamic theory of justice. Different from other justice theories, digital justice theory does not really give the definite, only, and correct answer. Instead, digital justice relies on everyone to promise, fulfill, practice, and realize it (Zhao Lei and Cao Jianfeng 2020).

Bibliography

Adam, Smith. 2015. *The Theory of Moral Sentiments*. Trans. Jiang Zhiqiang, et al. Beijing: The Commercial Press.

Bodenheimer, Edgar. 2004. *Jurisprudence: The Philosophy and Method of the Law*. Trans. Deng Zhenglai. Beijing: China University of Political Science and Law Press.

Cheng, Xiao. 2019. "Protection of Personal Information from the Perspective of the Compilation of Civil Code." *China Legal Science*, 4th issue.

Daniel, Solove. 2006. *The Digital Person: Technology and Privacy in the Information Age*. New York: New York University Press, 2006.

David, C. Vladeck. 2014. "Machines without Principles: Liability Rules and Artificial Intelligence." *Washington Law Review*, 89th issue.

David, Edmond Neuberger. 2020. "How to Judge a Case with the Help of Science and Technology" Trans. Ge Feng. August 10. <http:///www.infzm.com/contents/ 119170>.

Deloitte and Ali Research. 2019. "The Approach of Data Assets: Data Assets Valuation and Industry Practice." <http://www.d-long.cn/eWebEditor/uploadfile/2019103011190887534744.pdf>.

Bodenheimer, Edgar. 1962. *Jurisprudence: The Philosophy and Method of the Law*. Trans. Deng, Zhenglai. 2004. Beijing: China University of Political Science and Law Press.

Fan, Jinxue. 2003. "The Theory of Right Concept." *China Legal Science*, 2nd issue.

Francis, Bacon. 1983. *The Essays of Francis Bacon*. Trans. Shui Tongtian. Beijing: The Commercial Press.

Gao, Fuping. 2019. "The Legal Basis of Processing of Personal Information: A Perspective of Interests Related to Personal Information." *Journal of Comparative Law*, 2nd issue.

Gao, Zhihong. 2020. "The Connotation of the Contemporary Rule of Law in the View of Public Interest and Its Realization Path", *Tribune of Political Science and Law*, 2nd issue.

Guo, Daohui. 1997. *On Benefit Distribution and Adjustment in Legislation, Xiangjiang Law Review (Vol. 2)*. Changsha: Hunan Publishing House.

Gustav, Radbruch. 2001. *Aphorism of Legal Wisdom*. Trans. Shu Guoying. Beijing: China Legal Publishing House.

He, Yuan, ed. 2020. *Data Law*. Beijing: Peking University Press.

Hoshino, Echi. 2004. *Person in Private Law: Focusing on the Civil Law and the Property Law*. Trans. Wang Chuang. Beijing: China Legal Publishing House.

Hume, David. 1996. *A Treatise on Human Nature*. Trans. Guan Wenyun. Beijing: The Commercial Press.

Li, Guojie. 2014. "Data Sharing: The Premise of Modernization of National Governance System in the Age of Big Data." *China Information Weekly*, August 25.

Li, Yan. 2008. "The Transformation Relationship among Civil Legal Interests, Rights and Interests." *Social Sciences Review*, 3rd issue.

Liang, Shangshang. 2016. "Public Interest and the Interest Measurement Theory." *Tribune of Political Science and Law*, 6th issue.

Liu, Zegang. 2020. "The Uncertainty of Big Data Privacy and Its Response Mechanism." *Zhejiang Academic Journal*, 6th issue.

Lord Justice Briggs. 2017. "Ultimate Reform: The Way of Delivering Just and the Approach of Accessing to Justice: British Online Court's Concept, the Scope of Acceptance, and the Basic Stages" Trans. Zhao Lei. *China Review of Administration of Justice*, 2nd issue.

Lv, Zhongmei. 2005. *The Way of Communication and Coordination: On Civil Law Protection of Civil Environmental Rights*. Beijing: China Renmin University Press.

Ma, Changshan. 2019. "The Fourth Generation of Human Rights' under the China Review of Administration of Justice Background of Smart Society and Its Protection", *China Legal Science*, 5th issue.

Mei, Xiaying. 2019. "Between Sharing and Control the Limitations of Private Law and the Building of Public Order in Data Protection." *Peking University Law Journal*, 4th issue.

Peng, Chengxin. 2004. "From Interest to Right: Justice as the Linkage and Core." *Law and Social Development*, 5th issue.

Peter, Stein, and Shand John. 2004. *Legal Values in Western Society*. Trans. Wang Xianping. Beijing: China Legal Publishing House.

Phil, Mcnally, and Inayatullah Sohail. 1988. "The Rights of Robots." *Futures*, 2nd issue.

Priscilla, M. Regan. 1995. *Legislating Privacy: Technology, Social Values and Public Policy*, Chapel Hill: University of North Carolina Press.

Prosser, William L. 1960. "Privacy." *California Law Review 48*, 3rd issue.

Qi, Yanping. 2015. *Evolution of the Ideology of Human Rights*. Ji'nan: Shandong University Press.

Rawls, John. 1988. *A Theory of Justice*. Trans. He Huaihong, et al. Beijing: China Social Sciences Press.

Richards, Neil M., and Daniel J. Solove. 2007. "Privacy's Other Path: Recovering the Law of Confidentiality." *Georgetown Law Journal*, 1st issue.

Sun, Ping. 2018. *To Protect Our Information*. Beijing: Peking University Press.

Sylvia, Kierkegaarda, Watersb Nigel, Greenleafc Graham, Bygraved Lee, A., Lloyde Ian, and Saxbyf Steve. 2011. "30 Years on – The Review of the Council of Europe Data Protection Convention." *Computer Law & Security Review*, 27th issue.

Thomas, Nagel. 1978. *The Possibility of Altruism*. Princeton, NJ: Princeton University Press.

Trachtman, Joel P. 2013. *The Future of International Law: Global Government*. Cambridge: Cambridge University Press.

Tu, Yongqian. 2019 "The Humanity Analysis of Rights: Concurrently Discussing the Independent Compilation of Personality in the Forthcoming Civil Code of PRC." *Tribune of Political Science and Law*, 2nd issue.

Wang, Dongsheng. 2019. *Criminal Law Protection of Personal Information*. Beijing: Law Press.

Wang, Guanghui. 2015. *Human Rights Law*. Beijing: Tsinghua University Press.

Wang, Tianen. 2018. "Information Civilization: A Key to a New Understanding of Development." *Social Sciences in China*, 6th issue.

Warren, Samuel D., and Louis D. Brandeis. 1890. "The Right to Privacy." *Harvard Law Review 4*, 5th issue.

Westin, Alan F. 1967. *Privacy and Freedom*. New York: Athenum.

Xie, Yuanyang. 2015. "The Value of Personal Information from the Perspective of Information Theory with a Review of the Protection Mode of Rights to Privacy." *Tsinghua University Law Journal*, 3rd issue.

Yan, Lidong. 2019. "Exploring Data Rights from the Perspective of 'Bundle of Rights'." *Oriental Law*, 2nd issue.

Yang, Chunxue. 2005. "The Rejuvenating of Homo Economicus: A Discussion and Defence on New Synthesis." *Economic Research Journal*, 11th issue.

Yuval, Noah Harar. 2017. *Homo Deus: A Brief History of Tomorrow*. Trans. Lin Junhong. Beijing: CITIC Press.

Zhang, Jianwen. 2018. "Contribution and Limitation of the Grishin Law: A Review of the Draft of the First Robot Law of Russia." *Journal of East China University of Political Science and Law*, 2nd issue.

Zhang, Li, ed. 2019. *Data Governance and Data Security*. Beijing: Post & Telecom Press.

Zhang, Wenxian. 2019. "Human Rights Jurisprudence in the New Era." *Human Rights*, 3rd issue.

Zhang, Wenxian. 2020. "Constructing the Legal Order of an Intelligent Society." *Oriental Law*, 5th issue.

Zhang, Yuanquan. 2009. "Right to Information Self-Determination in Germany." *China Doctoral Forum of Public Law*.

Zhao, Hong. 2017. "Current Situation of Protection of Right to Informational Self-determination in China and Trend Prospect of Its Legislation." *China Law Review*, 1st issue.

Zhao, Lei, and Cao, Jianfeng. 2020. "Digital Justice Is Coming." *China Information Weekly*, August 25.

Zhou, Hanhua. 2020. "Legal Nature of Personal Information Protection." *Studies in Law and Business*, 3rd issue.

Zhou, Sijia. 2020. "Clarification of the Relationship between Rights to Personal Data and Rights to Personal Information." *ECUPL Journal*, 2nd issue.

Zhou, Yanyun and Yan, Xiurong. 2016. *Digital Labor and Karl Marx*. Beijing: China social sciences press.

CHAPTER 2

Core Topics of Data Rights Legislation

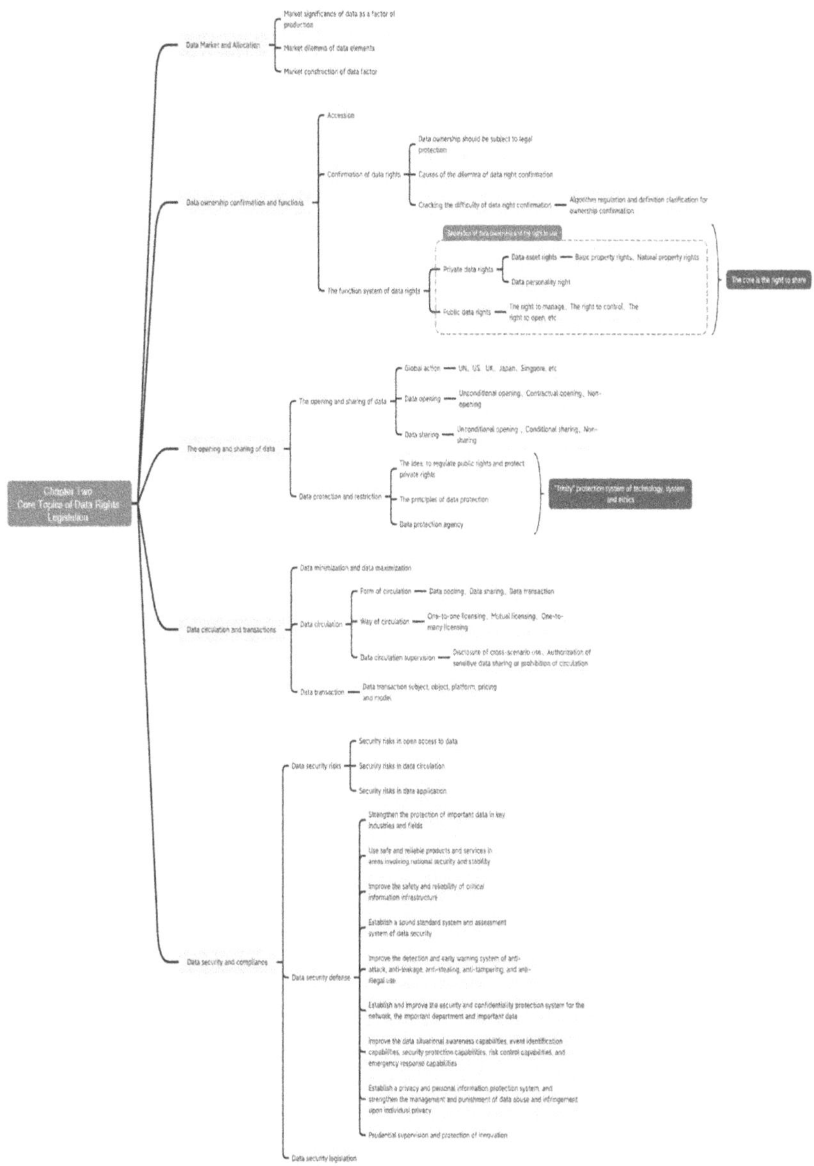

Awareness of digital rights began in the 1970s with legislation on personal data protection as the major symbol. Based on legal, academic, and mathematical foundations, digital rights legislation focused on addressing core issues such as the data market and distribution, confirmation of data ownership rights and the powers of such rights, data openness and sharing, data circulation and transactions, and data security and compliance. Promoting the development of the data factor market and using data as a basic factor to participate in distribution played a guiding role in the development of the digital economy, guiding enterprises to pay more attention to data as a production factor, increasing productivity, and accelerating the birth of new formats, new models, and a new digital economy. Confirmation of data rights ownership is the logical starting point for the clarification of data ownership structure. This clarifies the rights and responsibilities of data subjects and the distribution mechanism of data property rights, before going on to build a credible data rights system. Data openness, sharing, transactions, and exchanges are important ways of data circulation and an important prerequisite for maximizing the value of data. Data security and compliance is at the core of data rights legislation. The purpose is to protect data and prevent attacks, leakage, stealth, tampering, and illegal use.

Data Market and Allocation

After the Fourth Plenary Session of the 19th CPC Central Committee, the Party proposed that data can be used as a factor of production to participate in contribution-based distribution. The *Opinions of the Central Committee of the Communist Party of China and the State Council on Building a More Complete Factor Market Allocation System and Mechanism* outlined the basic policy of data as a production factor for the first time, the core of which was to "promote the openness and sharing of government data," "enhance the value of social data resources," and "strengthen data resource integration and security protection." On October 29, 2020, the *Proposals of the Central Committee of the Communist Party of China on Formulating the Fourteenth Five-Year Plan for National Economic and Social Development and the Long-term Goals for 2035*, adopted at the Fifth Plenary Session of the 19th CPC Central Committee, clearly requires the promotion of "the market-oriented reform of land, labor, capital, technology, data and other factors." Changes from the *Opinions* to the *Proposals* reflect that China's attitude to the market and the allocation of data as a production factor is moving from the stage of being spontaneous to conscious. Regarding data as a new production factor, firstly, emphasizes the importance of data as a national basic strategic resource and, secondly, reflects the fact that China pays more attention to the cultivation of the data factor market and the construction of the data system.

Market Significance of Data as a Factor of Production

Factors of production is a category of economics. "It refers to the sum of various social resources required for social production and operation activities, and is all the basic factors necessary to maintain the operation of the national economy and the production and operation of market entities" (Shen Rong 2020). In different social backgrounds and different ages the content of production factors are very different. In the era of agriculture, land and labor were the most important production factors. By the beginning of the twentieth century, the second industrial revolution was coming to an end; social productivity had been greatly improved; and economic activities had gradually moved toward industrialization, scale, and organization. At this time organization itself became the key to production. Since then, with the improvement of productivity and the change of production methods, the role of technology has gradually emerged and become a factor of production. In the era of the digital economy, data can not only help us better organize and plan production and operations, it can also help us make more accurate judgments and more effective forecasts, thereby creating great wealth for society.

In this context, data was surely regarded as a factor of production (Guo Xiaonbei 2020).

> Data, as a factor of production, reflects an important change: with the acceleration of the digital transformation of economic activities, the multiplier effect of data in improving productivity and data has become a new production factors with the most prominent features of the times. (Liu He 2019)

Its great significance is reflected in three aspects. First, the participation of data in production, which has a multiplier effect on other factor resources, can improve productivity and contribute to the creation of new products and services, thus boosting economic growth. Second, the participation of data in distribution has a substitution effect on the original production factors of labor, land, capital, and technology. The changes to the economic structure and the factors involved will have a profound impact on income distribution. Third, with high liquidity, low cost, long-term infinity, and economic externalities, data has a wide-ranging radiating effect on various sectors of the national economy, helping to increase total factor productivity (Guo Xiaobei 2020). According to incomplete statistics, digitalization has contributed more than 40 percent of labor productivity growth in the United States over the past ten years.

> Currently, the value of data is growing in the global economy. The competition among major countries for data resources is getting fiercer as countries strive to take the commanding height in the development of the digital economy. As the value of data continues to spill over, the position of data in the economy and society is rising, and the connotation of data is undergoing changes. (Wang Qiang and Chen Qiyun 2020)

Data as a production factor is becoming a new variable that changes the international competitive landscape.

The changing context—from data to data resources, from data resources to big data, from big data to data factor, and from data factor to its marketization—reflects and embodies important trends in the development of modern economic systems represented by the digital economy. Compared with traditional production factors such as land, labor, capital, and technology, data has some clear features: complex subjects, complex ownership, abundance, close cross-correlation of factors, and a multiplication of value spillover effects (Table 6). At the same time, it also holds out value in its derivation, sharing, and non-consumption.

> As such, it does not impose any restriction on growth because of limited supply like natural resources do, and provides the foundation and possibility for continuous growth and sustainable development. Data has become a key production factor of the digital economy. It will also participate in circulation and distribution in a market-oriented way, infusing in traditional market factors the characteristics of the digital age or even turning them into more advanced production factors. (Zhang Hanqing 2020)

At the same time, the data factor will be the most important means of production in the era of new infrastructure. New infrastructure will bring about wide application of 5G, the development of intelligent applications, and the emergence of new business forms and new models, all of which are based on data. "No data, no application; no application, no intelligence."

Table 6. Comparison of Data with Other Factors

Content of Comparison	Land	Labor Force	Capital	Technology	Data
Subject characteristics	Single subject	Single subject	Complex subject	Complex subject	Complex subject
Ownership transfer model	Clear ownership	Clear ownership	Clear ownership	Clear ownership	Complex ownership
Resource scarcity	Scarce resource	Scarce resource	Relatively scarce resource	Relatively scarce resource	Abundant resource
Cross-correlation of factors	Relatively independent	Partly overlapped	Partly overlapped	Partly overlapped	Closely overlapped
Value spill-over effect	Inconspicuous spillover	Inconspicuous spillover	Conspicuous spillover	Conspicuous spillover	Multiplied value

Source: 2020. *Data Elements: Open Class for Leading Cadres*, Ed. Yang Tao, Beijing: People's Daily Press.

The Market Dilemma of the Data Factor

As a new production factor in the era of digital economy, data has the characteristics of atomicity, non-structuredness, non-scarcity, heterogeneity, non-exclusiveness, zero marginal cost, and increasing returns to scale, which create many problems and challenges in all aspects in the data life cycle, such as data rights definition, data openness, data pricing, data transactions, data utilization, data security and compliance, and data destruction.

To begin with, coordination is weak. The report to the 19th CPC National Congress pointed out that "The Party exercises overall leadership over all areas of endeavor in every part of the country." In this vein, Party governance over data is both a trend and something necessary. To achieve this, we need good data coordination, but China is far from a strong country in this regard in terms of relevant law, policy, and technology. On the one hand, data coordination is insufficient at the national level. Since 2015, the inter-ministerial joint conference for promoting the development of big data has played an important coordinating role, but a series of problems remain difficult to solve. One particular problem is how to create a more professional and more refined overall decision-making and implementation process which is a must if we are to build a hyper-scale data market in the future. At the national level, more than 70 percent of the State Council's constituent departments, directly affiliated ad hoc agencies, and directly affiliated institutions have issued big data-related documents and initiated the construction of relevant big data systems within their scope of responsibility. However, problems such as data aggregation barriers, segmentation, and repetitive construction are still prominent. Cross-regional, cross-departmental, and cross-system coordination is still very difficult, resulting in a lack of synergy. On the other hand, at the local level, since the new round of institutional reform which started in 2018, more than twenty provincial-level governments, including those of Shandong, Guangdong, Guangxi, Zhejiang, and Guizhou, have established big data institutions (Table 7). However, due to the lack of unified guidance and standards at the national level, the names, administrative levels, and responsibilities of these big data institutions, located in various provinces and cities, are not aligned. Some are at the bureau level, such as the Shandong Provincial Big Data Bureau, and some are at the deputy-bureau level, such as the Guangdong Provincial Government Service Data Administration. In terms of affiliation, some are subordinate to the provincial government like the Big Data Development Administration of Guizhou Province, some to the general office of the provincial people's government like Guangdong Provincial Government Service Data Administration, or the department of industry and information technology like Shaanxi Provincial Government Data Service Bureau, or the provincial development and reform commission like Fujian Provincial Big Data Administration. Such differences in institutional affiliation and functions have resulted discrepancies in operating mechanisms.

Table 7. The Establishment of Provincial Big Data Management Institutions after the Structural Reform in 2018

Province	Institution	Superiority	Level
Shandong	Shandong Provincial Big Data Bureau	Provincial Government Agencies	Bureau Level
Guangdong	Guangdong Provincial Government Service Data Administration	Departmental Management Agency of the Provincial Government Office	Deputy Bureau Level
Guangxi	Guangxi Zhuang Autonomous Region Big Data Development Bureau	Autonomous Region Government Agency	Bureau Level
Zhejiang	Zhejiang Big Data Development Administration	Departmental Management Agency of the Provincial Government Office	Deputy Bureau Level
Chongqing	Chongqing Big Data Application Development Administration	Municipal Government Agency	Bureau Level
Anhui	Anhui Provincial Data Resources Administration	Provincial Government Agency	Bureau Level

(*continued*)

Table 7. Continued

Province	Institution	Superiority	Level
Guizhou	Guizhou Province Big Data Development Administration	Provincial Government Agency	Bureau Level
Fujian	Digital Fujian Construction Leading Group Office (Provincial Big Data Administration)	Departmental Management Agency of Provincial Development and Reform Commission	Deputy Bureau Level
Jilin	Jilin Provincial Government Service and Digital Construction Administration	Provincial Government Agencies	Bureau Level
Henan	Henan Big Data Administration	Departmental Management Agency of the Provincial Government Office	Deputy Bureau Level
Shaanxi	Shaanxi Provincial Department of Industry and Information Technology (Provincial Government Affairs Data Service Bureau)	The Ministry of Industry and Information Technology concurrently serves as the Government Data Service Bureau	—

Source: Collated from public data.

Data legislation awaits a breakthrough. As a new production factor, data has a relatively complex rights system. From a global perspective, the confirmation of data ownership is a huge challenge, which is reflected in both legal confirmation and technical confirmation. "Unclear data ownership seriously hinders the market-oriented allocation of data as a production factor, and even brings compliance risks to enterprises" (Liu Li 2020).

> Currently in China, breakthroughs are urgently needed in the legislation on data openness, data transactions, and data security. First of all, in terms of data openness, the *Regulations on the Disclosure of Government Information of the People's Republic of China* is not yet well-aligned to the development pattern of data openness and improvements to it are required in regard to the principles, platforms, and management

> systems of data openness. Second, data ownership and transactions occur in diverse, changeable, and complex ways. Last but not least, data security adds to the difficulty of data right ownership confirmation. (Shi Yang et al. 2020)

In comparison, Western countries have made breakthroughs in the past years by issuing many dedicated legal documents.

> The United States supports government data openness with a series of laws such as the *Freedom of Information Act*, *the Electronic Freedom of Information Act*, and the *Privacy Act*; The United Kingdom provides oversight and mandatory restrictions for government data openness with regulations such as the revised *Freedom Protection Act* and the *Public Sector Information Reuse Directiv*e. (Ye Runguo and Chen Xuexiu 2016)

In contrast, although the *Cybersecurity Law* and the *Civil Code of China* provide for the protection of personal information and data, they lack specific lower-level regulations and implementation rules. In this sense, China clearly lags behind some Western countries in the practice of digital rights protection legislation (Tian Weilin 2018). Also, these are not sufficient to solve the problem of data factor market legislation well.

Moreover, it is difficult to regulate and supervise the data market. The integration of digital technology and market systems has overturned the relationship structure between data subjects in the data market, and has also brought new competition rules and supervision methods. The current market supervision rules were mostly formulated in the era of the agricultural economy and the industrial economy, and they are not compatible with the development of the digital economy at many points (Shi Yang et al. 2020). "In terms of data technology, we are already at the forefront of the times, and we are undoubtedly lagging behind in terms of the institutional supply of data regulation and supervision" (Liu Xiaojuan 2017). At the same time, there remain some outstanding problems: First, there is a lack of legislation regarding digital rights, data transactions, data openness, privacy protection, etc., and a digital legal system has not yet been formed. Second, the standards are not clear and only a very limited number of options are available when it comes to the means of supervision and control. Many areas lack clear rules and the criteria of legitimacy are uncertain. Although the *Cybersecurity Law* authorizes "the Ministry of Industry and Information Technology to be responsible for the overall coordination of cybersecurity work and related supervision and management,"[1] this type of supervision is more a general supervision rather than specialized supervision, and there is a lack of detailed implementation rules for supervision. There is not yet any dedicated mechanism or institution in place to coordinate efforts to promote data supervision, or any specialized technology-based supervision institution. Third, the legislative technique adopted is the traditional empirical approach where a general legislation prevails over a specific one, therefore the liability provisions are general, penalties are light, and there is basically a lack of operability.

Data Factor Market Construction

Since data is a new factor of production, development of a data market should be driven by three wheels: law, technology, and ethics.

> The "invisible hand of the free market" and the "visible hand of macroeconomic regulation and control" must be used well. Also, efforts should be made to form a structure in which the roles of the market and the government are well balanced, complementary, coordinated, and mutually promoting.[2]

Concerted efforts in many aspects should be made to promote the construction of a data factor market with clear ownership, orderly circulation, and efficient allocation, which lets data play the key role in boosting productivity of the market economy, gets different industries connected, optimizes the structure of economic development, and shapes new competitive advantages in the era of the digital economy.

A public service platform for data circulation should be established throughout society. The construction of a basic platform will be of great significance to improving the data factor market. In terms of development prospects, with the accelerated development of new technologies such as

1 See Article 8 of the *Cybersecurity Law of the People's Republic of China*.

2 See the speech by General Secretary Xi Jinping on May 26, 2014, when he presided over the 15th collective study of the Political Bureau of the 18th CPC Central Committee.

5G, blockchain, artificial intelligence, and quantum informatics in the next ten years, the data factor market infrastructure will be faced with great challenges. Taking the new infrastructure construction efforts as an opportunity, progress should accelerate toward an integrated national data center system to establish and improve the public service system for data factor circulation for government-to-government data sharing, government-to-enterprise data openness, enterprise-to-government data collection, and enterprise-to-enterprise data exchange.

> The first is to deepen and promote the integration and data sharing of e-government systems, build a national data sharing and exchange system, and promote the sharing of government data across regions, departments, and levels. The second is to improve the public data openness system, formulate data openness processes and plans, and offer access to relevant data sets under the premise of strengthening security and privacy protection. The third is to sort out channels for governments at all levels to collect data from social organizations and for social organizations to report data to the government, establish a unified data acquisition and cooperation mechanism between governmental and non-governmental organizations in accordance with laws and regulations, and promote the connection between governmental and non-governmental data platforms. The fourth is to build a full-process data factor circulation platform covering match-making for data transactions, transaction supervision, pricing, and dispute arbitration, and clearly define the mechanisms for data registration, evaluation, pricing, transaction tracking, and security audits. (Shi Yang et al. 2020)

On the above basis, we will build a new ultra-large data infrastructure system and a "national data network that features effective connection between eastern China's data resources and western China's computing power. In the meantime, we will establish regional data centers according to national strategies for the coordinated development of the Beijing-Tianjin-Hebei region, the Guangdong-Hong Kong-Macao region, the Yangtze River Delta, and the Pearl River Delta in a bid to form a new pattern of coordinated development of the eastern, central, and western regions of the country supported by data.

A market environment that facilitates the circulation of data as a production factor should be created. The do this, we need to adhere to market-based resource allocation; follow the principles of openness and sharing, effective utilization, security, and efficiency; give full play to the resource advantages of both the government and the market; and make efforts to strengthen data pricing, access supervision, fair competition, cross-border circulation, and risk prevention so as to create a healthy and sustainable data market environment.

> First, in terms of organization and management, a joint mechanism for the promotion of data factor allocation should be established at the ministerial level, and a comprehensive data management department should be set up to promote in good coordination data factor allocation management and supervision. Second, in terms of institutional building, progress should be accelerated toward the formulation and promulgation of basic laws and regulations such as the *Data Security Law of the People's Republic of China*, the *Personal Information Protection Law of the People's Republic of China*, the *Data Property Law of the People's Republic of China*, and the *Data Transaction Law of the People's Republic of China* so as to provide a legal basis and regulatory bottom line for the efficient allocation of data as a production factor. Third, in regard to enforcement, it is necessary to speed up the formulation of implementation rules and methods for the definition of data property rights, data openness and sharing, market system construction, personal information protection, data security, and cross-border data flow. Fourth, special forces should be organized to find out the scale of national data resources as soon as possible and establish a catalog and list of national data assets so as to lay the foundation for better management of data factor resources at the national level. (Wang Lei 2019)

The deep integration of data as a production factor with other new factors should be promoted. Big data makes a smarter world. "Integration is a general trend within our reach, and it is our common pursuit for technological progress."[3] The implementation of the Data Plus strategy and the promotion of the deep integration of data as a production factor and other new factors are of great significance for the upgrading of the industrial value chain. Therefore, it is necessary to find ways to establish a data legislation framework where data serves as the linkage between the talent chain, the technology chain, the industrial chain, the innovation chain, and the capital chain so as to promote the establishment of a modern industrial system featuring coordinated development of the digital economy, the real

3 See the speech by Sun Zhigang, Secretary of the CPC Guizhou Provincial Committee and Chairman of the Standing Committee of the Provincial People's Congress, at the opening ceremony of the 2018 China International Big Data Industry Expo on May 26, 2018.

economy, governance technology, modern finance, and rural revitalization (Shi Yang 2020). First, we should promote the in-depth integration of data as a production factor with the real economy, so that the data industry can find a better development direction, maximize its value, and promote the transformation and upgrading of the real economy. Second, we should promote the in-depth integration of data as a production factor and rural revitalization, and implement the national digital countryside strategy to better tackle problems related to agriculture, rural areas, and farmers and push for a rural industrial revolution. Third, we should promote the in-depth integration of data as a production factor and services for people's livelihoods so that "data does more, and people run fewer errands," effectively improving the quality of people's life. Fourth, we should promote the in-depth integration of data as a production factor and social governance, improve governance capabilities and modernize the governance system, and truly realize the governance pattern where people watch over data and computing runs on the cloud.

Data Ownership Confirmation and its Powers and Functions

We are still in the exploratory stage for the establishment of a data ownership confirmation mechanism, which is a field attracting wide attention from industry, academia, and policy makers. Confirming the ownership of the data factor is essential for the clarification of data assets and the effective allocation of data resources. Since the 13th Five-Year Plan period, the state has repeatedly requested data ownership confirmation. The *13th Five-Year Plan* for *National Informatization* pointed to the acceleration of legislation on data ownership and data management. The *Guiding Opinions of the General Office of the State Council on Promoting the Standardized and Healthy Development of Platform Economy* (GBF [2019] No. 38) requires the exploration of the establishment of rules and procedures for data resource ownership confirmation, circulation, transaction, application, and development, and the strengthening of data privacy protection and data security management. During a meeting of the 13th

National People's Congress, the Finance and Economics Committee proposed to make clear "rules on data ownership, rights, and transactions." During the 19th CPC National Congress, General Secretary Xi Jinping clearly put forward the requirement of "establishing systems related to data resources ownership confirmation, openness, circulation, and transactions; and improving the data property rights protection system." However, the legislation has not yet met the requirements relating to data ownership. Article 127 of the newly promulgated *Civil Code* stipulates: "Where there are laws particularly providing for the protection of data and online virtual assets, such provisions shall be followed." In essence, this avoids the topic of data ownership as it adopts the approach of "negative-affirmation" and fails to fully reflect the value orientation and policy requirements of the state to strengthen data property rights protection (Jiang Fan 2020). The ownership of data determines the distribution of data value and benefits, and the division of data quality and security responsibilities (Jingdong Law Research Institute 2018, p. 10).

> On the one hand, the unclear ownership of data may cause ownership disputes in subsequent development and use; on the other hand, it is difficult to define the ownership of rights and responsibilities and ensure data security and personal privacy when big data analysis and association are carried out with ambiguous data attribution. (Wang Hailong et al. 2018)

These problems severely hampered data sharing and openness, as well as data circulation, transactions, and property rights distribution. They are the core issues that need to be resolved through data rights legislation.

Accession. Accession refers to the combination of things belonging to different owners to form inseparable things or things with new properties (Xie Zaiquan 2003, p. 505), which is mainly achieved in three forms: processing, combining, and mixing.[4] Accession is one of the methods of

4 Combining refers to the situation where things belonging to different owners are combined together and can be identified, but it is difficult or too expensive to divide. Mixing refers to the situation where things belonging to different people are combined and cannot be recognized, or the cost is too high. Processing refers to the transformation of movable properties owned by others to make a new property. Among them, the main difference between combining and mixing is: after

obtaining ownership and an important means of confirming the ownership. It has an indispensable position in the world's legal systems. Modern civil law countries or regions generally stipulate accession rules in their property laws, and common law countries have also established accession basis in their property legal systems. Example include Articles 547 to 577 of the *French Civil Code*,[5] Article 950 of the *German Civil Code*,[6] Article 246 of the *Japanese Civil Code*,[7] and Article 814 of the *Civil Code* of Taiwan, China.[8] Accession plays an important role in confirming the ownership of things, promoting the use of things, increasing social wealth, and reducing transaction costs (Xie Zaiquan 2003, p. 505). As a production factor, data is the most fundamental proposition in the digital economy era. Its complexity far exceeds that of oil, coal, and even capital in the industrial revolution era. To achieve mass production of data, the collection of large amounts of data is required. The problem we face, and urgently need to

mixing, the state of the property before mixing can no longer be identified. After combining, the property before combining can still be identified.

5 Articles 547 to 550 of the *French Civil Code* are discussed in Chapter I, Title II "Of the Right of Accession to What is Produced by a Thing," and Articles 551 to 577 are the contents of Chapter II, Title II "Of the Right of Accession to What Unites or Incorporates Itself with a Thing."

6 Article 950 of the *German Civil Code*: (1) A person who, by processing or transformation of one or more substances, creates a new movable thing acquires the ownership of the new thing, except where the value of the processing or the transformation is substantially less than the value of the substance. Processing also includes writing, drawing, painting, printing, engraving or a similar processing of the surface; (2) On the acquisition of ownership of the new thing, the existing rights in the substance are extinguished.

7 Article 246 of the *Japanese Civil Code*: (1) When processing movable property for others, the ownership of the processed product belongs to the owner of the material. However, when the price significantly exceeds the price of the material due to processing, the processor acquires ownership of the object. (2) When the processor has provided some materials, the processor shall obtain ownership if the price, plus the price generated by the processing, exceeds the price of other materials.

8 Article 814 of the *Civil Code* of the Taiwan Region of China: If the movable property is processed by others, the ownership of the processed product belongs to the owner of the material. However, if the value added by processing exceeds the value of the material, the ownership of the processed product belongs to the processor.

resolve today, is the ambiguity of data ownership and the difficulty of data rights confirmation, which will pave the way for data pooling for higher efficiency, lower costs, better organizational methods, and better distribution of benefits (Yang Dong 2020). In the case of accession, since the data properties are closely integrated, it is practically impossible or highly difficult to separate the combined, mixed or processed data properties. Therefore, it is necessary to use the accession rules to confirm the ownership of the accessed data so that it continues to exist in a form, but cannot be restituted or separated. It is also necessary to create a set of accession rules in the digital rights legislation to ensure that the accessed data becomes new data and appears in the form of single ownership, without allowing the parties to forcibly separate and request restoration.

The definition of confirmation of data rights. The definition is a necessary and indispensable tool for solving legal problems. Without a strict definition, we cannot think about legal problems clearly and rationally (Rheinstein 1945). At present, there are many opinions in academia and industry about the connotations of data ownership confirmation, and no consensus has yet been formed. Du Zhenhua believes that "data ownership confirmation is to clarify the ownership of data from different sources in legal form" (Du Zhenhua and Cha Hongwang 2016)—"to determine the right holder of the data, that is, who has the ownership, possession, use, and beneficiary rights of the data, and has the responsibility to protect personal privacy, etc." (Du Zhenhua 2015). Zhou Linbin and Ma Ensi proposed, from the perspective of law and economics, that "the confirmation of big data ownership is to clarify the definition of the initial property rights of big data, including clarifying the nature, content, and ownership of big data rights" (Zhou Linbin and Ma Ensi 2018). Based on the perspective of data transactions, the Beijing Big Data Transaction Service Platform provides:

> Data ownership confirmation refers to ownership confirmation guidance given in regard to data rights holders, the nature of the rights, data sources, and time of obtaining such rights, period of use, data usage, data volume, data format, data granularity, nature of data industry and data transaction methods for the purpose of clarifying the relationships between the two parties of a data transaction in terms of their responsibilities and rights so as to guide the parties involved in the transaction

> to complete the data transaction in a scientific, uniform and safe manner. (Peng Yun 2016)

From the definition above, it is not difficult to see that the purpose of confirmation of data ownership is to encourage innovation, increase positive externality spillovers, and reduce the impact of information asymmetry so as to maximize effective demand, or to get as close as possible to what Ronald Coase referred to as a "world of zero transaction costs." To do this we need to tackle three problems: One is about the subject of data rights, that is, who should enjoy the benefits attached to data; the second is about the object of data rights, that is, which data is regulated by data legislation; the third is about the content of data rights, that is, what are the specific powers and functions a data subject enjoys.

International practice of data right ownership confirmation. Internationally, there have been continuous attempts to ascertain data right ownership. For example, through the *General Data Protection Regulation* and the *Regulation on the Free Flow of Non-personal Data*, the EU has established the dual structure of "personal data" and "non-personal data." For any "personal data" related to an identified or identifiable natural person, its rights belong to the natural person. For "non-personal data," that is, those other than "personal data," companies enjoy the "data producer rights." However, the EU's attempts to confirm data rights ownership were unsuccessful; the division between "personal data" and "non-personal data" was inconsistent with existing practices. The scope of personal data is too broad. In the digital age, there is almost no data that cannot be combined or processed to be associated with specific natural persons. Therefore, the same data set often contains both personal data and non-personal data. It may be very difficult to not only distinguish between the two types, but also to achieve the desired effect. Contrary to the EU, the United States has adopted a pragmatic approach to data ownership confirmation. Based on the structure of conventional rights to privacy in the United States, it uses "the right to information and privacy" to resolve the threat posed by the Internet to private information, formulating industrial laws in the fields of finance, medical care, and communications, supplemented by industrial self-discipline mechanisms, and has formed a relatively flexible system. Currently, when confirming the ownership of data rights, it is necessary to make full use of the experience of the EU and the US, focusing on the following four "musts." First, we must fully consider the different phases of data economy development and our specific national conditions. Second, we must take personal privacy and sensitive data protection as the redline. Third, the main purpose must be data circulation and sharing. Fourth, digital technology must be used to empower data rights ownership confirmation (PWCC 2020).

Cracking the difficulty of data rights confirmation. Research on data rights confirmation must give due consideration to the production mechanism of data rights and explore the social foundation that underlies it, especially "the context of the problem, the social environment, and the change of cultural conception" (Yu Baihua 2017). To address the issue of confirmation of data rights and construct the content of these rights and their transfer systems, we need to make good use of both systems and technology. Currently, the most urgent task lies with legislation to clarify the ownership of data rights. Traditionally, data rights ownership confirmation required the submission of ownership certificates and an expert review, but this lacked technological credibility—there are uncontrollable factors such as tampering. Taking into account the special characteristics of data assets, currently two types of technologies may help solve the problem of data rights ownership confirmation. In scenarios where data needs to be transferred and traded in physical forms and ownership needs to be clarified, blockchain technology is recommended: The immutability of the blockchain, as well as the digital signature, the consensus mechanism, smart contracts, and other related technologies can be helpful when confirming data rights ownership and, at the same time, it records and monitors the production, collection, transmission, use, and the benefits of data throughout the whole process, providing a solid technical foundation for data sharing and circulation. Specifically, the owners, producers, and users of data assets join the blockchain network as important nodes, and use the blockchain to synchronize consensus to record in detail every step of the generation, circulation, and transactions of the data. It not only stores the data itself, but also records the identity and operation history of all parties related to the data asset, which is witnessed by all nodes within the consensus, allowing no one to shirk or deny anything that has happened in the chain. In this way, all participants can contribute their own data assets and supervise asset circulation and profit distribution through smart contracts, sharing among them both the benefits and risks, thus greatly promoting the circulation of data assets. As data flows are shared across different business entities, reorganization and analysis of data can generate new data and it can be difficult to divide the data among the multiple participating parties. In such a scenario, the right to use and operate data is particularly important. Therefore, it is recommended that multi-party secure computing be used so that, without changing the actual possession and control of the data or the ambiguity of ownership, technological support can be provided for data circulation and sharing. With multi-party secure computing platforms, we will be able to move computing power to the data end, so ensuring that corporate data security and individual privacy protection, data sharing and utilization, as well as business innovation can still be sufficiently supported (PWCC 2020).

Confirmation of personal data ownership. The legal subject of personal data is an individual, and the data has both personal and property attributes and contains within it the value of personal dignity and freedom, as well as commercial value and the value of public management (Jingdong Law Research Institute 2018, p. 55). Except as clearly provided by national laws, individuals should have ownership of their data, that is, the right to personal data. "Natural persons have data rights to their personal data in accordance with the law, and no organization or individual may infringe with such rights."[9] Individuals have the right to possess, use, and dispose of personal data, and obtain benefits accordingly. Personal data rights specifically include the right of access,[10] the right to rectification,[11] the right to erasure/to be forgotten,[12] the right to restrict processing,[13] the right to data portability,[14] and the right to object.[15] Specifically, for the collection

9 See Article 11 of *Data Regulations of Shenzhen Special Economic Zone (Draft for Comment).*

10 See Article 15 of *General Data Protection Regulation* (GDPR).

11 See Article 16 of *General Data Protection Regulation* (GDPR).

12 See Article 17 of *General Data Protection Regulation* (GDPR).

13 See Article 18 of *General Data Protection Regulation* (GDPR).

14 See Article 20 of *General Data Protection Regulation* (GDPR).

15 See Article 21 of *General Data Protection Regulation* (GDPR).

of personal data, work should be done clearly on the basis of classification. Except for the data expressly required by national legislation, the scope of collection should be determined by the users on their own. Personal data should be stored in a personal data center or a personal data account. Other individuals or institutions can only be authorized to use it for a limited period of time, and must accept necessary supervision and management for that (Wei Lubin 2018, p. 40–4).

Confirmation of corporate data ownership. "Corporate data refers to the data actually controlled and used by an enterprise, including commercial data, such as financial data and operational data, as well as user data legally collected and used by the enterprise" (Shi Dan 2019). Similar to personal data, corporate data is privately owned data. Except for the scope defined by special regulations, corporations have the ownership to their own data, that is, the corporate data rights. It should be noted that corporate data is different from the data held by the corporation, because the personal data of customers held by the corporation is not corporate to the enterprise; the corporation should not possess ownership of consumers' personal data. Within the scope of any contract, the corporation may only have a limited right to use customer data. That is, the ownership of corporate data and the data held by the corporate are not the same. Correspondingly, there are two main types of domestic claims on corporate data rights: One gives corporations extensive rights to the data they hold (including collected user personal data), the other classifies the data held by corporations and claims that the corporations have rights to some types of data. At present, paradoxically, the first viewpoint is mainly advocated by scholars, while the second is mainly advocated by practitioners (Xu Wei 2019). Based on the complexity and particularity of data, after a comprehensive examination of the views of experts and scholars such as Long Weiqiu (2018), Xu Ke (2017), Ding Daoqin (2017), and Yang Lixin (2016) we are more inclined to defer to the opinions of practitioners, that is, it is necessary to divide corporate data into different types and claim different rights for different types of data. For example, Ding Daoqin divides data into basic data and value-added data. For basic data, users, as data providers, possess the ownership of personal basic data; for value-added data, data processors possess the ownership of the value-added data generated by processing, editing, and analyzing basic data. Similarly, Yang Lixin and Chen Xiaojiang divide data into raw data and derivative data. The main value of the distinction between the two is: The enterprise has absolute rights to the latter and, with derivative data as the object, data exclusive rights should be established as a kind of property right or, more specifically, a new type of intellectual property right. Although Ding Daoqin and other scholars divide the two types of data based on whether the data is identifiable, judging from their more detailed explanations the division seems to be actually based on whether the data has been "processed" by the corporation (Xu Wei 2019). With this understanding, the confirmation of corporate data ownership also complies with the general rules of the accretion theory.

Confirmation of the ownership of public data. "Public data refers to the texts, data, images, audio, video, and other information resources generated and managed by the government in the process of performing its duties according to law, and recorded and stored in a certain form."[16] There are mainly two types of public data: people's data and government data. People's data is generated by the people and is not privately owned data, nor is it personal data. However, under normal circumstances, the people are not clearly defined subjects and, with unspecificity, cannot assume the role of data subjects. Therefore, it would be inappropriate to directly assign the right to people's data to the people. Consequently, the ownership of people's data is transferred to the government, and the government shall formulate management standards for it.[17] In addition, due to the nature of the government[18] as a public authority, government data is not private data but public data, which should be regarded as a state-owned asset. The

16 The concept of "public data" comes from the definition of "public data" in Article 2 of the *Regulations on the Application of Public Data Management of Chengdu*.

17 Among them, as special public data, collective data has a specific generating subject, which is a "public" with a clear scope, such as class collectives, village collectives, etc. At this time, its management can be formulated by the government, or through collective and independent negotiation, or a combination of the two.

18 Governmental affairs departments refer to the party committees, people's congresses, government, CPPCC, supervisory committees, courts, procuratorates, and public institutions and social organizations authorized by laws and regulations to have administrative functions. (See Article 3, paragraph 2 of the A*dministrative Measures for the Sharing of Xi'an Municipal Affairs Data Resources*.)

corresponding government data rights are mostly owned by the state in legislative practice, and the government exercises its right to their management and use. For example, Article 7 of the *Administrative Measures for the Sharing of Municipal Government Data Resources of Xi'an* stipulates that:

> The ownership of government data resources belongs to the state and falls in the scope of state-owned asset management. The municipal government authorizes the municipal big data industry development management authority to exercise the power of overall management of data resources, take charge of the overall management, authorize development, utilization and value increase, and provide supervision and guidance related to Xi'an's municipal government data.

Article 4 of the *Interim Measures for the Management of Municipal Government Data Resources of Changsha* stipulate that: "The ownership of the data generated and collected by the government authorities at all levels in Changsha, according to their statutory duties, shall belong to the People's Government of Changsha." Article 12 of the *Regulations on Open and Shared Government Data of Guiyang Municipality* stipulates: "Administrative agencies have the right to manage and use the government data they collect in accordance with the law. Article 21 of the *Data Regulations of Shenzhen Special Economic Zone (Draft for Opinions)* stipulates that:

> Public data is a new type of state-owned asset, and its data rights are owned by the state. The Shenzhen Municipal Government exercises the data rights of public data in the region on behalf of the city, and authorizes the city data coordination department to formulate public data asset management measures and organize their implementation.[19]

In addition, the *Administrative Measures for the Sharing of Municipal Affairs Data Resources of Xi'an* also provides for "the powers and connotations of government data rights in Article 6, that is, the right to government data resource includes ownership, the right to manage, collect, use, and derive income. Article 8 defines the right to collect, manage, and use

19 See Article 21 of *Data Regulations of Shenzhen Special Economic Zone (Draft for Comment)*.

government data, that is, "government departments have the right to collect, manage, and use relevant government data resources in accordance with their statutory functions. Article 9 stipulates the right to use government affairs data and the right to income derived from that data, that is:

> [A]s authorized by the municipal big data industry development and management agency, relevant enterprises and other entities have the right to use relevant government data resources and the right to benefit from the reuse of data resources.

Separation between data ownership and the right to use data. In the industrial economy, the right to control and the right to use (by the owner) were actually one (Jiang Qiping 2012). In the digital age, on the contrary, ownership (more specifically the right to control, which is part of ownership) and the right to use are being separated. The *Opinions of the Chengdu Municipal People's Government and the Chengdu Municipal Committee of the Communist Party of China on the Overall Promotion of Covid-19 Pandemic Control and Economic and Social Development and Striving to Achieve the Economic and Social Development Goals of 2020* clearly requires "improving the management of public data operations and services, and exploring and promoting the separation of data ownership and the right to use." In the future, the right to use will be more important than ownership. Rather than possessing it, it is better to use it. The essence is to offer open access to one's own resources to exchange and connect with others.

> The global economy is moving away from the material world and moving closer to the non-physical bit world. At the same time, it is moving away from ownership and moving closer to the right to use. It is also moving away from copy value and moving closer to network value. At the same time, it is heading towards a world that is bound to come, where more and more remixes continue to occur. (Kelly 2016, p. 242)

There is already a widespread practice of separating ownership and the right to use. Although most people are studying the legal structure of data ownership, facts show that data ownership is not very important. What matters more is who owns the right to use the data and what value the data can generate. The key to data property rights lies in the separation of ownership and the right to use, which is changing the old economic order. Data has the characteristics of being non-consumable, reproducible, shareable, divisible, non-exclusive, and having zero marginal costs. On the one hand, data is a special commodity with value and use value. On the other hand, it is capital and has the characteristics of expansion. Based on these characteristics digital labor has become the source and carrier of value emerging in the era of big data. The basic laws of data labor have enhanced the depth and breadth of global value chain reconstruction, and brought new ways of competition and growth. Data power brings profound changes to data relations, and this change is detonating a broader economic and social movement, driving a competitive economy toward a sharing economy. Sharing is an unstoppable and transformative force. In the future, more and more social resources will begin to be shared. The essence of the sharing economy is to "weaken ownership and release the right to use." The right to share makes it possible to separate data ownership and the right to use, forming a shared development pattern of "not asking for ownership, but for the right to use." The theory of shared value will surely become a revolutionary theory after the theory of surplus value.

The power and function system of data rights. "Data rights are the right of the right holder to make independent decisions, control, process, and derive income and compensation for damage to specific data in accordance with the law."[20] Through the analysis of the confirmation of ownership of personal data, corporate data, and public data, it can be found that data is divided into "private data" and "public data." From the perspective of the implementing entities, data rights can be divided into public data rights and private data rights. The subject of public data rights is the state, and it is the state's power to manage and restrict data; the state also has the power to manage, supervise, and protect data. Public data rights are divided into three elements. The first is the power to manage, that is, the state's jurisdiction and judicial power over domestic data covering the entire life cycle of production, transmission, and transaction. The second is the power of control, that is, the state takes effective measures to protect the authenticity and integrity of the data in the territory. The third is the power to manage

20 See Article 4 of the *Data Regulations of Shenzhen Special Economic Zone* (*Draft for Comment*).

open disclosure, that is, to disclose and share public data with the rest of society. From another perspective, this is also the obligation and responsibility of a modern state, and an important measure to promote the modernization of the national governance system and governance capabilities. Corresponding to data power, private data rights lie more but not entirely within the scope of civil law. In the civil law system, these rights are divided into personal rights and property rights, according to the different objects of the rights. Based on this principle, data rights should also be divided into data personal rights and data property rights (Zhu Baoli 2019). Data personal rights include data personality rights and data relation-related rights. As for the overall level of rights, data rights are a general upper concept, while data property rights are a lower concept, classified by the content of rights. Data property rights, like other property rights, are a group of behavioral collective rights and a bundle of other rights, including the right to possess, use, benefit from, and dispose of such property.

Data Openness and Sharing

Openness and sharing are important social attributes of data. In order to adapt to the times, it is necessary to explore the construction of a data openness and sharing system, and introduce data protection laws and policies, so that the public have channels with which to obtain and use data. Currently, data openness is making progress in various countries and regions, with the United States and Britain leading the way. In China, data openness focuses on government data, as government data openness has become a national strategy and a series of laws, regulations, and policies have been promulgated to promote the openness, sharing, and utilization of government data. Data protection is the prerequisite and cornerstone of data openness, and "establishing a mechanism to ensure security"[21] is a basic principle of data openness in all countries. Data openness is the

21 See *Interim Measures for the Administration of the Sharing of Governmental Information Resources* (GF [2016] No. 51).

sublimation of the value of data protection. Through "analysis, mining, and research on shared and open data"[22] and the "development of network data security protection and utilization technologies,"[23] it will further "promote the openness of public data resources, promote technological innovation and the development of economic society."[24] Balance between incentives for data openness and data protection promotion is the only way to equilibrium between the value of data openness and protection. However, to properly handle the relationship between "encouraging openness and ensuring effective protection" and to pay equal attention to prudential regulation and innovations in protection, further exploration is still needed institution-wise.

Data openness in the United States can be traced back to the disclosure of government information. The cornerstone of the system is the theorists who held sway at the time of the War of Independence and George Washington's discourse on the right to know. The provisions on freedom of speech and freedom of the press in the United States Constitution provide protection for government information disclosure. For example, the first amendment reads:

> Congress shall make no law respecting an establishment of religion, or prohibiting the free exercise thereof; or abridging the freedom of speech, or of the press; or the right of the people peaceably to assemble, and to petition the Government for a redress of grievances.[25]

In 1789, the U.S. Congress enacted the *Housekeeping Statute*, which stipulated that executive departments must disclose information in a unified publication. The head of an executive department may prescribe regulations for "the custody, use, and preservation of its records, papers, and

22 See Article 30 of the *Regulations on Promoting the Development and Application of Big Data of Guizhou Province.*

23 See Article 18 of the *Cybersecurity Law of the People's Republic of China.*

24 See Article 18 of the *Cybersecurity Law of the People's Republic of China.*

25 In January 22, 1945, Associated Press executive director Kent Cooper popularized the phrase the "right to know" in *New York Times*: The citizen is entitled to have access to news, fully and accurately presented. There cannot be political freedom in one country, or in the world, without respect for "the right to know."

property." The United States successively adopted the *Federal Registration Act* (1935) and the *Federal Administrative Procedure Act* (1946), and created the *Federal Registration Daily*, which specifically publishes information about the federal government, stipulating that the public can request information disclosure from the government, but the government has the right to refuse. In practice, the government often invokes Article 3 of the *Federal Administrative Procedure Act*: "to be kept secret in the interests of benefit of the public," and other abstract provisions to reject request for information that should have been disclosed. In 1966, the United States adopted the *Freedom of Information Act*, which completely changed the situation, stipulating that:

> [T]he public has the right to request access to records from any federal agency. Federal government agencies are obliged to make a decision on the request of the public. If the request is rejected, it must explain the reasons and inform the applicant that it can file a reconsideration or lawsuit. Decisions made by federal government agencies on whether information should be disclosed can be subject to reconsideration or judicial review.[26]

After that, under pressure from the public and the news media, the United States Congress revised the *Freedom of Information Act* many times and enacted the *Privacy Bill of Rights Act* and the *Government in the Sunshine*

26 The *Freedom of Information Act* was passed in 1966. It is a law that stipulates the disclosure of government information by various agencies of the United States Federal Government. In principle, all documents of the institutions should be accessible to the public. However, certain public and private interests should be protected by way of exceptions; all information opening requests for information equally and judicial relief. Its main content is to stipulate the rights of the people in obtaining administrative information and the obligations of administrative agencies in providing administrative information to the people. It requires federal administrative agencies and independent management agencies to publish various information in the "Federal Register" and provide the public with documents and records that do not fall within the scope of exemption from publication as specifically provided by the law. The *Freedom of Information Act* has a landmark significance in the history of open government affairs in the US, and is an important symbol of the citizens' right to know, from an idea to a reality (See Li Yunchi 2012).

Act. Data openness thus started in the United States.[27] On January 21, 2009, Barack Obama issued the *Memorandum of Transparency and Open Government* on the first day of his presidency, proposing three principles: "The government should be transparent, the government should be participatory, and the government should be collaborative."[28] He also directed that:

> [T]he Chief Technology Officer, in coordination with the Director of the Office of Management and Budget (OMB) and the Administrator of General Services, to

27 *The Freedom of Information Act*, the *Privacy Act*, and the Government in the *Sunshine Act* constitute an important basis and guarantee for the U.S. Federal Government's open data system, and focus on seeking a balance between the public's information access and privacy protection. They play an important role in the disclosure of government information and protection of citizens' privacy (See Lu Jianying 2013).

28 Government should be transparent. Transparency promotes accountability and provides information for citizens about what their government is doing. Information maintained by the federal government is a national asset. My administration will take appropriate action, consistent with law and policy, to disclose information rapidly in forms that the public can readily find and use. Executive departments and agencies should harness new technologies to put information about their operations and decisions online and readily available to the public. Executive departments and agencies should also solicit public feedback to identify information of greatest use to the public; government should be participatory. Public engagement enhances the Government's effectiveness and improves the quality of its decisions. Knowledge is widely dispersed in society, and public officials benefit from having access to that dispersed knowledge. Executive departments and agencies should offer Americans increased opportunities to participate in policymaking and to provide their government with the benefits of their collective expertise and information. Executive departments and agencies should also solicit public input on how we can increase and improve opportunities for public participation in government; government should be collaborative. Collaboration actively engages Americans in the work of their Government. Executive departments and agencies should use innovative tools, methods, and systems to cooperate among themselves, across all levels of government, and with non-profit organizations, businesses, and individuals in the private sector. Executive departments and agencies should solicit public feedback to assess and improve their level of collaboration and to identify new opportunities for cooperation.

> coordinate the development by appropriate executive departments and agencies, within 120 days, of recommendations for an *Open Government Directive*.[29]

In May of the same year, the United States established the world's first open data portal, Data.gov,[30] which required all federal government departments to provide data regularly and quantitatively. Government budgets, expenditure and elections are the foci of the Open Government Plan. In December 2012, Obama signed the *National Strategy for Information Sharing and Information Safeguarding* and announced the Big Data Research and Development Plan. In May 2013, Obama signed the *Making Open and Machine Readable the New Default for Government Information*, requiring the federal government to fully open data, and stipulates that the default state of new and modernized government information resources shall be open and machine readable. In 2014, the United States promulgated the *DATA Act* to comprehensively promote data openness. In January 2019, U.S. President Donald Trump signed the *Open Government Data Act*, requiring full openness of government data based on the categorization of "machine-readable data required, open by default, open license, or worldwide public domain dedication required, and innovation."[31] With this, data openness in the United States became

29 The three principles of the *Open Government Directive* are "Transparency," "Participation," and "Collaboration," which require reducing the backlog of the *Freedom of Information Act* and publishing more databases on government websites. Opening up website data enables the public to understand government information and promote public discussion.

30 Early federal government data open websites include: FedStats.gov, the first website established by the U.S. government in 1997 to fully disclose federal government data, and the USA spending.gov and Recovery.gov websites established in 2007. Since the launch of the *Open Government Directive*, the U.S. federal government has begun to more actively explore how to better open data through integrated websites. Data.gov was launched by the U.S. General Services Administration (GSA) in May 2009. It has forty-seven moderate data sets and has grown from hundreds of data sources (including federal agencies, states, counties, and cities) to more than 200,000 Data sets. Data.gov sets an example for other open government data directories. Since 2009, hundreds of countries, states, and cities around the world have launched their own open government data websites.

31 § 3562. Requirements for Government data.

truly legalized, which was an important milestone in the history of the United States' open data movement.

The open data movement in the UK started in the 1970s. In 1984, the UK promulgated the *Data Protection Act* and the *Utilization of Local Government Information Act*, followed by the *Local Government Access to Information Act*, and the *Access to Medical Reports Act*. These laws include content relevant to government data openness. To a certain extent this became the bud of the British government's open data system. In 1989, the UK revised its *Official Secrets Act*. After 1990, a series of laws and regulations such as the *Citizens Charter*, *Open Government*, and *Code on Access to Information* were successively formulated, which strongly promoted the openness of government data. In this process, the continuous development of democracy, the civil rights movement, and the construction of the rule of law further promoted the legalization of the British government's open data system. In 2000, the United Kingdom formally passed the *Freedom of Information Act 2000*, although the *Freedom of Information Act* did not fully take effect until 2005. The completion of this legislative process marked the beginning of a new period in the development of the British government's

---

(a) Machine-Readable Data Required: Open Government data assets made available by an agency shall be published as machine-readable data.

(b) Open by Default: When not otherwise prohibited by law, and to the extent practicable, public data assets and non-public data assets maintained by the Federal Government shall:

(1) be available in an open format; and

(2) be available under open licenses.

(c) Open License or Worldwide Public Domain Dedication Required: When not otherwise prohibited by law, and to the extent practicable, open Government data assets published by or for an agency shall be made available under an open license or, if not made available under an open license and appropriately released, shall be considered to be published as part of the worldwide public domain.

(d) Innovation: Each agency may engage with non-governmental organizations, citizens, non-profit organizations, colleges and universities, private and public companies, and other agencies to explore opportunities to leverage the public data assets of the agency in a manner that may provide new opportunities for innovation in the public and private sectors in accordance with law and regulation.

open data system.[32] In 2010, the UK officially launched the national open data website, Data.gov.uk. Since 2011, the United Kingdom has issued three editions of the *UK National Action Plan for Open Government*, paving ways in the five priority areas of open data, government accountability, fiscal transparency, citizen empowerment, and transparency of natural resources. These plans were enacted to further emphasize the commitment to completely open government data, with a view to improving public services, promoting national economic growth, and increasing the transparency of governance. In 2012, the UK issued the *Open Data White Paper: Unleashing Potentials*, proposing to build a transparent government through open data, while at the same time providing resources for business innovation and improving public services. A series of strategic measures were proposed. In the same year, the UK revised the *Freedom of Information and Protection of Privacy Act*, requiring government departments to publish data in a machine-readable manner while, at the same time, regulating the fees and copyrights for open data. After the G8 summit in 2013, the UK issued the *G8 Open Data Charter UK Action Plan*, which proposed to focus on the opening of four key databases, including national statistics, national maps, national elections, and national budgets; fourteen areas of high-value data were also proposed in the charter. The latest *Open Government Partners UK National Action Plan 2016–2018* proposes to open up multiple data sources, such as business information, natural resource information, contract and procurement data, government donation funding data, election data, and plans to further improve and advance data-driven technology applications and encourage participation in data openness. It can be said that the UK

32 *Freedom of Information Act* 2000 of the UK stipulates that anyone has the right to request information from a public authority, and the authority must give the requested information immediately if it is readily available. The law also provides for the establishment of information commissioners and special committees to accept and respond to relevant complaints from the public. If the government department subject to the complaint fails to provide the information according to law, the Information Commissioner has the right to request it, or a special committee will issue an execution order to it. In terms of public exemption, the *Freedom of Information Act* stipulates eighteen situations, including information related to national security, information that damages national defense, and information that damages international relations.

has been quite successful in promoting public service improvement and innovative development with open public data. In the 2015 World Wide Web Foundation's survey and analysis of open data in eighty-six countries around the world, called the "Open Data Barometer," the UK ranked first with full marks.

Relatively speaking, data openness and sharing is still in its infancy in China. Specifically, China lacks convenient data acquisition channels and sound user-government dialogue mechanisms. Relevant laws and regulations remain to be improved, and the depth and breadth of data openness are insufficient. In the past two years, China listed open data in its agenda and set it as a national strategy. During the second collective study session of the Political Bureau of the CPC Central Committee, General Secretary Xi Jinping emphasized the need to "promote the integration and openness and sharing of data resources, ensure data security, and accelerate the construction of a digital China." Premier Li Keqiang pointed out in a teleconference on the reforms to streamline administration and delegate power, improve regulation, and upgrade services that "more than 80 percent of China's information and data resources are in the hands of government departments at all levels, and it is a huge waste not to share them." In August 2015, the State Council formally issued the *Outline of Action to Promote the Development of Big Data* (GF [2015] No. 50), which clearly required "building a unified and open platform for national government data by the end of 2018," and "accelerating the openness and sharing of government data, promoting resource integration, and improving governance capabilities." In October of the same year, "implementing the national big data strategy and promoting the opening and sharing of data resources" was formally written into the document issued at the Fifth Plenary Session of the 18th CPC Central Committee. In September 2016, the State Council successively issued the *Interim Measures for the Administration of the Sharing of Government Information Resources* and the *Guiding Opinions of the State Council on Accelerating the Promotion of Internet Plus Government Services*, providing policy guidance for government data openness. In December 2016, the *"Thirteenth Five-Year" National Informatization Plan* made the Data Resource Opening and Sharing Action and the "Internet Plus Government Services" Action priority actions. Article 69 of the *E-commerce*

Law of the People's Republic of China, promulgated in August 2018, stipulates that "the state shall take measures to promote the establishment of a public data sharing mechanism and promote the use of public data by e-commerce operators in accordance with the law," as a partial tentative response to the open data system, answering the call for open access to and use of domestic data.

The goal of data openness. Only by clarifying the goals of data openness can we set data openness on a good track. By analyzing the data openness policies of China, the United States, the UK, and other countries, it can be concluded that the purpose of China's data openness, especially open government data, is to:

> [P]romote the healthy development of the digital economy, improve government governance capabilities and service levels, and stimulate market vitality and innovation in society.[33]

Data openness in the United States was originally intended to satisfy the public's request for information, that is, to satisfy citizens' right to know. Afterwards, they vigorously promoted the openness of government data in order to "make the government open to an unprecedented height [...] ensure public trust and establish a transparent, public participation and collaborative system. Opening up will strengthen our democracy and increase the efficiency and effectiveness of the government" (Barack Obama 2009). British data openness is committed to realizing the value of open data, especially the value to politics, the economy, and society. For example, the *G8 Open Data Charter: UK Action Plan 2013* proposes to make UK "the most transparent government in the world" and "maintaining Britain's position as a global leader on open data." The *Open Data White Paper: Unleashing Potential* hopes that under the theme that "transparency drives prosperity," the British government can truly achieve

33 See Article 1 of the *Interim Measures for the Administration of the Sharing of Governmental Information Resources*, Article 1 of the *Interim Measures on the Openness of Public Data of Shanghai*, Article 1 of the *Interim Measures for the Administration of Public Data Opening and Security of Zhejiang Province*, and Article 1 of *Government Data Sharing and Opening Regulations of Guiyang*.

transparency and "ensure that everyone can benefit from transparency and open data." The *Open Government Partnership UK National Action Plan 2013–2015* pointed out that the UK should be built into the "world's most open and transparent government" to achieve "faster growth, better public services, less corruption and less poverty."

The principle of data openness. China's data openness system has a rather general statement concerning the principle of data openness: "Disclosure of government information by administrative organs shall adhere to disclosure being the norm and non-disclosure the exception, and observe the principles of justice, fairness, legality, and convenience for the people";[34] or, government information disclosure should be "demand-oriented, secure and controllable, based on categories and levels, with unified standards, convenient and efficient";[35] or, relevant work should "feature good coordination and planning, be promoted comprehensively with services provided proactively and free of charge and management in accordance with the law."[36] The United States and the UK have more scientific and detailed regulations on data openness principles, and there are usually not one but multiple such principles. For example, the U.S. *Freedom of Information Act* fundamentally determines the principle that government data should be "active, free, and completely open by relevant government departments," and the *Open Government Directive* puts forward the three principles of "government transparency, citizen participation, and collaboration." The *Open Data Charter* stipulates the five principles of open data by: default, quality and quantity data, usability by all, releasing data for improved governance, and releasing data for innovation. The *Public Sector Transparency Board: Public Data Principles* states fourteen principles, such as:

> [P]ublic data will be released in a reusable, machine-readable format; public data will be released under the same open license, and public data will be timely and fine-grained; public data will be freely available to use in any lawful way.

34 See Article 5 of *Regulations of the People's Republic of China on Disclosure of Government Information*.

35 See Article 4 of *Interim Measures Public Data Opening of Shanghai*.

36 See Article 3 of *Government Data Sharing and Opening Regulations of Guiyang*.

Classification for data openness. Data classification before disclosure is an innovation of China's. In the current data openness system, data is mainly divided into three types as far as disclosure is concerned: unconditional access, conditional access, and no access. Article 25 of the *Administrative Measures for E-Government and Government Data of Shandong Province* clearly states that:

> Government data within the scope of openness is divided into two types: unconditional access and access on request. For government data of unconditional access, citizens, legal persons and other organizations can directly obtain them on the open government data website. Where citizens, legal persons, and other organizations request certain government data, the relevant departments of the people's government at or above the county level shall handle the request in a timely manner in accordance with the relevant national and provincial government information disclosure regulations.

The *Regulations on Open and Shared Government Data of Guiyang Municipality* do not expressly stipulate the classification for data openness, but from the analysis of the substantive significance given in Articles 18 to 22, it can be seen that there are mainly two types: unconditional access and no access. More specifically, the first paragraph of Article 18 stipulates the scope of no-access data, which includes those:

> (1) Involving state secrets; (2) Involving business secrets; (3) Involving personal privacy; (4) Other government data that must not be opened as required by laws and regulations.

The data of unconditional access consists of two parts: the data specified in paragraph 2 of Article 18, and the data not specified in the first paragraph. Sharing is a special kind of openness. Data can also be divided into three types for the purpose of sharing: unconditional sharing, conditional sharing, and no-sharing. For example, Article 9 of the *Interim Measures for the Administration of the Sharing of Government Information Resources* states:

> [G]overnment information resources are divided into three types: data for unconditional sharing, conditional sharing, and no-sharing. Government information resources that can be provided to all government departments for shared use belong to

> the unconditional sharing category. Government information resources that can be provided to relevant government departments for shared use or can only be partially provided to all government departments for shared use belong to the conditional sharing category. Government information resources that should not be provided to other government departments for shared use belong to the no-sharing category.

Data Circulation and Transaction

In the application scenarios of industrial digitalization and digital industrialization, data circulation is the "normal" while static data storage is the "abnormal." Data circulation is the prerequisite and basis for the realization of the value of data and it takes various forms such as data pooling, data sharing, and data transactions, which are made possible based on three types of permissions: one-to-one permissions, one-to-many permissions, and mutual permissions. China's data transaction market is still in the initial stage of development, and it is necessary to give full play to the power of both the market and the government to build a data transaction system that encourages compatibility. Specifically, we are to "support the research and development of data transaction technology and innovations in data transaction models, broaden data transaction channels, and promote efficient data circulation."[37]

Data Minimization and Data Maximization

"The European *General Data Protection Regulation* is one of the most important pieces of legislation for the protection of personal data in the world" (Ding Xiaodong 2018). This legislation is considered to be "the most stringent regulation of data protection in the history of data legislation." Compared to the United States, the EU places more emphasis on

37 See Article 58 of *Data Regulations of Shenzhen Special Economic Zone (Draft for Comment)*.

"protection" in the balance between the protection and utilization of personal data. This is conducive to protecting personal privacy, but there is concern in the EU that this may further widen the gap in the development of the Internet between the EU and the United States. The *General Data Protection Regulation* highlights the principles of "empowering users" and "strict regulation of enterprises." This is welcomed by the European Consumer Organization, but aroused opposition from internet companies. In the digital age, the kind of policy adopted for personal information with data at its core is related to the development of big data and artificial intelligence, and the trend of data application. The United Sates and the EU are basically the same in terms of the principle of "empowering users," but have different positions on several other key issues.

The first is the different attitudes toward encouraging and restricting data development. The United States regards big data as a national strategy. In 2019, the U.S. digital economy was the largest in the world, reaching $13.1 trillion (US). Since 2012, the United States has successively issued policy documents, such as the *Big Data Research and Development Initiative* (2012), *Big Data: Seizing Opportunities, Preserving Values* (2014), and *Federal Big Data Research and Development Strategic Plan* (2016), and established a big data senior steering group to encourage the development of the data industry, which means that the United States will continue to maximize the role of data. Meanwhile, the EU has proceeded cautiously and independently in the direction of "data minimization." During the past twenty years, the EU has artificially restricted the development of the Internet through legislation and other external factors. The result is that the EU basically has no world-leading internet platforms today. Under the guidance of the "data minimization" principle, it will be difficult for the EU to develop a worldwide data industry platform in the future.

The second is a sharp contrast on consumer policy orientation. As one of the leading countries in terms of internet data platform development, the United States has chosen a policy orientation of compromise and balance between data development and data protection, highlighting the neutrality of personal data. The EU, on the contrary, as a data consumer, places more emphasis on the protection of personal data and privacy. If personal data is considered neutral, the principle of "empowering users" will be in exactly the middle point between data openness and transparency of personalized service information and the protection of personal privacy, leaving it to the user to decide which side they would like to go further. If personal data is considered negative, openness and transparency will be restricted, and the protection of personal data emphasized. One advantage is that consumers in the EU will enjoy more data security and privacy protection. For example, the *General Data Protection Regulation* strengthens the "right to be forgotten," which is conducive to the "incognito" and "account cancellation" of users on the Internet. One disadvantage is that EU consumers will lose the opportunity to access a greater number of personalized services.

The third is a completely different policy orientation toward enterprises. The *General Data Protection Regulation* emphasizes that "European laws apply in Europe," that is, if companies located outside the EU want to provide services within the EU, they must also comply with EU laws and regulations.

> This will have a wide-ranging impact on data giants and platforms who are based outside of the EU but run businesses within it. Overall, the *General Data Protection Regulation* gave European privacy regulators the power to impose high fines on companies, which could reach 4% of the company's global annual sales. (Jiang Qiping 2018)

By way of contrast, U.S. data legislation better reflects the trend of application outside of domestic jurisdiction, which is more in line with the law enforcement needs of cross-border data retrieval and puts the United States first in the legislative design. For example, the *Clarifying Lawful Overseas Use of Data Act*[38] increases the law enforcement authority of U.S. law enforcement agencies on data stored abroad, and at the same time allows law enforcement agencies of "eligible foreign governments" to access U.S. stored data. However, according to the act, most developing

38 The *Clarify Lawful Overseas Use of Data Act* originated from a lawsuit between Microsoft and the FBI regarding cross-border data retrieval. Since the original legislation did not clarify the enforcement of overseas data, the act intensified the call for legislation on cross-border data retrieval by law enforcement agencies. The legislative process was completed in just over a month, in March 2018.

countries, including China, are not regarded as "eligible foreign governments," which shows that the United States puts its own interests first and tries to dominate the formulation of the rules of cross-border data retrieval. This policy permits its law enforcement agencies to extend their long arms into the cyberspace of other countries, damaging the judicial sovereignty and national security of other nations.

Data Circulation

With the rapid expansion of the digital market, data openness, sharing, and exchange has become a trend. It can be said that "the legal circulation and utilization of data is the key to the development of the big data industry, and data ownership is the logical starting point for data utilization and circulation and data industrialization" (Ding Daoqin 2017). However, data circulation[39] is also accompanied by many issues, such as ownership, quality, compliance, and security, which have become bottlenecks that restrict data circulation.

Data circulation formats. The free flow of data is the "data normality" in the digital age, which is an inevitable requirement for the openness, unboundedness, and sharing of cyberspace. "Data should not be defined by its storage, but by its circulation."[40] Data circulation has three main formats: data pooling, data sharing, and data transaction. Data pooling mainly exists between institutions connected by capital, or some other kind of interest, and the flow of data is restricted by the internal rules and regulations of these institutions. The *Guiding Opinions on Accelerating the*

39 Data circulation can be defined as the process in which data stored in some information systems is used as the circulation object and is transferred from the supplier to the demander according to certain rules (See Cloud Computing and Big Data Research Institute of China Academy of Information and Communications Technology 2018).

40 Kevin Kelly believes that personal data is the big future. All businesses are data businesses. Data should not be defined by its storage, but by its circulation. With the continuous development of cloud technology, the ability to intervene in the network is more important than the data actually owned.

Development of Modern Logistics in the Circulation Sector of China (SGF [2008] No. 53) puts forward that "[w]e should encourage the construction of public logistics network information platforms and support business enterprises and logistics enterprises to realize the sharing of resources, data and information through the Internet and other advanced technologies." Data sharing mainly exists between cooperative institutions, and the flow of data is subject to inter-institutional contracts. But the premise is that:

> We should maintain national security and public security, keep state secrets and business secrets, protect personal privacy, and protect the legitimate rights and interests of data rights holders. No unit or individual may use data sharing and openness to engage in illegal and criminal activities.[41]

Data transaction refers to the exchange of data between the supplier and the demander through a third-party data trading platform in accordance with the transaction rules and pricing mechanism that they abide by. "Data transactions shall conclude a contract in accordance with the law, clarifying the data quality, transaction price, submission method, and data usage."[42]

Data circulation method. Data circulation is essentially a permission to use the data, and this permission can take three forms: one-to-one permissions, one-to-many permissions, and mutual permissions. These three types of permissions comprehensively build a model for data circulation and social utilization. Among them, one-to-one data permission means that the data owner only provides data to a specific subject, allowing it to use the data; this is a common data circulation method. It may be included in the business cooperation between enterprises, where one party permits the other party to use data within a specific range; it may also be a separate permission-to-use-data contract, such as an open API agreement. Mutual permission by two or more data owners to use data is mutual data permission, which is a behavior of jointly using the data generated by each. This

41 See Article 25 of the *Regulations on Promoting the Development and Application of Big Data of Guizhou Province.*

42 See Article 43 of the *Regulations on the Development and Application of Big Data of Hainan Province.*

kind of permission to use data is essentially a mutual permission method, which can also be called data sharing. The first basic characteristic of data sharing is that the subjects are limited to a specific scope and there must be at least two subjects; the second is that the specific subjects have permission to use the data owned or controlled by all the subjects within a certain scope based on a mutual permission-to-use mechanism. Data sharing can enable subjects in the scope to use existing data resources more fully, avoiding unnecessary labor and the corresponding costs, such as those required for data collection and data acquisition. The shared data can be regarded as the common data resource of the subjects within the scope. Therefore, the principle of data sharing is to transfer one party's rights to use data to other parties to realize data sharing and pooling. One-to-many data permissions refers to the permission given to unspecified subjects by the data owner, and its fundamental feature is that its data users are the public or whoever in society that needs to use the data. There are two types of one-to-many permissions: free permission and conditional permissions. The free permission to use means that specific data is clearly defined as "data with unconditional access," and can be accessed without any conditions by unspecified social entities. In contrast, conditional permission to use is permission to use the data given by the data owner to an unspecified party who needs to use the data, but with clearly stated conditions, including the purpose of use, the qualification of the user, and consideration for such use. The conditional data permission is essentially a kind of data transaction that allocates data resources to those who need to use the data through market mechanisms to realize the social utilization of data (Gao Fuping 2019).

Data circulation supervision. Data circulation supervision should be based on classification and managed according to different data circulation methods, and privacy security analysis and control should be ensured at each link of data circulation so that every link of data circulation and usage can be queried, managed, and controlled.

> For the affiliated use mode, data sharing mode and data transaction mode, three different regulatory strategies should be adopted: disclosure of cross-scenario use, authorization for the sharing of sensitive data, and prohibition of sensitive data circulation. For the affiliated enterprise model, attention should be paid to issues such as user authorization and the protection of the right to know for cross-scenario use of

> affiliated enterprise data, and the establishment of a security system for private data storage and access control. For the partner sharing model, attention should be paid to issues such as user authorization for data sharing between different companies, and user authorization for encrypted transmission of private data. For the data transaction mode, attention should be paid to issues such as user authorization for data transaction (multilateral authorization for non-sensitive data sharing), disclosure of transaction rules, and prohibition of private data circulation.
>
> (Zhang Minchong 2016)

In addition, the Japanese experience in data circulation supervision is worth examining. First, the Japanese government believes that the free development of the data circulation market may lead to data monopoly by super-large enterprises. In June 2017, the *Report of Study Group on Data and Competition Policy* issued by the Japan Fair Trade Commission stated:

> Encouraging data circulation and data collection by companies will help companies improve their products and services, thereby driving company operations and market development into a virtuous circle. The free development of the data circulation market may gradually produce super-large enterprises with superpowers in data monopoly, thereby reducing the space for the development of start-ups and small and medium-sized enterprises.
>
> (Japan Fair Trade Commission Competition Policy Research Center 2017)

Anti-monopoly agencies must be established to supervise international internet giants. In February 2019, the Japanese government announced that it would establish an anti-monopoly regulatory agency to review large technology companies such as Facebook and Google. This agency will be responsible for examining competition, protecting personal data, and making anti-data-monopoly recommendations. On March 6, 2019, the Japanese government ruled that the *Anti-Monopoly Law* applies when foreign internet giants illegally collect and use Japanese personal information. This is regarded as "abuse of dominant position" in *anti-monopoly law*.

Data Transaction

The digital economy has entered a new era of data-driven development. Cultivating the market of the data factor and promoting the circulation of data transactions is an inevitable requirement for economic and social innovation and development. On October 11, 2020, the *Implementation Plan for Comprehensive Pilot Reform in Shenzhen to Build the City into a Pilot Demonstration Zone for Socialism with Chinese Characteristics (2020–2025)* clearly stated that research and analysis shall be conducted into building a data trading market, or supporting data trading, based on existing trading venues. On September 18, 2020, the *Implementation Plan for the Establishment of Beijing International Big Data Exchange* proposed to explore the construction of Beijing International Big Data Exchange. On August 11, 2020, the Beibu Gulf Data Exchange was inaugurated and established in Nanning, dedicated to giving full play to the role of data as a "new energy" driving economic development. Since the CPC Central Committee and the State Council issued the *Opinions on Building Better Mechanisms for Market-based Factor Allocation* on April 9, 2020, all localities accelerated the building of the data factor market and focused on promoting the construction of trading platforms for data resources, forming a new high tide for data exchange construction following the establishment of the Global Big Data Exchange in Guiyang in 2015.

Data transaction subjects. The subjects in the legal relationship of data transactions include all the parties that enjoy rights and assume obligations in a data transaction relationship. They can be categorized as data suppliers,[43] data demanders[44], and data trading service

43 A data supplier shall meet the following requirements: (1) There is no record of major violations of data laws and regulations within one year; (2) It is registered with the data trading service agency and has been reviewed and approved; (3) Data can be safely delivered to the data demander; (4) It shall comply with the rules and regulations of the data trading service agency. Administrative agencies and organizations authorized by laws and regulations to manage public affairs shall not participate in data transactions as data suppliers. (See Article 8 of the *Interim Measures on Data Transaction Management of Tianjin Municipality (Draft for Comment)*.)

44 A data demander shall meet the following requirements: (1) There is no record of major violations of data laws and regulations within one year; (2) It is registered

agencies.[45] Among them, "data suppliers and data demanders refer to citizens, legal persons, and other organizations that conduct data transactions through data trading service agencies. Data trading service agencies rely on data trading service platforms to provide data trading services for the supplier and the demander."[46] From the perspective of market economics, data transaction subjects are equivalent to subjects in the data factor market (in a certain sense). They refer to commercial subjects that engage in activities of business data in the market of the data factor, and enjoy operational autonomy in accordance with the law.[47]

---

with the data trading service agency and has been reviewed and approved; (3) The transaction data can be secured; (4) It shall use the data in accordance with the agreement between the data supplier and demander. The re-identification of personal information is prohibited, and the transacted data shall be destroyed in time as agreed upon completion of use; (5) It shall comply with the rules and regulations of the data trading service agency. (See Article 9 of the *Interim Measures on Data Transaction Management of Tianjin Municipality* (*Draft for Comment*).)

45 The data trading service agency shall meet the following requirements: (1) It shall apply for registration of market entities in accordance with the law; (2) There is no record of major violations of data laws and regulations within one year; (3) It shall be able to guarantee the security of data transaction services; (4) The data trading service platform is deployed in China; (5) It shall not use the data or data derivatives of the data suppliers and demanders without authorization. The data trading service agency shall perform the following obligations: (1) Organize and supervise data transactions, settlement and delivery; (2) Review the legality of data sources provided by data suppliers; (3) Monitor data violations; (4) Formulate and implement punishment rules for transaction violations; (5) Manage data trading service platforms; (6) Accept and resolve complaints about data transactions; (7) Other obligations required by laws and regulations. (See *Article 10 of the Interim Measures on Data Transaction Management of Tianjin Municipality (Draft for Comment)*.)

46 Electronic transactions are data transactions conducted through the data trading service platform, and non-electronic transactions are data transactions conducted offline. (See Article 7 of the *Interim Measures on Data Transaction Management of Tianjin Municipality (Draft for Comment)*.)

47 See Article 101 of the *Data Regulations of Shenzhen Special Economic Zone* (*Draft for Comment*).

Data transaction objects. Transaction data[48] is the object in the legal relationship of data transactions and the object to which the rights and obligations of the subjects are directed. "All data that are obtained in accordance with the law and cannot be processed to identify a specific data supplier or restored, can be traded."[49] However, data under one of the following circumstances cannot be traded: (1) Data involving national security, public safety, and personal privacy; (2) Data involving business secrets without the authorization and consent of the legal right holder; (3) Data involving personal information without the explicit consent of the personal information subject; data involving the personal information of the minor over the age of 14 without the express consent of the minor or his guardian; data involving the personal information of the minor under the age of 14 without the explicit consent of his guardian; (4) Data obtained by fraud, deception, misleading statements, or from illegal channels; (5) Data that is expressly prohibited by other laws, regulations or legal agreements.[50]

Data trading platform. The development of data trading platforms is a milestone in the development of data trading (Mu Huijun 2016). A data trading platform is to data trading what the stock exchange is to securities trading—a data trading platform is at the core of a data transaction that realizes the free circulation of data among different rights. In terms of function, "a data trading service platform should have functions such as user management,[51] transaction management,[52] order

48 Transaction data refers to the legitimate data for the transaction between the data supplier and demander. (See Article 38 of the *Interim Measures on Data Transaction Management of Tianjin Municipality* (*Draft for Comment*).)

49 See Article 14 of the *Interim Measures on Data Transaction Management of Tianjin Municipality* (*Draft for Comment*).

50 See Article 15 of the *Interim Measures on Data Transaction Management of Tianjin Municipality* (*Draft for Comment*).

51 *Interim Measures on Data Transaction Management of Tianjin Municipality* (*Draft for Comment*) Article 23 The data trading service platform shall support functions of user management such as user registration and verification, user login, password retrieval, registration information modification, and password modification.

52 *Interim Measures on Data Transaction Management of Tianjin Municipality* (*Draft for Comment*) Article 24 The data trading service platform shall support data suppliers to retrieve demand information, publish transaction data, deliver transaction data, and handle online complaints, and shall support data demanders to retrieve

management,[53] and platform management."[54][55] In terms of performance, "a data trading platform shall establish a safe, reliable, manageable, and traceable data transaction environment, formulate rules for data transactions, information disclosure, and self-regulation, and take effective measures to protect personal privacy, business secrets and important data."[56] The establishment of a data trading platform has standardized data transactions and made pricing mechanisms more reasonable. At present, China has established the Guiyang big data trading platform, the Zhongguancun big data trading platform, and the Central China big data trading platform.

Data transaction pricing. Data pricing is the logical starting point for data transactions, and a form of monetization of data value (Key Laboratory of Big Data Strategy 2019, p. 138). There is a huge difference in data pricing compared with the pricing of other assets. The value of data assets is mainly derived from the business income generated directly or indirectly. However, since the data itself can be copied without damage, and the income generated in different business scenarios can be superimposed,

---

transaction data information, release data requirements, manage purchase lists, make evaluations, and file online complaints.

53 *Interim Measures on Data Transaction Management of Tianjin Municipality (Draft for Comment)* Article 25 The data trading service platform shall support functions of order management such as online order placement, order modification, cancellation, deletion, query, and online payment, and shall save and record the data transaction electronic agreement between the supplier and the demander, review the cancellation of the delivered order, and set the maximum payment time for the order, automatically cancel the expired unpaid order.

54 *Interim Measures on Data Transaction Management of Tianjin Municipality (Draft for Comment)*. Article 26: The data trading service platform shall have functions of platform management, such as supply and demand information management, transaction data billing management, security management, transaction auditing, log management and support data trading service agencies to review user registration information and release information, release and modify notice announcements, query and export order information and payment information, and backup and restore system data.

55 See Article 22 of the *Interim Measures on Data Transaction Management of Tianjin Municipality (Draft for Comment)*.

56 See Article 59 of the *Data Regulations of Shenzhen Special Economic Zone (Draft for Comment)*.

the value of specific data assets is different from the value of traditional assets. It is not a fixed value, but a dynamic value that changes with a variety of factors. Because data is different from other commodities in being easy to copy and spread but difficult valuate, it is impossible for data exchanges to simply borrow the pricing models of financial exchanges and commodity exchanges. The bidding modes of traditional exchanges are generally continuous bidding and call bidding, which involve many-to-many relationships, while data transactions are generally one-to-one or one-to-many. Different types of data require different pricing mechanisms, but on the whole:

> Data trading platforms should construct data asset pricing from multiple dimensions such as real-time, time span, sample coverage, integrity, data type and level, and data mining potential, and coordinate with evaluation agencies of data value to reasonably evaluate the value of data assets.[57]

At the same time, from the legislative stance:

> The government should be promoted to formulate data pricing rules and evaluation criteria of data value, encourage the establishment of evaluation institutions of data value, promote market-oriented reform of data factor pricing, and guide market entities to exercise autonomy of data factor pricing in a reasonable manner in accordance with the law.[58]

Data transaction mode. "The data factor market can use a variety of legitimate methods such as autonomous transactions and trading platforms to carry out data transaction activities."[59] "Data transactions can generally take two forms: electronic transactions and non-electronic transactions."[60] The essence of data transactions is the transfer of data

57 See Article 60 of the *Data Regulations of Shenzhen Special Economic Zone* (*Draft for Comment*).

58 See Article 80 of the *Data Regulations of Shenzhen Special Economic Zone* (*Draft for Comment*).

59 See Article 58 of the *Data Regulations of Shenzhen Special Economic Zone* (*Draft for Comment*).

60 See Article 6 of the *Interim Measures on Data Transaction Management of Tianjin Municipality* (*Draft for Comment*).

property rights, including the transfer of data property ownership, the transfer of the right to use data property, and the transfer of data *jus fruendi* (Li Wenlian and Xia Jianming 2013). The transfer of data property ownership means that the owner of the data property rights transfers the ownership to the demander of the data property rights. Ownership of data property rights is generally highly targeted, and is a data product that can be directly applied after analysis. The transaction model based on the right to data use is characterized by the transaction of leasing data and retrieving data. The most typical business model is the leasing of databases, such as Chinese journal databases and various paper retrieval databases. Users pay a certain fee to obtain the right to use the database for a certain number of times or within a certain period of time. The data *jus fruendi* transaction model means that the data demander uses the data provided by the data supplier to obtain profits and then distributes the benefits with the data supplier.

Data Security and Compliance

Data security and compliance is a new important aspect and a new important content of national security, and it is a comprehensive issue involving technology, law, supervision, and social governance. To ensure data security, the establishment of legal regulations is an important prerequisite and a key link. General Secretary Xi Jinping has repeatedly emphasized that "national security is the top priority" and clearly required that "national data security must be effectively guaranteed"; "the coordination of policies, supervision, and laws must be strengthened, and the construction of laws and regulations must be accelerated." On September 8, 2020, China put forward the *Global Initiative on Data Security* at a high-level meeting of the International Seminar on "Seizing Digital Opportunities for Cooperation and Development" to express China's propositions in the field of data security, that is, to correct deviations at critical moments to prevent cyberspace from falling into the trap of a clash of civilizations and Cold War thinking. Data security derives not only from technology, but also from various risks and crises caused by the openness, circulation, and application of data. To prevent data security risks and promote data legal compliance, it is necessary to develop technologies, talents, and systems required to maintain security and compliance, and build a three-dimensional and multi-dimensional data security defense and compliance system.

Data Security Risks

Weak risk and security awareness, poor security and reliability of critical information infrastructure, hackers and vulnerabilities, data terrorism, and the lack and lag of laws have increased the frequency of the damage caused by data risks. In particular, it has been more common for data related to the national interest, public security, trade secrets, individual privacy, and military research and production to be attacked, leaked, stolen, tampered with, or used illegally. Data security has become the most urgent core issue in the digital age.

Security risks in open access to data. Data risks in open access to data are the main threats faced at the national level as data openness has become a national strategy. In July 2013, General Secretary Xi Jinping pointed out: "Big data is the 'free' resource of the industrial society. Whoever has the data has the initiative." The scale of data owned by a country, and the country's ability to use it, has gradually become an important part of the overall national power. The right to possess and control data will become the core power of the country, in addition to land, sea, and air rights. Open access to data has made state sovereignty in the digital age increasingly antagonistic, posing a serious threat to national security. Thus, the struggle for data sovereignty has become a salient strategy. The United States places strict restrictions on open access to data, emphasizing that open access must be balanced with national security, law enforcement, and privacy protection. That is, open government data should apply only under the premise of complying with the nine "clauses of exemption from disclosure of information" of the *Freedom of Information Act*. The nine "clauses of exemption from disclosure of information"[61] are:

> (1) matters that are specifically authorized under criteria established by an Executive order to be kept secret in the interest of national defense or foreign policy and are in fact properly classified pursuant to such Executive order; (2) related solely to the internal personnel rules and practices of an agency; (3) specifically exempted from disclosure by statute; (4) trade secrets and commercial or financial information obtained from a person and privileged or confidential; (5) inter-agency or intra-agency memorandums or letters that would not be available by law to a party other than an agency in litigation with the agency; (6) personnel and medical files and similar files the disclosure of which would constitute a clearly unwarranted invasion of personal privacy; (7) certain records or information compiled for law enforcement purposes; (8) contained in or related to the control by an agency responsible for the regulation or supervision of financial institutions; (9) geological or geophysical information and data, including maps, concerning wells.

Security risks in data circulation. Data security risks in data circulation are mainly concentrated in data collection, data transmission, and data storage. In the process of data collection, there may be security threats such as data corruption, data loss, data leakage, data stealing, and privacy leakage. To tackle these risks in the process of data collection, it is necessary to adhere to the principle that "whoever collects the data should be responsible,"[62]

> Clarify the purpose of data collection, and ensure the legality, legitimacy, and necessity of data collection. Necessary measures should be taken to keep the environment, facilities and technology of data collection under control to ensure the integrity, consistency and authenticity of the data, and to ensure that the data is not leaked during the collection process."[63]

61 See "Exemption from Disclosure of Information" in Article (b) of the *Freedom of Information Act*.

62 See Article 13 of the *Regulations on Big Data Security Control of Guizhou Province*.

63 See Article 19 of the *Management Measures on Data Security of Tianjin Municipality (Interim)*. In addition, in 2014, six farmers' associations, including the American Farm Bureau Federation, Soybean Association, National Corn Growers Association, and Farmers Union, joined forces to reach the "Privacy and Security Principles for Farm Data" on the collection of farmland data with six giant agricultural technology providers (ATPs), headed by Deere and Monsanto. These

The main security issues faced by data in the process of transmission include confidentiality, integrity, and authenticity. Problems include data being monitored and tampered with. Especially in the environment of wireless network transmissions, data security issues in network transmission are particularly prominent. In this regard, "to transmit data, one should reasonably select transmission channels and take necessary security measures to prevent data from being stolen, leaked, and tampered with."[64] "Corresponding control measures should be taken according to the data security level to ensure the security and reliability of data transmission."[65] The security problems of data storage management are prominently manifested as risks, such as uncertain data associated permissions, access control problems, and insufficient storage capacity.

> Therefore, according to the type, scale, purpose, security level, and importance of the data, we need to choose appropriate systems, media, facilities and equipment with corresponding security performance and protection levels to store the data,

---

basic principles include: (1) Farmers have the property rights and absolute control rights of their own farm data. (2) Farmers allow agricultural technology providers to share data with "stakeholders with an economic interest." (3) Access and use of farm data should be granted only with the affirmative and explicit consent of the farmer—this will be by contract agreements. (4) Farmers have the freedom to choose to participate or not to participate in data collection and sharing. (5) Once a farmer chooses to withdraw and requests that their data be destroyed, the provider must destroy and return the data. (6) There is a prohibition on the use of farm data by the provider to speculate in commodity markets. These principles reflect the following demands: First, the access and use of data collection should be specified in a contractual manner, and user permission should be obtained. Users have absolute control over the data, they can freely choose to enter and exit, and they can request destruction and return of data. The second is to allow service providers to share data with "stakeholders with an economic interest." This is because modern society is built on the basis of specialized division of labor, and user services are often provided by a group of companies that cooperate closely, and necessary data sharing is a prerequisite for obtaining collaborative services. The third is that the use of data must not cause potential substantial damage to farmers (not for speculation in commodity markets).

64 See Article 19 of the *Regulations on Big Data Security Control of Guizhou Province.*

65 See Article 20 of the *Management Measures on Data Security of Tianjin Municipality (Interim).*

> and take appropriate technical and management measures to ensure the security of the storage systems and the stored data.[66]

Security risks in data application. Data processing, exchange, use, destruction, and service outsourcing are the main links prone to security risks in data application. "When processing data, the original data should be properly protected and shall not be arbitrarily changed or forged; and there must not be any destructive changes and permanent loss of data caused through malicious processing."[67] "Personal data may be processed only if the data subject has unambiguously given his consent."[68] "In data exchange, the integrity and availability of the data shall be maintained. The exchange of data shall be carried out legally, and the parties to the exchange shall not impersonate others or defraud the exchange of data by other means."[69]

> Data shall not be used for illegal purposes. Data obtained through illegal means such as attacks, stealing, malicious access, is not allowed to be used. The use of data for advertising, marketing and promotional activities shall not interfere with the normal production and life of the person involved, and shall not harm the legitimate rights and interests of the person involved or any other person.[70]
>
> When destroying data, the method of destruction and the requirements for destruction shall be reasonably determined according to the needs of big data security management. When destroying important data such as public data and data involving trade secrets and personal information, a security risk assessment shall be conducted.[71]
>
> If a service outsourcing business involves the collection, storage, transmission or application of data, a security agreement shall be signed with the service provider in accordance with the law. Security guarantee measures shall be taken, and data export, copy, and destruction shall be supervised.[72]

66 See Article 19 of *Regulations on Big Data Security Control of Guizhou Province.*

67 See Article 20 of *Regulations on Big Data Security Control of Guizhou Province.*

68 *Directive 95/46/EC of the EU on the protection of individuals with regard to the processing of personal data and on the free movement of such data* stipulates: "Member States shall provide that personal data may be processed only if: (a) the data subject has unambiguously given his consent."

69 See Article 21 of *Regulations on Big Data Security Control of Guizhou Province.*

70 See Article 22 of *Regulations on Big Data Security Control of Guizhou Province.*

71 See Article 23 of *Regulations on Big Data Security Control of Guizhou Province*

72 See Article 16 of *Regulations on Big Data Security Management of Guiyang Municipality.*

As for the situation in other countries, we may take Germany as an example. The *German Federal Data Protection Act* stipulates that "the collection, processing, and use of personal data are permitted only when permitted or required by this law or other laws or with the consent of the data owner."[73]

Data Security Defense

To prevent data security risks and effectively ensure data security, it is necessary to build a three-dimensional data security defense system covering all aspects. The State Council's *Action Outline for Promoting the Development of Big Data* lists "strengthening security control, improving management, and promoting healthy development" as the three major tasks, and clarifies specific priorities in relevant work. As a strategic guidance for big data development in China, it fully reflects the top-level design and overall planning of big data security at the national level, and provides a policy basis and action guide for big data security in China.

The protection of important data in key industries and fields needs to be strengthened. This is to strengthen the protection of information concerning key systems, key industries, and important fields in the country, especially data and information involving national interests, public security, trade secrets, personal privacy, military research and production. According to the *Measures for the Administration of Data Security (Draft for Comment)* issued by the Cyberspace Administration of China, "the term 'important data' means data whose divulgation may directly affect national security, economic security, social stability, and public health and security, such as undisclosed government information and extensive information on population, genetic health, geographical conditions, and mineral resources."[74] To protect important data in key industries and fields, and to eliminate technical loopholes, defense vulnerabilities, and management

73 See section 4 of *German Federal Data Protection Act* (acceptance of data collection, processing, and use).

74 See Article 38 of *Measures for the Administration of Data Security (Draft for Comment)*.

weaknesses to the greatest extent, the key lies in strictly implementing the relevant provisions of the *Cybersecurity Law* and the *Regulations on Classified Protection of Cybersecurity*. In particular, "personal information and important data collected and produced by critical information infrastructure operators during their operations within the territory of the People's Republic of China shall be stored within China."[75] "Measures such as data classification, important data backup and encryption shall be taken."[76] Also, special protection measures shall be taken for confidential data involving the national interest, trade secrets, personal privacy, and sensitive data, and the principle of "three determinations and four clears" shall be implemented. Specifically, the "three determinations" are academic definitions, legal restrictions, and policy confirmations, which should be followed in the definition of national interests, trade secrets, personal privacy, and sensitive data. In the absence of policy confirmation, the definition of national interests, trade secrets, personal privacy, and sensitive data must be legally restricted or academically defined. The principles of "four clears" means: First, it is necessary to be clear about the boundaries and use of data sharing in various fields, systems, and departments, especially the boundaries, scope, and use of open government data. Second, it is necessary to be clear about the scope and boundaries of data security, responsible parties and specific requirements for data collection, transmission, storage, use, and openness. Third, it is necessary to be clear about the government's authority, scope, and method in the overall utilization of big data in the market through open forms such as contracts. Fourth, it is necessary to be clear about the rights, responsibilities, and obligations of the subjects of personal information collection.

Safe and reliable products and services must be used in areas involving national security and stability. It is necessary to plan and design an autonomous and controllable next-generation internet with Chinese characteristics, and pay more attention to security issues in the network convergence technology, terminal mobility, and terminal access of the new-generation

75 See Article 37 of *Cybersecurity Law of the People's Republic of China*.

76 See Article 21 of *Cybersecurity Law of the People's Republic of China*.

or next-generation equipment from the perspective of technology, products, and services. According to the *Cybersecurity Law*:

> Network products and services shall comply with the compulsory requirements of relevant national standards. Providers of network products and services shall not install malware. When a provider discovers any risk such as security defect and vulnerability of its network products or services, it shall immediately take remedial measures, inform users in a timely manner, and report it to the competent department in accordance with relevant provisions. Providers of network products and services shall continuously provide security maintenance for their products and services, and shall not terminate the provision of security maintenance within the stipulated period or the period agreed upon by the parties.[77]

"Key network equipment and specialized network security products shall, in accordance with the compulsory requirements of relevant national standards, pass the security certification conducted by qualified institutions or meet the requirements of security detection before being sold or provided."[78]

The safety and reliability of critical information infrastructure shall be improved. General Secretary Xi Jinping emphasized that "critical information infrastructure in the fields of finance, energy, power, communications, and transportation is the like the central nervous system of economic and social operations. It is the top priority of network security, and it is a possible target for major attacks." Critical information infrastructure mainly refers to the products, services, systems, and assets on which the operation of the social economy depends heavily. Being "critical" means having high relevance with a lot of important things hinged on it. Once the critical infrastructure is damaged, there will be paralysis, and social and economic operations will be severely affected. At present, China has not clearly defined the scope or set the standards for the security protection of critical information infrastructure. This is a weak point that urgently needs to be shored up. From a global perspective, the core of each country's network security legislation is to protect the critical information infrastructure. Strengthening the security protection of the critical information

77 See Article 22 of *Cybersecurity Law of the People's Republic of China*.
78 See Article 23 of *Cybersecurity Law of the People's Republic of China*.

infrastructure is not only an urgent need in China's currently grave data security situation, but also an inevitable requirement to effectively ensure national security. The level of security and reliability of critical information infrastructure is mainly reflected in four aspects: first, business continuity capability—that is, uninterrupted and reliable supply capability; second, the independent control of key equipment—that is, the realization of the country's independent design, manufacturing, controllable management and use of major information products, facilities, equipment, and technologies; third, institutionalization of the sensitive data storage and circulation; fourth, the primary responsibility for critical information infrastructure. To strengthen the security guarantee of critical information infrastructure, the core lies in "protecting critical information infrastructure from attack, intrusion, interference and damage,"[79] and the key lies in "the focus of protection based on the rules for graded protection of cybersecurity."[80] Specific measures can be found in Article 32, Article 33, Article 34, Article 35, Article 36, Article 37, Article 38, and Article 39 of the *Cybersecurity Law* and various specific provisions of the *Regulations on the Security Protection of Critical Information Infrastructure*.

A sound standard system and assessment system needs to be established for data security. Standards are the universal language of the world. Data security cannot be separated from the requirement of "standards," and data compliance needs standards to be in place first. The improvement of the standards system and assessment system for data security can specifically include the following six aspects: First, focus on research work for and formulation of basic standards, technical standards, application standards, and management standards for data. Second, lead in the research and application of standards for data security in key areas such as individual privacy, e-commerce, and national security, as well as areas prone to security issues. Third, research to form a security standards system covering the entire process of data collection, storage, transmission, mining, disclosure, sharing, use, and management. Fourth, for key objects such as data platforms and data service providers, evaluations must be conducted on data reliability

79 See Article 5 of *Cybersecurity Law of the People's Republic of China*.
80 See Article 31 of *Cybersecurity Law of the People's Republic of China*.

and security as well as application security, and there must also be sound risk detection, warning, and evaluation. For key industries and important departments, the national security department shall conduct the security assessment of critical information infrastructure and the assessment of sensitive data, and issue licenses afterward. Fifth, the assessment monitoring system and real-time monitoring system of data and network security, as well as the ability to perceive, detect, and respond to the threat of big data cyberattacks need to be improved. Sixth, efforts are to be made to speed up the implementation of security assessment on cross-border data flow, strengthen data transfer security testing and assessment, and ensure the security of data in the global flow. In addition, it is necessary to:

> [S]trengthen the publicity and training of national, industry and local standards for data security, and guide and encourage data operators to refer to relevant standards for data security to improve data security protection capabilities.[81]
>
> It should focus on the national big data strategy [...] establish a sound big data security management system, build the local standard system, the evaluation system and the guarantee system of big data security.[82]

Also,

> [I]t is necessary to encourage responsible units for security to use blockchain and other new technical means to optimize the general structure of data aggregation, strengthen trust certification and anti-tampering design, and improve the level of big data security protection.[83]

In addition,

> [E]nterprises, scientific research institutions, colleges and universities, and related industry organizations should be encouraged and supported to conduct research, formulation, and collaborative research on big data security-related standards, and promote the formation of national, industry and local standards.[84]

81 See Article 8 of *Management Measures on Data Security of Tianjin Municipality (Interim)*.

82 See Article 5 of *Regulations on Big Data Security Control of Guizhou Province.*

83 See Article 22 of *Regulations on Big Data Security Management of Guiyang Municipality.*

84 See Article 43 of *Regulations on Big Data Security Control of Guizhou Province.*

> And legally established big data industry organizations should be supported to formulate industry security norms and service standards in accordance with laws, regulations and articles of association, conduct self-discipline management of their members' big data security behaviors, organize big data security education and business training, promote big data security cooperation and exchanges, and improve the level of big data security management and the quality of employees.[85]

The anti-attack, anti-leakage, anti-stealing, anti-tampering, and anti-illegal use detection and early warning system needs to be improved. Data attacks, data leakage, data stealing, data tampering, and illegal use of data should be the subject of early warning systems. Attacks, leakage, stealing, tampering, and illegal use are often mingled and occur at the same time. They are the top priority for the early warning systems that prevent damage to data systems. The essence of building a data security detection and early warning system is to comprehensively

> [T]ake prevention, management, and disposal strategies and measures to prevent big data from being attacked, invaded, interfered, destroyed, stolen, tampered with, deleted, and illegally used, and to ensure the authenticity, integrity, validity, confidentiality, and controllability of big data.[86]

At the same time:

> [T]he analysis, prediction and evaluation of big data security risks should be strengthened, and relevant information should be collected; if big data security incidents such as large-scale hacking or virus spread are discovered, early warning information should be released in a timely manner, preventive response measures should be proposed, and the responsible person for big data security should be guided and supervised to do security precautions.[87]

To prevent data from attacks, leakage, stealing, tampering, and illegal use, it is necessary to establish an encryption mechanism and a traceability mechanism for management systems at the source, along the process, and throughout the entire system, and establish a three-in-one security

85 See Article 17 of *Regulations on Big Data Security Management of Guiyang Municipality*.

86 See Article 3 of *Regulations on Big Data Security Control of Guizhou Province*.

87 See Article 33 of *Regulations on Big Data Security Control of Guizhou Province*.

technology guarantee mechanism for data security, application security, and operating system security.

Network security and confidentiality protection systems should be established and improved. The establishment of a data security and confidentiality protection system should include a standardized system from the management and technical levels, which should comprehensively enhance the overall capabilities of data security, confidentiality, and protection. From a management perspective, the data security and confidentiality protection system can be divided into system management, asset management, technology management, and risk management. The technical perspective means that data security can rely on mainly electromagnetic protection technology, communication security technology, information terminal protection technology, and network security technology. First, the most basic is "to formulate a security management system for data security personnel, sign a security responsibility letter and confidentiality agreement, and regularly conduct security training."[88]

Second,

> [C]ryptography technology, management of cryptographic facilities and systems shall be used in accordance with the relevant regulations of the country's cryptography management, and keys shall be generated, distributed, accessed, updated, backed up and destroyed in accordance with regulations.[89]

Third,

> Responsible units for security should establish an internal security management control and support mechanism based on the life cycle, scale, and importance of the data, and the nature, category, and scale of the unit, and identify the person in charge of security management and implement security management responsibilities for different positions; operators of critical information infrastructure should also set up special security management agencies.[90]

88 See Article 15 of *Management Measures on Data Security of Tianjin Municipality (Interim).*

89 See Article 18 of *Management Measures on Data Security of Tianjin Municipality (Interim).*

90 See Article 10 of *Regulations on Big Data Security Management of Guiyang Municipality.*

Improvements are needed in data situational awareness capabilities, event detection capabilities, security protection capabilities, risk control capabilities, and emergency response capabilities. The situational awareness capability refers to the ability to establish a qualitative or quantitative indicator system that integrates multi-party alarms and traffic information through aggregation, correlation, fusion, merging, and other methods to achieve the purpose of accurately grasping the situation. The core of the event detection capability lies in accurate "prediction," that is, through the collection, analysis, and calculation of massive data of cyberattacks before an attack event occurs, to discover abnormal behaviors and laws of cyberattacks, and to effectively identify the attack source and network risk points. The development trend of network and data security incidents can also be accurately predicted, leaving cyberattacks nowhere to hide. In terms of security protection capabilities, it is necessary to make preparations and protections to ensure that data owners avoid danger, infringement, and accidents, and to protect all aspects of data application and processing. Risk control capability formulates, selects, and implements treatment plans through risk identification, determination, and measurement, thereby reducing or even eliminating the possibility of risk occurrence, while reducing losses at the same time. In terms of emergency response capabilities, the top priority is to improve the emergency response plan, to include joint responses, data recovery, data disaster recovery, and other subsystems.

> Data operators should comply with relevant laws and regulations, refer to data security standards, perform data security protection obligations, and establish data security management responsibility, assessment and evaluation systems, as well as data security complaint reporting systems. They should formulate data security plans, implement data security protection technical measures, and carry out data security risk assessments. They should also formulate emergency plans for data security incidents, handle and report data security incidents in a timely manner, organize data security education and training, and accept supervision by relevant departments, as well as social supervision.[91]

91 See Article 7 of *Management Measures on Data Security of Tianjin Municipality* (*Interim*).

Efforts should be made to establish a privacy and personal information protection system and strengthen the management and punishment of data abuse and infringement of personal privacy. The protection of privacy and personal information runs through all aspects of the entire process of data collection, storage, transmission, transaction, and application. The key is to regulate the behavior of all stakeholders. First, in the data collection stage, it mainly involves three parties: individuals, the government, and enterprises. For individuals, the most important thing is to cultivate awareness of privacy and personal information protection; for the government and enterprises, it is necessary to standardize their data collection methods, and clarify the legal and social responsibilities of government departments, enterprises, industries, and netizens in the data society. Second, in the data processing stage, which mainly involves the government, enterprises, and industrial organizations, the main purpose is to establish a personal data processing review mechanism and a desensitization and decryption guarantee mechanism for data operators. Third, in the data transaction stage, due to the involvement of multiple parties it is extremely easy to leak private and personal information. Thus, a sales permission mechanism must be established, as well as a transfer registration mechanism and a cross-border flow review mechanism for personal data. Fourth, in the data application stage, a multiple-participant reporting mechanism, a traceability mechanism, and an accountability mechanism for personal data privacy leakage must be established.

The relationship between prudential supervision and protection of innovation should be properly handled. Supervision and innovation are a pair of contradictions. They are both opposed and unified. On the one hand, regulation stimulates innovation. On the other hand, innovation promotes continuous changes in regulation. It is not an empty talk to say that:

> The relationship between the development of innovation and the guarantee of security shall be properly handled, and supervision should be conducted prudentially and innovation should be protected; the confidentiality management rules and measures shall be explored and improved, and the security of data shall be effectively guaranteed.[92]

92 See the State Council's *Action Outline for Promoting the Development of Big Data* (GF [2015] No. 50).

Only by correctly handling the relationship between data supervision and innovation, mastering the balance, innovating in supervision and supervising innovation, achieving prudential supervision, protecting innovation, coordinating between the two, and achieving healthy development can we realize a virtuous circle of development featuring "regulation–innovation–reregulation–re-innovation." Thus, we must (1) continuously upgrade our innovation in big data development, (2) strengthen the supervision of the big data development and innovation process, (3) improve the supervision and coordination mechanism of big data development, (4) establish a risk early warning mechanism, and (5) strengthen international and regional cooperation in the supervision of big data development.

Data Security Legislation

Data security has become a major issue relevant to national security and development interests. Special legislation on data security has a special strategic significance. Without data security, there will be no national security. To solve data security problems, legislation is fundamental, while technology offers support. On September 7, 2018, the Standing Committee of the 13th National People's Congress announced its legislative plan, and the *Data Security Law of the People's Republic of China* (hereinafter referred to as the *Data Security Law*) was included in the list of draft laws with relatively mature conditions, to be submitted for deliberation during the term of office. On June 28, 2020, the twentieth meeting of the Standing Committee of the 13th National People's Congress reviewed the *Data Security Law* (*Draft for Comment*).

The *Data Security Law* (*Draft for Comment*) has a broad scope and many highlights, which are mainly reflected in the following aspects. First, in terms of legislative concepts, it adheres to the holistic approach to national security, and systematically builds on the concept of data security governance, which fully reflects the huge leap in thinking from "management" to "governance" of the country, as well as the strategy and wisdom of "China's governance." Second, in terms of legislative technique, it introduces a dynamic balance mechanism for multiple interests, and always adheres to the basic principle of "equal attention to security and development." Third, in terms of legislative content, it establishes the basic framework of the data security system. The established protective jurisdiction measures, the data security collaborative governance systems, the international co-operation mechanisms, and the legal status in data transactions have laid the foundation for the development and improvement of a future data security system.

As a new law born out of many years of efforts, the *Data Security Law* (*Draft for Comment*) represents a historic step forward in the process of data security legislation in China. There are many notable points, yet there are still shortcomings that need to be tackled. First, the position of the law in the overall legislative system is not very clear. The *Data Security Law* is an important part of the national security legal system. It forms a complete basic legal system in the digital field together with the *Cybersecurity Law* and the *Personal Information Protection Law*, which is still in the making. The *Personal Information Protection Law* should deal with data security issues from the perspective of protecting personal privacy, while the *Data Security Law* should be the main defense of national security, with data "self-reliance" and "national security and public security" as the regulatory focus. The relationship between the *Data Security Law* and the *Cybersecurity Law* has aroused considerable controversy within judicial and theoretical circles, and has led to some speculation. Second, the overall coordination is poor. A key point to consider is how to coordinate between the *Data Security Law* and the *Civil Code*, the *Cybersecurity Law*, the *Personal Information Protection Law*, and other relevant laws. Third, operability is also an issue. Compared with the *General Data Protection Regulation*, the provisions of the *Data Security Law* (*Draft for Comment*) are rather general. Most of them are only principles. Some clauses are more like slogans, without substantive content, and a large number of compliance systems need to be refined before they can be effectively implemented and applied in reality. Fourth, alignment with international convention is insufficient. "Chinese laws are going to the world, and the most likely is the law of the digital economy." The *Data Security Law* should keep its Chinese characteristics while aligning sufficiently with international rules. As a domestic law, it may be subject to scrutiny by the international society in the perspective of international rules. It is necessary, therefore, to take precautions and to fully consider the compliance of domestic laws with international rules, agreements, and international laws, and do a good job in dispute assessment and litigation plans under the framework of international law to provide better solutions for data security.

Data security legislation needs to fully consider the background of the digital society and the development of digital technologies, and avoid using industrialization thinking to formulate laws for the digital society. Efforts should be made to amplify China's voice in the international community, especially in the making of international rules in cyberspace where there are currently no such rules. First, it is necessary to clarify the position of the *Data Security Law*, put in the *National Security Law* as the upper-level law, correctly handle the relationship between the *Data Security Law* and other laws under the guidance of the holistic approach to national security, and more clearly define basic concepts such as data, data security, data activities, online data processing, data belonging to controlled items, and domestic data. Second, the regulation scope of the *Data Security Law* must be clarified, and "open access to government data" should be included in the legislative plan of the National People's Congress, and be separately legislated. Because the *Data Security Law* is mandatory, its logical starting point and main content should be data security, which needs to be specific and clear. Third, it is necessary to further define the responsibilities of public security agencies, national security agencies, and national cyberspace administration agencies, improve the data classification and staging system, and establish a data property rights system, and an administrative implementation and settlement agreement system. In addition, complaints and reporting channels should be unblocked, legal responsibilities should be strictly enforced, and data rights protection should be further strengthened.

Bibliography

Cloud Computing and Big Data Research Institute of China Academy of Information and Communications Technology. April 2018. "White Paper on Key Technologies of Data Circulation (Version 1.0)."

Ding, Daoqin. 2017. "The Binary Division of Basic Data and Value-added Data." *Law and Economy*, 2nd issue.

Ding, Xiaodong. 2018. "What Are Data Rights? From the Perspective of the Protection of Data Privacy in the European *General Data Protection Regulation.*" *East China University of Political Science and Law Journal*, 4th issue.

Du, Zhenhua. 2015. "Exploration of Data Right Confirmation in Big Data Application." *Mobile Communications*, 13th issue.

Du, Zhenhua, and Cha, Hongwang. 2018. "Realistic Considerations of Data Property Rights System." *Chongqing Social Sciences*, 8th issue.

Gao, Fuping. 2019. "Data Circulation Theory: The Basis of Rights Allocation of Data Resources." *Peking University Law Journal*, 6th issue.

Guo, Xiaobei. 2020. "Achieving Multi-factor Organic Linkage by Industrial Digitization." *Economic Information Daily*, April 16, 2020, A01 edition.

Jiang, Fan. 2020. "You Quanrong, Representative of the National People's Congress: Strengthening the Protection of Data and Network Virtual Property." *Economic Daily*, May 27, 2020, 8th edition.

Japan Fair Trade Commission Competition Policy Research Center. 2017. "Report of Study Group on Data and Competition Policy."

Jiang, Qiping. 2012. "Digital Ownership Requires Separation of Domination and Use Rights." *China Internet Week*, 5th issue.

Jiang, Qiping. 2018. "Personal Data Protection, 'Degree' Is a Difficult Problem." *People's Daily*, June 6, 22nd edition.

Jingdong Law Research Institute. 2018. *EU Data Charter: <General Data Protection Regulation> GDPR Review and Practice Guidelines*. Beijing: Law Press.

Kelly, Kevin. 2016. *The Inevitable*, Trans. Zhou Feng, et al. Beijing: Publishing House of Electronics Industry.

Liu, He. 2019. "Insist and Improve the Basic Socialist Economic System." *People's Daily*, November 22, 2019, 6th issue.

Liu, Li. 2020. "Research on the Dilemma and Countermeasures of the Market Allocation of Data Asset Elements." *China Management Informationization*, 14th issue.

Li, Wenlian and Xia, Jianming. 2013. "Business Model Innovation Based on 'Big Data.'" *China Industrial Economics*, 5th issue.

Liu, Xiaojuan. 2017. "Government Responsibilities for Big Data Supervision-Focusing on Privacy Protection." *Chinese Public Administration*, 7th issue.

Long, Weiqiu. 2018. "Re-discussion on the Property Right Path of Enterprise Data Protection." *Oriental Law*, 3rd issue.

Mu, Huijun. 2016. "Relevant Analysis of the Construction of Domestic Big Data Trading Platforms and Trading Situations: Taking the Central China Big Data Exchange as an Example." *China CIO News*, 9th issue.

Obama, Barack. 2009. "Memorandum on Transparency and Open Government." Weekly Compilation of Presidential Documents.

Peng, Yun. 2016. "Research on Data Right Confirmation in Big Data Environment." *Modern Science Technology of Telecommunications*, 5th issue.

PWCC. 2020. "White Paper on Data Asset Ecology: Building a New Era of Sustainable Digital Economy." <https://www.pwccn.com/zh/services/consulting/publications/white-paper-on-data-asset-ecology-nov2020.html>.

Rheinstein, Max. 1945. "Education for Legal Craftsmanship." *Iowa Law Review*, no. 408.

Shen, Rong. 2020. "Accelerating the Development of Technology Factor Market to Promote Social and Economic Progress." *Forum on Science and Technology in China*, 5th issue.

Shi, Dan. 2019. "Legal Protection and System Construction of Enterprise Data Property Rights." *Electronical Intellectual Property*, 6th issue.

Shi, Yang, Wang, Jiandong, and Guo, Qiaomin. 2020. "Challenges and Countermeasures for China to Build a New Data Element Market System." *E-Government*, 3th issue.

Tian, Weilin. 2018. "The Connotation, Current Status and Basis of Public Big Data Information Security Legislation." *Henan Social Sciences*, 7th issue.

Wang, Hailong, Tian, Youliang, and Yin, Xin. 2018. "Blockchain-based Big Data Confirmation Scheme." *Computer Science*, 2nd issue.

Wang, Lei. 2019. "Advancing the Market-oriented Allocation of Data Elements: Bottlenecks and Countermeasures." *China Economic & Trade Herald*, 24th issue.

Wang, Qiang, and Chen, Qiyun. 2020. "Data Elements: Features, Applications, Status and Development." <https://mp.weixin.qq.com/s/uMOqdK3D3OIEaKe5HIgY-A>.

Wei, Lubin. 2018. *Analysis of Property Rights of Data Resources. Shandong University Doctoral Dissertation.*

Xie, Zaiquan. 2003. *Civil Law of Property Rights (Volume 1).* Taipei: Taiwan San Min Publishing House.

Xu, Ke. 2017. “Data Protection and Other Triple Approaches-Comment on Sina Weibo’s Unfair Competition Case.” *Journal of Shanghai University*, Social Science Edition, 6th issue.

Xu, Wei. 2019. “Reflection on the ‘Triple Authorization Principle’ of Enterprise Data Acquisition and Type Construction.” *SJTU Law Revie*, 4th issue.

Yang, Dong. 2020. “Improving the Benefit Sharing Mechanism of Data as a Factor of Production.” *Study Times*, May 1, 2020, A3 edition.

Yang, Lixin, and Chen, Xiaojiang. 2016. “Derivative Data Is the Object of Data Exclusive Rights.” *Chinese Social Sciences Today*, July 13, 2016, 005th Edition.

Ye, Runguo, and Chen, Xuexiu. 2016. “Problems and Suggestions for Security Guarantees of Open and Shared Government Data.” *Information Technology and Standardization*, 6th issue.

Yu, Baihua. 2017. “The Judgment of Interests in Right Determination.” *The Jurist*, 6th issue.

Zhang, Hanqing. 2020. “Big Data Becomes a New Driving Force for High-Quality Economic Development.” *Economic Information Daily*, April 16, 2020, A06 Edition.

Zhang, Minchong. 2016. “Patterns and Problems of Big Data Flow.” *Information and Communications Technologies*, 4th issue.

Zhou, Linbin and Ma, Ensi. 2018. “Law and Economic Analysis of Big Data Confirmation.” *Journal of Northeast Normal University, Philosophy and Social Sciences Edition*, 2nd issue.

Zhu, Baoli. 2019. “Definition of Data Property Rights: Multidimensional Perspectives and System Construction.” *Legal Forum*, 5th issue.

CHAPTER 3

Difficulties in Data Rights Legislation

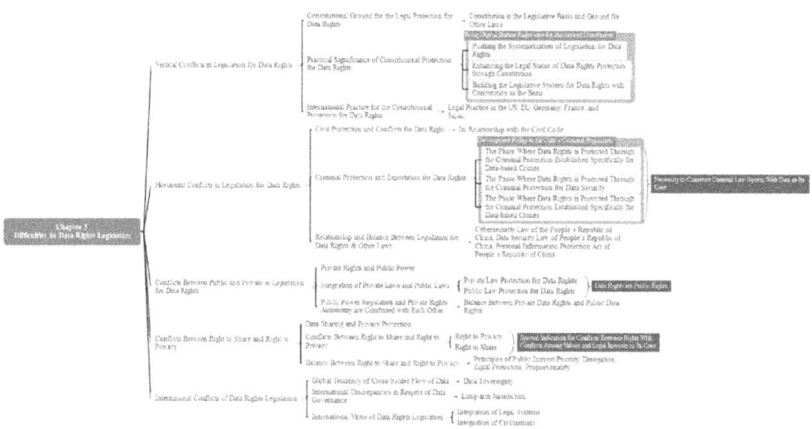

Digital science and technology, advancing at an unprecedented rate, is pushing vigorously for a change in the existing world order, with the boundaries of current laws and regulations being challenged constantly. This brings forward a series of new opportunities as well as challenges for international data governance. Nowadays, the approach to international data governance, led by the EU and the United States, has shown new tendencies on a variety of levels, ranging from legislation to execution, and to international competition. Against this background, it is necessary and important to move faster toward the rule of law in the digital sphere in China. Since digital rule of law is still in the exploratory stage in China, data rights legislation is confronted with many problems that need to be solved, including—without limitation—vertical conflicts, horizontal conflicts, conflicts between public and private domains, international conflicts, etc. Thus, for the purposes of maintaining China's data sovereignty and promoting the development of the digital economy in China , special attention shall be paid to the particularities of the data factor, the rules for the balance of interests shall be set in a more scientific and flexible way, and all conflicts in the process of data rights legislation shall be handled appropriately and effectively when designing specific systems in this regard.

Vertical Conflicts in Data Rights Legislation

The vertical conflicts in legislation refer to the conflicts among legal documents at different levels, mainly the unconformities between the constitution and other laws (Liu Shen 2003). As people become more dependent on data, the traditional concept of human rights in the constitutional sense will appear narrower. As citizens' demand for self-determination, self-management, and self-selection in respect of personal data grow stronger, the concept of human rights tends to expand faster in the digital world, and to place digital human rights under constitutional protection will be a response to this realistic demand. Making data rights constitutional rights is an important safeguard for the digital society; therefore, it is necessary to push data rights to a higher level in the legal system by inscribing it in the constitution. If data rights can be protected by the constitution, other data rights legislation will surely align with it soon. In the long run, constitutional protection for data rights will lay the foundataion for a normative system as specialized laws will join as the legal ground for data rights protection and other laws and regulations will provide support. Whereas some countries have incorporated personal data protection provisions into their constitutions, this has not yet happened in China.

Constitutional Ground for the Legal Protection for Data Rights

The constitution "is the fundamental law of the State and has supreme legal authority."[1] In accordance of Article 5 of the *Constitution of the People's Republic of China*, no laws or administrative or local rules and regulations may contravene the constitution. The primary principle for the legislation and formulation of the other laws is to keep their legal nature in line with the articles and philosophies of the constitution, and the form and formulation of other laws shall rely upon their constitutionality, for the latter is the foundation of modern legislation. At the macro level, the constitution leads and adjusts other laws, providing them with logical premises and regulative principles, while at the micro level, the other laws can further enhance and consolidate the legal status of the constitution by providing supplementary construction thereof. In a word, it is an important embodiment of the principle of the rule of law that a modern law-based society ensures the core status of the constitution in the national legal system. The constitution provides the legal ground for any other legal forms by its supreme legal authority and fundamental status in the legal system, and regulates as well as controls the legitimacy of any other legal forms through the principle of constitutionality, so that under the guidance of the principle of constitutional supremacy a nation's legal system can be systemized and operated in an orderly fashion, and the organic utility of a nation's legal institution can be secured (Mo Jihong 2007).

With the coming of the age of the digital civilization, the provisions and the underlying legal philosophy of the current constitution can no longer meet the practical needs for data rights protection. When we make new laws with sound rights protection as the value orientation and the happiness of the people as the ultimate pursuit, it will be inevitable that these laws will conflict with the rights originally provided for in the constitution. Thus, to meet people's new needs and expectations the priority is to connect proposed data rights legislation with the constitution so that constitutional support is made available. Up to thirty-two nations (including, but not limited to, Russia, Sweden, Hungary, Yugoslavia, Spain, Portugal, and Greece) have incorporated "personal data" into their constitutions as part

1 See the *Preamble of the Constitution of the People's Republic of China.*

of their fundamental rights when enacting or amending their constitutions (Yao Yuerong 2012, p. 111). The *Constitution of the People's Republic of China* has provided fundamental guidance for data rights legislation: On the one hand, data owners, data controllers, and data processors shall take the constitution as the fundamental code for conducting their activities in the area of data, and their fundamental rights relating to data shall be interpreted in accordance with the constitution. In addition to the aforementioned, they shall also shoulder the responsibility to maintain the dignity, as well as the enforcement of, the constitution. On the other hand, data rights legislation shall be based on the *Constitution of the People's Republic of China*. In China, constitutional protection for data rights is realized indirectly through the protection of other related fundamental rights. Articles 37, 38, 39, and 40 of the *Constitution of the People's Republic of China* are deemed to be legal bases of great importance (see Table 8). Even though no exact words such as "data rights protection" are present in the above articles, through the protection of citizens' fundamental rights, such as personality rights, the right to freedom, and the right to privacy, the inviolability of personal data can be protected indirectly, which provides the constitutional basis for data rights legislation. According to Article 33 of the constitution, "the State respects and preserves human rights." However, "human rights" is not a concept that has remained or will remain unchanged; on the contrary, it evolves with the needs of the economy, society, and realities on the whole before being put under the protection of the constitution (Zhao Yingjie and Sun Ruidong 2020). With the coming of the digital age, it is necessary to review the concept of "human rights" based on the concept of "data man," so that the status and dignity of people can be safeguarded, "digital human rights" can be put under better protection, and the legal order enhanced (Ma Changshan 2019). Since digital human rights are a reflection of human rights in the digital world, it is reasonable to bring digital human rights under the auspices of the constitution. Data rights share the same features as constitutional fundamental rights in both form and substance; they are in accord with the requirement to constantly expand the content and variety of constitutional fundamental rights of a modern society, and regulate data rights as part of citizens' fundamental rights.

Table 8. The Source of Constitution for Data Protection

Articles	Content
Article 33	All persons holding the nationality of the People's Republic of China are citizens of the People's Republic of China. All citizens of the People's Republic of China are equal before the law. The state respects and protects human rights. Every citizen is entitled to these rights and, at the same time, must perform the duties prescribed by the Constitution and the law.
Article 37	Freedom of the person of citizens of the People's Republic of China is inviolable. No citizen may be arrested except with the approval or by decision of a people's procuratorate or by decision of a people's court, and arrests must be made by a public security organ. Unlawful detention or deprivation or restriction of citizens' freedom of the person by other means is prohibited, and unlawful search of the person of citizens is prohibited.
Article 38	The personal dignity of citizens of the People's Republic of China is inviolable. Insult, libel, false accusation, or false incrimination directed against citizens by any means is prohibited.
Article 39	The residences of citizens of the People's Republic of China are inviolable. Unlawful search of, or intrusion into, a citizen's residence is prohibited.
Article 40	Freedom and privacy of correspondence of citizens of the People's Republic of China are protected by law. No organization or individual may, on any ground, infringe upon citizens freedom and privacy of correspondence, except in cases where, to meet the needs of state security or of criminal investigation, public security or procuratorial organs are permitted to censor correspondence in accordance with procedures prescribed by law.
Article 41	Citizens of the People's Republic of China have the right to criticize and make suggestions regarding any state organ or functionary. Citizens have the right to make to relevant state organs complaints or charges against, or exposures of, any state organ or functionary for violation of the law or dereliction of duty; but fabrication or distortion of facts for purposes of libel or false incrimination is prohibited.
Article 51	Citizens of the People's Republic of China, in exercising their freedoms and rights, may not infringe upon the interests of the state, of society, or of the collective, or upon the lawful freedoms and rights of other citizen.

Source: Collated from public data.

Practical Significance of Constitutional Protection for Data Rights

We should promote the systematization of data rights legislation by providing constitutional protection for data rights. To address the various problems encountered in legal theory and legal practice, which arose from a misunderstanding of the relationship between the constitution and other legal forms, we should reconstruct this relationship based on the acknowledgment that the constitution is the fundamental law (Mo Jihong 2007). Based on the fundamental features of data rights protection, it is necessary to put data rights legislation within the framework set by the constitution, clarify the relationship between data rights legislation and the constitution, and take the constitution as the starting point to promote data rights legislation. Fundamental changes have occurred in respect of data protection in the age of the digital civilization, and the importance of data rights increases day by day; however, our civil, criminal, and other laws have failed to provide appropriate protection, making data rights protection an unsettled issue of some significance. Thus, it is necessary to push the systematization of legislation for data rights protection by way of the constitution. The connection between data rights protection and the constitution demands the data rights legislation system to be in accordance with the constitution and other constitutional laws. Meanwhile, constitutional protection for data rights will push for improvements in data rights legislation, solving existing problems such as fragmentation, low status in the legal system, and poor effectiveness and operability. Though quite a few relevant rules and regulations have been promulgated, the completion of the legislative system for data rights protection still needs to be driven by constitutional protection.

We are to enhance the legal status of data rights protection by way of the constitution. "Constitution, as the mother of laws, forms the basis of other legal institutions, and impacts other laws through the pervasion effects of its objective value system, sequentially shapes social orders" (Yang Xueke 2020, p. 1). This shows that the rights and laws recognized and approved by the constitution share the same authority as the supreme law, or have great influence nationwide, and ought to be complied with by all the people. Once put under constitutional protection, data rights will be recognized as fundamental rights, and data rights legislation will move from a theoretical level to legislative practice. Although the constitutional basis for data rights protection can be demonstrated theoretically, acknowledgment at the constitutional level is still necessary data rights to become citizens' fundamental rights, making data rights protection more authoritative, reliable, and fair. Thus, if data rights and data rights legislation can be recognized by the constitution, the fundamental legal status of data rights legislation will be ensured and the legal status of data rights protection enhanced. Whether due to the basic or special attributes of data, data rights have already entered the purview of the constitution in various forms, which makes the connection between data rights and the constitution an inevitable challenge.

We need to build the data rights legislation system on the basis of the constitution. State power cannot merely stay on the periphery of civil society; state power must participate in civil society in all forms. Furthermore, the administrative function of the state has expanded into various areas, such as society, economy, and culture, experiencing significant development in content (Osuga Akira 2001, p. 51). Due to the expansion of state power and balancing between state interests and individual interests, the constitutional protection described above seems to be more pertinent now than at any other time (Wu Changhong 2014, p. 45). Germany has added the right of self-determination to general personality rights, while France has incorporated personal data protection into its constitution, as a direct result of their citizens' clamor for these rights—which represent a basic practice of countries worldwide. The effective regulation and protection of personal data is a precondition upon the adequate safeguard of data rights, and it is only upon the adequate safeguarding of data rights that infringement of the same can be prevented, data space protected, and the maximal value of data unleashed. Thus, the legislative system for data rights shall contain, without limitation, the basic concepts of data rights and have as its purpose the protection of these rights, principles for application, a legislative model, a legislative hierarchy, and specific rules, as well as formulate a set of legal institutions in accord with the constitution.

International Practice for the Constitutional Protection of Data Rights

"Give back morality what belongs to morality, law what belongs to law, and criminal law what belongs to criminal law" (Herbert L. Packer 1988, p. 296). We need to build a systematic and standardized data protection mechanism. Our protection for data needs to go beyond the current legal framework and act upon international conventions by referring to advanced overseas experience while conforming to our national conditions.

The right to privacy is constitutionally protected in the United States through judicial interpretation. It is expressly stipulated by the Fourth Amendment of the *Constitution of the United States*:

> The right of the people to be secure in their persons, houses, papers, and effects, against unreasonable searches and seizures, shall not be violated, and no warrants shall issue, but upon probable cause, supported by Oath or affirmation, and particularly describing the place to be searched, and the persons or things to be seized.

The Supreme Court held that the Fourth Amendment protected people rather than places, and that an individual's legitimate right to privacy is entitled to constitutional protection, *Katz v. United States*.[2] In 2011,

2 Katz, the defendant, was charged with transmitting wagering information by telephone (commonly known as "reporting the winning number") from Los Angeles to Miami and Boston in a public telephone booth. The defendant was convicted by the District Court upon the confirmation of evidence of the petitioner's end of telephone conversations, overheard by FBI agents who had attached an electronic listening and recording device to the outside of the public telephone booth from which he had placed his calls. Unsatisfied with this judgment, the defendant petitioned the Supreme Court, which held that the recording shall be excluded for its violation of the *Fourth Amendment of Constitution of the United States*: The Supreme Court supported the petitioner's argument, with seven out eight judges voting in his favor. The court delivered the following opinion: "The Government's eavesdropping activities violated the privacy upon which the petitioner justifiably relied

the court held in *Carpenter v. United States*[3] that an individual's legitimate privacy shall be free from intrusion, and further explained "a legitimate expectation of privacy." With the scope and nature of the right to privacy having expanded into the digital world, the protection of the right to privacy has expanded to all aspects of citizens' pursuit of data freedom. With such features as flexibility, feasibility, and certainty, the *Constitution of the United States* can be modified so as to conform to its citizens' demand for rights, thus providing certainty and clarity. Although the right to privacy is not directly mentioned in the *Constitution of United States*, this right has been put under constitutional protection by reason of judicial interpretations in actual cases.

Data protection is treated as a fundamental right by the EU, which has a similar legal status to an EU treaty. The *Charter of Fundamental Rights of the European Union* is one of the fundamental pillars for data protection in the EU, as well as a key legal document that secures the right to surveillance in respect of national data security. Article 8 stipulates that:

---

while using the telephone booth, and thus constituted a 'search and seizure' within the meaning of the Fourth Amendment, which shall be excluded from the trial." But, in the meantime, the Supreme Court also clarified in its judgment: "Although the surveillance in this case may have been so narrowly circumscribed that it could constitutionally have been authorized in advance, it was not in fact conducted pursuant to the warrant procedure which is a constitutional precondition of such electronic surveillance."

3 In 2011, to catch Carpenter, the suspected leader of a robbery gang, the FBI obtained seven days' worth of cell phone location records by court warrant to analyze the track of Carpenter, upon which charge the latter was sentenced to more than 100 years in prison. Then Carpenter petitioned the courts, arguing that the FBI obtained these phone location records in violation of the "legitimate expectation of privacy." The Supreme Court issued a declaration of certiorari in 2016, holding that the petitioner was entitled to the "legitimate expectation of privacy" in respect of his phone location records, but the government's acquisition of Carpenter's cell site records was a lawful Fourth Amendment search.

> Everyone has the right to the protection of personal data concerning him or her. Such data must be processed fairly for specified purposes and on the basis of the consent of the person concerned or some other legitimate basis laid down by law. Everyone has the right of access to data which has been collected concerning him or her, and the right to have it rectified. Compliance with these rules shall be subject to control by an independent authority. (Gloria González Fuster 2014, p. 1–2)

Therefore, it is clear that "people" are treated as the specific subjects of rights, while all the relevant authorities are regarded as the subjects of duty, highlighting the fact that the EU treats data security as a fundamental right of the "people." With these dynamic changes to data protection, the *Charter of Fundamental Rights of the European Union* can be relied on by any nation, enterprise, and individual in the world. The *General Data Protection Regulation*, also known as the "EU Charter of Data," is supported by powerful institutions with surveillance authority to protect personal data; its influence has already been mapped globally.

As to Germany, personal information is highly valued and has been placed under the protection of *Basic Law for the Federal Republic of Germany*. Article 1 stipulates: "Human dignity shall be inviolable. To respect and protect it shall be the duty of all state authority." Article 2 stipulates: "Every person shall have the right to free development of his personality insofar as he does not violate the rights of others or offend against the constitutional order or the moral law." Article 10 stipulates: "The privacy of correspondence, posts and telecommunications shall be inviolable." The three aforementioned articles provide not only constitutional protection for personal dignity and personality rights, but also the inviolability of personal information. Within the domain of exercising legitimate rights, self-management and self-determination are the primary conditions for the protection of "personal dignity." According to Germany's Federal Constitutional Court, privacy, self-determination, and personal dignity are the three objects of highest importance when considering the protection of personality rights. The German Federal Constitutional Court proposed the concept of the "right of information self-determination" for the first time in its population census of 1983, holding that the disclosure to the government of personal information shall be subject to a citizens' right to self-determination. Thus, the "right of information self-determination" not only represents the self-determination of "personal dignity," it also relates to personality rights. To sum up, the "right of information self-determination" is entitled to constitutional protection.

In France, personal data protection is placed under direct constitutional protection. Personal data protection is highly valued and laws are employed to regulate procedural issues, such as the scope, collection, and usage of personal data, and also specific legal liabilities for infringement thereof. *Act NO.78–17 of 6 January 1978 on Data Processing, Data Files and Individual Liberties*, enacted in 1978, is a law formulated specifically for information security. The *Digital Republic Law*, taking effect in 2016, has clear stipulations regarding issues such as the digital economy, open access to data, and data access, having built a strong personal data protection system. The *French Data Protection Act*, which took effect in 2018, enlarged the scope of subjects and duties in respect of personal data protection, as well as providing clarification on the authorities in charge. In 2018, a bill to amend the constitution was passed by the National Assembly "to punish the extension and unreasonable use (of personal data)," which was then incorporated into Article 34 of the *French Constitution*. Thus, from specific laws, to bills, to the constitution, the path for the constitutional protection of personal data in France was clarified gradually.

In Japan, information protection was incorporated into the constitution by the expansion of the right to privacy. *The Constitution of Japan* stipulates in Article 11:

> The people shall not be prevented from enjoying any of the fundamental human rights. These fundamental human rights guaranteed to the people by this Constitution shall be conferred upon the people of this and future generations as eternal and inviolate rights.

and:

> All of the people shall be respected as individuals. Their right to life, liberty, and the pursuit of happiness shall, to the extent that it does not interfere with the public welfare, be the supreme consideration in legislation and in other governmental affairs.

Article 13: Since "fundamental human rights" and the "right to the pursuit of happiness" are stipulated in the aforementioned articles, the extension of this constitutional protection for rights not yet specified in the constitution is justified. The Tokyo Court held that the right to privacy is part of the "fundamental human rights." Following the "Post Feast" Case in 1964, the connection between the right to privacy and the "right to the pursuit of happiness" was expounded by court in the "Tokyo Student's Federation" Case in 1969 and, in the "Criminal Record Inquiry by the Japan Federation of Bar Associations" case in 1981, the judge clearly pointed out that regulations regarding personal information shall be enhanced so as to better protect an individual's right to privacy. Therefore, one can deduce that Japan's constitution has placed information protection under its protection.

Horizontal Conflicts in Data Rights Legislation

The horizontal conflicts in legislation refer to the "difference" in content as between laws at the same legal level, which is also called "discrepancy."[4] Here, "between laws at the same legal level" means between laws, between administrative regulations, between local regulations, or between rules (Hu Jianmiao 2020). Where laws and administrative regulations fail to provide for a certain issue and the issue does not fall within scope of the exclusive legislative authority of the central government, local governments will promulgate their own regulations to attend to local needs. This will likely bring about the result that where there are different laws and regulations on one issue, discrepancies are highly likely to occur. When it comes to data rights legislation, horizontal conflicts can be discrepancies between the data rights legislation and relevant stipulations in the civil law, criminal law, cybersecurity law, data security law, personal information protection law, or any other related laws. This is essentially a discrepancy born out of insufficient legal

4 The *Legislation Law of the People's Republic of China* stipulates in Article 60: "For any discrepancy between a draft law and the relevant provisions of any other law, the proposer shall provide an explanation and a handling opinion and, when necessary, a proposal on amending or repealing the relevant provisions of the other law at the same time."

adaptability as data protection evolves constantly toward the ultimate goal of better serving the people by providing equal, efficient, and reasonable legal protection, and safeguarding national data security, public data security, and personal data security.

Civil Law Protection of Data Rights and Related Conflicts

The civil law protection of data. Civil law protection largely focuses on the personal interests contained in the data, which may be considered the ultimate goal and the core value orientation of data protection. Infringement of personal interests by the breach of relevant civil stipulations may happen in a variety of forms, such as the illegitimate disclosure, modification, distortion, illegal commercial utilization, and illegal deletion of personal data; thus, the personal rights attributes of data demand that its content shall contain personal independence, personal freedom, personal dignity, etc. Besides, the property rights attribute of data is also significant; the subject of data with property rights of a certain type shall realize protection for those property rights. Balancing data property rights and data use, as well as giving full play to the data factor, will enhance the efficiency of the society and economy; thus it is feasible to provide the data owners with the right to free disposal, the right to limit transfer, the right to revoke modification, the right to anonymity, the right to compensation for damage, etc. Thus, based upon the data's property rights attribute, civil protection is made available for data owners. Civil protection for data has been realized, step-by-step, through the settlement of varieties of realistic data security issues, and data's personality rights attribute and property rights attribute have been embodied step-by-step, concurrently, making civil protection for data an established fact. The development of the civil rights theory highlights a process during which protection for rights has been improved, the scope of protection expanded, and the gap in the protection narrowed, and the emerging dual attributes of data has become a significant legal phenomenon.

Limitation of the civil protection for data. While people have become more aware of civil protection for data, systematic, normative, and specific protection for data is not yet in place, which seems to be somewhat lagging behind compared to the fast iteration and updating of science and technology. Such a gap tends to hamper effectiveness in respect of data protection. The first reason for such a deficiency is the lack of a civil protection system for data. Since data rights legislation is still in its initial stage in China, relevant laws, regulations, and rules appear to be scattered, repetitive, and fragmented; very few articles can be applied directly and fail to cover the full data life circle, which limits the effective application of relevant laws to some extent, and even hinders the establishment of the entire civil protection system for data. The second reason is that relevant civil stipulations for data protection are not very specific. Article 127 of *Civil Code* stipulates: " Where there are laws particularly providing for the protection of data and online virtual assets, such provisions shall be followed." Even though this article clearly stipulates the protection of data, its content is still too general, giving no detail as to the connotation and extension of the concept of data containing no words like "right." Besides, the civil law is rather unclear about the application of information and data, failing to stipulate the relationship between the two: data can take the form of information, while information can be the carrier of data. The third reason is that civil protection for data is weak in operability. The most relevant civil stipulations for data protection fail to take into account the complexity and diversity of the scenarios for data use, with the result that civil stipulations lag behind what is required by the latest development in related fields. Thus, even though many relevant regulations have been proposed, civil protection for data still lacks realistic practicability (Huang Xiaomin 2020).

The relationship between data rights legislation and the *Civil Code*. If data rights protection is confused with personal information protection under the *Civil Code*, it is obvious that the legislative significance of the latter, which is a fundamental law, will be affected directly, and civil laws may be reduced to their previous condition of fragmentation and, likely, the authority and unity of fundamental laws will be adversely affected. Data rights legislation for and the *Civil Code* are two different but complementary areas, and data rights protection, the core component of the rising data rights law, is a brand new legal concept. If traditional personal information protection is applied mechanically in the area of data rights protection, incompatibility will be inevitable and discrepancies will arise therefrom.

This will damage the scientific nature of legislation, with conflicts emerging during the application process. For such reasons, it is necessary to clarify ideologically that the purpose of data rights legislation is to protect those rights by the formulation of basic principles and the creation of institutions with data rights protection as their central task, thus forming a new legal system. Data rights law is obviously different from the *Civil Code*, and the two shall not be conjoined. Even though data rights legislation can overlap and coincide with the *Civil Code* to some extent, the two are fundamentally different in that the former aims at data rights protection while the latter aims to establish a basic civil system—they play different roles in the legal system. Only when we recognize the relationship between data rights legislation and the *Civil Code* will data rights legislation be able to focus on realistic problems and constitute appropriate institutions, instead of being confined by the traditional civil law system (Zhou Hanhua 2020).

Criminal Law Protection of Data Rights and Relevant Expectations

In recent years, data leakage has happened with increasing frequency and massive data-related crimes, such as Meituan selling users' personal information; Trip.com's website vulnerablities; and leakage of check-in records from chain hotels have caused a negative impact and even panic in society (Wei Xiaowen 2020). Personal data is closely connected with personal interests, so to protect citizens' personal data from theft, illegal spreading, and leakage, it is necessary to enhance criminal law protection of data. As for the specific path leading to such protection, there are generally three steps: criminal law protection of data rights as affiliation of other rights, criminal law protection of data rights by way of data security protection, and criminal law protection directly and specifically against data crimes.

The first step. The cyberspace and computers are committed to anonymity and this, somehow, incites traditional crimes and brings about a variety of challenges and problems for criminal legislation and judicature (Britz 2016, p. 69). On the one hand, data protection can only be realized in association with the protection of existing rights, such as the right to privacy, the right to know, the right to freedom, and personality rights. On the other hand, a series of new rights including, without limitation, the right to be forgotten and the right to portability, have arisen from data protection. Therefore, relevant laws such as the *Privacy Act*, the *Electronic Communications Privacy Act*, the *Wiretap Act*, and the *Children's Online Privacy Protection Act* have been promulgated in the United States, and it is not hard to tell that all the aforementioned laws are targeted at the right to privacy. The *Act on the Protection of Personal Information* of Japan stipulates in Article 16: "A personal information handling business operator shall not handle personal information without obtaining in advance a principal's consent beyond the necessary scope to achieve a utilization purpose specified pursuant to the provisions under the preceding Article," and stipulates in Article 23: "A personal information handling business operator shall, in case of altering a utilization purpose, in advance inform a principal of the contents to be altered or put them into a state where a principal can easily know." Undoubtedly, these two aforementioned articles focus on the right to know. However, data is typically intangible and not limited by time or space; thus it is inadequate and risky to protect data as an affiliation to rights such as the right to privacy and the right to know; a stringent, comprehensive, and detailed data security law is necessary to regulate data-related crimes. With the emergence of new features for rights, as well as new explanations for concepts, the hysteresis quality of criminal regulation for data rights protection, and the efficient regulation and stringent control of data-based crimes, has become a major concern.

The second step. The *Federal Data Protection Act* stipulates in Article 1[5] that the purpose of this act is to protect personal data. Legal protection for personal information is also stringent in Denmark. Its *Act on Processing of Personal Data* stipulates that even the spreading of information about citizens' private lives will be subject to criminal punishment. With the *Data Protection Act* as the guiding legal document and regulations including, without limitation, *Communications Regulations*, *Guiding Principles to Communication Data Protection*, the *Regulation of Investigatory Powers*, etc., as support, the UK has built a model of law-based data protection with multiple functions, such as data protection, data management, and

5 *Federal Data Protection Act* stipulates in Article 1: "The purpose of this Act is to protect the individual against his right to privacy being impaired through the handling of his personal data."

data surveillance. *The Vienna Declaration on Crime and Justice: Meeting the Challenges of the Twenty-first Century*[6] stipulated the definition and types of computer crime in detail, while nations in the world have achieved a basic consensus in respect of fighting computer crime, so that any behavior that damages the integrity and completeness of a computer system may be viewed as a crime; this has played a part in coping with illegal access to computer information (Nisida Noriyuku 2007, p. 104–5). The *Convention on Cybercrime*[7] integrated the experience of EU members in fighting cybercrime, and defined cybercrime as "action directed against the confidentiality, integrity and availability of computer systems, networks and computer data as well as the misuse of such systems, networks and data" (Zhao Bingzhi and Yu Zhigang 2004, p. 155). Where trade secrets or state secrets are the subject of illegal information access, such behavior will be prosecuted as an infringement of trade secrets or the illegal acquirement of state secrets (Wang Qianyun 2019). Even though data rights have not been mentioned in the relevant laws of each nation, these rights have been covered by the criminal law through concepts such as data security, information security, cybersecurity, and computer security.

The third step. The path for the criminal protection of data is conditional upon the confirmation of criminal liability for data-based crimes; however, the latter is preconditioned upon the clarification of official charges for data-based criminal behaviors, which is the premise for the criminal law to function effectively. *The Penal Code of Japan* has stipulated a series of relevant illegal acts, such as: the unlawful opening of letters, unlawful disclosure of confidential information, breaking into a residence, and concealment of letters (Hong Li 2004, p. 407). *The German Criminal Code* has set six criminal accusations including, without limitation, violation of

6 Vienna Declaration on Crime and Justice: Meeting the Challenges of the Twenty-first Century, the official website of United Nations, April 17, 2000. <https://www.un.org/zh/documents/treaty/files/A-CONF.187-4-REV.3.shtml>.

7 In November 2001, twenty-six member states of the European Commission, together with the officials from thirty other nations, including America, Canada, Japan, and South Africa, signed this convention; from that point, the Convention on Cybercrime has become the first international convention aimed at fighting cybercrime.

privacy of spoken word, violation of privacy of correspondence, data espionage, etc., to regulate data-based crimes.[8] Article 252[9] and Article 253 (I) of the *Criminal Law of the People's Republic of China* stipulates that the illegal obtaining, concealment, destruction, and sale of citizens' personal information are criminal behaviors, which will be prosecuted as an infringement of citizens' right to communication freedom and infringement of citizens' personal information.[10] With data and the values contained therein as the entry point, and taking into account the characteristics of traditional system of criminal charges in other nations, it is feasible to build an effective criminal protection system for data rights. The construction of a criminal protection system for data rights can be realized in three steps: first, the creation of reasonable institutions for data collection and use; second, the formulation of unified system for data protection, which may standardize the operations regarding data, elevate personal data protection to legal rights, or even fundamental rights, and clarify the fundamental legal hierarchy of personal data in the legal system; and third, the clarification of legal liabilities and obligations for data-based crimes, and the formulation of a punitive compensation system. Thus, it is urgent that a specific, reasonable, and unified data-centric criminal protection system for data rights be constructed.

8 *The German Criminal Code*, translated by Xu Jiusheng and Zhuang Jinghua. Beijing: Law Press China, 2000, p. 156–8.

9 The *Criminal Law of the People's Republic of China* stipulates in Article 252: "Those infringing upon the citizens right of communication freedom by hiding, destroying, or illegally opening others' letters, if the case is serious, are to be sentenced to one year or less in prison or put under limited incarceration."

10 The *Criminal Law of the People's Republic of China* stipulates in Article 252: "Those infringing upon the citizens right of communication freedom by hiding, destroying, or illegally opening others' letters, if the case is serious, are to be sentenced to one year or less in prison or put under limited incarceration."

Relationship and Balance between Data Rights Legislation and Other Laws

The predicament for data rights protection under the current rights system. The current legal system in China has provided certain protection for personal data rights, mainly focusing on the regulation of fundamental rights, personal information, and other data (see Table 9).

> Restricted by the scope and method of regulation, solutions provided by the current legal system in respect of personal data protection is not adequate, rendered as the degree of protection, support and push being insufficient, and the rules for data transaction and data use being lacking, which, with the obstruction regarding law enforcement growing, results in the legal system's being increasingly unable to meet challenges arising from the large-scale collection, transmission, and use of personal data. (Lian Yuming 2017)

Theoretically speaking, personality rights are mainly protected as civil rights, and legal protection that can incorporate data is very limited. From the perspective of theories regarding the right to privacy, relevant legal protection is, in the main, realized privately; however, data is more about public social order, therefore protection for the right to privacy shall be limited by the public interest. When perceived from the perspective of "real rights" theories, which emphasize "one right for one object," data protection largely focuses on "multiple rights for one property," which goes against the basic principle of real rights. From the perspective of creditors' rights theories, creditors' rights focuses on the contractual relationship between enterprises and users; however, data rights are complex and flexible in nature, which hinders the establishment of profitable contractual relationship between data providers and users, and render contract terms regarding creditors' rights and obligations inapplicable. Pursuant to intellectual property rights theories, intellectual properties are innovative and creative in nature, so data protection, applicable to multiple subjects for each item under protection, follows a mechanism that is clearly incompatible with the nature of intellectual property. In short, legislation for data protection in China has shortcomings such as vague concepts, a diversified system, a limited scope of regulation, and a lack of clear and unified enforcement system, mechanism, and agency.

Table 9. Collation of the Important Articles Regarding Protection for Privacy, Information, or Data under Current Legal System

Laws	Articles	Content
Law of the People's Republic of China on the Protection of Minors (2020 Revision)	Article 63	No organization or individual shall conceal, destroy, or illegally delete minors' letters, diaries, emails, or other online communications contents.
	Article 72	Information processors that handle the personal information on minors through the Internet shall follow the principles of legitimacy, fairness, and necessity. To process the personal information on minors under the age of 14, the consent of minor's parents or other guardians shall be obtained, unless as otherwise prescribed by laws and administrative regulations. Where a minor, his parent or any other guardian requests the information processor to correct or delete the minor's personal information, the information processor shall take measures in a timely manner to correct or delete such information, except as otherwise prescribed by laws and administrative regulations.
Criminal Law of the People's Republic of China (2017 Version)	Article 252	Those infringing upon the citizens right of communication freedom by hiding, destroying, or illegally opening others' letters, if the case is serious, are to be sentenced to one year or less in prison or put under criminal detention.
		Postal workers who open, hide, or destroy mail or telegrams without authorization are to be sentenced to two years or less in prison or put under criminal detention. Whoever sells or provides any citizen's personal information in violation of the relevant provisions of the state shall, if the circumstances are serious, be sentenced to imprisonment of not more than three years or criminal detention in addition to a fine or be sentenced to a fine only; or be sentenced to imprisonment of not less than three years but not more than seven years in addition to a fine if the circumstances are especially serious.

Table 9. Continued

Laws	Articles	Content
	Article 253	Whoever sells or provides to any other person any citizen's personal information obtained in the course of performing functions or providing services in violation of any relevant provisions of the state shall be given a heavier penalty in accordance with the provisions of the preceding paragraph. Whoever illegally obtains any citizen's personal information by stealing or other methods shall be punished in accordance with the provisions of the first paragraph. Where an entity commits any crime as provided for in the preceding three paragraphs, the entity shall be sentenced to a fine, and its directly responsible person in charge and other directly liable persons shall be punished according to the provisions of the applicable paragraph.
Law of the People's Republic of China on Maternal and Infant Health Care (2017 Version)	Article 34	Personnel engaged in the work of maternal and infant health care shall strictly abide by the professional ethics and keep secrets for the parties concerned.
Law of the People's Republic of China on Commercial Banks (2015 Version)	Article 6	Commercial banks shall protect the legal rights and interests of the depositors against the encroachment of any entity or individual.
	Article 29	Commercial banks shall follow the principles of voluntary deposit and free withdrawal, paying interest to depositors and keeping secret for depositors the handling of individual savings deposits. Commercial banks have the right to refuse any entity or individual to inquire about, freeze, or deduct individual savings accounts, unless it is otherwise prescribed by law.

(continued)

Table 9. Continued

Laws	Articles	Content
Postal Law of the People's Republic of China (2015 Version)	Article 3	The freedom and privacy of correspondence of citizens shall be protected by law. No organization or individual shall infringe upon the freedom and privacy of correspondence of citizens under any pretext, provided unless required to protect national security or investigate criminal offenses. Public security organs, national security organs, and prosecutorial organs may inspect the correspondence of citizens under statutory procedures. Except as otherwise provided for by law, no organization or individual shall inspect or withhold mails or remittances.
Law of the People's Republic of China on the Protection of Consumer Rights and Interests (2014 Version)	Article 14	In purchasing and using commodities or receiving services, consumers shall be entitled to human dignity, respect for their ethnical mores and customs, and legal protection of personal information.
	Article 29	In collecting and using the personal information of consumers, business operators shall adhere to the principles of legality, rationality, and necessity, and expressly state the purposes, methods, and scope of collection, and use of such information, and obtain the consent of consumers. Business operators collecting or using the personal information of consumers shall disclose their rules for the collection or use of information, and may not collect or use information in violation of laws, regulations, and agreements with consumers. Business operators and their employees must keep strictly confidential the collected personal information of consumers and may not divulge, sell, or illegally provide such information to others. Business operators shall take technical and other necessary measures to ensure information security, and prevent the personal information of consumers from being divulged or lost. If the divulgence or loss of personal information of consumers occurs, or may occur, business operators shall immediately take remedial measures. Business operators shall not send commercial information to consumers without the consent or request of consumers or with a clear refusal from consumers.

Table 9. Continued

Laws	Articles	Content
Law of the People's Republic of China on Prevention and Treatment of Infectious Diseases (2013 Version)	Article 68	Where the disease prevention and control institutions purposely divulge information and materials relating to personal privacy of an infectious disease patient, a pathogen carrier, a suspected infectious disease patient, or persons in close contact with such patients shall take relevant legal liability.
Prison Law of the People's Republic of China (2012 Version)	Article 7	The dignity of a prisoner shall not be humiliated, and his personal safety, lawful properties, and his right to defend, petition, complain, accuse, as well as other rights, which have not been deprived of or restricted according to law, shall not be violated.
	Article 47	A prisoner may, in accordance with the relevant regulations, meet with his relatives and guardians during the service of his sentence.
Law of the People's Republic of China on Resident Identity Cards (2012 Version)	Article 6	The resident identity card shall be designed by the department for public security under the State Council. And the resident identity cards shall be uniformly made and issued by public security organs. The resident identity cards shall be readable both visually and by computer, and the contents read visually and by computer shall be limited to the items prescribed in the first paragraph of Article 3 of this Law. Public security organs and the people's police shall keep confidential citizen's personal information gained through making, issuing, examining, or seizing resident identity cards.
	Article 20	Any of the people's police who divulges a citizen's personal information gained through making, issuing, examining, or seizing his resident identity card and thus infringing upon the citizen's lawful rights and interests shall be legally liable.

(continued)

Table 9. Continued

Laws	Articles	Content
Statistics Law of the People's Republic of China (2010 Version)	Article 9	Statistic agencies and statistics personnel shall keep confidential the national secrets, trade secrets, and personal information they have access to in the process of doing statistical work.
Passport Law of the People's Republic of China (2007 Version)	Article 20	Anyone who impairs the legitimate rights and interests of any citizen due to divulging the personal information of that citizen, which he has access to in the course of making or issuing a passport, shall be subject to legal liability.
Law on Practicing Doctors of the People's Republic of China (1998 Version)	Article 37	Anyone who divulges the privacy of patient and causes serious consequences shall take relevant legal liability.

Source: Articles above are incomplete collection, collated from public data.

The relationship between data rights legislation and other relevant laws. One key issue appurtenant to data rights legislation is maintaining its connection and supportive relationship with other laws, that is, the issue of "the role in the legal system." The role of data rights in the legal system reflects its authority, function, and value when compared against other rights. From the perspective of value, the *Data Security Law* (*Draft*) plans and balances data circulation and protection, emphasizing both development and security; the *Personal Information Protection Law* (*Draft*), meeting the needs of the times, provides strong support for the realization of the national informatization strategy and the construction of a strong country in the field of information. The *Cybersecurity Law* facilitates the construction of a solid network infrastructure and an orderly cyberspace, and shall exert great influence on China's participation in the formulation of international rules regarding cyberspace (Li Haiying 2015). On the one hand, data rights legislation can satisfy the demand for data security and institutional supply; on the other hand, it can also meet people's growing need for data rights. When perceived from the perspective of content, the *Data Security Law* (*Draft*) focuses on national security in respect of important data; the *Personal Information Protection Law* (*Draft*) highlights issues such as personal information rights and data protection; the *Cybersecurity Law* pays attention to key issues such as information infrastructure protection and cybersecurity monitoring; while data rights legislation focuses on the regulation of data security, data exploitation and use, and the protection of rights and interests of data, etc., especially the protection of "data man's" rights. In terms of their positions and levels in the legal system, the *Data Security Law* (*Draft*) and the *Personal Information Protection Law* (*Draft*) are the core laws for the implementation of the holistic approach to national security prescribed in the *National Security Law*. The content of the *Cybersecurity Law* involving data will gradually be replaced by stipulations of the *Personal Information Protection Law* and the *Data Security Law*. Data rights legislation, as the fundamental law in the digital arena, shall play the important role of regulating data relations.

Table 10. Basic Framework for the Legal Documents Regarding the Protection of Privacy, Information, or Data

Date Issued	Legal Documents	Relevant Content
December 2012	*Decision of the Standing Committee of the National People's Congress on Strengthening Information Protection on Networks*	It clearly stipulates the requirement for personal digital information protection for the first time by way of legal document.
July 2013	*Provisions on Protecting the Personal Information of Telecommunications and Internet Users*	It stipulates in detail the requirements for telecommunications service operators and internet information service providers in respect of the rules for the collection and use of users' personal information, information protection measures, etc.
November 2016	*Cybersecurity Law of the People's Republic of China*	It incorporates personal information protection into the scope of network security, and stipulates about personal information protection particularly in its Chapter IV "Network Information Security."
March 2017	*General Provisions of the Civil Law of the People's Republic of China*	It establishes specific article for personal information protection at the level of civil fundamental law.
May 2017	*Interpretation of the Supreme People's Court and the Supreme People's Procuratorate on Several Issues concerning the Application of Law in the Handling of Criminal Cases of Infringing on Citizens' Personal Information*	It stipulates comprehensively and systematically that upon conviction for the offense of infringement of a citizens' personal information, the defendant shall be convicted and sentenced. It also clarifies the issues regarding relevant law application.

Table 10. Continued

Date Issued	Legal Documents	Relevant Content
December 2017	*Information Security Technology and Personal Information Security Standard*	It clarifies the compliance requirements for the collection, storage, use, and sharing of personal information in the form of national standards.
August 2018	*E-Commerce Law of the People's Republic of China*	It is the first written law in China to make comprehensive stipulations about electronic commerce.
January 2019	*Announcement of the Office of the Central Cyberspace Affairs Commission, the Ministry of Industry and Information Technology, the Ministry of Public Security, and the State Administration for Market Regulation on Carrying out Special Campaigns against Mobile Internet Application Programs Collecting and Using Personal Information in Violation of Laws and Regulations*	It was issued by the Office of the Central Cyberspace Affairs Commission, the Ministry of Industry and Information Technology, the Ministry of Public Security, and the State Administration for Market Regulation jointly for the purposes of assessing the collection and use of personal information, supervising and punishing crimes, and certificating the security of APP.
August 2019	*Provisions on the Cyber Protection of Children's Personal Information*	It is the first legislation specifically for children regarding network protection. This Provision, as a milestone legal document, protects children's personal information for their full life circle, and covers the collection, storage, use, transfer, disclosure, deletion, etc., of such information.

(*continued*)

Table 10. Continued

Date Issued	Legal Documents	Relevant Content
November 2019	*Notice by the Secretary Bureau of the Cyberspace Administration of China, the General Office of the Ministry of Industry and Information Technology, the General Office of the Ministry of Public Security and the General Office of the State Administration for Market Regulation of Issuing the Measures for the Determination of the Collection and Use of Personal Information by Apps in Violation of Laws and Regulations*	It is issued by the Secretary Bureau of the Cyberspace Administration of China, the General Office of the Ministry of Industry and Information Technology, the General Office of the Ministry of Public Security, and the General Office of the State Administration for Market Regulation jointly for the purposes of regulating the verification of the illegal collection of personal information through APP, as well as providing a reference for enterprises in respect of the legal collection and use thereof.
May 2020	*Civil Code*	It stipulates the right to privacy and emphasizes clearly that natural persons possess the right to privacy and his/her personal information shall be protected by law. The processing of such information shall be in compliance with the principles of legitimacy, rightfulness, and necessity.
June 2020	*Data Security Law of the People's Republic of China*	The draft of which was first reviewed by the 13th Standing Committee of the National People's Congress at its 20th meeting.
October 2020	*Personal Information Protection Act of the People's Republic of China*	The draft of which was first reviewed by the 13th Standing Committee of the National People's Congress at its 22th meeting.

Source: Collated from public data.

Coordination between data rights legislation and relevant laws. Data rights legislation is the collective term for legal norms regulating the legal relationship between data owners, data controllers, and data processors. With the right to privacy, information, and data as the main objects of study, with ownership rights and use of data during its full life circle as the main content of study, a data rights system is the main feature of study. Data rights legislation absorbs the content regarding information protection in the *Personal Information Protection Law* (*Draft*), integrates stipulations regarding data development in the *Data Security Law* (*Draft*), and deepens arguments regarding cyberspace sovereignty and national security in the *Cybersecurity Law*. On the one hand, it approaches data privacy and data security from the perspective of individuals; while on the other hand, it considers China's position and influence in the international community from the perspective of the state. *The Legislation Law of the People's Republic of China* stipulates in Article 4: "Legislation shall be conducted according to the statutory power and procedures, on the basis of the overall interests of the State, and to maintain the unity and dignity of the socialist legal system." Balance and coordination between laws is a basic feature of the legal system of socialism with Chinese characteristics, as well as a basic requirement for us to adhere to and to keep improving the socialist rule of law with Chinese characteristics. Data rights law is not intended as a replacement of any traditional legal branch; it attempts to adopt an interdisciplinary method and make good use of the knowledge graph covering all existing legal branches to respond comprehensively to and keep trying to resolve the legal risks and problems constantly arising in the digital age. Thus, data rights legislation focuses on common issues shared by all legal branches in the digital area. It integrates elements of the traditional legal branches horizontally, breaks through the barriers of legal branches vertically, and forms an endogenous, integral, and cooperative legal study framework for data rights to explore the universal rules covering the whole life circle of data through different research angles and legal perspectives.

Public-Private Conflicts in Data Rights Legislation

Data rights are not only private rights belonging to individuals, they are also a kind of public power relevant to the development of enterprises, the functioning of society, and national security. Data rights possess both a private right attribute and a public right attribute, with the former focusing on the protection of private interests and the latter focusing on the protection of public interests. Here, "public interest" includes not only societial interests and national interests, but also the interests of enterprises and various organizations and groups. Conflicts exist in many aspects where the right of data self-determination goes against the free flow and use of data, where the private rights enjoyed by individuals go against public power, and where private interests are balanced with public interests. Moreover, such conflicts can be somewhat connected, overlapping, and tangled with one another. Data rights and data power are a unity of opposites, and it is necessary for data rights legislation to separate private rights from the public power contained in data rights and balance between the two, with private data rights compromised to an appropriate level and the regulation of public data power strengthened, so as to construct a data rights system with public and private integration, promote data circulation and sharing, and provide important support for effective data governance.

Private Rights and Public Power

"Rights are the legal expression of interests in essence. The more interest human production generates, the more diverse rights will become" (Ma Changshan 2020). In a digital society, "data is both a paradigm of right and a narrative of power." (Key Laboratory of Big Data Strategy 2020, p. 61). Here, data rights, as rights of the individual, are mainly about embodying and protecting individual interests and are essentially the interests and qualifications of individuals with respect to data. The "individual" here means being private, emphasizing private rights. While data power emphasizes the public attribute of data, with the subjects thereof being public institutions and social organizations, and the objects thereof being the public interests protected by law, such power amounts to public power. Subjects of both private data rights and public data power may be the processers, controllers, or transmitters of data. Conflicts in respect of the rights and interests of data inevitably arise among private entities, public power holders, and data owners.

Rights are private rights in essence, which normally refers to power granted to individuals by operation of the law for the realization of their interests. In a society of private rights, the political proposition that men are born equal is expressed and protected through the equality of capacity for civil rights in civil law. "Private rights enjoyed by civil subjects in civil laws and conducts are the sole legitimacy basis and legal ground for the existence of administrative agencies" (Liu Kaixiang 2020). Civil laws are typical private laws, and the thread that lies under the whole of the civil code is a private right, that is, the grant, exercise, and protection of private rights. The entitlement to legal protection of a personal right as civil right, and its status among other personal rights, is confirmed by the chapter "Personality Rights" of the *Civil Code*, which also forms the basis for the further construction of the comprehensive legal system for data protection under a data rights system. Against the background of digitalization, with issues such as protection for personal privacy, boundaries for the use of corporate data, and benefit distribution regarding data transactions being problematic under many circumstances, data rights have become increasingly important. However, the reality is that there remains a lacuna in data legislation, which causes a predicament for rights protection, forming a big obstacle for the digital industry's development.

In essence, power is public (power), which refers to state power rather than the individual rights enjoyed by citizens. Public power is comprised of legislative power, judicial power, and administrative power, which shall be held and wielded by the state or, more specifically, by different agencies, exclusively. Whether it is economic power, political power, or social power, the subjects thereof shall always be public institutions and social organizations, and the direct objects thereof shall always be public interests protected by law. "It is the function of the constitution and administrative laws to regulate the exercise of public power" (Zhang Qianfan 2012, p. 5), which sets the "redline" for the exercise of public power, making sure that public power is more of a duty than a kind of authority. In the age of big data, "the government, as the organization holding public power, shall regulate the generation, storage, transfer, and use of personal data through public laws for the purposes of national security, public security, and public welfare" (Wu Weiguang 2016). Data is power, and power is data. As data becomes a representation of a kind of power that we cannot go without, whoever owns data holds power; thus, a new data power system is in the making.

The natural conflicts between public power and private rights.

> Conflicts between private rights and public power actually happen between the administrative agencies that represent the authority and the administrative counterparts that represent private entities, the key issue of which is the protection of personal data upon the realization of social interests. (Liu Dexue 2014, p. 126)

The duty of the state is to ensure sound protection of the data rights of citizens and this surely includes protecting private rights from the intrusion of public power. However, where the scope and intensity of exercising public power is excessive, intrusion into citizens' data freedom is inevitable. The *Constitution of the People's Republic of China* stipulates in Article 38: "The personal dignity of citizens of the People's Republic of China is inviolable. Insult, libel, false accusation or false incrimination directed against citizens by any means is prohibited." This covers both infringement by other civil entities and intrusions by public power, granting individuals the right to participate in the data processing by public authorities and providing them with constitutional protection. Where private rights are harmed by administrative agencies, the subject of the private rights are entitled to the right to request the administrative agency involved to be held to account for the damage caused. The *Administrative Procedure Law of the People's Republic of China* stipulates in Article 12: "The people's courts shall accept the complaint claiming that an administrative agency has otherwise infringed upon personal rights, property rights, or other lawful rights and interests filed by citizens, legal persons, or other organizations." The scope of application of data rights protection is quite narrow in the domain of private rights in China, mainly focusing on the protection of citizens' personal information and right to privacy. Generally, the protection of citizens' private rights is inadequate. Public power exists for the realization and enjoyment of private rights by citizens. Restricting public power equals protecting private rights, which means that data rights and data power are both supporting and countering each other concurrently.

Integration of Private Laws and Public Laws

Where the subjects are private entities and the conflicts arise from the exercise of private rights, such conflicts shall be regulated by private laws; where the subjects are administrative agencies and the interests represented are public interests, the conflicts shall be regulated by public laws.[11]

> The reason why public law theories and private law theories differ in regard to the effectiveness of the same legal behavior is that their theoretical systems and value pursuits are different. In practice, there are more and more conditions where public law behaviors interweave with private law behaviors, i.e., there are private law behaviors under public laws and public law behaviors also exist under private laws. (Jiang Bixin 2019)

With the coming of the digital age, data rights have extended from "the area of private law," where the "personality rights" are traditionally distinguished from the "right to privacy," to "the area of public laws," resulting in its compound nature "across the public law arena as well as the private law arena." "Laws are aimed at not only protecting individual interests

11 Public law and private law are an important classification under the continental law system, first enunciated by Domitius Ulpianus. Domitius Ulpianus proposed the theoretical basis for public laws and private laws, based on the difference between societal interests and individual rights. Public laws, mainly the constitution and the criminal law, focus on the administrative function of the state for the protection of society's interests where national rights are involved. Private law, mainly civil law and commercial law, focus on the equal relationship between individuals, for the purpose of protecting individual rights (Jiang Ping and Mi Jian , 1987. *Basics for Roman Law*. Beijing: China University of Political Science and Law Press, p. 8).

but also pursuing the preservation of social public interests and social order" (Zhang Huilin 2013, p. 55). Thus, based upon traditional private law protection, data rights are entitled to the dual protection of public and private law.

Private law protection for data rights. Generally speaking, society's interests are realized indirectly by prior legal protection for private interests. From the perspective of the civil law, property rights and interests, as well as personality rights and the interests contained in data rights, are confirmed under the *Civil Code*,[12] which establishes data rights' status for private law protection. Upon the promulgation of the *Civil Code*, whether it is the explanation and application of the personal information protection norms under existing laws such as the *Cybersecurity Law*, the *E-Commerce Law*, or the legislation in respect of personal information protection and the ownership of data rights such as the *Data Security Law*, shall be preconditioned upon full respect for and protection of a natural person's data rights and interests. Opinions or legislation deviating therefrom shall be in violation of the *Civil Code*. The Committee on Data Protection (UK) stated: "Protection for personal data is not solely aimed at establishing an individual right, instead, it intends to construct a legal framework where individuals, personal data, and the overall rights of society can be balanced" (Cmnd. 7341, pp. 18, 42). However, it would be inappropriate to put personal data rights and interests and the right to privacy (together) in the book of personality rights of the *Civil Code*; data rights need to be guaranteed by a separate private law for the realization of the different rights and interests of data owners.

Public law protection for data rights. As Roman thinker Marcus Tillius Cicero once said: "*Salus populi suprema lex esto*" (Let the good of the people be the supreme law). Public law, mainly the constitution and criminal law, is the law governing the administrative function of the state. It is about state power and it protects social interest.

> In the domain of public law, the parties involved in legal regulation are the state and individuals. The reason why state power is above personal rights is that the ultimate

12 See the stipulation in Article 127 of the *Civil Code*: "Where any laws provide for the protection of data and network virtual property, such laws shall apply."

> aim of the state power is the realization of public interests of society. (Wang Xiuxiu 2016, p. 100)

How advanced a legal system is depends on its stipulations on social interests. Article 1035 of the *Civil Code* of China stipulates the legal ground for personal information's public law protection,[13] which includes informed consent, the public interest or a natural person's legitimate rights, and public information. Public security forms an important part of social interests and is usually in tension with personal data rights, which makes it the primary cause for the limitation of the latter. The *Personal Information Protection Law* (*Draft*), promulgated in October 2020, defines personal information as a "right and interest" in Article 1,[14] forming the basis for providing public law protection for data rights (as a new type of right). "Though the data privacy of an individual citizen is the individual's private interest, it may concern public interests such as national security under certain circumstances." (Wang Xuehui and Zhao Xin 2015). It is fair to say that the value of public law protection for data rights lies mainly in the realization of social interests, such as digital order, digital human rights, and digital justice; while private law protection for data rights puts more emphasis on the value of equality and personal data rights. This shows that law may be oriented more toward personal data rights or social interests and legal protection for data rights and interests tend to vary accordingly.

Data rights as a new type of public right. Whether under the *Civil Code* or the *Personal Information Protection Law* (*Draft*), personal information is

13 See the stipulation in the first paragraph of Article 1035 of the *Civil Code*: "The processing of personal information shall be in compliance with the principles of lawfulness, justification, and within a necessary limit, and shall not be excessively processed; meanwhile, the following conditions shall be satisfied: (1) consent has been obtained from the natural person or his guardian, unless otherwise provided by laws or administrative regulations."

14 See the stipulation in Article 1 of the *Personal Information Protection Law* (*Draft*): "Purposes of this law include protection of personal rights and interests of data, regulation of personal information processing, safeguarding the order of free flow of personal information, and enhancing the rational use of personal information."

defined as an interest, not a right. Individuals are entitled to rights such as the right to consent, the right to know, the right to correct, and the right to delete[15] in respect of their own information. These cover the full life cycle of personal data processing and actually establish individuals' full control of their own information. Data rights are both constitutional rights and civil rights. They possess features of personality rights and property rights concurrently, making them a new type of rights that can be divided into multiple bundles of rights including, without limitation, the right of possession, the right to use, the right to earnings, the right to share, and the right to cross-border transmission, upon different conditions of application. "Personality rights are traditional civil rights, while personal data rights are brand new public rights, which emerges newly from the large-scale application of computers" (Paul M. Schwartz and Daniel J. Solove 2011). Just as legal scholar Zhou Hanhua suggested, "where personal information rights are defined within the framework of traditional civil rights, and personal information protection is incorporated into private personality rights together with the right to privacy, logical contradictions and practical conflicts will be inevitable" (Zhou Hanhua 2020). Thus, what our legal system is confronted with is the protection of partial interests in data processing and use, which can only be done by the regulation of data rights by the public legal system. The significance of data rights and independent public rights is that not only can data owners challenge other civil entities, they may also challenge administrative agencies, forcing governmental agencies to respect and protect personal rights to data.

Balance between Private Data Rights and Public Data Rights

"One major function of law is to regulate and reconcile various interests that conflict with each other, whether an individual interest or society

15 See Article 1037 of the *Civil Code*: "A natural person may retrieve or make copies of his personal information from the information processers in accordance with law. Where the person discovers that the information is incorrect, he has the right to raise an objection and request corrections or other necessary measures to be taken in a timely manner."

interest" (Bodenheimer 2017, p. 414). In the digital age a large amount of data lies within the control of the state and enterprises and, with the rising of "administrative states," public power grows, expands, and arbitrarily intrudes into "the private domain." Generally speaking, private data rights and public data power are confrontational; they compete with each other and provide checks and balances for each other in cyberspace. Thus, the purpose of data rights legislation has developed from the protection of the right to privacy and personal rights to comprehensive protection when balancing and coordinating of multiple rights and interests.

Concession of private data rights. As we move from traditional information protection to the *General Data Protection Regulation*, private data rights protection has gone from weak to strong protection. But such protection, be it weak or strong, is bound to bring imbalance in regard to data rights. The concession of private data rights is for the purpose of removing data barriers, facilitating data circulation, and maximizing data value. What lies between concession and limitation is sharing. The sharing of rights is necessary for data development and serves as an important means to push data rights from imbalance to balance. From the perspective of rights, sharing and possession represent the essential difference between data rights and real rights. "The right to share is as important to data rights as the right of possession to real rights, which indicates the inevitable trend from "making the best of property" to "making the best of data." (Key Laboratory of Big Data Strategy 2019, p. 266). Private data rights need to give way to the public interest and national security, but it is also necessary to prevent governmental power from expanding beyond proper limitation, making sure that governmental power is kept at a reasonable distance from personal rights and interests.[16]

16 Per the legislative practice around the world, it is normal to see that in the weighing of society's interests, legislators provide governmental agencies with delegated power to limit people's fundamental rights by law. For instance, the Basic Law for the Federal Republic of Germany stipulates in the first paragraph of Article 2: "Every person shall have the right to free development of his personality insofar as he does not violate the rights of others or offend against the constitutional order or the moral law," and the Constitution of PRC stipulates in Article 51: "Citizens of the People's Republic of China, in exercising their freedoms and rights, may not

Restriction on public data power. The exercise of public data power may have an impact on those public interests protected by law. The reason why public data power needs to be restricted is that, for the purposes of safeguarding social public interests and national security, the intervention of public power in the process of collecting and using citizens' personal data have already become an established fact. Private data rights need to be regulated by law, but data shall not be monopolized by individuals, and it is improper to sacrifice the public interest for personal data rights protection. It is the top priority of the government to keep data, a new product of the digital society, under control, and this calls for certain restrictions on and the regulation of relevant public data power so that the exercise of data rights can be maintained within a reasonable scope and appropriate channels. However,

> [R]egulating data public power does not mean undermining the authority of it. This should be done on the basis of sound relevant rules and procedures. (Key Laboratory of Big Data Strategy 2020, p. 93)

Within the process of legislation for data rights, it is necessary to follow the idea that "power shall be governed by law," and avoid the arbitrary exercise and expansion of public data rights, so that the private data rights can be better protected.

The legislative system for data rights with the unification of public law and private law.

> Practice of the rule of administrative law follows two main logics in China: one is the legality consideration with constrain of public power and protection of private rights as its core; and the other is the optimality consideration with improvement of governmental efficiency as its core. (Zhu Xinli and Tang Mingliang 2009)

Data rights lay emphasis on two major points. One is that private data rights are closely connected with personal dignity, personal freedom,

---

infringe upon the interests of the state, of society or of the collective, or upon the lawful freedoms and rights of other citizens." Personal rights and society's interests are frequently in conflict; thus, it is necessary to balance personal rights protection with society's interests. It is only when these issues are resolved that the legal system will function as it was designed.

property rights and the interests of data owners, and the other is that the realization of private data rights represent social value, that is, common, shared, and collective. Personal data is indispensable for data subjects to realize the purposes of their social interactions, the free circulation of personal data, the development of politics and the economy, and the formation of a sound legal system. "The regulation of big data technology shall adopt a model that combines public power regulation and private rights self-regulaiton" (Wu Weiguang 2009). To deal with data infringements of both public law and private law, it is necessary for public law and private law to avoid the disadvantages of regulation and make the best of their complementary advantages by constructing a "protection model where the public law can cooperate with private law" to cope with infringements of citizens' data rights, so that such infringements are limited by aspects of substantiality, procedures, and relief. By so doing, the conflicting demands for data rights protection can be satisfied.

Conflicts between the Right to Share and the Right to Privacy

The era of the digital economy has seen data sharing become the foundation for data circulation and the development of the digital industry. However, data sharing may damage the subject of digital rights as a result of the misuse of personal data, such as data leakage. The right to share is the essence of data rights, and it is realized via the welfare property rights of data and the usufruct rights of public data. It thus becomes possible to separate the right to use data from data ownership, and form a basic pattern of sharing where people seek not to own, but to use data (Key Laboratory of Big Data Strategy 2020, p. 5). The right to share refers to specific personality rights enjoyed by a natural person to control his/her own personal information and life and domain, which are irrelevant to public and group interests. The reason why conflicts between the right to share and the right to privacy emerge is because of the conflict between public interests and personal interests and the discrepancies between property interests and personality interests, which creates an enormous problem in the field of law and legislation for data rights.

Data Sharing and Privacy Protection

> Sharing is the innate requirement of big data development and for sharing; open access to data is indispensable. However, privacy protection requires that data and information are kept confidential. Thus, data openness with sharing as the goal will inevitably lead to serious privacy infringements in the era of big data. (Wu Xinghua 2017)

Data sharing is a norm, a specific approach, and a way of action for data subjects to control the level of transmission and the way of use for the data they produce or add value to. The premise of promoting the orderly and healthy development of data sharing lies in distributing data rights and interests among data subjects in a law-based, fair, and effective way (Chen Bing and Gu Dandan 2020). In August 2015, the State Council stated in the *Action Plan for Promoting Big Data Development* (GF [2015] No. 50) that:

> [We] should vigorously promote connection of, open access to, and sharing of government information systems and public data, accelerate the integration of government information platforms, eliminate information isolation, and advance toward the opening of data resources toward society.

This is in fact a policy proposal in support of the principle of sharing.

Rules and regulations protected personal privacy in the German and French criminal codes as early as in the nineteenth century.[17] Besides, the Spanish *Criminal Code* stipulated the "crime of privacy infringement, privacy reveal, and residence invasion" in Chapter 10, and the Italian *Criminal Code* stipulated the "crime of illegal invasion of private life" in order to crack down on illegal obtaining and revealing to the public, and

17 Germany issued a criminal code in 1871, which stipulated the crime of private secrets infringement. Also, France made stipulations on the infringing of personal privacy in Article 226-1 of the criminal code.

the spreading of other's private information. Also, the "crime of revealing secret," Article 134 of the *Penal Code of Japan*, restricts workers in the pharmaceuticals industry from revealing "other's secrets acquired through business" without "reasonable reason" in order to protect patients' personal privacy, under limited circumstances. The United States has focused on the protection of its citizens' right to personal privacy by introducing a series of federal laws aimed at providing legal protection for private information, protecting privacy in public law, and restricting private data processing in specific industries and domains. The *Model Penal Code* was adopted by many American states in 1962. The privacy terms contained therein protects the right to privacy in multiple specific laws.[18] More and more countries and regions are strengthening legislation on personal privacy and data protection, including the execution of a series of rules, conventions, and stipulations related to the right to privacy protection.[19]

18 Article 250.12 of the *Model Penal Code* 1962 stipulated the punishments for privacy infringements. Similar regulations could be seen in Article 552(a) of the *Privacy Act of 1974*, Article 1681(b) of the *Fair Credit Reporting Act of 1970* and Article 1030(a), (4) and (5) of *Computer Fraud and Abuse Act* enacted in 1984. Besides, the *Electronic Communications Privacy Act of 1986* is a significant statutory law that protects privacy in the realm of e-commerce. The *Video Privacy Protection Act of 1988* prevents the illegal reveal of video rents and sale records. The *Cable Television Consumer Protection and Competition Act of 1992* restricts the publication of personally identifiable information (PII) of cable television subscribers. The *Telephone Consumer Protection Act of 1991* restricts telephonic solicitations and the use of automatic telephone equipment. The *Health Insurance Portability and Accountability Act of 1996* explicitly defines the concept and scope of health information protection. The *Children's Online Privacy Protection Act of 1997* was enacted due to concerns about the misuse of children's information, arising from an investigation by Federal Trade Commission (FTC) into KidsCom.com, which violated rules concerning the Uniform Personal Data Act (UDPA). All states implemented the *Data Breach Notification Laws* in 2018, which requires individuals and government entities to provide notification of breaches of personal information and relevant events that affected clients and individuals. The *California Consumer Privacy Act of 2018* also protects personal privacy in all respects.

19 Relevant regulations on personal information protection can be seen in the following laws: *Guidelines on the Protection of Privacy and Transborder Flows of Personal Data*, OECD (1980), the *Convention for the Protection of Individuals with regard to Automatic Processing of Personal Data* by Council of Europe, the

The second paragraph of Article 1032 of the *Civil Code* of China stipulates that "privacy is the undisturbed private life of a natural person and his private space, private activities, and private information that he does not want to be known to others." The first paragraph of Article 12[20] of the *Law of the People's Republic of China on Prevention and Treatment of Infectious Diseases* is a rule related to personal privacy, including information and documents. It is stipulated in the third paragraph of Article 4 of the *Mental Health Law of the People's Republic of China* that "the relevant entities and individuals shall keep confidential the name, portrait, address, employer, and medical records of the patients with mental disorders and other information from which the identities of the patients with mental disorders may be inferred." The second paragraph of Article 39[21] of the *Regulation*

Privacy Act 1988 by Australia, the *Guidelines for the Regulation of Computerized Personal Data Files* by UN General Assembly in 1990, the *Privacy Act 1993* by New Zealand, the *Directive 95/46/EC of the European Parliament and of the Council on the Protection of Individuals with Regard to the Processing of Personal Data and on the Free Movement of Such Data* by the European Parliament and of the Council in 1995, the *Directive 95/46/EC on Data Protection* by the European Union in 1995, the *Personal Information Protection and Electronic Documents Act* by Australia in 2001, the *Act on Promotion of Information and Communication Network Utilization and Information Protection 2001* by South Korea, the *Additional Protocol to the Convention for the Protection of Individuals with regard to Automatic Processing of Personal Data, regarding supervisory authorities and transborder data flows* by Council of Europe in 2001, the *Act on the Protection of Personal Information* by Japan in 2003, the *APEC Privacy Framework* by APEC in 2004, the *Generally Accepted Privacy Principles* by American Institute of Certified Public Accountants (AICPA) in 2009, the *Convention for the Protection of Individuals with Regard to the Processing of Personal Data* by Council of Europe in 2012, and so on.

20 It is stipulated in Article 12 of *Law of the People's Republic of China on Prevention and Treatment of Infectious Diseases (2013 Amendment)* that "disease prevention and control institutions and medical agencies shall not divulge any information or materials relating to personal privacy."

21 It is stipulated in the second paragraph of Article 39 of *Regulation on the Prevention and Treatment of HIV/AIDS (2019 Revision)* that "no entity or individual may publicize the name, address, working entity, portrait, and materials of disease history of any HIV-infected individual, AIDS sufferer, or any of his/her family members, or any other information from which his/her identity can be inferred."

on the Prevention and Treatment of HIV/AIDS protects patients' private information. The first paragraph of Article 1 of *Decision of the Standing Committee of the National People's Congress on Strengthening Information Protection on Networks* stipulates that "the state protects electronic information by which individual citizens can be identified and which involves the individual privacy of citizens." Article 43 of the *Law of the People's Republic of China on Public Libraries* stipulates that "public libraries shall appropriately protect readers' personal information, borrowing information and other information that may involve the privacy of readers and shall not sell or otherwise illegally provide it to others." Besides which, terms of privacy protection exist in a number of laws, regulations, departmental rules, and relevant legal explanations, such as the *Public Security Administration Punishments Law of the People's Republic of China*,[22] the *Tort Law of the People's Republic of China*,[23] the *Civil Procedure Law of the People's Republic of China*,[24] and the *Provisions of the Supreme People's*

22 It is stipulated in Article 42 of *Public Security Administration Punishments Law of the People's Republic of China* that "anyone who commits any of the following acts shall be detained for not more than 5 days or shall be fined not more than 500 yuan. If the circumstances are relatively serious, he/she shall be detained for not less than 5 days but not more than 10 days, and may be concurrently fined not more than 500 yuan: (2) Insulting any other person openly or making up stories to defame any other person: (6) Peeping into, sneaking photos, wiretapping, or spreading the privacy of any other person."

23 It is stipulated in Article 62 of *Tort Law of the People's Republic of China* that "a medical institution and its medical staff shall keep confidential the privacy of a patient. If any privacy data of a patient is divulged or any of his/her medical history is open to the public without the consent of the patient, causing any harm to the patient, the medical institution shall assume the tort liability."

24 It is stipulated in Article 68 of *Civil Procedure Law of the People's Republic of China* that "evidence shall be presented in court and cross-examined by the parties. Evidence that involves any state secret, trade secret, or individual privacy shall be kept confidential, and if it is necessary to present such evidence in court, such evidence shall not be presented in open court." It is stipulated in Article 134 of the *Civil Procedure Law of the People's Republic of China* that "a people's court shall try civil cases openly, except those involving any state secret or individual privacy or as otherwise provided by law." It is stipulated in Article 156 of *Civil Procedure Law of the People's Republic of China* that "the public may consult effective written

Court on Several Issues concerning the Application of Law in the Trial of Cases involving Civil Disputes over Infringements upon Personal Rights and Interests through Information Networks.[25]

Conflicts between the Right to Share and the Right to Privacy

Data rights have the right to share as its core, and the central concern of the sharing system is the balance between data rights and the interests of individuals, and the public interest over data. "The sharing system corrects the preference to private interests over public interests in our previous approach to data, and instead proposes and advocates a new approach that pursues a balance between private interests and public interests" (Key Laboratory of Big Data Strategy 2020, p. 40). The right to share is not only the requirement of data development, the balancing of data rights and real rights is essential. According to the first paragraph of Article 1032 of the *Civil Code*, "a natural person enjoys the right to privacy. No organization or individual may infringe upon the other's right to privacy by prying into, intruding upon, disclosing, or publicizing other's private matters." It suggests that the right to privacy enjoyed by citizens in accordance with the law is a fundamental right to personality, which entitles the denial of their personal information to others, thus leaving their personal life uninterrupted;[26] this covers three fields: self-determination

judgments and rulings, except where the content involves any national secret, trade secret, or individual privacy."

25 It is stipulated in the first paragraph of Article 12 of *Provisions of the Supreme People's Court on Several Issues concerning the Application of Law in the Trial of Cases involving Civil Disputes over Infringements upon Personal Rights and Interests through Information Networks* that "where a network user or NSP discloses through network a natural person's individual privacy such as genetic information, medical records, health inspection materials, criminal records, home address, and private activities, or any other personal information, which causes damage to any other person, and the infringed party requests the assumption of tort liability by the network user or NSP, the people's court shall support such a request."

26 The right to privacy contains rich connotations, but the definition of it is inconsistent. The *Universal Declaration of Human Rights* 1948 clearly proposed that

privacy, space privacy, and information privacy. Thus, whereas the right to share highlights the free flow and sharing of data—representing public interests and property interests—the right to privacy represents personal interests and personality interests. It is unavoidable that the conflicts between the two will emerge.

The *right to share v. self-determination privacy right*. The so-called self-determination privacy right refers to the right of citizens to determine and make choices concerning their personal matters and way of life. For instance, citizens enjoy the right to self-determination regarding contraception, termination of pregnancy, homosexuality, euthanasia, and ways to raise and educate their children (Allen and Turkington 2004, p. 371–2). Self-determination privacy rights ensure that citizens can manage their own affairs according to their true thoughts without interference from others so that their status as an independent individual can be maintained. On the one hand, frequent data sharing easily leads to infringement of self-determination privacy rights as it may disclose the consequences of citizens making a choice on their own right to privacy. On the other hand, data sharing may be seriously damaged if self-determination privacy protection is claimed excessively or abused. The establishment of the right to share makes it possible that several subjects can exist concurrently in data, and each of them enjoys independent and complete data rights rather than sharing a right. The right to share helps to coordinate conflicts between different data subjects by providing a value basis for settling conflicts involving data interests. Against such a background, excessive claims, or abuse of self-determination privacy protection, by citizens will restrict the collection and utilization of some data, thus obstructing the realization of the economic and social value of the data as a resource.

privacy of residence and communication shall not be violated. Article 12 states that "no one shall be subjected to arbitrary interference with his privacy, family, home, or correspondence, nor to attacks upon his honor and reputation. Everyone has the right to the protection of the law against such interference or attacks." Article 8 of *European Convention on Human Rights* 1950 stipulated that "everyone has the right to respect for his private and family life, his home, and his correspondence." The above-mentioned sources of international law make the right to privacy a fundamental human right, drawing international attention to privacy protection.

The *right to share v. the right to space privacy*. "The right to space privacy is a civil right which provides that the specific private space of a party shall not be illegally watched, invaded, and interfered" (Wang Liming 2007). It is applicable to both traditional physical spaces and virtual spaces, such as mobile communication, diaries, communications, electronic chat rooms, and email. Specifically, the right to space privacy has two characteristics: first, the target it protects is private space;[27] second, the behaviors it prevents are illegal intrusions, including physical and nonphysical intrusions.[28] However, space privacy protection may obstruct the effective operation of data sharing. For example, navigation systems such as Baidu Maps and Google Maps provide exceptional convenience for users, but the sharing of location data is essential for their operation. However, location data is part of space privacy data as it is related to an individual's geographic position. As a result, the conflict between data sharing and space privacy protection is worsening, resulting in damage to privacy space protection in the case of a data sharing intrusion. The right to privacy intends to protect individuals' not to have their private space intruded by others. However, secrets in and peace of private space, and control of personal data, may be intruded during data sharing. As a result, conflicts between the right to share and the right to privacy have increased.

The *right to share v. the right to information privacy*. "The right to information privacy was born in the first place mainly as a right of passive defense. It refers to the right that personal information owned by citizens shall not be disclosed without permission" (Wang Yan and Ye Ming 2019). With the development of computers, big data, and other technologies, once personal information has been disclosed on the internet it will be

27 Private space, including tangible and intangible space, refers to personal space that can exist in the private realm.

28 With the development of technology, physical intrusion is rarely seen. Intrusions of space privacy can be established as a result of "snooping", such as a wiretap and surveillance of things, such as phone calls and email. The regulation of space intrusions is justified; such behaviors harm the benefits one may reasonable expect of space privacy enjoyed by rights holders. Prohibiting private space harassment aims to ensure a stable life enjoyed by rights holders in their private space (Wang Yan and Ye Ming 2019).

hard to retract or return it to its original state. Thus, the right to information privacy is gradually transforming from passive defense to positive utilization (Wang Liming 2009), stressing control over the use of personal information. On the one hand, apart from some public data resources controlled by the government, most of the data on personal behavior on the internet is, at present, controlled by internet companies that are likely to abuse data and infringe personal information privacy due to their pursuit of self-interest as they are "economic man" by nature. On the other hand, strictly protecting the right to privacy may burden data subjects. For example, for data collectors there are the costs of giving notices, making revisions, and deleting data. Even though such burdens may be justifiable, they would, all the same, dampen the willingness of data subjects to share data. The right to share is intended to promote data sharing and it focuses on the protection of data property rights and interests. On the contrary, the right to privacy pays more attention to personality interests. That is why there is conflict between the right to share and the right to privacy.

Balance between the Right to Share and the Right to Privacy

The settlement of disputes is one of the basic functions of law: the law must seek to balance multiple types of interest. The right to share and the right to privacy are not completely opposite. Generally, benefits measurement through legal means is applied to resolve conflicts of rights in judicial practice. To be more specific, the approach to measure benefits is to calculate the value of disposition rights according to the measure of the benefit, after measuring the benefits claimed by the subjects to the dispute when the rights claimed are in conflict with each other (Wang Suyuan and Ren Erxin 1999). In order to realize a balance between the right to share and the right to privacy, some basic principles must be complied with, such as the principle of public interest priority, the principle of derogation, the principle of proportionality, and the principle of equal protection. Work must also be done to tackle basic questions concerning the right to share and the right to privacy, clarify the scope and limitations of the two, strictly stipulate the procedure for the realization of the right to share, strengthen supervision of the enforcement of the right to share, and improve the accountability and relief systems in the case of an infringement of the right to privacy by the right to share.

The principle of public interest priority. As Aristotle put it, "man is by nature a social animal," since their lives involve social relationships, people need to shoulder certain social responsibilities. The principle of public interest priority means that personal interests shall be restricted when it is necessary to do so for the protection of public interests (Wang Xuehui and Zhao Xin 2015). Germany takes the public right to know as the priority when public interests conflict with the rights of individuals.[29] In China, the exercise of rights shall not infringe the public interest in the constitution[30] and other laws.[31] Thus, the principle of public interest priority is a basic idea of legislation in a law-based society, and no subject shall infringe the social commonwealth during the exercise of rights. Laws in other countries and regions, including both constitutions and laws of other branches, accept the basic principle that the public interest takes priority (Liang Shangshang 2016).

The principle of derogation. "Derogation legally refers to the suspension and restriction of rights. The principle of derogation features unilateral restriction on the right to privacy" (Lin Min 2017). When applying this principle, the value of the relevant interests shall be balanced before

29 It is stipulated in the second paragraph of Article 19 of *Basic Law for the Federal Republic of Germany* that in no case may the essence of a basic right be affected.

30 It is stipulated in Article 13 of *Constitution of the People's Republic of China* that "the lawful private property of citizens may not be encroached upon. The state protects by law the right of citizens to own private property and the right to inherit private property. The state may, for the public interest, expropriate or take over private property of citizens for public use, and pay compensation in accordance with the law."

31 It is stipulated in Article 15 of *Open Government Information Regulation of the People's Republic of China* that "for government information relating to a trade secret, individual privacy or the like, whose public disclosure would harm the lawful rights and interests of any third party, an administrative agency shall not disclose to the public such government information unless the third party consents to its public disclosure, or the administrative agency deems that its withholding would materially affect the public interest."

making a decision; the more valuable interests will be protected through the derogation of the right to privacy. It is stipulated in Article 17 of the *International Covenant on Civil and Political Rights* of the United Nations that the right to privacy can be derogated, and countries may declare the derogation of its citizen's right to privacy, including suspending the protection of private life secrets or limiting the scope thereof. As a member state of the *Universal Declaration of Human Rights*, China applies the principle of derogation to the protection of the right to privacy and this principle is applicable to the protection of the right to privacy of public figures who have gained material and spiritual interests from society that are unavailable to other citizens, thus balancing privacy interests against such gains (Tang Kaiyuan 2005).

The principle of equal protection. There can be compromise between different rights. When the right to share conflicts with the right to privacy, certain concessions can be made between the two rights within a certain range to find a balance between the two, based on mutual tolerance. Both the right to share and the right to privacy are basic rights of citizens and they each have their own value. The right to share acts as a driver of the digital economy and protects user rights and interests in data. The right to privacy entitles the right holder to control his/her personal life. The two are both protected by law. It is stipulated in Article 51 of *Constitution* of China that "citizens of the People's Republic of China, in exercising their freedoms and rights, may not infringe upon the interests of the state, of society, or of the collective, or upon the lawful freedoms and rights of other citizens." It establishes the spirit of equal protection of rights. Both the right to privacy and the right to share are legitimate rights that should be acknowledged by law, and there should be no differences in their level and position in the legal system. Equal protection is also a principle required by morality—data rights legislation shall both protect personal dignity and take into consideration the effective operation of the right to share.

The principle of proportionality. The principle originates from the spirit of Article 20 of the British *Magna Carta*—making the punishment fit the crime.[32] Germany was a pioneer in defining this as a basic principle of administrative law, which is also viewed as a basic and immutable article in value measurement in countries that have constitutional courts (Li Xiuqun 2007, p. 147). The principle of proportionality requires a tradeoff between planned goals and ready-to-adopt methods when the government takes administrative action. This has two sub-principles—appropriateness and necessity. The former requires that the government adopt measures that are helpful to reach administrative goals, while the latter, or the "least harm principle," requires that of all the methods available to achieve the administrative goal the government should choose the one that is the least intrusive into citizens' rights (Zhou Youyong 2005, p. 51). Therefore, the principle of proportionality shall apply to the right to share and the right to privacy so that infringement and harm to citizens' rights can be minimized, while the right to share shall apply to data that is deemed to have the necessity to be shared following legal procedures.

International Conflicts in Data Rights Legislation

Today, according to the World Economic Forum, we are entering the new era of globalization 4.0, a time of digitalization-driven globalization. Cross-border data flow is becoming an important force driving globalization as data becomes global as assets and flows more freely in the world. At present, countries around the world are actively drafting and proposing policies and regulations on data governance strategy on the basis of their own core values, making cross-border data flow and data sovereignty new issues in international politics. However, a general consensus has yet to

32 For a trivial offense, a free man shall be fined only in proportion to the degree of his offense and a serious offense correspondingly, but not so heavily as to deprive him of his livelihood. In the same way, a merchant shall be spared his merchandise and a villain the implements of his husbandry, if they fall upon the mercy of a royal court. None of these fines shall be imposed except by the assessment on oath of reputable men of the neighborhood (Chen Guohua 2016, p. 36–7).

be reached on the regulation of cross-border data flow and principles of data sovereignty. It is difficult for countries to agree on issues regarding international data governance due to differences in their legislative concepts and administrative systems. As a result, international conflicts may emerge. In Chinese data rights legislation we should macroscopically coordinate institutional differences with other countries and balance between domestic law and international law. We should also embark on a mission of legal modernization, formulating and promoting a more scientific approach to legalization under the umbrella of international data governance, while advancing the digital economy and ensuring security.

Global Tendency of Cross-border Data Flow

In the era where data means productivity, cross-border data flow, as the core issue of digital trade and the strategical frontier of major powers benefit game, is becoming an important feature in the promotion of new globalization. However, problems brought about by cross-border data flow inevitably provokes concerns about personal privacy, national security, and the future economy; this is due to differences in economics, politics, and the law, resulting in conflicts between the legal jurisdictions of sovereign states and data iniquities. Data sovereignty, as part of state sovereignty, retains features of supremacy and exclusivity. Due to the different systems in different countries, no global governance mechanism and system has yet been formed to accommodate the diverse demand of various countries for legislation and data flow. This is a major difficulty in data rights legislation.

Cross-border data flow has had a significant impact on the traditional perception of state sovereignty, undermining state sovereignty and giving birth to data sovereignty. Data sovereignty refers to the power enjoyed by the state to generate, disseminate, manage, control, use, and protect data within its jurisdiction. In the era of big data it is an inevitable requirement that all countries safeguard their state sovereignty and independence, and combat data monopoly and hegemony. Data sovereignty includes the following rights: data jurisdiction, the right to independence over data, the right to equality over data, and the right to self-defense over data (Key Laboratory of Big Data Strategy 2020, p. 190). Data sovereignty is an important part of state sovereignty and a manifestation and natural extension of state sovereignty in data space. In practice, against the backdrop of the growing significance of data sovereignty, the question of how to ensure their own sovereignty and take a dominant position in the protection of interests such as order, freedom, and development, security has become the focus of countries around the world. At present, the existence and significance of data sovereignty has been recognized through various international agreements and national laws in China and abroad. However, a global definition of data sovereignty has yet to be made.

The United States, as the first country to develop a data sovereignty strategy, has formed the most comprehensive data sovereignty strategy system with over 130 relevant acts. The *Clarifying Lawful Overseas Use of Data Act* (CLOUD Act) issued in 2018 is an outstanding example.[33] The *CLOUD Act* targets new problems that have emerged during access to cross-border data, solving key sovereignty-related problems that appear in two data flow situations, that is, data needed for law enforcement is stored overseas and foreign law enforcement agencies need to access data stored in America. As for the EU, they apply the *GDPR*.[34] The European Data Protection Board requires the data controller to enter into a data transmission agreement with the data recipient; see *Guidelines 2/2020 on articles 46 (2) (a) and 46 (3) (b) of Regulation 2016/679 for transfers of personal data between EEA and non-EEA public authorities and bodies (for public consultation)*, issued in February 2020, which provides a relatively flexible and convenient data transmission path from public institutions

33 The U.S. *Clarifying Lawful Overseas Use of Data Act* 2018, expressly entitles American law enforcement agencies access to user data stored overseas by companies who have a business in the US, broadening the power of American law enforcement power to seize data overseas. America has also signed an agreement on bilateral data access with the United Kingdom.

34 The *General Data Protection Regulation* (GDPR) provides that it is only when the data protection ability of the data controller beyond the EU is equal to one from the EU that data can be transmitted overseas. It is also regarded as the strictest and most extensive data protection rule in history.

of the European Economic Area to institutions in third countries and international organizations. To sum up, the *CLOUD Act* of the United States, the *GDPR* of the EU, and other data governance systems build up regulations and rules in line with their own interests, with data sovereignty at their core to protect their own data resources from infringement while acquiring and governing more data resources overseas. Russia strongly pursues localization of data sovereignty; they have strict local storage regulations on cross-border data. A typical example is the *Sovereign Internet Law*[35] which came into force on November 1, 2019, constituting the system

35 In order to strengthen network sovereignty through legislation, Russian cross-party MPs collectively proposed the *Federal Communication Law and Amendments to the Federal Law on Information, Information Technologies and Information Protection*—also called the *Stable Runet Act* or *Sovereignty Internet Law*. It was agreed by the State Duma of Russia on February 12, 2019, officially passed by Russian Federation Council on April 22, 2019, and came into force on November 1, 2019. But rules relating to the national domain name system did not become effective until January 1, 2021. The Sovereignty Internet Law mainly talks about the establishment of network sovereignty, or an autonomous and controllable network through legislation from five aspects. The first is domain name autonomy, which stipulates that Russia has to establish a national system able to receive domain name information and an autonomous address resolution system in order to replace the current domain name service system in cases of emergency. All networks' critical national interests should use this system. To a certain extent, it established an autonomous internet. The second stipulates that the Federal Service for the Supervision of Communications, Information Technology and Mass Media, is responsible for the design, construction, and rules for use of the domain name system. At the same time, the act highlights the significance of regular drills for the government, telecommunications companies, and the owners of technology and networks in order to identify threats and take corresponding measures. The third is the management and control platform. The law stipulates that internet service providers have the responsibility to show the regulatory department how to guide the internet data flow to the routing node administrated by government so that domestic internet data does not go through to foreign servers, which minimizes the circulation of Russian users' data to foreign countries. Telecommunications companies have a duty to provide a centralized management flow should an emergency occur. For example, they should add equipment to the communication network to identify the flow origin. The fourth is active disconnection, which requires the Federal Service for Supervision of Communications, Information Technology and Mass Media (Roskomnadzor), to maintain the stability of Russian network. They can cut connections with

of data sovereignty protection in Russia with *Federal Law of 27 July 2006 No. 152-FZ on Personal Data* and other relevant laws.

In China, the concept of sovereignty in cyberspace is evolving quickly. In August 2015, the State Council issued the *Action Outline for Promoting the Development of Big Data* (GF [2015] No. 50), which addressed the issue of China taking full advantage of the scale of data to [...] enhance protection capacity for cyberspace data sovereignty, safeguard national security, and effectively improve China's national competitiveness. The outline officially lifts big data and data sovereignty up to a national strategy. Against the backdrop of the global trend of data sovereignty legislation, China has begun to build up its own system of cyber and data sovereignty in recent years. From the perspective of legislation, China added the concept of cyberspace sovereignty in the *National Security Law of the People's Republic of China*[36] and the *Cybersecurity Law of the People's Republic of*

external internet resources if they find that the Russian internet has been damaged, and control the communications network used by the public while ensuring the stable operation of the external internet. It is also empowered to make decisions on threats and take action to eliminate them. The fifth is overall planning of technology. The act proposes principles of routing choice and methods of tracking and monitoring. It also required that the Centre for Monitoring and Managing the Public Communications Network under Roskomnadzor be set up to analyze the contents of calls transmitted by external telecommunications companies, and information in national data transmission systems, in order to maintain the security of Russian internet. (Zhao Hongrui et al. 2019)

36 See Article 25 of the *National Security Law of the People's Republic of China* states that "the state shall build a network and information security guarantee system, network and information security protection capability; strengthen innovation research and development and the application of network and information technologies; realize the controllable security of the core technologies crucial to the infrastructure network and information and the information systems and data in important fields; strengthen the network management to prevent, frustrate, and legally punish network attacks, network invasion, network information theft, the dissemination of illegal and harmful information and other network-related infractions of law and crimes; and maintain the state's sovereignty, security, and development interests in the cyberspace."

China,[37] which protects sovereignty, security, and the development of cyberspace by operation of law so that behavior in cyberspace is expressly required to be administered by and subject to national sovereignty. However, there are few laws about cyberspace at present, and most of the existing ones were established with regulations and departmental rules that enjoy relatively little legal effect, and which lack effective support from superior laws. Since the requirement for a security assessment for cross-border transfer of critical information infrastructure in the *Cybersecurity Law of the People's Republic of China* was carried out in 2017,[38] the relevant authorities have improved administrative policies and systems of data cross-border flow through regulations or normative documents (see Table 11).

37 See Article 1 of the *Cybersecurity Law of the People's Republic of China* states that "this Law is developed for the purposes of guaranteeing cybersecurity; safeguarding cyberspace sovereignty, national security, and the public interest; protecting the lawful rights and interests of citizens, legal persons, and other organizations; and promote the sound development of economic and social informatization."

38 It is stipulated in Article 37 of the *Cybersecurity Law of the People's Republic of China* that "personal information and important data collected and produced by critical information infrastructure operators during their operations within the territory of the People's Republic of China shall be stored within China. If it is indeed necessary to provide such information and data to overseas parties due to business requirements, a security assessment shall be conducted in accordance with the measures developed by the national cyberspace administration in conjunction with relevant departments of the State Council, unless it is otherwise prescribed by any law or administrative regulation."

Table 11. Main Terms Concerning Cross-border Data Flow in China

Documents	Date of Declaration	Department of Declaration	Relevant Provisions
Personal Information Protection of the People's Republic of China (Draft)	October 21, 2020	Legislative Affairs Commission under the Standing Committee of the National People's Congress	Chapter III Rules on the Cross-Border Provision of Personal Information. Article 38: Where a personal information processor truly needs to provide personal information to any party outside the territory of the People's Republic of China for business needs, the following conditions shall be satisfied: (1) A security assessment organized by the national cyberspace administration has been passed in accordance with Article 40 of this Law; (2) Personal information protection certification has been conducted by a specialized institution according to provisions issued by the national cyberspace administration; (3) A contract has been concluded with the overseas recipient,

			agreeing on both parties' rights and obligations, and supervision is conducted to ensure that personal information processing activities of the overseas recipient meet the personal information protection standards provided in this law; (4) Other conditions provided by law or administrative regulations, or by the national cyberspace administration. Article 39 Where a personal information processor provides personal information to any party outside the territory of the People's Republic of China, it or he shall notify individuals of the overseas recipient's identity, contact information, processing purposes, processing methods, categories of personal information, the methods in which individuals exercise the rights provided in this law over the overseas recipient, and other matters, and obtain the individuals' separate consent.
			Article 41 Where it is necessary to provide personal information to any party outside of the territory of the People's Republic of China for international judicial assistance or administrative law enforcement assistance, an application shall be filed with the relevant

(continued)

Table 11. Continued

Documents	Date of Declaration	Department of Declaration	Relevant Provisions
			competent department for approval according to the law. Where any international treaty or agreement concluded or acceded to by the People's Republic of China provides for the provision of personal information to parties outside the territory of the People's Republic of China, such provisions shall prevail. Article 42 Where an overseas organization or individual engages in personal information processing activities that damage the rights and interests relating to personal information of citizens of the People's Republic of China or compromise the national security or public interests of the People's Republic of China, the national cyberspace administration may include it or him in a list of those the provision of personal information to whom is restricted or prohibited, make an announcement, and take measures such as restricting or prohibiting the provision of personal information to it or him.
Data Security of the People's Republic of China (Draft)	July 3, 2020	Standing Committee of the National People's Congress	Article 10 The country actively carries out international exchanges and cooperation in the realm of data to establish global rules and standards concerning data security, in order to promote the security and free flow of cross-border data.

Master Plan for the Construction of Hainan Free Trade Port	June 1, 2020	Departments and Institutions of the CPC Central Committee, Central Committee of the Communist Party of China, State Council	11. Facilitate data flow. Launch pilot projects on the security management of cross-border data transfers to explore and develop a convenient and secure cross-border data transfer mechanism within the framework of national security management system for cross-border data transfers.
Information security technology—Personal information security specification (GB/T 35273-2020)	March 6, 2020	General Administration of Quality Supervision, Inspection and Quarantine of the People's Republic of China, and Standardization Administration of the People's Republic of China	9.8 Transfer of personal information overseas. Where personal information collected and produced during the operation in People's Republic of China is transferred overseas, the controller of personal information should comply with national regulations and standards.

(continued)

Table 11. Continued

Documents	Date of Declaration	Department of Declaration	Relevant Provisions
Measures for the Administration of the Lin-gang Special Area of China (Shanghai) Pilot Free Trade Zone	August 20, 2019	People's Government of the Shanghai Municipality	Article 35 (Internet Infrastructure) The Lin-gang Special Area shall build sound international communication facilities, accelerate the construction of a new generation of information infrastructure, improve broadband access capabilities, network service quality and application level, and create a secure and facilitative channel exclusively for international internet data. Article 36 (Cross-border Data Flows) The Lin-gang Special Area shall focus on key fields such as integrated circuits, artificial intelligence, biomedicine, the headquarters economy, conduct security assessment on cross-border data flows on a pilot-program basis, and establish certification of data protection capabilities, review data circulation backups, cross-border data circulation, transaction risk assessments and other data security management mechanisms. Article 37 (Protection of Intellectual Property and Data) The Lin-gang Special Area shall launch a pilot program of international cooperation rules, and increase efforts to protect patents, copyrights, trade secrets, and other rights and data, and voluntarily participate in leading global exchanges and cooperation in the digital economy.

Framework Plan for the New Lingang Area of China (Shanghai) Pilot Free Trade Zone	July 27, 2019	State Council	9. Implements the orderly and secure cross-border flow of data over the international internet. Sound international communication facilities shall be built, the construction of 5G, IPv6, cloud computing, the Internet of Things, the Internet of Vehicles, and other next-generation information infrastructure shall be accelerated, broadband network access capabilities and the quality and application level of network services in the New Area shall be improved, and a safe and facilitative channel exclusively for data on the international internet shall be established. The New Areas shall be supported in focusing on key fields such as integrated circuits, artificial intelligence, biomedicine, and headquarters economy; conducting the security assessment of cross-border flow of data on a pilot-program basis; and establishing certification of data protection capabilities, review data circulation and backup, and deal with cross-border data circulation, trading risk assessment, and other data security management mechanisms. A pilot program of international cooperation rules shall be launched; efforts to protect patents, copyrights, trade secrets, and other rights and data shall be intensified, and exchanges and cooperation in leading the global digital economy shall be joined voluntarily.

(*continued*)

Table 11. Continued

Documents	Date of Declaration	Department of Declaration	Relevant Provisions
Measures for the Security Assessment for Cross-border Transfer of Personal Information (Exposure Draft)	June 13, 2019	Cyberspace Administration of China	Full text.
Regulation of the People's Republic of China on the Administration of Human Genetic Resources (Order No. 717 of the State Council of the People's Republic of China)	May 28, 2019	State Council	Article 27 Where it is necessary to transport, mail or carry the materials of China's human genetic resources out of China for the purpose of conducting scientific research through international cooperation by using China's human genetic resources or for any other particular circumstances, the following conditions shall be met, and a certificate of exit of human genetic resources issued by the science and technology administrative department of the State Council shall be obtained, provided that: (1) It causes no harm to China's public health, national security and public interest; (2) The entity has legal person status; (3) There is a specific overseas partner and a reasonable exit use; (4) The materials of human genetic resources are legally collected or from a legal preservation entity; (5) The application has

			passed the ethical review. Where the materials of China's human genetic resources are transported, mailed, or carried out of China, customs formalities shall be based on the certificate of exit of materials of human genetic resources. Article 31: The science and technology administrative department of the State Council shall retain experts in biotechnology, medicine, health, ethics, law, and other aspects to form an expert review committee to conduct technical reviews of the applications for the collection and preservation of China's human genetic resources, scientific research through international cooperation, and the transport, mailing, and carriage of materials of China's human genetic resources out of China, filed in accordance with the provisions of this Regulation. Review opinions shall be taken as the basis for making approval decisions. Article 38 Whoever, in violation of this Regulation, transports, mails, or carries the materials of China's human genetic resources out of China without approval shall be punished by the customs office in accordance with the provisions of laws and administrative regulations.

(continued)

Table 11. Continued

Documents	Date of Declaration	Department of Declaration	Relevant Provisions
Measures for the Administration of Data Security (Consultation Paper)	May 28, 2019	Cyberspace Administration of China	Article 28 The export of personal information shall be governed by the relevant provisions. Article 29 Where a domestic user accesses the domestic internet, the traffic shall not be routed overseas.
Information security technology—Security Impact Assessment Guide of Personal Information (Consultation Paper)	June 11, 2017	National Information Security Standardization Technical Committee	6.1 Influence assessment of classical personal information processing 6.1.1 Classical situations of assessment Generally, a security assessment of personal information shall be carried out concerning personal information processing before personal information is transferred overseas 6.1.2 Security assessment before personal information is transferred overseas Assessments should refer to the relevant requirements in the GB/T *Information Security Technology—Guidelines for Data Cross-Border Transfer Security Assessment*.

Information Security Technology—Guidelines for Data Cross-Border Transfer Security Assessment (Consultation Paper)	August 30, 2017	National Information Security Standardization Technical Committee	Full text.
Measures for the Security Assessment for Cross-border Transfer of Personal Information and Important Data (Consultation Paper)	April 11, 2017	Cyberspace Administration of China	Full text.

(*continued*)

Table 11. Continued

Documents	Date of Declaration	Department of Declaration	Relevant Provisions
Cybersecurity Law of the People's Republic of China (Order No. 53 of the President of the People's Republic of China)	November 7, 2016	Standing Committee of the National People's Congress	Article 12 The state shall protect the rights of citizens, legal persons, and other organizations to use the network in accordance with the law; promote the popularity of network access; provide better network services; provide the public with safe and convenient network services; and guarantee the orderly and free flow of network information in accordance with the law. Article 37 Personal information and important data collected and produced by critical information infrastructure operators during their operations within the territory of the People's Republic of China shall be stored within China. If it is necessary to provide such information and data to overseas parties due to business requirements, a security assessment shall be conducted in accordance with the measures developed by the national cyberspace administration, in conjunction with relevant departments of the State Council, unless it is otherwise prescribed by any law or administrative regulation.

Interim Measures for the Administration of Online Taxi Booking Business Operations and Services	July 27, 2016	Order of the Ministry of Transport, the Ministry of Industry and Information Technology, the Ministry of Public Security, the Ministry of Commerce, the State Administration for Industry and Commerce (revoked), the General Administration of Quality Supervision, Inspection and Quarantine (revoked), and the Cyberspace Administration of China	Article 27 An online taxi booking platform company shall observe the relevant state provisions on network and information security, and the personal information collected and business data formed shall be stored and used in the Chinese mainland, with a storage life of not less than two years. The aforesaid information and data may not be flowed out, unless otherwise as provided for in laws and regulations.

(*continued*)

Table 11. Continued

Documents	Date of Declaration	Department of Declaration	Relevant Provisions
Measures for the Administration of Population Health Information (for Trial Implementation)	May 5, 2014	National Health and Family Planning Commission (revoked)	Article 10: Entities in charge may not store population health information in any server outside China and may not host or lease any server outside China.
Regulation on the Administration of Credit Investigation Industry	January 21, 2013	State Council	Article 24: For information collected inside China, credit investigation institutions shall arrange, save, and process it inside China. To provide information to overseas organizations or individuals, credit investigation institutions shall abide by the laws, administrative regulations, and the relevant provisions of the supervisory and administrative department of credit investigation under the State Council.
Notice by the People's Bank of China Regarding the Effective Protection of Personal Financial Information by Banking Institutions	January 21, 2011	People's Bank of China	6. Personal financial information acquired inside China shall be stored, processed, and analyzed inside China. Unless otherwise provided by law, regulation, or the provisions of the People's Bank of China, no banking institution may provide personal financial information acquired inside China to any party outside China.

Source: Collected according to published documents.

International Discrepancies in the Realm of Data Governance

The international society has generally reached the consensus that data is a fundamental strategic resource which makes data governance one of the core topics in dialogues concerning global cyberspace governance. That the object of international data governance is gradually expanding from personal data to non-personal data suggests that cooperation and competition on data between countries keeps growing. A main obstacle to the international data rights legislation lies in failure to establish a global governance system and structure that satisfy various needs for data flow due to the divergence of regulations insofar as cross-border data flow is concerned. Under such (global) circumstances, it is urgent that a regulation system for cross-border data flow be promoted, and that the internal logical relationships and external support of regulations relating to data governance, data sovereignty, and the data economy be studied. By doing so, the national ability of data governance will be improved.

Long-arm jurisdiction in the realm of cross-border data flow. American and European countries apply an aggressive data sovereignty strategy to expand their power of law enforcement on cross-border data through long-arm jurisdiction. The *CLOUD Act* authorizes American regulators, law enforcement agencies, and the judiciary to acquire data stored overseas by American companies through internal legal procedures, and permits recognized and qualified foreign governments to obtain data from American companies for investigation and law enforcement purposes, thus negating data localization (Jingdong Law Research Institute 2018, p. 21). The adequacy rule in the *GDPR* and the *Council of Europe Convention for the Protection of Individuals with regard to Automatic Processing of Personal Data (Convention 108)* take localization of facility, or data, and cross-border data flow, as significant regulation objects.[39] However, emerging economies,

39 The nationality jurisdiction stipulated in Article 3 of *General Data Protection Regulation (GDPR)* exceeds the scope applicable in traditional regulations. It may bring challenges to the integrity of right to enforce the law owned by other sovereign states. The GDPR permits the conditional cross-border transfer of personal data through the following methods where: (1) the Commission has decided that a country, a territory, one or more specified sectors, or an international organization

including China and Russia, mainly apply a defensive approach to data sovereignty, addressing data governance and local law enforcement through data localization. Therefore, long-arm jurisdiction authorizes the acquisition of foreign data that is not available to traditional regional governance, but this deepens conflicts on data jurisdiction and executive power with other countries. The spread of long-arm jurisdiction will definitely affect the global data legislation structure. Its justification is that it provides a special method to regulate data flow, but it also brings new problems to the global governance system.

Divergence of rules on cross-border data flow. In order to effectively deal with data-related crimes, it is necessary to reform extraterritorial jurisdiction, but the precondition and guarantee to make it effective is to respect cyberspace sovereignty. As a component of the sovereignty principle, extraterritorial jurisdiction is in nature integrated with data sovereignty. Thus, any law that may infringe sovereignty, or has actual influence on it, should be assessed as to its reasonableness. The unilateral framework of data acquisition set up through the *CLOUD Act* places the power of the United States above the spirit of mutual respect, mutual trust, and collective governance, attacking the data sovereignty of countries with non-qualified governments. The European Union actively promotes free data flow between its member states to form a uniform digital market strategy. By contrast, it requires that an adequacy agreement be reached when transferring data from the EU to third countries, and only countries that meet the adequacy requirements will receive adequacy protection. All in all, an internationally agreed rule of cross-border data flow has yet to take shape and there is no global rule to regulate international divergence—all sovereign states

provides an adequate level of protection the transfer of European data to foreign countries, territories, or sectors does not require any specific authorization; (2) the methods of receiving approval of contractual articles, binding corporate rules, codes of conduct, and criteria of certification from the EU are applicable to organizations and companies; and (3) under specific derogation situations, such as the express consent of the data subject. It means that any institution, regardless of whether it is situated in Europe or not, may be subject to the regulation if it involves the processing of personal data on European citizens. Therefore, in reality, the regulation has become a worldwide law and long-arm jurisdiction.

strive for data jurisdiction on the basis of their own national benefit and, as a result, national governance on data sovereignty is further complicated.

International conflicts in global data governance. Data sovereignty represents the power and justification of a country to govern data relevant to itself, thus the issue of definition becomes key in the establishment of a global system with rules on data governance. "Internationally, more and more countries and regions have begun to build their data sovereignty systems from the legal perspective for the purpose of data governance." (He Bo 2017). The *CLOUD Act* of the US, the *GDPR* of the EU, and other data governance systems build up regulations and rules in line with their own interests to protect their own data resources from infringement, while broadening benefits by acquiring and governing more data resources overseas. With more and more emerging economies becoming involved with cyberspace governance, the traditional model of legislation, whereby European countries and the United States act as leaders, has been broken, and the creation of a new global legal system for data governance is forming. But a huge challenge has emerged during the process—finding a subtle balance between the compromise needed for a common standpoint and the protection of special interests needed by all member states. On the whole, the international legal system on data resources is in its formative stage. While a consensus has been reached with regard to some significant problems, a binding international law or a customary international legal system has yet to be created. Therefore, we should accelerate the improvement of rules and regulations relevant to data sovereignty at the state level and make full use of the experience and approach learned from cooperation with other countries in order to promote the establish of a data governance system in line with our interests while strengthening our international influence in this regard.

The International Value of Data Rights Legislation

It was made clear in the *Proposals for Formulating the 14th Five-Year Plan (2021–2025) for National Economic and Social Development and the Long-Range Objectives Through the Year 2035* that "we should actively joint the establishment of international rules and standards in digital domain." However, there are huge differences in the standpoints held by other countries, and it is impossible to form a coordinated system on global data governance in a short time. Hence, we should speed up legislation for data rights and determine which structural governance system of cross-border data flow is appropriate for China to become a digital economy power. The power to dominate rules will thus be strengthened.

Data rights are key to the integration of domestic and international law.

> From the perspective of the source of law, the globalization of law is actually the coordination and integration of domestic laws and international laws. (Gao Changfu 2008)[40]

Cross-border data flow has become a significant part of globalization and digitalization. National laws in sovereign states compete with one another, which has led to shaping international laws that are not dominated by any one country. Nowadays, though countries have reached a consensus on the application of international law in respect of cyberspace international relations and data protection, conflicts have been frequent when trying to establish principles and specific international regulations on data, especially when it comes to some existing laws and regulaitons in some developed western countries who are more likely to impose principles that protect their own interests, resulting in conflicts with developing countries, including China.

Data rights are characterized by private right attributes, public power attributes, and sovereign attributes. To be more specific, data rights consist of sovereign rights that embody the dignity of a state, public power that represents the public interest, and data rights that highlight personal well-being (Key Laboratory of Big Data Strategy 2019b, p. 160). We should build up international regulations, data rights systems, and the international legal

40 Domestic law, a counter concept of international law, is classified according to the establishment and applicable subject of law. It is made for a specific country and applicable in the scope of its own sovereignty. The subject of domestic law generally involves an individual or an organization, but countries could be included under this specific legal relationship (Gao Changfu 2008).

community through global cooperation to avoid mutual attack. From the perspective of global rules of legal development, various laws continue to integrate in the path to achieving global integration. What is more, data rights become a significant driver during the integration of domestic law and international law because of the positive interaction between them.

Data rights laws promote the establishment of a community with a shared future in cyberspace. The *Constitution of the People's Republic of China* expressly stipulates that "we should promote the building of a community with a shared future for mankind,"[41] indicating that the spirit of community with a shared future for mankind has become present in every aspect of the building of China's legal system, and serves as the fundamental spirit guiding China's foreign exchanges and participation in international governance in the new era. The idea of building a community with a shared future in cyberspace has taken shape as a new governance concept under the guidance of the spirit of a community with a shared future for mankind. The reform of the international system on data governance has now entered a key stage, and the building of a community with a shared future in cyberspace is growing into an international commonality that respects national data sovereignty under the framework of international law.

> Legalization of international relations attempts to safeguard rights and strengthen the duties of human community and promote the level of international governance legalization through the compliance and enforcement of international law by all countries. As a result, a community with a shared future for mankind with fairness, justice, reasonableness, and democracy will be built up. (Reidenberg 1993)

Aimed at redefining the rights and obligations concerning resource allocation in cyberspace, the data rights law embodies the ideology, values, and philosophy of the internet era. At present, the transformation of internet governance reflects an overall trend of reform in the development

41 It is pointed out in the preface of the *Constitution of the People's Republic of China (2018 Amendment)* that "China consistently carries out . . . peaceful coexistence, sticks to the path of peaceful development, and seeks a reciprocal win-win open strategy in developing diplomatic relations and economic and cultural exchanges with other countries, and promotes the building of a community with a shared future for mankind."

of international data governance and data rights law. An innovative solution proposed by China for international cyberspace governance represents China's wisdom in the promotion of the building of a community with a shared future in cyberspace.

Data rights law will promote the building of an integrated society and world order. Historically, the application of science and technology has boosted exchange and integration between societies, since the transmission of technology itself is a process of integration. However, at present, as the world is going through great changes not seen in the past century, conflicts have become unavoidable. They vary between the Internet and blockchains, from social order to ethical norms, and from digital economy to digital governance. Building a community with a shared future of cyberspace needs not only an integration of interests, but an agreement on common human values. As such, recognition cannot be reached in the short term; we have to consistently promote societal change in the digital era to realize this. As President Xi Jinping pointed out at the Conference on Dialogue of Asian Civilizations:

> each civilization is the crystallization of human creation, and each is beautiful in its own way. The aspiration for all that is beautiful is a common pursuit of humanity that nothing can hold back. Civilizations don't have to clash with each other; what is needed are eyes to see the beauty in all civilizations. (Xi Jinping 2019)

Integrating civilization is helpful to achieve value orientation for world order. Amid the attack of a new round of digital revolution, countries all over the world are thinking about and seeking systems and rules in the digital era; data rights law will push the building of a more reasonable and fairer digital societies. Thus, an effective solution to promote integration and order is to digitalize society; data rights law will become the key power of integration and reconstruction.

Bibliography

Allen, Anita L., and Richard C. Turkington. 2004. *Privacy Law: Cases and Materials*. Trans. Feng Jianmei, et al. Beijing: China Democracy and Legal System Publishing House.

Bodenheimer, Edgar. 2017. *Jurisprudence: The Philosophy and Method of the Law*. Trans. Deng Zhenglai. Beijing: China University of Political Law and Science Press.

Britz, Marjie. 2016. *Computer Forensics and Cyber Crime: An Introduction*. Trans. Dai Peng, et al. Beijing: Publish House of Electronics Industry.

Chen Bing, and Gu Dandan. 2020."Rethinking and Restructuring of the Rational Way of Data Sharing in Digital Economy: From the Perspective of Data Typing." *Journal of Shanghai University of Finance and Economics*, 3rd issue.

Cmnd. 7341. 1978. *The Lindop Report into Data Protection*. London: HMSO.

Fuster, Gloria González. 2014. *The Emergence of Personal Data Protection as a Fundamental Right of the EU*. New York: Springer International Publishing.

Gao Changfu. 2008. "A Brief Discussion on Legal Globalization: Also on the Interaction between International Laws and Domestic Laws." *Journal of Jishou University Social Sciences*, 3rd issue.

He Bo. 2017. "Legal Practice and Suggestions of Data Sovereignty." *Information Security and Communications Privacy*, 5th issue.

He, Yuan., ed. 2020. *Data Law*. Beijing: Peking University Press.

Hu Jianmiao. 2020. "How to Understand 'Legal Discrepancy'." *Study Times*, October 14.

Huang Xiaomin. 2020. "Analysis of Several Issues Regarding the Civil Protection for Personal Data in Big Data Age." *Legality Vision*, 8th issue.

Jiang Bixin. 2019. "Validity of Legal Acts: The Similarity and Difference between Public Law and Private Law." *Journal of Law Application*, 3rd issue.

Jingdong Law Research Institute. 2018. *European Union Data Charter: Commons and Guide to Practice on General Data Protection Regulation (GDPR)*. Beijing: Law Press China.

Key Laboratory of Big Data Strategy. 2019a. *Block Data 5.0: Theory and Method of Data Sociology*. Beijing: CITIC Press.

Key Laboratory of Big Data Strategy. 2019b. *Data Rights Law 1.0: Theoretical Basis*. Social Sciences Academic Press (China).

Key Laboratory of Big Data Strategy. 2020. *Data Rights Law 2.0: The System Construction*. Beijing: Social Sciences Academic Press.

Li Haiying. 2015. "The Value Orientation and Institutional Choice of the Cybersecurity Law." *China Information Security*, 9th issue.

Li, Hong. 2004. *The Essentials of Japanese Criminal Law*. Beijing: China Procuratorial Press.

Li Xiuqun. 2007. *The Study of the Horizontal Effect of Constitutional Rights*. Doctoral Thesis of China University of Political Science and Law.

Lian Yuming. 2017. *Big Data Blue Book: China Big Data Development Report No. 1*. Beijing: Social Sciences Academic Press.

Liang Shangshang. 2016. "Public Interest and the Interest Measurement Theory." *Tribune of Political Science and Law*, 6th issue.

Lin Min. 2017. "The Conflict and Coordination between the Right to Know and the Right to Privacy in Open Government Information." *Library and Information Science*, 2nd issue.

Liu Dexue. 2014. "An Analysis of the Conflicts among Rights in Respect of Personal Data Protection." In *Legal Protection of Personal Data: Perspectives from Mainland China, Hongkong, Macao, and Taiwan*, edited by Chen Haifan, et al. Beijing: Social Sciences Academic Press.

Liu Kaixiang. 2020. "An Analysis of the Boundary between Public Power & Private Rights in Civil Code and Its Meaning." *Social Governance Review*, 7th issue.

Liu, Xin. 2003. *Conflicts of Domestic laws and Legislative Countermeasure*. Beijing: China University of Political Law and Science Press.

Ma Changshan. 2019. "'The Fourth Generation of Human Rights' under the Background of Smart Society and Its Protection." *China Legal Science*, 5th issue.

Ma Changshan. 2020. "Governance Logic and Legalization of the Digital Society." *Science of Law (Journal of Northwest University of Political Science and Law)*, 5th issue.

Magna Carta. 2016.Trans. Chen Guohua. The Commercial Press.

Mo Jihong. 2007. "The Relationship between Constitution and Other Legal Forms." *Journal of Shanghai University of Political Science and Law*, 6th issue.

Nisida Noriyuku. 2007. *On Specific Provisions of Japanese Criminal Law*. Trans. Liu Mingxiang, et al. Beijing: China Renmin University Press.

Osuga Akira. 2001. *On the Right to Existence*. Trans. Lin Jie. Beijing: Law Press China.

Packer, Herbert. 1988. *The Limits of the Criminal Sanction*. Redwood City: Stanford University Press.

Reidenberg, Joel R. 1993. "Rules of the Road for Global Electronic Highways: Merging the Trade and Technical Paradigms." *Harvard Journal of Law and Technology*, 6.

Schwartz, Paul M., and Solove, Daniel J. 2011. "The PII Problem: Privacy and a New Concept of Personally Identifiable Information." *New York University Law Review*, 86th issue.

Tang Kaiyuan. 2005. "Balance between Keeping Government Information Public and Confidential". *Seeker*, 8th issue.

The German Criminal Code. Trans. Xu Jiusheng, et al. Beijing: Law Press China.

Wang Liming. 2007. "Contents of Rights to Privacy". *Zhejiang Social Sciences*, 3rd issue.

Wang Liming. 2009. "New Developments on Right to Privacy." *Renmin University Law Review*, 1st issue.

Wang Qianyun. 2019. "The Criminal Law System on Data Security Crime under the Background of Artificial Intelligence." *Legal Forum*, 2nd issue.

Wang Suyuan, and Ren Erxin. 1999. "Study on Conflict of Right and Disposition." *Journal of Lanzhou University*, 1st issue.

Wang Xiuxiu. 2016. "Personal Data Rights: The Legal Protection Mode from the Perspective of Society Interests." Academic Dissertation for PHD of East China University of Political Science and Law.

Wang Xuehui, and Zhao Xin. 2015. "On Public Law and Private Law Protection of Privacy: From the Perspective of 'Big Data Era' Personal Information Privacy." *Hebei Law Science*, 5th issue.

Wang Yan, and Ye Ming. 2019. "Conflicts and Balances between Personal Data and Privacy Protection in the Era of Artificial Intelligence." *Theory Journal*, 1st issue.

Wei Xiaowen. 2020. "Criminal Protection for Citizens' Personal Information." *Nan Fang Lun Kan*, 7th issue.

Wu, Changhong. 2014. *Research on the Criminal Protection for Personal Data*. Shanghai: Shanghai Academy of Social Science Press.

Wu Weiguang. 2009. "The Governance of Big Data Technology by Collaboration of Private Rights and Public Power." *Journal of Cyber and Information Law*, 1st issue.

Wu Weiguang. 2016. "Criticism on Private Protection for Personal Data Information under the Background of Big Data Technology." *Political Science and Law*, 7th issue.

Wu Xinghua. 2017. "Data Sharing and Privacy Protection." *Journal of Shandong University of Science and Technology*, 4th issue.

Xi Jinping. 2019. "Keynote Speech at the Opening Ceremony of the Conference on Dialogue of Asian Civilizations." *China Daily*, No. 5, May 15.

Yang Xueke. 2020. "Digital Constitutionalism." *Academic Dissertation for PHD of Jilin University*.

Yao, Yuerong. 2012. *Personal Data Protection under Constitutional Perspective*. Beijing: Law Press China.

Zhang Huilin. 2013. "On Restrictions to Private Rights for Public Interests: From the Perspective of Remedies for Over-Restricted Ownership." Academic Dissertation for PHD of Jilin University.

Zhang Qianfan, ed. 2012. *Constitutional Law*. Beijing: Peking University Press.

Zhao Hongrui, Wang Hongwei, Zhang Chunlei, and Wang Heyong. 2019. "Contents, Features and Strategies in Russian Latest Sovereignty Internet Law". September 11. <http://lawyeredu.pkulaw.cn/index.php?m=content&c=index&a=show&catid=11&id=1138>.

Zhao Yingjie, and Sun Ruidong. 2020. "Analysis on the Human Rights Attribute of Environmental Rights from the Perspective of Constitution." *Journal of North China University of Science and Technology (Social Science Edition)*, 3rd issue.

Zhao, Bingzhi, and Yu, Zhigang. 2004. *Comparative Study on Computer Crimes*. Beijing: Law Press China.

Zhou Hanhua. 2020. "Legal Orientation of Personal Information Protection." *Studies in Law and Business*, 3rd issue.

Zhou Youyong. 2005. *Research on the Basic Principles of Administrative Law (2nd Edition)*. Wuhan University Press.

Zhu Xinli, and Tang Mingliang. "The Two-Dimensional Structure of the Construction of Law-based Government: Legality, Optimality, and Their Interaction." *Zhejiang Academic Journal*, 6th issue.

CHAPTER 4

Institutional Innovations in Data Rights Legislation

Legislation coordinates social ideals and social reality, or to put it differently, legislation lies between the well-regulated state of society and the reality. This is particularly true for data rights legislation. It not only upholds and helps realize justice, but also creates order. By putting together data rights relations and data rights rules, data rights legislation realizes the effective combination, regulation, and protection of data rights relations, minimizes the cost of data use, and improves the efficiency of data resources allocation. From the perspective of realistic needs, data protection needs to go beyond the limits of private rights protection and beyond the principle of informed consent; balance between industrial development and social justice; create a more open, inclusive, and friendly data ecosystem; keep the rules dynamic and flexible; establish a support system that is more in line with our value pursuits through a bottom-up and distributed rule generation mechanism; and form a data protection regulation and legislation system that better meets realistic needs. In the exploration of data rights legislation we have been trying to create an institutional system that covers data management, data classification, data rights and interests, data evidence systems, and data ethics in the hope of contributing to relevant theoretical discussions and the improvement of relevant rules.

Data Management System

> The convergence of information technology with the economy and society has triggered a rapid growth of data, and data has become a fundamental strategic resource for a country. Big data is exerting an increasingly important impact on global production, circulation, distribution, and consumption activities, as well as on economic operation mechanisms, social lifestyles, and national governance capabilities. (State Council of the People's Republic of China 2015)

Facing the trend of huge amounts of data scattered at various sources and in diverse formats, institutional innovation in data management is key to the sustainable development of big data, and high-quality data development has become a must. It was proposed at the 19th CPC National Congress that efforts were to be made to build a digital China, while the *14th Five-Year Plan* emphasizes "establishing fundamental systems and standards for data property rights, data transaction and circulation, cross-border data transmission, and data security protection, and promoting the development and utilization of data resources." The realization of these set goals is predicated on having high-quality data. In this context, ensuring data quality through sound regulation, establishing data standards, and creating a data management system from the perspective of full life cycle data management will offer a scientific guide to, and play a leading role in, putting data to its best use.

Data Quality

"Data quality is the extent to which the attributes of the data meet explicit and implicit requirements when used under given conditions" (State Administration for Market Regulation and China National Standardization Management Committee 2018, p. 1). Data quality is the basis for the development and application of big data, and a symbol of how well the digital civilization develops.

> In order to maximize the value of big data and restrain its adverse effects, so that personal security, social security, and national security can be effectively maintained, it is imperative to build a data quality management system under the guidance of the basic principles of data protection. (Qi Aimin and Pan Jia 2015)

Data quality determines data value. The world is witnessing a global movement driven by data, technology, and social media—a movement with great potential to create more responsible, efficient, responsive, and effective governments and businesses, and spur economic growth. *The Open Data Charter*, signed by the leaders of the G8 member countries in June 2013, clearly defines the quality and quantity of data. On the one hand, high-quality data should be compiled; on the other hand, timely, comprehensive and accurate high-quality data should be made available.[1] Open

1 *The Open Data Charter*, Principle 2: Quality and Quantity. We recognize that governments and the public sector hold massive information that may be of interest to citizens. We also recognize the time it may take to produce high-quality data and the importance of consulting with each other and with countries and wider open data users to determine which data needs to be prioritized for release or improvement. We will release timely, comprehensive and accurate high-quality open data. As far as possible, the data will be in its raw, unmodified form and at the finest level of granularity available; ensuring that the information in the data is written in a clear and intelligible language for all to understand, although translation into other languages is not required under this *Charter*. We also need to ensure that data is adequately described so that consumers have enough information to understand data's strengths, weaknesses, analytical limitations and security requirements, how to process the data, and release data early enough to allow users to provide feedback—and, thereafter, make revisions to ensure that the highest standards of open data quality are met.

data has become the core of this global movement, and data quality has become the key to the effectiveness of open data. In July 2020, Article 57 of *the Data Regulations of Shenzhen Special Economic Zone (Consultation Paper)* issued by the Shenzhen Justice Bureau stipulates: Market entities of the data factor shall establish and improve the organizational structure and self-evaluation mechanism of data governance, organize and carry out data governance activities, strengthen data quality management, and promote the realization of data value. The value of big data is based mainly on the integration of high-quality data; isolated data is of no practical value. By developing a scientific and reasonable data quality management standards, we can realize the correlative fusion of data to maximize its value.

Current data quality assessment mechanism. International organizations such as the International Monetary Fund, as well as countries such as the United Kingdom and Sweden attach great importance to data quality management legislation. In general, data quality management legislation at the international level can be divided into three types: special laws and regulations for data quality management; normative documents; and general legislation that provides for the content of data quality management. For example, the International Monetary Fund's Data Quality Assessment Framework and General Data Dissemination System have provided a comprehensive framework for data quality assessment and management. China's data quality management legislation also includes the same three types of law, among which normative documents form the mainstay, with the regulation of data quality management usually found in data quality industrial standards; for example, the *Financial Data Security – Guidelines for Data Security Classification*; *Guidelines on Classification and Gradation of Industrial Data (Trial)*; *Guidelines on Classification and Gradation of Securities and Futures Industry Data*; and *Guidelines on Data Governance for Banking Financial Institutions*.

Building data quality assurance mechanisms. In June 2018, the State Administration for Market Regulation and China National Standardization Management Committee released *Information Technology – Evaluation Indicators for Data Quality*, which clearly points out that data traits include six aspects: normalization, integrity, accuracy, consistency, time-efficiency, and accessibility (See Table 12). First, normalization. Normalization refers to the degree to which the data conforms to data standards, data models, business rules, metadata, and authoritative reference data. Among them, the data standards refer to the rules and benchmarks in the naming, definition, structure, and the value range of the data; the data model is a graphical and textual representation of the analysis, which identifies the data that organizations need to fulfill their mission, functions, goals, objectives, and strategies, as well as manage and evaluate the organization. Metadata refers to data about data or data elements (which may include its data description), as well as data about data ownership, access rights, storage paths, and volatility. Authoritative reference data is the authoritative reference source. Second, integrity. Integrity refers to the degree to which a data element is given a numeric value as required by prevailing data rules. Third, veracity. Veracity refers to the degree to which the data accurately represents the true value of the object it describes. Fourth, consistency. Consistency refers to the degree to which the data does not contradict data used in other particular contexts. Fifth, time-validity. Time-validity refers to the accuracy of the data over time. Sixth, accessibility. Accessibility refers to the degree to which the data can be accessed (State Administration for Market Regulation and the China National Standardization Management Committee 2018, p. 1). The object of constructing a data quality assurance mechanism is to normalize and guide the overall life cycle of data according to the above six characteristics, and realize the legalization of data quality management through a data quality evaluation mechanism.

Table 12. Data Quality Evaluation Indicators

Traits	Indicator	Description
Normalization	Data Standards	Measurements of data conforming to data standards Note 1: When evaluating data quality, it is necessary to collect the standards followed in naming, creating, defining, updating and archiving data, including international standards, national standards, industry standards, local standards, or related regulations Note 2: As important as, or even more important than, data archiving, the destruction of old data in a complete data rule generally has a more detailed and enforceable regulation
	Data Models	Measurements of data conforming to data models Note 1: A data model is a means of visually describing the structure of organized data and is a specification for data representation Note 2: When evaluating data quality, it is necessary to check whether there is a clear and understandable data model definition its organization of the data
	Metadata	Measurements of data conforming to the metadata definition Note: Metadata standards, description, or characterization of other data to make it easier to retrieve or use information. When evaluating data quality, check whether a scrutable metadata document is provided

Table 12. Continued

Traits	Indicator	Description
	Business Rules	Measurements of data conforming to business rules Note 1: Business rules are authoritative principles or guidelines used to describe business interactions and establish rules for the results and integrity of actions and data behaviors Note 2: Evaluating data quality requires checking for the existence of business rules for good archiving
	Authoritative Reference Data (Authoritative Reference Source)	Reference data is a collection or classification of values used as a reference for systems, application databases, processes, reports, transaction records, and master records Note: Reference data lists need to be collected when evaluating data quality
	Security Codes	Security codes are rules for security and privacy, including data permission management and data desensitization processing, etc.
Integrity	Data Element Integrity	According to the requirements of business rules, the degree of assignment of data elements in the data set that should be assigned
	Data Record Integrity	According to the requirements of business rules, the degree of assignment of data records in the data set that should be assigned

(continued)

Table 12. Continued

Traits	Indicator	Description
Accuracy	Correctness of Data Content	Whether the data content is expected data
	Compliance of Data Format	Whether the data format (including data type, value range, data length, data accuracy, etc.) meets the expected requirements
	Data Repetition Rate	A measure of unexpectedly duplication for a specific field, record, file, or data set
	Data Uniqueness	A measure of the uniqueness of a specific field, record, file, or data set
	The Occurrence Rate of Dirty Data	A measure of invalid data outside the correct field, record, file, or data set
Consistency	Consistency of the Same Data	The consistency of the data when the same data is stored in different locations or used by different applications or users. When data changes, the same data stored in different locations is modified synchronously
	Consistency of Linked Data	Check the consistency of the linked data according to the consistency constraint rules
Time-efficient	Correctness Based on Time Quantum	The degree to which the number of records or frequency distribution based on the date range meets the business requirements
	Correctness Based on Time Point	The degree to which the number of records or frequency distribution or latency based on a timestamp meets the business requirements
	Time Sequence	The relative timing relationship between data elements of the same entity in the data set
Accessibility	Access	Accessibility of data when needed
	Availability	The availability of the data within the set effective life cycle

Source: State Administration for Market Regulation and the China National Standardization Management Committee 2018.

Data Standards

Standards are like a shared language of the world. Big data standards are the "license" that we use to enter the international big data market. Whoever sets the standards has the greatest influence, and whoever masters the standards will take the commanding height. General Secretary Xi Jinping emphasized that it is an important and urgent task to strengthen standardization work and implement a standardization strategy. Standards promote innovation and lead to progress. As one of the basic guarantees for the sound development of the big data industry, data standards determine the quality of development and only high standards can bring high-quality results. For the sound and orderly development of the big data industry, we urgently need to establish a set of sound reference standards. We should strive to increase recognition for our big data standards in the international arena, vigorously implement a standardization strategy, accelerate data standardization development, further promote the integration of all kinds of standards, and endeavor to take a dominant role in developing big data international standards through relevant explorations. It is only by these efforts that we can occupy the commanding height in global data resource allocation, keep an upper-hand position in the rapidly changing world of international data competition, and lead the development of the digital revolution.

Current situation of data standards system construction. In July 2015, the General Office of the State Council issued *Several Opinions on Strengthening the Service for and Supervision of Market Entities through Big Data Application* and, in August 2015, the State Council issued the *Action Plan to Promote Big Data Development*, both of which put forward explicit requirements for establishing a data standard system.[2]

2 *Several Opinions on Strengthening the Service for and Supervision of Market Entities through Big Data Application* affirmed the important role of big data in market supervision and services, and proposed the division of major tasks to "Establishing a big data standard system, and studying and formulating relevant big data; accelerate the establishment of technical standards for government information collection, storage, disclosure, sharing, use, quality assurance

> [B]ased on the industrial and regional characteristics of big data development, many regions have set up their own local technical committees for big data standardization, to gradually advance the development of local big data standards in order to form a safe, reliable, standardized, convenient and efficient local big data standard system, and serve the development of the local big data industry. (Big Data Standards Working Group of National Technical Committee for Information Technology Standardization and China Electronics Standardization Institute 2020)

For example, provinces such as Guizhou, Guangdong, and Shandong have respectively set up provincial big data standardization technical committees; Inner Mongolia has established its Standardization Technical Committee on Cloud Computing and Big Data; Shanxi Province has its Standardization Technical Committee on Cybersecurity and Big Data Information Technology; and Shanghai set up the Technical Committee of Standardization for Public Data. Relying on these provincial standardization technical committees, each region has developed its own local standards. For example, Guizhou Province has more than ten local standards on government data, such as *Government Data – Open Data Core Metadata*; *Government Data – Operating Instructions on Data Opening*;

---

and safety management; guide the establishment of standards for information sharing and exchange between enterprises." *The Action Plan to Promote Big Data Development* systematically deployed our country's big data development work, introducing a standard and normative system in the policy mechanism. The promotion of the big data industry standard system accelerated the establishment of data and statistical standards systems for government departments, public institutions, and other public institutions, and promoted the formulation and implementation of key common standards, such as data collection, government data opening, index standards, classification catalogs, exchange interfaces, access interfaces, data quality, data transactions, technical products, security and confidentiality—and accelerated the establishment of a big data market transaction standard system to carry out standard verification and application pilot demonstrations; establish a standard compliance evaluation system, giving full play to the role of standards in cultivating the service market; improving service capabilities; supporting industry management; and actively participating in the formulation of relevant international standards.

and *Government Data – Guidelines on Data Classification and Gradation.* Focusing on the supply-side structural reform of agriculture in the Shandong Province, Shandong Province has developed ten local standards for agricultural big data, which include: the *Agricultural Big Data Standard System* and the *Agricultural Big Data – Basic Requirements for Data Processing.* Based on the cloud platform construction of "Cloud-on-Northern Xinjiang, the Inner Mongolia Autonomous Region developed local standards such as: *Guidelines for Public Big Data Security Management*; *Big Data Platform – Norms for Data Access Quality*, and *Standards for the Compilation of Big Data Standard System* so as to promote government data sharing and exchange, using high-quality public data.

The path of innovation in the data standard system. A sound standards system is the inherent requirement of the sustainable development and a sign of the maturity of data quality management. *Guide for standardization, Part 1: Standardization and related activities – General vocabulary* (GB/T 20000.1–2002) defines "standardization" as follows: "In order to obtain the best order within the established range and promote common benefits, establish common use and repeated use clauses for actual or potential problems, as well as activities like the compilation, publication, and application of documents." Thus, the construction of a data standard system requires the development of a series of standards, such as data collection, data processing, data circulation, data pricing, open access to data so as to form a scientific and efficient data order, and the promotion of the common interests of relevant subjects to maximize the political, economic, and social benefits derived from access to data. The industrial foundation of the digital economy is constantly growing, and the internationalization of some companies is gradually deepening. Thus, the construction of a data standard system is required to break through single "localization" strategies so as to provide a more diversified data flow mechanism for enterprises to realize global development and effectively balance the interests of security, development, and openness.

Full Life Cycle Data Management Framework

The premise of data value realization is the correct understanding, management, and utilization of data throughout its life cycle.

> In 2014, the European Commission released the *Data-driven Economy Strategy*, focusing on an in-depth study of innovation mechanisms based on the big data value chain and proposing to vigorously promote the "Data Value Chain Strategic Plan" to generate value at different stages of the data value chain through a coherent EU ecosystem with data at its core. The concept of the data value chain is the life cycle of data, from data generation, verification and further processing to the utilization and reuse of new products and services. (Big Data Standards Working Group of National Technical Committee for Information Technology Standardization and China Electronics Standardization Institute)

"By comparing some typical data life cycles at home and abroad, we found that multiple life cycle models include core links such as data collection, data processing, and data utilization" (Chu Jiewang and Xia Li 2020). Based on the core links as well as the characteristics of data, i.e., systematic generation process, cyclic organizational process, and accumulated data resources, full life cycle data management can be divided into six links: data collection, data processing, data preservation, data sharing, data analysis, and data reuse. Among them, data collection mainly includes demand confirmation and data acquisition; data processing mainly includes data screening, data reconstitution, and data integration; data preservation mainly includes data archiving, data storage, and data maintenance; data sharing mainly includes open access to data and data dissemination; data analysis mainly includes value assessments, time-validity assessments, and comprehensive value judgments; and data reuse mainly includes the reuse and regeneration of data.

The above six links and their sub-links constitute a closed data life-cycle management framework. It is a loop that goes around each data utilization subject. Effective data collection and data sharing is the most important link in the full life-cycle management of data and has important practical significance in promoting the safe and free flow of data among different subjects and fully releasing and utilizing the value of data.

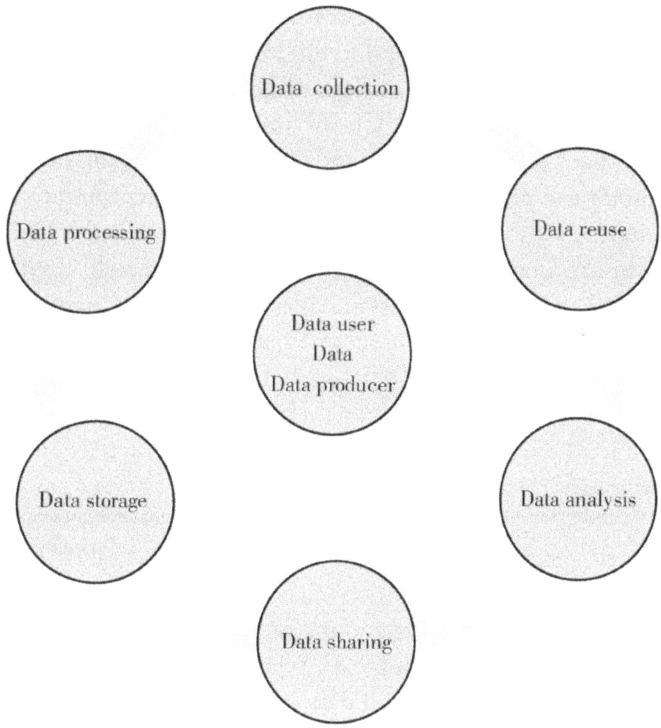

Figure 3. Data Overall Life-cycle Management Framework

Data Classification System

Data rights legislation should not only fully reflect the characteristics of the digital era and actively respond to the challenges brought by the recent changes to the law, it should make special institutional arrangements for products of the digital era. The data classification system is a system that allows the law to stipulate differentiated data protection frameworks and policies for different types of data according to the specific requirements of the regulators. A data classification system will play an important role in supporting and promoting the realization of the goals of market-based pricing for the data factor, autonomous and orderly data flow, and efficient and fair allocation of data resources, as well as solving the problems of data ownership confirmation, data security, and privacy protection. Classifying data from the perspective of the data subject, data processing, and data protection, and determining the methods and principles of data classification according to application scenarios, as well as determining the strategies and measures for data classification and protection, will help build a rights system that can effectively protect the rights and interests of individuals while fully ensuring free data circulation and giving full play to the advantages of the digital economy.

Significance of Data Classification

"From the perspective of connection, data grading and data classification are both for data protection, which is usually referred to as classification-based data protection, because grading can also be understood as a form of data classification" (Liu Yun 2020). Scientific and reasonable data classification is important for sound data grading. Proper data grading ensures the highest possible level of protection for the most important and valuable data, while reducing unnecessary cost concerning compliance (Li Songtao and Xie Zongxiao 2019).

> In the context of social transformation, economic transition, and the iterative development of science and technology, new interests and rights demands related to data have sprung up, and different data rights subjects have put forward new claims and caused changes to the legal system for data protection. (Li Xiaoyu 2019)
>
> Subjects who are "data generators" have gradually realized the necessity or importance of personal data protection, while subjects who are "data controllers" or "data users" experience both the importance of data and the pressure of privacy protection in the processing of personal data. There is not always harmony between these two categories of data subjects and the value of personal data protection or fair use will be more evident when the two pursuit different or even exactly opposite interests. (Zhang Wenliang 2018)

Therefore, the classification of data is a basic requirement for the legal guarantee of personal data protection, which is an important measure to promote the healthy development of the digital economy and a practical need to maintain a sound digital ecology.

Current Status of Data Classification

Article 19 of the Data Security Law (Draft) states:

> The State protects data by staging and classification according to its importance in socio-economic development, and the degree of harm to national security, public interests or the legitimate rights and interests of citizens and organizations caused by tampering, destruction, disclosure, illegal acquisition or use of data.

In reality, the basis for data classification varies, from compliance requirements such as statutes/standards, to usefulness, value, and ownership of data assets, and to the sensitivity level and risk profile of the data. In summary, the classification of data can be explored from the perspectives of the data subjects, data processing, and data protection.

Data Classification from the Perspective of Data Subjects

From the perspective of data subjects, data can be divided into personal data, corporate data, public data, and data from other organizations. Personal data is all data that can be used to identify a person. This can include, but is not limited to, data regarding all aspects of a person's physical, psychological, intellectual, family, social, economic, and cultural facets. This data not only matters to personal rights, such as reputation, health status, criminal records, and social circles, but also matters for property rights when it comes to writings and property. "Personal data takes 'identifiability' as a constitutive element in determining its content." To protect the rights of a person, that data needs to be linked and trace to a specific individual; in legal terms this process of associated tracking is called "identification" (Li Yang and Li Xiaoyu 2019a). For this reason, both common law and civil law systems use "identifiability" as the criterion for determining personal data. However, there are some differences between legal systems.[3] Article 4(1) of the EU *General Data Protection Regulation* states that: "'Personal data' means any information relating to an identified or identifiable natural person (data owner), who can be identified directly or indirectly, in particular by reference to such identifiers as name, ID number, location data, and online identification, or by reference to one or more elements specific to that natural person, such as physical, physiological, and genetic attributes; psychological, economic, and cultural features; or social identity." The definition of personal data adopts a broader standard, combining direct identification and indirect identification. Influenced by this, the mainstream view of Chinese academic circles holds that the substantive standard for the identification of personal data is "identifiability" (Gao Fuping and Wang Wenxiang 2017; Cheng Xiao 2018; Yu Chong 2018). The legislation also adopts a broad and vaguely determined standard of "direct + indirect identifiability" for personal data.[4]

3 In the United States, a country that advocates freedom of behavior and has the most developed network data industry, personal data is defined in a restrictive manner by lawmakers and judges in terms of legislation, interpretation, and application, emphasizing the associative characteristics of personal data. Different from the United States, Germany, which is deeply influenced by Immanuel Kant's philosophy that "man is the purpose," advocates the supremacy of personal dignity and personal freedom. Thus, in Germany, granting natural persons the right to self-determination with respect to personal data is aimed at protecting personal dignity and freedom. If individuals are unable to decide whether their data and information can be collected, stored, and used by others at their own will, human dignity and personal freedom will become empty words. Accordingly, the level of protection of rights to personal data, which has constitutional significance, should take precedence over the protection of economic interests.

4 For example: Article 76 (5) of *the Cybersecurity Law*, adopted in 2016; *the Decision on Strengthening the Protection of Network Information*, passed by the Standing Committee of the National People's Congress in 2012; and Article 4 of *the Regulations on the Protection of Telecommunication and Internet Users' Personal Information* all adopt identifiability as the criterion to define personal data. Among them, the data that can directly identify a specific natural person includes his/her

"Corporate data refers to the data actually controlled and used by a corporate, including commercial data such as financial data and operational data, as well as user data legally collected and used by the corporate" (Shi Dan 2019). The former belongs to non-public commercial data, which is mainly included in the category of transaction secrets for protection, while the latter belongs to commercial data, for which there is no clear stipulation in the law. As such, there remains a lacuna in the law. On the whole,

> Corporate data is data that is scarce and can bring economic benefits to the corporate in the form of symbols or codes. Different from traditional physical objects, corporate data is non-material and intangible, which needs to rely on a certain carrier to exist and has the characteristics of objective non-exclusiveness and non-losing of use. (Li Yang and Li Xiaoyu 2019b)

"Different from the attributes of strong personality rights, weak property rights of personal data, and the social attributes of public data, corporate data embodies the attributes of strong property rights and weak personality rights" (Li Yang and Li Xiaoyu 2019a).

According to Locke's "labor property theory"[5] and Bentham's "utilitarianism theory," substantial investment by a corporation may be regarded as a basic element of corporate data. Specifically, the labor property theory holds that people can claim property rights to things that are mixed with their own labor, and that people are entitled to the benefits of their actions (Locke, translated by Ye Qifang and Zhai Jounong 2009, pp. 17–19). Corporate data is data with economic value generated by a substantial investment, including human, material, and financial resources. Other

---

personal name, ID card number, fingerprints, genetics, social security number, and portrait data. Data that can indirectly identify a specific natural person includes gender, age, occupation, education, marriage, interests, hobbies, sexual preference, habits, and financial status.

5 The labor property theory is usually used to justify the protection of ownership of physical property and, since corporate data is an intangible object, the labor property theory cannot explain the justification for the protection of corporate data rights and interests. However, the concept of a romantic creator behind the labor property theory is helpful to understand the rationality for the protection of corporate data rights and interests.

competitors or individuals should pay reasonable consideration when using corporate data, otherwise the value concept of fairness will be violated. Utilitarianism focuses not only on the interests of a specific individual right holder, but also on the interests of the general majority (Li Wei 2019).[6] In the digital age, all parties in the market are eager for corporate data. If all types of free-riding behaviors are permitted in market competition, the enthusiasm for corporate investment will be undermined, with the result that the supply of corporate data products and the benefits they bring to the entire society will reduce.

"Public data is non-exclusive and non-competitive public goods in nature" (Li Xiaoyu 201), and the associated interest is essentially collective interest (Zeng Junping 2006).[7] Public data is a general term for all kinds of data resources acquired nationwide through legal procedures by the state or by state organs on behalf of the state in the course of performing their duties in accordance with the law and administrative regulations so as to meet the management or other needs of social public utilities. The massive public data resources created during the continuous aggregation of data does not only profoundly affect the business ecosystem, but also promotes innovation in the government's social and public utility management model (Wang Yongqi 2019).

> Public data involves all aspects of social production and life. Although managed by the government or more specifically some relevant authorities on behalf of the state, it is open to the public for inquiry, and compared with personal data, it is public in nature as a kind of resource, not privacy, not exclusive, and integral. (Wu Changhai and Chang Zheng 2017)

The use of public data differs from the use of physical objects in that the use and disposal of the latter can lead to both the destruction of the objects and the payment of consideration by the user; while the use of the

6 Some scholars also call it the "principle of greatest happiness."

7 Collective interest means that there is a common opportunity to profit within the group—a common space of interest. In terms of public data resources, individuals, enterprises, or other organizations, members of social groups are free to use public data, reflecting the collective view of individualism.

former, an abstract object, does not lead to the destruction of the data. In other words, the non-competitive nature of public data as a public good means that the marginal cost of incremental consumption is zero, and it should be made available free of charge (Li Xiaoyu 2019). From the perspective of constitutive elements, public data should possess three aspects: openness, sharing, and free use. Openness means that public data should be public and that any subject may have unrestricted access to the data. Openness provides a prerequisite for the use of public data, and excludes non-public, confidential data from public data. Sharing indicates that public data is essentially a public resource that cannot be exclusively owned by individuals or institutions, but should be shared by all members of society. Free use emphasizes the right of each subject to use public data reasonably, according to his/her own will, and enjoy the benefits of public data brought about by data development.

"Other organizations" is a long-standing and widely used term in China's legislation, which can refer to, or not refer to, a subject in a legal sense. When it does not refer to a legal subject, it is not really a legal term (See Table 13). When it does refer to a legal subject, it has a clear definition as a legal term.

> Since 1989, when *the Administrative Procedure Law* juxtaposed "other organizations" with "citizens" and "legal persons," and especially since Article 40 of the *Opinions of the Supreme People's Court on Several Issues Concerning the Application of the Civil Procedure Law of the People's Republic of China* clearly defines the definition and types of other organizations. The word "other organization" gradually formed into a specific term and expression with fixed meaning in the sense of a subject, that is, it is specially used to refer to the third type of subject other than natural person and legal person. (Tan Qiping 2017)

According to Article 52 of the *Judicial Interpretation of the Civil Procedure Law*, "other organizations" refers to organizations that have been legally established which have certain organizational structures and properties, but do not have corporate capacity. Based on this, "other organizations," within the meaning of the subject, should have the right to data ownership, and the data of other organizations should be regarded as a type of data from the perspective of the data subject.

Table 13. "Other Organizations" as Non-Subject in Current Laws

Serial Number	Legal Name	Article	Usage
1	Archives Law	Article 6, 7, 11, 13	Organs, groups, enterprises, institutions, and other organizations
2	Asset Appraisal law	Article 12	Relevant state organs or other organizations
3	The Charity Law	Article 61, 70	Charities and other organizations
4	Law on Promoting the Transformation of Scientific and Technological Achievements	Article 17, 24, 26, 27, 39	Enterprises or other organizations. Enterprises, research and development institutions, institutions of higher learning, and other organizations; as well as State, local enterprises, and institutions, as well as other organizations or individual
5	The Food Safety Law	Article 140	Social groups or other organizations
6	Law on the Protection of Rights and Interests of the Elderly	Article 7, 35, 37	State organs, social groups, enterprises, and other organizations; charities and other organizations; professional services and other organizations
7	The Espionage Act	Article 7	Organs, groups, and other organizations
8	Environment Protection Law	Article 36	State organs and other organizations using financial funds
9	Law on the Protection of Consumer Rights and Interests	Article 45	Social groups, other organizations, and individuals
10	Trademark Law	Article 3	Groups, associations, or other organizations

Table 13. Continued

Serial Number	Legal Name	Article	Usage
11	Agriculture Law	Article 13, 44	Enterprises, research institutions, and other organizations; supply and marketing cooperatives, rural collective economic organizations, farmers' professional cooperative economic organizations, other organizations, and individuals
12	Public Security administration Punishment Law	Article 52	State organs, people's organizations, enterprises, institutions, or other organizations
13	Road Traffic Safety Law	Article 6	Organs, troops, enterprises, institutions, social groups, and other organizations
14	The People's Mediation Law	Article 34	Townships, streets, social groups, or other organizations
15	Statistics Act	Article 7, 21, 41	State agencies, enterprises, and other organizations, as well as individual businesses and individuals; enterprises, institutions, or other organizations
16	Patent Law	Article 10, 18, 19	Foreigners, foreign enterprises, or other foreign organizations
17	Circular Economy Promotion Law	Article 15, 25, 37	Sellers or other organizations; state organs and other organizations using financial funds; waste recycling enterprises and other organizations
18	Anti-drug Law	Article 3, 16	State organs, social groups, enterprises, institutions, and other organizations

(*continued*)

Table 13. Continued

Serial Number	Legal Name	Article	Usage
19	Popularization of Science and Technology Law	Article 3	State organs, armed forces, social organizations, enterprises and institutions, rural grassroots organizations, and other organizations
20	The Accounting Law	Article 2	State organs, social groups, companies, enterprises, institutions, and other organizations

Source: Tan Qiping 2017, 4th issue.

Data Classification from the Perspective of Processing

From the perspective of data processing, data can be divided into two types: native data and derivative data, according to the way the data content is generated. Native data is data that does not depend on existing data and is generated through legitimate recording and storage. "The generation of native data starts from having nothing, and being recorded and stored is an important technical characteristic of native data" (Li Yanan 2018).

> Single pieces of native data are not included in the discussion. Data as a kind of resource should be what we usually refer to as big data. Native data includes data with and without economic value. As datasets accumulate and quantitative accumulation triggers qualitative change, their availability and economic value gradually exceed those of personal data. (Zhu Mingjie 2019)

"Derivative data refers to systematic, readable, and good-to-use data produced through processing, computing, and aggregation based on algorithms after native data is recorded and stored. This may include data on using habits, shopping preferences, credit records, etc." (Yang Lixin 2016). Derivative data has value in its use and exchange, and is the object of the data trading market. Compared with native data, derivative data are featured by processing, computing, aggregation, and the like. In reality, it can be tricky to distinguish between native data and derivative data. Even though Article 1038 of the *Civil Code* clearly provides that: "An information processor shall not disclose or tamper with the personal information he collects and stores, and shall not illegally provide to others the personal information of a natural person without the latter's consent, unless the information, after being processed, cannot be used to identify any specific individual and cannot be restored to its original status." However, with the rapid development of digital technology, the data acquisition ability of data controllers and data processors has greatly improved, and it is difficult to define whether a certain piece of native or derivative data belongs to an individual, a data controller, or a data processor. If such data is attributed solely to individuals, the allocation of data resources may be hampered by a cumbersome and costly definition process, resulting in a loss of social welfare. If it is attributed to the data controllers and data processors who obtained the data, it will be prone to problems such as data monopoly and violation of personal privacy (Zhang Liangliang and Chen Zhi 2020).

Data Classification from the Perspective of Protection

From the perspective of data protection, data can be divided into general data, important data, privacy data, sensitive/desensitized data, trade secret data, and national security data. Specifically, *Directive 95/46/EC/ on the Protection of Individuals With Regard to the Processing of Personal Data and on the Free Movement of Such Data*, adopted by the EU in 1995, and the *General Data Protection Regulation*, adopted in 2016, set out more detailed provisions on the criteria and scope of personal data, making the division of general data and sensitive data[8] (See Table 14).

8 The criteria for defining sensitive personal data: The preface and specific provisions of *Directive 95* do not mention the criteria for defining sensitive data, but the EU privacy protection supervisory authority, the Article 29 Working Group, released a report stating that the sensitive data referred to in *Directive 95* involves basic rights, such as privacy and the right to be free from discrimination. Article 51 of the preamble to the *General Data Protection Regulation* states that personal sensitive data is "particularly sensitive to the basic rights and freedoms of individuals," and the processing of this data may cause "material risks" to basic rights and freedoms. In

> The special legal system for trade secret data is the product of the industrial revolution and the rapid development of the market economy. Common law countries represented by the United Kingdom and the United States have formed special sector laws on trade secrets as early as the 18th century. (Xiang Liling and Shi Shangyuan 2005)

The *Regulations of the People's Republic of China on the Disclosure of Government Information*, adopted on April 3, 2019, made specific provisions on the contents of information involving state secrets, business secrets, and matters of personal privacy which needed to be controlled.[9]

---

general, it is defined by its impact on fundamental rights and freedoms. As for the delimiting of the scope of sensitive personal data, *Directive 95* considers that sensitive data includes data of "racial or ethnic origin, political views, religious or philosophical beliefs, trade union membership, personal medical treatment or sexual life." With the development of the economy and the change of the public's understanding of the position of sensitivity, the *General Data Protection Regulations* expanded the scope of personal sensitive data to include sensitive data on "racial or ethnic origin, political views, religious or philosophical beliefs, trade union membership, genetics, biometrics, personal medical care, sexual life, sexual orientation." Compared with *Directive 95*, the EU has added "genetic data, biometric data and sexual orientation data" to the list of prohibited data, taking into account the development of science and technology and the change of public attitudes toward data sensitivity.

9 Article 14 of *the Regulations of the People's Republic of China on the Disclosure of Government Information* stipulates that government information defined as a state secret according to the law, government information prohibited from disclosure by laws and administrative regulations, and government information that may endanger national security, public security, economic security, or social stability after disclosure shall not be disclosed. Article 15 stipulates that administrative organs shall not disclose government information involving trade secrets and personal privacy that may harm the legitimate rights and interests of third parties. However, if a third party agrees to disclosure, or the administrative agency believes that non-disclosure will have a significant impact on public interests, it shall be disclosed.

Table 14. Main Types and Concrete Contents of Sensitive Personal Data in the EU

The Main Types	Concrete Content
Gene data	Personal data related to the heritage or genetics of a natural person, which may provide unique information about the physiology or health of a natural person, especially the unique information that can be obtained through the analysis of a biological sample of a natural person
Biological identification data	Based on special technology to process the personal data of natural persons related physical, physiological, or behavioral characteristics, which can identify or determine the unique identification of a natural person, such as a facial image or fingerprint data
Health-related data	Includes health care related services, such as disease, disability, disease risk, medical history, clinical treatment, or the physiological or biomedical status of the data subject, and tests carried out by doctors or other health professionals, hospitals, medical devices, or in vitro diagnostics
Other	Political views, religious or philosophical beliefs, status of union membership, sexual life, sexual orientation, racial or ethnic background

Source: Based on publicly available information.

Classification-based Data Protection

On the basis of data classification, different objectives are set for the protection of different categories of data. According to its identifiability, sensitivity, scale, and uncontrollability, data can be assigned different sensitivity levels (See Table 15). First, the principle of identifiability. Except for legitimate purposes that indeed require the identification of a specific data subject, data of a highly identifiable subjects should be de-identified before use so that it will not be used to identify the specific data subject without the help of additional data. Unless otherwise agreed upon with the data subject, data processing should cover only the fewest types and the smallest quantity of data as required to satisfy the data owner's authorized consent. For data with identifiability, ownership should be confirmed and no use or transfer of the same shall be permitted without authorization. Second, sensitivity. Data is sensitive, and for very sensitive data desensitization should be performed before use[10] so as to ensure reliable protection. Data should be encrypted for both storage and transmission in order to ensure confidentiality. For more sensitive data, special assessments should be conducted for the possible negative impact on owners should there be data leakage. If certain data induces a serious negative impact it should put under more careful protection, and regular assessment should be carried out for security. Third, scale. The large amounts of data stored in a system should first be classified, and then protected based on classification results. High-level data should go through integrity checks to ensure no damage has occurred during storage and transmission. High-quality data should be backed up regularly, and the validity of the backups should be verified. Fourth, uncontrollability. For data flows that may involve a change in the security protection level, the data security protection capabilities of each organization concerned should be fully assessed to ensure continuity and consistency of security protection measures during that flow. For access and acquisition by users, a more fine-grained access control, based on user attributes and behaviors, should be set in big data application scenarios. For data with a wide range of users and frequent flow, third-party security supervision shall be carried out frequently, and government supervision should be engaged when necessary (Gao Lei 2019).

10 Desensitization is similar to de-identification, but it pays more attention to privacy protection.

Table 15. Sensitivity Level and Method of Data Classification

Principles of Data Classification	Level of Importance	Criteria
The principle of identifiability	Confidential	Easy to identify a specific data owner without the need for additional information
	Sensitive	Easier to identify a specific data subject with only a small amount of related information is required
	Common	Difficult to identify a specific data owner and requires a large amount of correlating information (High, Middle, or Low)
The principle of sensitivity	Confidential	Information leakage will cause serious damage to the interests of data owners
	Sensitive	Information leakage will cause general damage to the interests of data subjects
	Common	Information leakage will only cause light damage to the interests of the data owner
The principle of scale	Confidential	Large amount of data with the highest quality
	Sensitive	Moderate amount of data with higher data quality
	Common	Small amount of data with average data quality
The principle of uncontrollability	Confidential	The external flow frequency of data is high and the number of users is large
	Sensitive	Both external flow frequency of data and the number of users is moderate
	Common	The external flow frequency of data is low and the number of users is small

Source: Gao Lei 2019, 5th issue.

Classification-based protection is the basic approach to data management. The *Outline of Action to Promote the Development of Big Data* required "scientific and standardized use of big data and effective protection of data security." The *Outline of the 13th Five-Year Plan for National Economic and Social Development of the People's Republic of China* further states: "establish a security management system for big data, implement classified and graded management of data resources, and guarantee safe and efficient credible applications." From a practical point of view, China still lacks a comprehensive management system covering the full life cycle of big data, and there are blind spots in our policies and regulations (Wang Shan 2011). Existing data use standards and norms may not yet be very effective and there are still gaps in compliance supervision (Li Lu and Jiao Chengpeng 2018). Currently, the network- and system-centered security protection model suffers from problems such as poor match between security measures with protection objectives, and the failure to achieve the anticipated protection. Classification-based protection, with data asset classification at the core, identifies and classifies data for better security management, and creates security policies based on data confidentiality, integrity, availability, controllability, and other factors. This is why we need to advance the transformation of data security protection from the network- and system-centered model to the data asset-centered model.

Data classification is not the end, but the starting point of data compliance. According to *Data Age 2025*, a white paper released by the International Data Corporation, the total volume of global data is expected to reach 163ZB in 2025, which is ten times the current amount. Rapid data growth is a new challenge for data management and a long-term issue that we will have to deal with for quite some time in the future. In the foreseeable future digital technology and related technical conditions will not likely be sufficient for data protection without distinction, so classification-based protection will remain a must for sound data security management and the guard against related risks. On the one hand, we must improve the classification-based data security management system.

> Sound and perfect data classification and grading security management system adapted to the big data environment needs to cover all parties involved in the factor market, including but not limited to government departments, enterprises and

> organizations holding data resources, third-party professional data service organizations, and clarify the main responsibility of data classification and grading security management of all parties. At the same time, it is necessary to implement policies based on the attributes and characteristics of data resources in various industries and fields, and formulate data classification and grading security management rules that are suitable for the development, utilization and circulation of data resources in this field. (Chen Tian and Liu Minghui 2020)

On the other hand, we must accelerate the formulation of data classification standards. More specifically, we need to explore key factors such as data format, characteristics, sensitivity, importance, and circulation scenarios in the context of digital technologies, such as Internet of Things, cloud computing, artificial intelligence, and 5G; clarify the practical problems that the standards should address; conduct in-depth research on the status of security management of various types of data; encourage all parties to participate in the preparation of standards; prepare data classification standards that are suitable for the new digital economy, which meet the new needs of a digital life and are in line with the new order of a digital society; and provide better guidance for data security management and security resource allocation.

Data Rights System

"The new technological revolution has triggered changes in the economic and social order, and has also posed new challenges to the current rights system" (Key Laboratory of Big Data Strategy 2019, p. 178). The current rights system, with a problematic understanding of the digital world and the corresponding approach to legal regulation as the basis, show some shortcomings that are difficult to deal with in practice. A new system needs to be put in place with big data as the foundation and it should be the result of a forward-looking and innovative approach to rights and interests as mankind moves toward a ternary world, meeting the needs of the coming era of a digital civilization. A data rights system represents an order based on data rights. It mainly includes the statutory data rights system, the data property rights system, and the data sovereignty system. Among them, the statutory data rights system elevates data rights to the level of rights stipulated by law; the data property rights system ensures that data right subjects enjoy, or can let others enjoy, the benefit or loss of the property interests in the data generated by their data processing behavior; the data sovereignty system is an extension of national sovereignty into data space, and is also the embodiment of the highest ownership of sovereign rights. Each of the three dimensions has its own emphasis, which together construct a set of institutional frameworks for the protection and utilization of digital rights.

Statutory Data Rights System

Statutory data rights is the starting point of research for the realization of data rights. Starting from the basic form of the right—although statutory data rights cannot be equated with the realization of data rights—it connects ideal data rights with actual data rights, and reprocesses ideal data rights to move it a step forward, thus is an inevitable choice leading to actual data rights. From a theoretical perspective, statutory data rights are an interpretation of the socialization of data rights. Interests are the external expression of rights and are the result of the socialization of rights (Chen Hongyan and Yin Kuijie 2014). From a realistic point of view, the creation of statutory data rights is the process of data rights concretization and the result of its actualization, which is an important guarantee for the realization of data rights.

> From the institutional perspective, the legalization of data rights is related to the basic economic system of a country or region. Only through the legalization of data rights, clarifying the data rights ownership, determining the types and contents of data rights, and realizing the institutional adjustment of data ownership, can the data ownership relationship of a country or region become a legal relationship, and consolidate and maintain the normal economic and social relations and order. (Key Laboratory of Big Data Strategy 2019, p. 187)

At present, data rights are not yet statutory and this does not meet people's expectations, resulting in conflicts and confrontation between ideal data rights and actual data rights in reality.

Statutory data rights provide legal stipulations and descriptions of the types, content, and effect of data rights, so that the realization of data rights are guaranteed by law. Statutory types of data rights means that only those types of data rights that are stipulated by law are legitimate, and no other types can be created or recognized by law, not even by reaching relevant agreements. The statutory content of data rights means that the content of data rights must be stipulated by law; no other content can be created and no agreement shall be valid if it contains anything inconsistent with the statutory content of data rights. The statutory effect of data rights means that the effect of data rights must be stipulated by law, which cannot be changed even if relevant agreements are reached. In the process of data rights legislation, legislators should restrict and protect data rights through the creation of reasonable laws so as to create a sound premise for the realization of data rights. In the process of private law practice, lawyers, jurists, and judicial officials must rationally protect data rights and interests, and provide realistic protection for the realization of data rights. In the process seeking relief for the damage caused to data rights, people should take a rational view. It is only by organically combining legislation, justice, relief, and people's rational concept of data rights that we can ensure the benign operation of a data rights.

Statutory data rights is a dynamic process. As a basic category of rights for human survival and development, data rights should be statutory rights, they should represent legitimate and reasonable interest claims, and should conform to the institutional requirements and value orientation of our times. Consequently, it is subject to economic, political, and cultural influences. Institutionally, the constitutive elements of the laws relating to data rights all have a bearing on the success of statutory data rights. We are in need of a substantive law dedicated to the protection of data rights and a corresponding procedural law. Cultural trends of a society can affect the progress toward statutory data rights. Although the digital age has come, the public awareness of data, data rights, and data rights law still needs to be improved; the lack of a data culture hinders the establishment and recognition of data rights. In terms of social development, statutory data rights reflect the current development level of a society in legal and social realms. At present, the value of data continues to increase, and mankind is marching toward the era of data rights. However, due to various factors related to social development, data rights have not yet attracted sufficient attention in society, and there is bound to be some delay in the establishment of statutory data rights. It would be meaningless if we go too fast in this aspect and surpass by a excessively large margin what social development actually requires.

Data Property Rights System

> In the digital economy, data has become the "new petroleum," intangible, but of great value. Clarifying the data property rights system is the primary issue facing the development of the digital economy, and it is also an important issue urgently needed to be solved by the legal system of the digital economy. (Shen Weixing 2018)

In January 2017, the European Commission published the report *Building a European Data Economy*, proposing three targets of the European Digital Single Market Strategy.[11] In this context, Europe has carried out research on non-personal data and the rights of data generators, and proposed the concept of new data property rights to regulate the market and transactions. In December 2017, General Secretary Xi Jinping pointed out during the second collective study session of the Political Bureau of the CPC Central Committee on the implementation of the national big data strategy that "we must build a digital economy with data as a key factor" and that "we must develop a system related to the identification, openness, circulation and trading of data resources, and improve the data property rights protection system." In March 2020, the *Opinions*

11 First, maximize the benefits of data and facilitate access to and sharing of machine-generated data; second, protect investments, assets, and confidential data, and create sound incentives for investment and innovation; third, ensure that data holders, processors, and service providers share equitably in the benefits within the value chain.

of the State Council and the CPC Central Committee on Building a Better Institutional Mechanism for Market-Based Factor Allocation proposed to "study and improve our understanding of the nature of property rights according to the nature of data." In October of the same year, the General Office of the CPC Central Committee and the General Office of the State Council issued the *Implementation Plan for the Comprehensive Pilot Program of Building Socialism with Chinese Characteristics with Shenzhen as a Demonstration Zone (2020–2025)*, giving Shenzhen the mission to take the lead in improving the data property rights system, and exploring new mechanisms for the protection and utilization of data property rights. In the process of the allocation of data as a production factor, the concept of data property rights has been repeatedly mentioned. The main reason is that there are currently no clear rules on how to own the data factor and how to allocate the property rights associated with it. Strengthening the protection of data property rights will not only better stimulate data circulation transactions and data product application, but also, and just as importantly, liberate and develop data productivity, cultivate the data factor market, and realize a digital economy led and supported by innovation.

The definition of data property rights is a necessary precondition for the effective allocation of the data factor. "The ownership of data property rights is a basic problem that needs to be solved in the development of the data industry. It determines how to allocate data value, obligations and responsibilities among different subjects" (Zhu Baoli 2019). "A just data property rights system should ensure reasonable distribution of rights and obligations based on legal relationships of property rights, and balance between the interests of multiple parties in society as much as possible" (John Rawls 1999, p. 5). The economist Harold Demsetz pointed out in his book, *Toward a Theory of Property Rights*, that "the generation of property rights is essentially a process of cost-benefit tradeoff. Property rights can only be generated when the benefits of internalizing the externalities by defining property rights outweigh the costs of doing so." Data has an economic basis when the benefits of confirmed data property rights are greater than the costs of it. The reason why the benefits of data property rights will increase is that the value of data has increased, acquiring property attributes, and even becoming a factor of production. The lawsuit between LinkedIn and hiQ, the fight between SF Express and Cainiao over logistics data, the data collection battle between Huawei and WeChat, and the Facebook data breach [...] all point to one central question: How to define and protect data property rights? Conditions are now ripe for confirming data property rights and a clear definition is a must throughout the life cycle of data.

The data property rights system is a product of government regulation of data flow, but practical adjustments need to be made in accordance with social efficiency to ensure a balance of interests between various parties and the public. As the object of data property rights, data is the foundation of the data property rights system. Natural persons, platform enterprises, government agencies, and data intermediaries may all become data benefitiaries. Data property rights are a cluster of rights, including the right to use, the right to earnings, the right to possess, and the right to dispose. The data property rights system is mainly to clearly define data ownership, data possession, data control, data use, data benefit, and data disposal. Data property rights are special in that their generation mechanism is fundamentally different from that of other asset property rights. Asset property rights are unique and exclusive, while data property rights are reproducible and non-exclusive. Data property rights can be defined with governance technology or through institutional design. However, the definition of data property rights is more complicated than the definition of other rights, and it is obviously inappropriate and unrealistic to simply apply the system of "one thing, one right." We shall put in place new jurisprudential rules predicated on this new digital civilization, which will allow data property rights to be shared by different subjects.

Data Sovereignty System

Since the twenty-first century, with the rapid development of the digital technology, cyberspace has become the fifth domain besides sea, land, air, and space. Cross-border data flow and storage have gradually become more common and convenient, which has impacted on the traditional concept of national sovereignty. As a result, data sovereignty has become the theoretical basis for countries to govern data, related technologies, and infrastructure. Originating from national sovereignty, data sovereignty is a new form of national sovereignty in this new context. As a product of national sovereignty in the digital era, data sovereignty starts in cyberspace, and it embodies, extends, and reflects national sovereignty. With the detachment of the concept of sovereignty from geographical elements, data sovereignty becomes a new branch of sovereignty and a major part of the sovereignty system. Data sovereignty involves the generation, collection, storage, analysis, and application of data that is related to the vital interests of the state, enterprises, and individuals, and bears unlimited value. Both international and domestic situations show that data sovereignty will become a new focus of attention for major countries, in addition to border defense, maritime defense, and air defense. Many countries and regions have already initiated data resource protection, data security system construction, and data infrastructure construction to strengthen data sovereignty and security protection capabilities as part of their national security efforts.

China is an active advocate and staunch defender of data sovereignty. With regard to national security, in August 2015, the State Council stated clearly that the object of the *Action Plan for Promoting Big Data Development* involved "Taking China's full advantage in data scale [...] to enhance protection capacity of cyberspace data sovereignty, safeguarding national security, and effectively improving China's national competitiveness." The *Cybersecurity Law of the People's Republic of China*, released in November 2016, states clearly in Article 37 that "personal information and important data collected and produced by critical information infrastructure operators during their operations within the territory of the People's Republic of China shall be stored within China." This fully reflects the great importance China attaches to data sovereignty. It can be said that data sovereignty has become an important requirement for countries who strive for equal participation and an appropriate position and influence in international cyber affairs and the safeguarding of national interests.

In April 2013, the North Atlantic Treaty Organization (NATO) officially released the *Tallinn Manual*, which provided that "states have the right to exercise control over cyber infrastructure and cyber conduct within their sovereign territory, and any interference with the cyber infrastructure of another State is a violation of sovereignty" (Zhu Lixin 2015). In June 2013, the 6th UN General Assembly adopted Article 20 of the resolution of the UN Group of Governmental Experts of Developments in the Field of Information and Telecommunications in the Context of International Security, which stated that "international norms and principles of state sovereignty and those originate from state sovereignty apply to information and communications technology activities carried out by states, as well as the jurisdiction of states over information and communications technology infrastructure within their territories." This confirms the existence of national sovereignty in cyberspace. In the *Tallinn Manual on the International Law Applicable to Cyber Warfare 2.0* (2017), Rule 1, "Sovereignty (General Principles)" explicitly rejects the "global commons doctrine" of cyberspace, arguing that:

> While (the global commons) characterization may be useful in an extra-legal context, the UN Group of Governmental Experts disagrees that it ignores those territorial attributes of cyberspace and cyber operations that implicate the principle of sovereignty. (Schmitt M. Tallin 2017, p. 12)

In accordance with Article 2 of the *Charter of the United Nations* and the relevant resolutions of the UN General Assembly, the international community has gradually developed a broad understanding that "the flow of information within or outside a sovereign state without the consent of the sovereign state is an infringement of state sovereignty." At present, the existence and importance of data sovereignty has been recognized by various international agreements and national laws, and its connotations have been continuously improved.

> The "data sovereignty theory," relying on the modern order of international public law, insists that data governance remains subordinate to traditional sovereignty, and it extends and develops from cyber sovereignty to technological sovereignty, while the "data freedom theory," based on the ideal of Internet cosmopolitanism, emphasizes data can flow freely without sovereign intervention and is mainly manifested as the long-arm jurisdiction over data and its controllers. In practice, the two theories of orders present a complex pattern of competition and intermingling. (Liu Tianjiao 2020)

To strike a balance between the two orders, it is necessary to construct an order based on data sovereignty, and adopt a positive attitude toward the value of efficiency in the digital era. The development of digital technology has given rise to the transmutation from "cyber sovereignty" to "data sovereignty," which has had a profound impact on the construction of international law and order (Huang Haiying and He Meng 2019). As the importance of data sovereignty continues to be highlighted, all countries are now concerned about how to safeguard their sovereign security, and how to gain a competitive edge in data sovereignty in matters of order and freedom, development, and security.

Safeguarding data sovereignty is of great practical importance to national security, economic development, and social stability. Countries with strong data control capabilities do not worry that their data will be plundered or used by others, while countries with weaker data control capabilities hope to increase their strengths for data management and use through international collaboration. At present, the policies related to data sovereignty mainly concentrate on data management and control, and countries' claims and practices on data sovereignty are demonstrated by their requirement to manage cross-border data flow. From an international perspective, more and more countries and regions have begun to build their legal systems of data sovereignty centered on data management (He Bo 2017). Therefore, only when we recognize the sovereign boundaries in cyberspace will we be able to ensure that there is a sound juridical basis for international law to be used to regulate data resources; that a specialized, systematic, and feasible international legal system can be formed on the basis of a consensus reached through consultation between sovereign states; that effective international legal regulation of data resources can be realized, and that compliance can be justifiably required from all countries following the principles of peace, cooperation, and development, as stipulated in the *Charter of the United Nations*. Otherwise, international law would not really be effective in the regulation of data resources. In this regard, to regulate data sovereignty and improve the international data governance system, we address issues of data security and data protection while focusing on the mining and usage of data resources. We should also respond to the risk of data sovereignty abuse with great caution, and build an institutional framework for data sovereignty in terms of cross-border flows based on data classification and the dissipation of data sovereignty abuse (from the perspective of a community with a shared future).

Data Evidence System

The development of digital technology has led to a transformation in the rule of law regarding evidence. The ascertainment of legal truth has always benefited from advances in science and technology. The ancient Chinese people had always conducted criminal investigations and identification with the science and technology available at the time. By the end of the nineteenth century, the Industrial Revolution had given rise to the third tide in scientific development, and applied science and technology advanced by leaps and bounds. The scientific activities derived from daily needs expanded the scope of independent evidence, extended independent human imagination, strengthened attention to evidence, and refined the judgment of evidence through technology. Data evidence is one more step forward from electronic evidence.

> Compared with electronic data in the early stage, big data evidence is featured with its large amount, and can prove the facts involved in a case by revealing the underlying pattern. This is already a qualitative change. At present, signs have appeared for using big data evidence to solve various evideance-related problems, and it is bound to develop further. Based on current judicial practice, it has become an urgent task to recognize the legal status of big data evidence and set evidence rules.
>
> (Liu Pinxin 2019)

Evidence-Centeredness

> In regard to the basis of judicial proof, human society has undergone two major transformations: the first one was from "testimony of deities" to "testimony of witness";

> the second one was from "testimony of witness" to "testimony of real evidence." As for the system of judicial proof or the system of evidence, the development of human society has, to a certain extent, embodied the law of "negation of negation," i.e., from free proof to unfree proof and then to relatively free proof.
>
> (He Jiahong and Liu Pinxin 2019, p. 1)

The formulation of legal provisions related to evidence, and the proving of facts of a case shall be evidence-based. This is a fundamental principle guiding the whole mechanism of evidence. In *On the Necessity and Basic Principles of Legislation on Criminal Evidence*, the Commission for Legislative Affairs of the Standing Committee of the National People's Congress pointed out that, although China does not yet have a dedicated law on evidence that makes a clear statement on the principle of being evidence-based, the legislature has long been paying special attention to this issue, and has invited renowned Chinese experts and scholars to discuss it. They agreed that, in order to better formulate a law on evidence, the relevant basic principles should first be established. In addition, the famous legal scholars, He Jiahong and Liu Pinxin, believe that:

> China should clarify the axiomatic principles that reflect the general law of judicial proof, such as seeking truth from facts, the evidence-based principle, direct speech, and combining regulated proof and free proof; as well as the policy principles that reflect legal values and social policies, such as compliance with legality, the principle of fairness and integrity and so forth.
>
> (He Jiahong and Liu Pinxin 2019, p. 1–101)

The theory of fact and the theory of reflection. There are a variety of views on evidence in legal circles, two of which are the most influential: one is the theory of fact; the other is the theory of reflection. The former insists that evidence is a fact that exists objectively or has occurred objectively. It is of the top priority. The latter argues that:

> Evidence is not the objective facts themselves, but the reflection of the objective facts in people's consciousness; it is of the second priority rather than the first, which means it is subject to the will of man and inseparable from the consciousness of man.
>
> (Wu Jialin 1981)

In short, the theory of fact holds that evidence is a fact; the theory of reflection regards evidence as the reflection of a fact. As for the relationship between the two, fact is the basis and the substantive aspect. There were two great debates on evidence, in the 1950s and 1980s, respectively, which revolved around these two theories of evidence, and relevant discussions continue to exist in the Chinese legal circle today.

Authenticity is what distinguishes fact from evidence. A fact is the real situation of things, and its essential characteristic is authenticity. The word "authentic" is similar in meaning to "actual." Hence, a fact is "a thing or event that actually occurs, or a tangible object or appearance that usually exists, and is indeed absolutely true rather than merely a speculation or opinion" (Xue Bo 2003, p. 825). In short, facts are "true" rather than "false." There are no "false facts," but there is false evidence. The two concepts of "fact" and "existence" can overlap. Whereas *Blackstone's Law Dictionary* defines a fact as "something that actually exists," in philosophy, existence is an ontological concept that refers to the objective world that does not depend on the consciousness of man; "the world is independent of my will" (Wittgenstein 1962, p. 94). Lenin pointed out: "If we grasp the facts from its whole sum or from the connection of the facts, then the facts are not only something more than eloquent, but also something well-documented; if we grasp the facts not from the whole sum nor from the connection, but fragmentarily and randomly picked facts out, then the facts can only be a kind of child's play, even worse than child's play." In a broad sense, evidence is information related to the facts which remain to be proved. According to Shannon, the founder of information theory, information is the elimination or reduction of uncertainty in people's knowledge of things. The data evidence system aims to eliminate or reduce the uncertainty of fact finding, which is undoubtedly of universal significance to human beings in their pursuit of fairness and justice.

Evidence-centeredness is what leads to fairness and justice before the law. Evidence-centeredness means that:

> In judicial practices, the fact-finding of a case must be based on evidence, and evidence must be taken as the cornerstone in judicial proof activities. In other words, judicial adjudication must be based on evidence, which is called the term "the principle of evidentiary adjudication."
>
> (He Jiahong and Liu Pinxin 2019, p. 86)

According to Taguchi Morikazu, a leading Japanese criminal jurist,

> [T]he facts that constitute the core elements of a crime must be found on the basis of evidence with evidence ability, and must only be found after investigation. The concept of "fact" and the concept of "based on evidence" have a special normative significance.

In practice, flawed criminal judgments occur for a number of reasons. These reflect ten misconceptions that exist in China's criminal justice system, its mechanisms, concepts, and other aspects.[12] Acknowledging these flaws is the first step to eliminating such mistakes; we must also take practical and effective measures to negate this problem. While it is true that we cannot completely obviate misjudged cases, but we must do our best to prevent them, and to strive to improve the litigation system and rules of evidence.

Evidential Significance of Data Rights

Data evidence is the result of the development of digital technology. We usually define data evidence as covering all evidence formed with the help of digital technology or electronic equipment, or all evidence that can prove the facts of a case which is expressed in electronic forms. With the development and application of digital technologies, information transmission has undergone disruptive changes, and traditional evidence has gradually been replaced by the new data evidence.

Standardized evidence.

12 The ten misunderstandings of today's criminal justice in China: (1) the deadline to solve the case against the regulations; (2) the investigation mode from confession to evidence; (3) the preconceived one-sided evidence; (4) the improper interpretation of scientific evidence; (5) the torture confessions that frequently happen; (6) unprincipled compliance with public opinion; (7) mutual restraint in name only; (8) the court trial pro forma; (9) overtime detention; and (10) misdemeanor without sufficient evidence. (He Jiahong 2014)

> A datamized and unified evidence standard is an evidence standard that is developed to meet the need of building complete evidence chains for different types of cases; applicable to public security, procuratorial, and judicial organs; and embedded in a data-based procedural system. It aims to concretize to a certain extent the requirement of "clear facts as well as solid and sufficient evidence". Digitalization is its essential feature, and unification is its derivative feature. The innovative practice of this standard has opened up the case handling process of public security organs, procuratorial organs and people's courts within a certain region, which represents the direction of evidence standard reform, enriches the relevant theoretical system, and provides a rectification mechanism for judicial decision-making.
>
> (Liu Pinxin and Chen Li 2019)

In practice, a datamized evidence standard has become an important aspect in the reform of the judicial system in Guizhou, Shanghai, Jiangsu, Sichuan, and some other places. Compared with traditional evidence, it is an effective way to solve conflicts about the legality and authenticity of evidence, such as "authentic therefore legal," "verified therefore legal," and "stable therefore legal."[13]

Scientific fact-finding.

> Classification is an important method for theoretical research on evidence. It is generally believed that the earliest academic research on the classification of evidence was conducted by the 18th century English jurist Jeremy Bentham, whose masterpiece *Theory of Judicial Evidence* was the first to propose nine methods of classifying evidence, including real evidence and human evidence, voluntary evidence and compulsory evidence, verbal evidence, sworn evidence and documentary evidence, direct evidence and circumstantial evidence, original evidence and hearsay evidence, and so forth. Since then, scholars of evidence law in various countries have deepened their research on the classification of evidence, although their criteria vary. In recent years, Chinese scholars have gradually agreed on the classification of evidence. They tend to

13 "Authentic therefore legal" means that the court will affirm the authenticity of the defendant's confession and directly conclude that the confession is lawful; "verified therefore legal" means that the truthfulness of the confession is inferred from the mutual verification among the confessed evidence and other evidence, while the lawfulness of the evidence collection procedure is inferred from this; "stable therefore legal" means that the authenticity of the confession is inferred from the stability of the confession, and the lawfulness of the evidence collection procedure is inferred from the authenticity of the confession.

> divide evidence into verbal evidence and real evidence, original evidence and derivative evidence, direct evidence and circumstantial evidence, and proof and disproof.
>
> (He Jiahong and Liu Pinxin 2019, p. 125)

Verbal evidence and real evidence focus on the content and presentation of evidence, while original evidence and derivative evidence focus on the provenance or source of information. Direct evidence and circumstantial evidence focus on the relationship between the main facts of the case, while proof and disproof focus on the facts asserted by the parties. Data evidence results from the intersection of law and technology.

> Along with the application various technological means in trials, the traditional rules of evidence have evolved, and testimony with audiovisual technology has put the traditional rules of verbal evidence in front of serious challenges; the traditional best evidence rule has begun to weaken, but the problems of that rule for electronic evidence are increasingly striking.
>
> (Chen Xuequan 2008)

As a result of the iteration of electronic evidence, data evidence can not only be used to trace the source of evidence, it also makes fact-finding more scientific.

From objective truth to legal truth.

> The relationship between objective truth and legal truth is just like that between absolute truth and relative truth. They are interdependent and can swap in some cases. Objective truth and legal truth cannot and should not be regarded as diametrically opposite, but as two aspects and two levels of truth in a case. Objective truth, like absolute truth, is kind of utopian, but it can be a pursuit that motivates police and judicial officers, which is quite meaningful.
>
> (Lei Jianchang 2004)

Simon, a leading British scholar, argues that "evidence is relevant if it logically proves or disproves some items that need to be proved. Even it may be tautological in etymology, there can be adequate reason to say that relevant evidence is the evidence that makes those items to be more likely or less likely proved." The characteristics of big data, such as objectivity and relevance, determine the characteristics of data evidence, such as professionalism and directness of its basis, objectivity, relevance, and authenticity of its content. As a concentrated embodiment of data evidence with high relevance, the evidential application of data and the datamization of evidence are not simply a play on words. They reflect the high relevance of data evidence, which is presented as a net spreading in space and a clear line in time, with clear nodes and a neat structure. Strengthening data collection, discovery, relevance, analysis of fact trajectory, and promoting crime risk warnings with the support of data not only adds new content to the law of evidence, it also provides a new direction for transforming the research paradigm of evidence law.

Legal Technology and Digital Justice

Legal technology is not something new, but it has never been so holographically integrated into our lives, or posed such a huge challenge to traditional legislation in various countries.

> When we look back on the evolution and development of the Internet, it is easy to see that the challenges and changes it has brought to traditional legal rules go from partial to panoramic, and from quantitative to qualitative.
>
> (Li Qian 2016)

An era led by legal technology is a brand new era, and laws of the previous era are no longer be applicable or suitable. According to Negroponte,

> I think of our laws as if they were fish baring and struggling on the deck. These dying fish are desperately gasping for air, because the digital world is very different. Most laws are made for a world of atoms, not bits. There is no place for national laws in the laws of computer space. (Negroponte 2017, p. 278)

Thus, a data-based legal order pushes legal thinking to a higher level. The development of technology brings difficult problems, but at the same time provides solutions. Changes and innovations in big data related judgments, the collection and application of big data, and the ways to put big data into effective use not only affect all aspects of social life, but also bring new opportunities for us to reflect on how we think about legal causality. "Humanity will eventually benefit from the development and advancement of technology and gain greater freedom and emancipation in the coming intelligent era" (Li Haiying 2016). The emergence of digital technology will change or even shatter the existing order and balance, thus bringing impact and change to the current legal system.

In the digital world, the law seems helpless in the face of overwhelming data flow, just like a person in front of a castle with its drawbridge up, going around it once and again but finding no entrance at all. Bodenheimer states:

> One of the fundamental roles of law is to make the numerous, varied, and diverse actions and relationships of human beings a kind of reasonable order, and to promulgate rules of conduct or standards of behavior that apply to certain actions or behaviors that should be restricted.
>
> (Bodenheimer 2017)

The limitations of the law in a digital world lie in the fact that data is naturally controlled by code, which does not submit to any intervention. Even if the law declares that someone owns a certain piece of data, the supposed owner will never truly be able to take the data under his/her control if this goes against what the codes allow. This is just like one cannot take an apple out of a computer screen. However, while the law cannot influence technology against the law of nature, it can influence the specific presentation of technology from the perspective of human behavior. In essence, if we are to find a way for the law to regulate the digital world, we must focus on controllable human behavior to establish a good data order. The birth of data rights shows that it is well-grounded and feasible in theory to protect it separately by law. More importantly, on the basis of clarifying data rights, legal rules concerning the right to personal data should be set up to regulate the collection, use, storage, transmission, and processing of data, thus forming a good order for data use and data protection.

In the digital era, everyone is both a producer and a consumer of data; no one can live without data. In line with this, every social relationship in human society has been directly or indirectly branded as "data-based," and the laws regulating these social relationships should also become data-based. Personal data and privacy are inextricably linked. However, since data has multiple values, such as in terms of personal freedom and dignity, commerce, and public administration, the remeasurement of interests in data protection and data use will, in theory, become the starting point and foundation of data law. A balance of interests is a requirement of civil law and social morality. The theory of balance of interests runs through the whole process of legal protection of personal data to achieve fairness and justice while optimizing the allocation of resources, which is also a direct manifestation of digital justice in the digital era. The rapid development of digital technology has made personal data complicated, and the conflict between private rights and public rights in personal data has become more and more intense. Whereas the legal protection of personal data is of prime importance; in the face of diversified and conflicting interests, the law is the best mechanism to strike a balance between unlimited needs and limited resources, which can arrange the priorities of different interests through legislative interest measurement.

Data Ethics System

Legislation is the universal means of international data protection, but this does not mean that law is the only means, much less an exclusion to other means of protection. As an important means of social regulation, legal norms, together with ethical norms and industrial self-discipline, constitute people's behavioral norms.

> As a kind of moral prospect that can guide our civilization forward, big data brings together the positive energy of value feedback or criticism instantly, making the society energetic, freer and more open, and both fair and efficient, which leads and promotes the development of human morality.
>
> (Yue Jin 2016)

Industrial self-discipline is a manifestation of ethics-based data protection according to industrial standards and corporate charters, besides laws and regulations to regulate corporate behavior (Priest 1998).

Ethics-based Protection of Data

Ethics in different eras have different and specific connotations. In the early days of cyberspace, spontaneously formed ethical norms played a major role in safeguarding data security. With the massive reshaping of the digital society, changes in traditional ethics are taking place silently, and inclusive coexistence is increasingly accepted as a code of conduct with ethical implications. To achieve intended goals in cyberspace, data ethics norms must be complied with.

Data ethics is concerned with the ethical issues that arise in the process of collecting and analyzing data, as well as in activities such as the use, description, dissemination, and open access to data in biomedical and social science research.

> Data has become an important strategic asset, and the huge social and economic benefits it brings inevitably lead to ethical issues regarding illegal collection, dissemination, and use of data, such as illegal acquisition and preservation of personal data, data misuse, undermined control of the data owner over data, data monopoly, unfair application of data, and biased guidance of data.
>
> (Chen Yi 2020)

At different stages, different subjects have different needs for data and different perceptions of data ethics. In 2016, the European Economic and Social Committee elicitated the ethical dilemmas that people would encounter at various stages in the data life cycle and divided them into ten categories: ownership, the right of control, the right to know, the right to privacy, trust, surveillance and security, digital identity, fulfillment of customization, de-anonymization, and digital divide. The ethical issues of data are inextricably linked to "people." People get involved in the digital world even before they are born, and continue to provide and use data at different awareness levels and in different ways throughout their lives.

> Digitalization has given birth to dataism, which is a philosophical expression of digitization. Dataism asserts that maximizing data flow and freedom of information are the highest good. In essence, dataism replaces human-centeredness with data-centeredness, and substitutes liberalism with dataism. Besides, the emphasis is put on freedom of data rather than that of mans.
>
> (Li Lun and Huang Guan 2019)

As Harari put it, "In the 18th century, human-centeredness changed from a God-centered worldview to a human-centered one, leaving God behind. In the 21st century, however, dataism may transform from human-centered to data-centered, leaving human behind" (Yuval Noah Harari 2017, p. 347). To avoid the drawbacks of dataism, to respect freedom and the rights of people, to promote regulated data sharing, and to oppose data abuse, we should advocate human-centered data ethics.

Data security is not only a matter of technology, but also a matter of weighing interests, values, and ethics. Data protection requires a system of rules regarding the ethics of collecting and disclosing personal information instead of just keeping secrets. The *Plan to Establish a National Committee for Ethics in Science and Technology*, which was adopted by the Central Commission for Comprehensively Deepening Reform, states that "we should pay close attention to improving institutional norms, advance governance mechanisms, strengthen ethical supervision, refine relevant laws and regulations and ethical review rules, and regulate various scientific research activities." The Fourth Plenary Session of the 19th CPC Central Committee proposed to "improve the system of ethical governance of science and technology." The *14th Five-Year Plan* also emphasizes the need to improve "the ethics system of science and technology." From the perspective of ethical norms, the governance of data protection in the era of a digital civilization should adhere to codes of ethics. In this aspect, American scholar Richard A. Spinello pointed out that "technology tends to develop faster than ethics, which may result in a lag effect and cause us great harm." He also proposed three principles of cyber ethics: autonomy, harmlessness, and informed consent.[14] In China, the academic circle has also established three ethical principles for the ethical issues arising from big data technologies: the principle of harmlessness, the principle of unity of rights and responsibilities, and the principle of respect for autonomy.[15] In general, we should focus on the meta-ethics of justice and its realization in the ethics system of the digital society, improve the system of data ethics protection, avoid the negative consequences caused by the technological alienation of big data, and strive to ensure justice for the data ethics system itself. In other words, we must focus on how to eliminate dehumanization, inhumanity, and non-liberty in the era of big data when formulating a relevant ethics system (Chen Shiwei 2016).

Co-governance and Self-Discipline of the Industry

Industrial self-discipline is a mode of regulating the behavior of enterprises by means other than laws and regulations, such as with the guidance of industrial and corporate charters (Priest 1998), which is a voluntary restraint of an enterprise's behavior (Maxwell et al. 2000). Co-governance and self-discipline of the data industry plays a vital role in supplementing

14 First, the principle of autonomy. Autonomy is the ability of individuals to determine their own lifestyles. When combined with personal data, it becomes the right of data owners to decide what their personal data is used for and what value is obtained. The second is the principle of harmlessness. One of the ways to protect personal data is causing no harm to the data owner when processing personal data. The third is the principle of informed consent. "Consent" is an expression of one's subjective will, which should be clearly understood by the data subject in terms of how and for what purpose the data will be processed, which means that informed consent is a prerequisite. (Spinello 1998)

15 The principle of harmlessness means that the development of big data technology should be people-oriented, concentrating on the healthy development of human society and the improvement of the quality of life; the principle of unity of rights and responsibilities means that the one who collects and uses data should shoulder corresponding responsibilities; the principle of respect for autonomy means the right to store, delete, and use, and know data should stay within the purview of the data generators (Yang Weidong 2018).

government regulation and law-based regulation, building a data industry ecosystem that is predicated on data protection and privacy, cracking down on illegal data flows, and mustering forces in the industry to pursue innovation.

Elinor Ostrom argues that:

> Leviathan or privatization is not the only effective solution. A large number of problems relating to common-pool resources in human societies are not addressed by the state or the market; self-organization and autonomy in human societies are actually institutional arrangements that are more effective for managing public affairs. (Ostrom 2000, pp. 22–50)

As a bridge between the government and enterprises, trade associations and chambers of commerce can guide market entities to regulate themselves through supervision, self-discipline, coordination, and other means, thus forming an organized "private order" corresponding to public order.[16] The motivation for industrial self-discipline can have six academic explanations: "the cost-profit theory," "the risk-avoidance theory," "the theory of protecting commons," "the system-oriented theory," "the market failure theory," and "the innovation-driven theory" (See Table 16). The factors above are taken into account when enterprises decide to participate in industrial self-discipline. For example, a report on industrial self-discipline in Australia categorized the motivations as: raising industrial standards, serving as a market tool, improving the information level, avoiding government regulation, and meeting legal requirements (Philip Eijlander 2005).

16 Private order refers to the self-regulatory mechanism reached by social individuals based on the personal relationships they automatically form, or organized groups they voluntarily join in a long-term relationship. In a state, private order can become a universal and formal legal system before they function partially as a supplement or substitute for public order under the constraints of national law.

Table 16. Theories on the Motivation for Industry Self-Discipline

Theory	Content
Cost-profit theory	According to the "cost-benefit theory," industry self-discipline has costs, including the input and expenses of members to develop and implement self-regulatory regulations. Meanwhile, industry self-discipline also has benefits, which are brought to its members by developing and complying with self-regulatory norms.
Risk-avoidance theory	The "risk aversion theory" argues that the most typical motivation is to avoid a negative corporate image. For example, some monopolies practice industry self-discipline, such as changing output and making price decisions to limit their monopoly rights in order to further curb the threat of reformists to their monopoly.
Theory of protecting commons	The "theory of protecting commons" claims the need to protect the "intangible commons," which are shared by all companies in modern industries, and to restrict the actions of individual companies that may harm the interests of the industry as a whole, which has led to the formation of such a system.
System-oriented theory	The "system-oriented theory" states that firms participate in the self-regulatory system for the purpose of maintaining the system. They may be motivated to join voluntary self-regulatory systems to seek legitimacy by strengthening their relationship with regulatory agencies, thereby reducing regulatory pressure from those agencies.
Market failure theory	The "market failure theory" argues that industry self-discipline is driven by some form of market failure, particularly market externalities, information asymmetries, imperfect private law, and the high costs of correcting market failures.
Innovation-driven theory	The "innovation-driven theory" believes that although self-discipline actually reduces market transparency, it increases social welfare through innovation in general. The gains from greater innovation usually outweigh the losses from less price transparency, so in this aspect innovation is indeed a driver of self-discipline.

Source: Chang Jian and Guo Wei, 2011, 1st issue.

From the perspective of the relationship between industrial self-discipline and government regulation, self-discipline can be divided into pure self-discipline, alternative self-discipline, and conditional self-discipline. Pure self-discipline refers to the kind of self-discipline performed by private groups. The government will simply accept it and never intervene as long as the self-discipline does not violate general values such as fair competition. Alternative self-discipline means that the right to initiate self-discipline rests with private actors, while the government monitors the process of regulation to protect the public interest. Conditional self-discipline, in which public regulation and private self disicipline are intertwined, is subject to the supervision of the government. From the perspective of the degree of government intervention, industrial self-discipline can be divided into mandatory self-discipline, approved self-discipline, compulsory self-discipline, and voluntary self-discipline.

> Mandatory self-discipline, means the framework is specified by the government. Authorized self-discipline, in which the organization formulates its own self-discipline plan, is implemented after the plan is submitted to the government for approval. Compulsory self-discipline is established because of the mandatory government regulation. Voluntary self-discipline is carried out without the state directly or indirectly intervening, promoting or ordering. (Black 1996)

According to its effectiveness, industrial self-discipline can be divided into voluntary consultation and competitive self-discipline. Voluntary consultation requires stakeholders to participate in the setting of standards and address information asymmetries through communication. In this way, industrial norms can be better adapted to the industrial environment, and can engage all parties to do everything they can to formulate the best risk responses that are less costly. Competition between different self-discipline actors is needed in the competitive self-discipline model. Consumers may choose from different self-discipline systems that compete with one another, which is of great help to effectively solving external problems and addressing information asymmetries. However, this model is only applicable where there are no significant externalities or information asymmetries, and may cause a "voluntary paradox."

> Competitive self-discipline can effectively curb anti-competitive behavior of self-discipline agencies, such as by creating access barriers and establishing price alliances, but where externalities are prominent, mandatory public regulation is a must to ensure that suppliers can meet minimum quality standards. (Ogus 1995)

Industrial self-discipline serves as a test bed for government policies and as a supplement for the abscense of legislation, but it still has limitations. First, industrial self-discipline may not be strict enough and the procedures may fail to meet the standards set by the courts. Opinions on the requirements of self-discipline may vary among different groups within an industry, and the guidelines established may change frequently. Second, industrial self-discipline lacks supervision and is usually poorly implemented. Foreign scholars, Mulligan and Goldman, argue that the lack of oversight and poor enforcement contributes to the lack of industrial self-discipline [...] the public, policy makers, and supporters of self-discipline are there just for formality's sake and to suppress necessary regulatory activities. The European Economic and Social Committee also points out that it is difficult to implement industrial self-discipline by reason that it is accountable to an independent entity and lacks legal support. Self-discipline only influence those who are unwilling to take the rules lightly, unless they become a mandatory obligation. Third, industrial self-discipline lacks legal remedy. Another problem in industrial self-discipline is that there is no effective legal remedy for victims. Policies developed by the industry provide little opportunity for a consumer to ask for relief or to lodge an appeal, and no compensation is available for policy gaps. Fourth, the cost of industrial self-discipline may make it more difficult for market entities to do business, or the burden will be shifted to consumers. Fifth, industrial self-discipline may be used for private interests; its procedures may be used to harm competitors or create access barriers, and may obstructing government regulation. Sixth, industrial self-discipline lacks openness and transparency and consumers are not able to fully participate. Therefore, consumers may not accept such norms.

> The ability to coordinate between services of industrial associations and other self-discipline organizations being increasingly imperative in the market, it is more prominent for large enterprises to play an active role in the market. The whole society will come to realize that enterprise benefits cannot be enhanced steadily and the

> whole industry cannot achieve sound and rapid development without industrial self-discipline and co-governance. (Li Baokuan and Ye Zijing 2019)

Industrial self-discipline "should neither be too rigid, or it will be as stagnant as backwater; nor too loose, or it will be as chaotic as rough seas." Industrial self-discipline should take co-governance as the core, and balance market vitality with order. It should also better the co-governance system where enterprises take responsibility, where democratic consultation is enforced, where society collaborates, where the public participates, and where science and technology support. By doing so, a community of industrial self-governance can be created in which every entity performs its obligations.

Digital Literacy

In 1994, Y. Eshet-Alkalai defined digital literacy as "the ability to understand and use various digital resources and information displayed by computers". In 1997, Paul Gilster formally introduced the concept of "digital literacy" in his book of the same name. According to him, digital literacy mainly includes the ability to acquire, understand, and integrate digital information. In August 2017, the International Federation of Library Associations and Institutions released the *IFLA Statement on Digital Literacy*, the world's first international and systematic statement on digital literacy. It points out that being digitally literate means being able to make maximum use of digital technologies in an efficient and logical manner to meet personal, social, and professional needs for information. All in all, "digital literacy is becoming universal and even serves as a prerequisite for other skills, which are demonstrated in the overall ability and competency of citizens to use information technology" (Sun Xuxin and Luo Yue 2020).

Social inequality has taken on new forms as human society evolves. Changes have taken place in the status of men and women from matrilineal to patrilineal clan societies; the polar opposites, formed by slave owners possessing slaves and land, have changed to the hierarchy of "exploitation" formed by landowners, who then exploit the peasants who work on the land; the extreme division between rich and poor formed by capitalists relying on the possession of the means of production and exploitation of workers' surplus value in the past have been transformed to a situation where contemporary capitalists rely on the purchase of shares to obtain dividends, and control enterprises and employees. Factors such as gender differences, means of production, tools of production, land, capital, economic status, and political power have always shaped the position of different social classes and groups, as well as the overall social structure. Digital inequality is a more profound embodiment and judgment of the socialization of digital technology. According to Professor Timothy Rook, who first proposed "digital inequality," the hallmark of digital inequality is the transformation from a historical class struggle to "information wars" in a new era between employers and employees, between producers and consumers, between the informed and the uninformed, between those who have access to technology and those who do not. In practice, digital inequality has gradually shifted from inequality of motivation, access, and effectiveness to inequality in the economy, society, culture, and information capital, and even in status and power in social networks (Yan Hui 2013, pp. 20–21).

The development of digital technology has created digital inequality to some extent. People and organizations are divided into three categories: those who generate data, those who have the means to collect data, and those who have the ability to analyze data, which is also known as the "data strata" in the era of big data. As a factor of production, data is a necessity just like food, clothing, housing, security, and education, and should be distributed fairly to citizens. Due to digital inequality, people are unable to share the fruits of advanced technology equitably, resulting in a situation of information "differentiation." In the digital age we are living in a sea of data, and all kinds of data is stored in cyberspace, an ocean of completely open data that requires an ethics-based data order. Owing to digital inequality, the situation of "the rich getting richer and the poor getting poorer" will certainly intensify. In other words, in this era data processors will use their technical advantages to obtain and exploit our privacy, while we, data generators, keep producing data that may expose and exploit our privacy. Nevertheless, we cannot, and are not able to, obtain and exploit the data belonging to the processors. Accordingly, in order to protect privacy and get a better deal with the value distribution of data, it is necessary to pay attention to both the building of data ethics and the enhancement of digital literacy of e-citizens.

The *14th Five-Year Plan* puts emphasis on "improving the digital skills of all." While we continue to use and rely on digital technology, this demands digital literacy for digital citizens in the digital age. The US Federal Government's *Plan of American National Educational Technology* and *Standards of Educational Technology of the USA* state that exemplary e-residency involves being "able to use digital information and tools in a safe, legal, and ethical manner." In his book *Digital Citizenship in Schools*, Mike Ribble, a researcher of digital citizenship education, stated that "digital citizens should be able to follow the related norms and behave appropriately and responsibly in the application of technology."

> While the requirements for citizens in the real world are mainly related to rights and duties, the basic requirements for digital citizenship refer to some of the qualities and norms that citizens must have in order to use technology for their practices and activities in the digital society. (Zhang Lixin and Zhang Xiaoyan 2015)

The *National Educational Technology Standards for Students: The Next Generation (Second Edition)* clearly defines the duties and rights of digital citizens. It asks for the ability to understand human, cultural, and social issues related to technology, as well as the ability to behave in accordance with legal and ethical norms. Based on the above, the basic requirements for digital citizenship can be summarized into four areas: awareness of data, digital information, digital competence, and digital culture.[17] These

17 Awareness of data mainly refers to the attitude digital citizens take toward technology. It is interpreted as the sensitivity digital citizens have to information technology and the consciousness of using information technology to serve their daily life, study and work, including the awareness of participating in digital life, the awareness of digital health, the awareness of digital security, and the awareness of responsibility. Digital information, mainly refers to the knowledge that e-residency should have to engage in life, study, work, recreation in the digital society. The information structure of digital citizens includes information technology system

four aspects not only comprehensively reflect the essential, composite, and interdisciplinary skills that are essential to the digital life of e-residency, but provide a way to maintain a harmonious ecology of cyberspace with which to create a digital world that is inclusive and all-embracing.

Bibliography

Anthony, Ogus. 1995. "Rethinking Self-discipline." *Oxford Journal of Legal Studies*, 15th issue.

Big Data Standards Working Group of National Technical Committee for Information Technology Standardization, China Electronics Standardization Institute. September 21, 2020. *White Paper on Big Data Standardization* (2020 Edition), Information Research Center of China Electronics Standardization Institute, <http://jl.cesi.cn/202009/6826.htm>.

Big Data Standards Working Group of National Technical Committee for Information Technology Standardization, China Electronics Standardization Institute. March 29, 2018. *White Paper on Big Data Standardization* (2020 Edition), Information Research Center of China Electronics Standardization Institute, <http://www.cesi.cn/201803/3709.htm>.

Black, Julia. 1996. "Constitutionalising Self-discipline." *Modern Law Review*, 59th issue.

Chang Jian, and Guo Wei. 2011. "The Position, Motivation, Model and Limitations of Industry Self-discipline." *Nankai Journal (Philosophy, Literature and Social Science Edition)*, 1st issue.

Chen Hongyan, and Yin Kuijie. 2014. "On the Legalization of Rights." *Journal of Northeast Normal University (Philosophy and Social Sciences Edition)*, 3rd issue.

---

itself, laws and regulations, health and safety involved in the application of information technology in various aspects of daily life, and knowledge related to the responsibilities and rights of digital citizens. Digital competence, mainly refers to the ability that digital citizens should have to use information technology to live, study, work, recreation, communication and shopping in the digital world, that is, digital life ability. Digital culture means the digital citizens should understand the unique culture in the digital world, abide by its ethical norms, and know its behaviors, etc.

Chen, Shiwei. 2016. "Ethical Governance of Big Data Technology's Alienation." *Studies in Dialectics of Nature*, 1st issue.

Chen Tian, and Liu Minghui. April 29, 2020. "Strengthen the Security Management of Data Classification and Classification, and Promote the Improvement of Market-Oriented Allocation of Data Elements." *China Academy of Information and Communications Technology*. <http://www.caict.ac.cn/kxyj/caictgd/202004/t20200429_280540.htm>.

Chen, Xuequan. 2008. "On the Impact of Technological Development on the Criminal Evidence System." *People's Procuratorial Semimonthly*, 1st issue.

Chen, Yi. 2020. "The Practice of EU Big Data Ethics Governance and Its Enlightenment to China." *Library and Information Service*, 3rd issue.

Cheng, Xiao. 2018. "Personal Data Rights in the Era of Big Data." *China's Social Research*, 3rd issue.

Chu Jiewang, and Xia Li. 2020. *Research on the Construction of Scientific Data Management System Embedded in Life Cycle Theory – Oxford University as an Example, Modern Intelligence*, 10th issue.

Edgar, Bodenheimer. 2017. *Juris Prudence: The Philosophy and Method of the Law*. Trans. Deng Zhenglai. Beijing: China University of Political Science and Law Press.

Elinor, Ostrom. 2000. *Governing the Commons: The Evolution of Institutions for Collective Action*. Trans. Yu Xunda, et al. Shanghai: SDX Joint Publishing Company.

Locke, *Two Treatises of Civil Government (Part 2)*. Trans. Ye, Qifang, et al. 2009, The Commercial Press, p. 17–19.

Gao Fuping, and Wang Wenxiang. 2017. "The Boundary of the Crime of Selling or Providing Personal Information of Citizens." *Politics and Law*, 2nd issue.

Gao, Lei. 2019. "Research on Hierarchical Protection of Personal Information in Big Data Applications." *Information Security Research*, 5th issue.

He, Bo. 2017. "Study on the Legal Practice and Suggestions for Countermeasures of Data Sovereignty." *Information Security and Communications Privacy*, 5th issue.

He Jiahong, and Liu Pinxin. 2019. *Law of Evidence*. Beijing: Law Press.

Huang Haiying, and He Mengting. 2019. "Interpretation of US Data Sovereignty Strategy Based on CLOUD Act." *Journal of Information Resources Management*, 2nd issue.

Key Laboratory of Big Data Strategy. 2019. *Data Rights Law 1.0: The Theoretical Basis*. Social Sciences Academic Press (China), p. 178; p. 187.

Lei, Jianchang. 2004. "On the Parallelism of Objective Truth and Legal Truth – From the Epistemological and Methodological Perspectives of Evidence." *Journal of Southwest Petroleum University (Social Sciences Edition)*, 1st issue.

Li Baokuan, and Ye Zijing. 2019. "The Position and Value of Industry Self-discipline in the New Mechanism of Social Co-Governance." January 21. <https : // www.financialnews.com.cn/ll/gdsj/201901/t20190121_153352.html>.

Li, Haiying. 2016. "Legal Challenges and Recommendations for Big Data." *Big Data Research*, 2nd issue.

Li Lu, and Jiao Chengpeng. 2018. "Research on Big Data Security Protection Strategy." *Cyberspace Security*, 5th issue.

Li Lun, and Huang, Guan. 2019. "Studies in Ethics." *Studies in Ethics*, 2nd issue.

Li Songtao, and Xie Zongxiao. 2019. "Analysis of Data Classification, Staging and Related Standards." *China's Quality and Standards Review*, 4nd issue.

Li, Qian. 2016. "The Change and Development of Legal Rules in the Era of 'Internet+'." *Administration Reform*, 3rd issue.

Liu, Pinxin. 2019. "On Big Data Evidence." *Global Law Review*, 1st issue.

Liu, Pinxin, and Chen Li. 2019. "The Datafied and Unified Evidence Standard." *Journal of National Prosecutors College*, 2nd issue.

Liu, Tianjiao. 2020. "Theoretical Distinctions and Practical Conflicts between Data Sovereignty and Long-Arm Jurisdiction." *Global Law Review*, 2nd issue.

Li, Wei. 2019. "Debate on the Concept of Utilitarianism: Hume and Bentham." *Academic Research*, 3rd issue.

Li, Xiaoyu. 2019. "Categorized Protection of Data Rights and Interests from the Perspective of Rights and Interests." *Intellectual Property Rights*, 3rd issue.

Li, Yanan. 2018. "The Realization of Regulation Path for Data Protection Behavior." *Academic Exchange*, 8th issue.

Li Yang, and Li Xiaoyu. 2019a. "Definition and Clarification of Corporate Data Boundaries in the Big Data Era – Discussing the Separation and Connection between Different Types of Data." *Fujian Forum (Humanities and Social Sciences Edition)*, 11th issue.

Li Yang, and Li Xiaoyu. 2019b. "The Nature of Corporate Data Rights and Interests in the Big Data Era and the Construction of Its Protection Model." *Xuehai*, 4th issue.

Liu, Yun. 2020. *Improve Data Staging and Classification Rules, Improve Network Data Security Legislation*, Cyberspace Administration of China, September 28, <http://www.cac.gov.cn/2020-09/28/c_1602854536494247.htm>.

Margot, Priest. 1998. "The Privatization of Regulation: Five Models of Self-discipline." *Ottawa Law Review 29*, 2nd issue.

Maxwell, John, Thomas Lyon, and Steven Hackett. 2000. "Self-discipline and Social Welfare: The Political Economy of Corporate Environmentalism." *Journal of Law and Economics*, 43rd issue.

Nicholas, Negroponte. 2017. *Digital Life*. Trans. Hu Yong, et al. Beijing: Publishing House of Electronics Industry.

Philip, Eijlander. 2005. "Possibilities and Constraints in the Use of Self-discipline and Co-Regulation in Legislative Policy: Experiences in the Netherlands-Lessons to Be Learned for the EU." *Electronic Journal of Comparative Law*, 9th issue.

Qi Aimin, and Pan Jia. 2015. "The Establishment of Data Rights, Data Sovereigns and Basic Principles of Big Data Protection," *Journal of Suzhou University (Philosophy and Social Sciences)*, 1st issue.

Rawls, John. 1999. *A Theory of Justice*. Cambridge: Harvard University Press.

Schmitt, M. Tallin. 2017. *Manual 2.0 on the International Law Application to Cyber Operations (2nd edition)*. Cambridge: Cambridge University Press.

Shen, Weixing. July 23, 2018. "Implementation of Big Data Strategy Should Pay Attention to the Construction of Digital Economy Legal System." *Guangming Daily*, 11th Edition.

Shi, Dan. 2019. "Legal Protection and Institutional Construction of Corporate Data Property Rights." *Electronic Intellectual Property*, 6th issue.

State Administration for Market Regulation, the China National Standardization Management Committee. 2018. *Information Technology – Evaluation Indicators for Data Quality*. China Standards Press, p. 1.

Sun Xuxin, Luo Yue, et al. 2020. "Digital Literacy in the Era of Globalization: Connotation and Evaluation." *Journal of World Education*, 8th issue.

Tan, Qiping. 2017. "On the Homogeneous Relationship between 'Unincorporated Organizations' and 'Other Organizations' in the Sense of Civil Subjects." *Journal of Sichuan University (Philosophy and Social Sciences Edition)*, 4th issue.

The State Council of the People's Republic of China. September 5, 2015. *Outline of Action to Promote the Development of Big Data*, the Chinese government website.

Wang Shan, et al. 2011. "Architecting Big Data: Challenges, Current Situation and Prospects." *Journal of Computer Science*, 10th issue.

Wang, Yongqi. 2019. "The legal Connotation of Public Data and its Regulatory Application Path." *Digital Library Forum*, 8th issue.

Wittgenstein. 1962. *Tractatus Logico-Philosophicus*. Trans. Guo Ying. Beijing: The Commercial Press.

Wu Changhai, and Chang Zheng. 2017. "Exploring Public Data Access and Openness in the Context of Big Data Economy." *Economic System Reform*, 1st issue.

Wu, Jialin. 1981. "On Subjectivity and Objectivity of Evidence." *Chinese Journal of Law*, 6th issue.

Xiang Liling, and Shi Shangyuan. 2005. "Comparison and Reflections of the Legislative Spirit of Information Secrecy in China and Foreign Countries." *Intelligence Theory and Practice*, 4th issue.

Xue, Bo. 2003. *English-Chinese Dictionary of Anglo-American Law*. Beijing: Law Press.

Yan, Hui. 2013. *Social Classes in China's Digital Society*. Beijing: National Library of China Publishing House.

Yang, Lixin. July 13, 2016. "Derivative Data Is the Object of Data Exclusive Rights." *Chinese Journal of Social Science*, No. 005.

Yu, Chong. 2018. "The Legal Benefit Attributes and Human Crime Boundary of Citizens' Personal Information in the Crime of Infringing Citizens' Personal Information." *Politics and Law*, 4th issue.

Yue, Jin. 2016. "The Moral Implications and Ethical Challenges of Big Data Technology." *Marxism & Reality*, 5th issue.

Yuval, Harari. 2017. *Homo Deus: A Brief History of Tomorrow*. Trans. Lin Junhong. Beijing: CITIC Press Group.

Zeng, Junping. 2006. "Collective Interest: A Theoretical Interpretation." *Financial Studies*, 9th issue.

Zhang Liangliang, and Chen Zhi. 2020. "The Cultivation of Data Element Markets Need to Speed Up the Improvement of the System of Data Property Rights." *Science and Technology China*, 5th issue.

Zhang Lixin, and Zhang Xiaoyan. 2015. "Discussion on Turning Digital Natives into Digital Citizens." *China Educational Technology*, 10th issue.

Zhang, Wenliang. 2018. "The Essence and Approach of Personal Data Protection Legislation." *Jiangxi Social Sciences*, 6th issue.

Zhu, Baoli. 2019. "Definition of Data Property Rights: Multi-Dimensional Perspective and System Construction." *Law Forum*, 5th issue.

Zhu, Lixin. 2015. "A Focus on the *Tallinn Manual*: A Look at the Rules of Cyber Warfare." *China Information Security*, 10th issue.

Zhu, Mingjie. 2019. "Analysis on the Contradictions and Legal Path of Data Rights Protection." *Gansu Finance*, 11th issue.

CHAPTER 5

Comparison of Data Rights Legislation Models

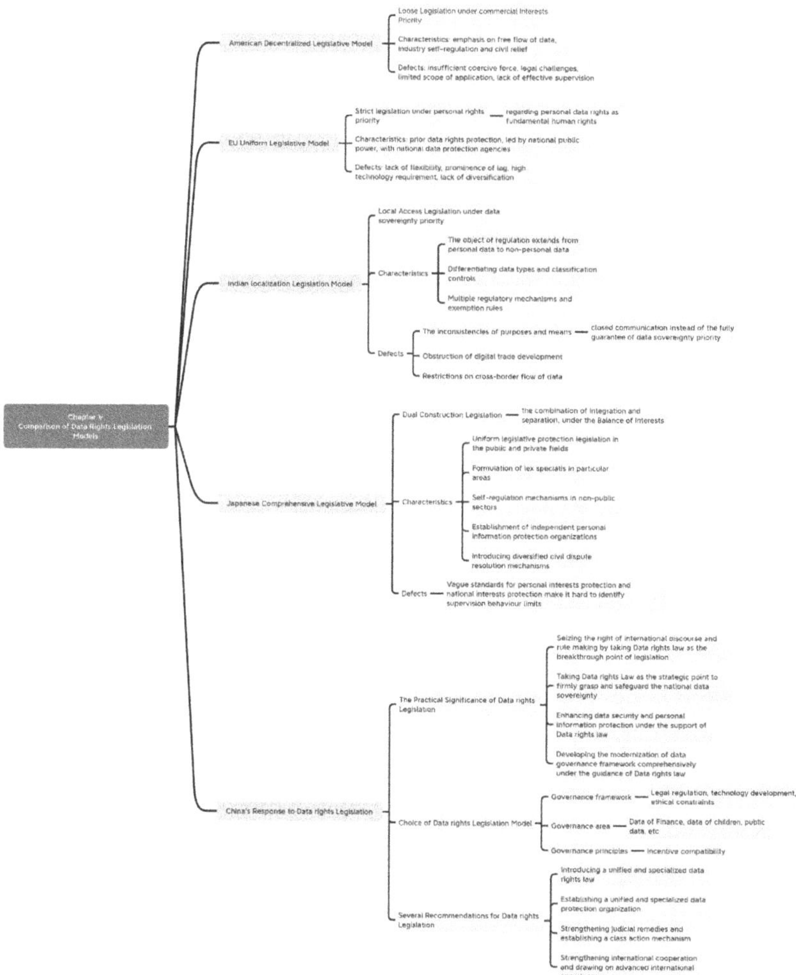

In the 1970s, as marked by the legislation for personal data protection, global legislation for data rights protection entered a prime time. By 2020, more than 140 countries and regions had promulgated legal norms on the protection of privacy, information, and data. With the development of digital technology, such as the Internet, big data, artificial intelligence, and blockchain, revisions have started to be made on extraterritorial personal data protection laws. Because of the divergence of historical and cultural backgrounds and the social and economic development of different countries, the models of data rights protection legislation are quite different, but can be categorized into four types: the decentralized legislative model represented by the US, the unified legislative model represented by the European Union, the localization legislative model represented by India, and the comprehensive legislative model represented by Japan. Each of the four models has its own advantages and disadvantages, and they have differences as well as commonalities. By objectively analyzing the advantages and disadvantages of the four legislative models, this chapter has drawn fully on the experience of the Japanese comprehensive legislative model, as well as the reasonable parts of the American model, the EU model, and the Indian model. Based on this, innovations are proposed to establish a data rights system with Chinese characteristics in line with China's national conditions.

Decentralized Model of the United States

The United States made the earliest, most abundant and complete theoretical research into legislative data rights protection. However, there is not, as yet, any specialized legislation and relevant stipulations are scattered in many federal laws. The United States has chosen a form of loose legislation that prioritizes commercial interests to form a unique American model, which features a combination of decentralized legislation and self-discipline.

The decentralized legislative model means that there are no basic laws for the protection of privacy, information, or data. Instead, the relevant legislation distinguishes between different fields and matters. The United States is a typical representative of this decentralized model, and stipulations regarding data rights protection are scattered in its complicated federal laws (Qi Aimin 2005). When discussing personal information or data protection in the context of American law, this includes privacy protection, which is the foundation of the U.S. Constitution and tort law. "In the U.S. Constitution and the common law, the right to privacy is regarded as a right to maintain integrity, independence and inviolability of personality." In order to protect it from public power, the Supreme Court of the United States recognized the right to privacy as a basic human right, although it was implicit in the Constitution in the early twentieth century. The *Fair Information Practice Guidelines* (FIPs) of personal information was established (see Table 17).[1] On this basis, the United States has formulated statutory laws in the field of information privacy protection, and confirmed that the norms relating to the right to privacy are scattered in the Constitution, tort law and other statutory laws, which can be divided into the following three levels: First, the general information privacy protection under the constitutional and common law system; second, the special law directed at sensitive personal information and high-risk groups of people who are vulnerable to privacy violation; and third, the "bottom-up" personal information protection provided by the *Federal Trade Commission Act*, from the aspect of "improper or deceptive behavior,"[2] which regulates commercial information privacy, data security, and other data-intensive business behaviors.[3]

1 See *International Comparative Research on Personal Information Protection*. China Financial Publishing House, 2017, p. 56.

2 According to the provision of Article 5 of *the Federal Trade Commission Act* prohibiting improper or deceptive acts or practices in or affecting business, if a merchant's privacy policy may mislead consumers, materially affect consumers' decisions on products and services, and lead to their irrational behavior, the act or practice is deceptive; if a merchant's behavior is likely to cause unavoidable significant harm to consumers and cannot bring corresponding benefits to consumers or competition, the act or practice is "improper."

3 See *International Comparative Research on Personal Information Protection*. China Financial Publishing House, 2017, p. 58.

Table 17. Legislation on Privacy Protection in the United States

Time	Name	Main Content
1792	*Fourth Amendment to the Constitution*	Citizens are free from unjustifiable search or seizure of their persons, residence, documents, or property
1966	*Freedom of Information Act*	Government agencies are required to make efforts to disclose information to the public, and the burden of proof is on the government
1970	*Fair Information Practice Guidelines*	Consumers have the right to rectification, and the errors in consumer reports do not apply to consumer behaviors
1974	*The Privacy Act*	Regulating the Federal Governments' handling of personal information, balancing public interests, and personal privacy
1978	*Right to Financial Privacy Act*	Without notification to or consent from their client, financial institutions are prohibited from disclosing any clients' financial records to the federal government at will, unless the federal government followed certain procedures and provided supporting documents accordingly
1980	*Right to Financial Privacy Act*	Regulating access to bank records by federal financial institutions
	The Privacy Protection Act of 1980	Establishing data standards of using newspaper and other media records for law enforcement agencies
1984	*Cable Communication Policy Act*	Closed circuit television operators are prohibited from using cable systems to collect users' personal information without prior consent
1986	*Electronic Communications Privacy Act*	Not only are government departments' not authorized to eavesdrop, all individuals and businesses are prohibited from eavesdropping on the content of communications
1988	*The Video Privacy Protection Act*	Provision relating to secure privacy protection for the purchase and rental of video

Table 17. Continued

Time	Name	Main Content
1994	*Drivers Privacy Protection Act*	Restrictions on the use and disclosure of personal vehicle records by state transport authorities
1996	*Health Insurance Portability and Accountability Act*	Protection of personal health information; patients' personal health information cannot be shared by any third party without the patients' consent.
1999	*Financial Services Modernization Act (Gramm-Leach-Bliley Act)*	Provides for means for financial institutions to process private personal information
2000	*Children's Online Privacy Protection Act*	Protects personal information processed on the Internet by online services. The collection and use of children's personal information without parental consent is restricted by the federal laws and regulations
2008	*Genetic Information Nondiscrimination Act*	Provides greater privacy and security protection on genetic data
2010	*Consumer Financial Protection Act of 2010*	Authorizes the Consumer Financial Protection Authority to regulate and protect financial privacy
2018	*California Consumer Privacy Act 2018*	Expands the scope of use, creates a series of consumer privacy rights, including access rights, deletion rights, the right to know, etc., and further increases the responsibility of enterprises to protect personal data
2020	*California Privacy Rights Act*	New data privacy rights are established, new obligations and responsibilities are imposed on businesses and service providers, and independent data regulators will be created to enforce California privacy laws and prosecute violations

Source: collated according to public information.

Personal information protection in the United States is regulated by the relevant laws on privacy from the federal level to the state level. Initially, these laws were aimed at avoiding the violation of individuals' right to privacy by public power, and are reinforced by the *1934 Restatement of Tort Law* which identified the serious violation of personal privacy without proper reason as a cause of civil action (Zhang Jiaxin 2019). The protection of its citizens' right to privacy originated from the provisions of the *Fourth Amendment of the Constitution*,[4] which provides that citizens are free from unjustifiable search or seizure of their persons, residence, documents, or property. Based on the Constitution's role shifting from the defender to the protector, the United States has gradually realized the necessity of dealing with citizens' privacy protection. In addition, the concepts and principles of privacy protection have been delivered by the legislature and courts to many other areas of privacy law, which promoted American personal information protection legislation. At the American legislative level, this can be divided into two levels: the federal level and the state level. At the federal level, there are approximately forty laws on personal information protection; at the state level, most states have made laws in this area. Among them, California has been in the forefront of privacy legislation because of its gathering of internet companies (Zhang Li 2019, pp. 163–4).

"The legislation of the US on personal information protection exists in various departments of privacy laws, with close relationship to the American privacy theory and its legal tradition" (Hong Hailin 2010, p. 99). The *Privacy Act of 1974*, which is recognized as the basic law of the United States on personal information protection is the most important one.

> Article 552(b) of the Act provides that "no institution may disclose any record in the record system to any other person or institution by any means of transmission without the concerned individual's written request or prior written consent."[5]

4 The *Fourth Amendment to the Constitution of the United States* provides that: "It is prohibited to infringe upon the right of citizens not to be subjected to unreasonable search and seizure of persons, residences, documents and property; search and seizure certificates may not be issued unless there is an oath or a solemn declaration of appropriate reasons, a specially designated place of search and a person or article being seized."

5 According to a 552(b) of the *Privacy Act*, "no institution may disclose any record in the recording system to any person or other institution by any means of

The current *Privacy Act* has 22 articles, which mainly address five aspects. The first is the scope of application. It applies only to organizations at or above the level of the federal ministries. The second is the protection of objects, which means the personal records protected by the administrative organs. The third is the rights of the information subjects, including the right to decide on the disclosure of information, and the right to access or to modify their own personal information; the fourth is the obligation of administrative organs, which refers to the obligation to collect and provide information, ensure data confidentiality, security and quality, and keep within the defined scope, and so on; the fifth is civil relief measures. If any administrative organ fails to change or review the information records of a particular individual upon request, or has violated the principle of "accuracy, relevance, timeliness, and completeness," or leads to wrong decisions against individuals, then that party shall have the right to file suit for civil compensation.

Relating to personal information in commercial use, the United States has made legislation mainly in the areas of finance, education, communications, health information, and consumer protection (Xiang Dingyi 2019). In the area of finance, the *Right to Financial Privacy Act* of 1978 provides that, without notice to or consent from their client, financial institutions are prohibited from disclosing their clients' financial records to the federal government at will, unless the federal government follows certain procedures and has provided supporting documents accordingly.[6] In the field of education, the *Family Education Rights and Privacy Act*, adopted in 1974, stipulates that educational institutions may not disclose a student's personal information unless they have obtained the consent of the adult students themselves or, in the case of a minor, the written consent of the student's parents. In the area of communications, the *Electronic Communication Privacy Act* of 1986 provides for the interception and disclosure of personal communications information by unauthorized third parties, with particular emphasis on the rule of not interfering with public

transmission without the written request or prior written consent of the individual concerned with the record."

6 See *International Comparative Research on Personal Information Protection*, China Financial Publishing House, 2017, p. 62.

communications without the approval of the court. In the field of health information, the *Health Insurance Portability and Accountability Act* of 1996 provides for the protection of personal health information; medical institutions may not use or share their patients' personal health information with any third party without the patient's prior consent. In the area of consumer protection, the *Consumer Privacy Rights Act* of 2012 emphasizes that consumers should be informed in time of the reuse of their personal information, especially regarding their right to know about privacy and security protection.

Clearly, the United States has adopted a decentralized legislative model that is mainly concentrated on, and applied to, the public arena, covering a wide range of protections relating to people's lives, which has also provided appropriate personal information protection in some special fields. The purpose of this model is to: seek a balance between the legal protection and reasonable use of personal information; to emphasize free data circulation; and to pay attention to industrial self-discipline and civil relief. The advantages are as follows. First, it restricts legislative power, since in this model, legislative power is scattered among different administrative organs, avoiding excessive expansion of any one of them. Second, it provides a flexible response to market demand. Due to legal instability, decentralized legislation is flexible and can provide a prompt response to social concerns. Third, it is conducive to the formation of a multiple protection pattern. "This legislative model can provide refined and better-targeted personal information protection, and can make some distinctions between different natures and acts of infringement to personal information" (Qi Aimin 2009b, p. 90). Fourth, this model helps promote the legislatures' initiatives in doing their jobs. However, a decentralized legislative model also has some disadvantages, which are mainly manifested in "the lack of centralized or unified legislation, the possibility of conflicts, duplication or inconsistency, and failure to provide coordinated and effective personal information protection on some occasions" (Qi Aimin c. 2009, p. 184).

The decentralized legislative model is mainly applied to the public arena, rather than private areas such as private groups and social organizations. With the rapid development of the market economy, the U.S. government is unwilling to over-intervene or enact legal constraints to personal information protection; rather, it intends to protect citizens' personal information security through industrial self-control, self-management, and self-restraint. Therefore, in the digital age, in the United States personal information in private areas is protected by relying on the "strong market power and personal behavior backed by the law " (Zhou Hanhua 2006, p. 102), which means that, in the private field, the United States has resorted to industrial self-discipline, which is guided by industrial associations or specialized agencies who provide codes of conduct and industrial guidelines to protect personal information (Jiang Po 2001, p. 443). Self-discipline is not completely laissez-faire; instead, it has a close relationship with the U.S. government and, strictly speaking, it falls under the government's guidance.

Industrial self-discipline in the United States takes norms as the core. The organizers formulate industrial norms so as to ensure conformity with the minimal legal requirements. The main forms are guidance for industry and online privacy seal programs. Guidance for industry is formulated by a self-discipline organization whose members have chosen to abide by industrial guidelines for personal information protection. For example, in June 1988, the American Online Privacy Alliance (OPA), whose membership included forty-six companies and groups, published its *Online Privacy Guidelines*, to be complied with by its members when collecting users' personal information. Online privacy seal programs promote personal information protection by issuing privacy authentication to institutions that meet the relevant norms and requirements (Jiang Po 2001, pp. 449–50). The program requires licensed websites to post their privacy authentication seals online, outlining their compliance with online personal information collection rules, and their various kinds of supervision and management measures (Zhou Xinyue 2013). There are many online privacy authentication seals in the United States at present. TRUSTe is one of the most famous organizations, whose certification and assurance programs consist of two parts: general privacy certification and verification and special certification (Li yuan 2016, pp. 62–3).

Compared with the decentralized legislative model, the industrial self-discipline model of the United States has some great advantages. On the one hand, as information technology is still developing rapidly, the self-discipline model can prevent legislation from restricting the application of new technologies especially when legislation comes out earlier than it perhaps should; and it can also prevent deviations that may occur when the government chooses one certain technology as the standard. Also, since personal information collection and processing can follow different processes in various fields, the industrial self-discipline model can fine-tune personal information protection measures so that they can be better targeted. However, this model also has obvious drawbacks. The first is its lack of coercive force. The self-discipline norms have no coercive power as state legislation does, and lack the options of judicial relief and clear dispute resolution procedures. The second is insufficient universality. Because industrial self-discipline is based on the will of individual enterprises, and although many well-known enterprises have participated, some still remain out of it. The third is the challenge to legitimacy. The self-discipline norms formulated by the industry usually emphasize the industries' "property rights" over information, which make for conflicts between personal information rights and the "information property ownership" of organizations (Spinello 1999, pp. 50–1). The fourth is the absence of effective supervision. There is no government supervision for industrial self-discipline and, when driven by interests, this may lead to some illegal behaviors, such as the creation of a monopoly, which is of particular concern.

Overall, the decentralized legislative model with industrial self-discipline has avoided the arbitrariness that results from unified legislation, met the requirements of the rapid technological progress and the digital economy development in the digital age, and has dealt with the changes. It has also avoided the adverse effects on technology, economic development, and social progress caused by rigid legislation (Ren Longlong 2017, p. 79). The United States model offers some experience that other countries may learn from. First, it has focused on the value and efficiency of personal information circulation. It is important to find a balance between personal information circulation and protection. Second, with the support of law, industrial self-discipline is able to deal with complex issues in industrial personal information management, saving some judicial costs. Third, at the federal level, the standards of personal information protection are set high so that they can be used to handle cross-border data flow risks and challenges in various aspects, and ensure the international circulation of personal information (Yang Ji 2012).

Unified Legislative Model of the EU

The ongoing global tide of data protection legislation in recent years has demonstrated many countries' concerns about data protection. As European countries legislate on data protection, their differences in the degree of legislative protection may affect the cross-border flow of personal data. In view of this, and in order to avoid unnecessary obstacles to integration within the EU out of concerns for data protection, the EU requires its members to adopt a uniform legislative model to fully protect their citizens' personal data, and to avoid the incomplete protection or non-compliance with the law. The EU's legislation on personal data protection is based on the long-existing theory of personality rights, with particular emphasis on the protection of the moral rights and personality interests of the concerned individuals. It provides a unified and scientific standard for personal data protection; however, this model also has the disadvantages of not taking into account the special features of personal data protection in various fields, and it lacks flexibility. Thus, it is hard to adapt this legislation to the evolving legal environment through adjustment.

Since the 1970s, the leakage and infringement of personal data have occurred frequently, which aroused the concern of European countries about personal data security. Due to the urgent need for data protection, some European countries have made special legislative attempts and formulated their own personal data protection laws step-by-step. In 1970, the State of Hesse, Germany, enacted the world's first special personal data protection law, the *Hessisches Datenshutzgeset* (Bennett and Rawls 1992, p. 48). In 1973, Sweden enacted the world's first personal data protection law at a national level, the *Swedish Data Protection Act* (Burkert H., pp. 43–70). In 1977, Germany also promulgated a national law of the *Federal Data Protection Act (Bundesdatenschutzgesetz)*. In 1978, France adopted *Law No. 78–17 of 6 January 1978 on information technology, files and freedoms* (Flaherty D. H. 1989, pp. 166–222). In 1981 Iceland adopted the *Personal Act on Data Protection and the Processing Act of Personal Data*. In 1984 the UK adopted *the Data Protection Act* (Bennett C. J. and John Rawls 1992). During the same period, Ireland also introduced relevant legislation, while Portugal, Belgium, the Netherlands, and other countries in Europe created their own personal data protection legislation, which had a profound impact on the later data protections throughout Europe (Zhang Xinbao 2015).

Shortly after its establishment, the EU took into account the reality of personal data circulation in its member states, and made an early decision to harmonize personal data protection legislation through an integration process (Pearce and Platten 1998). This included the adoption of uniform protection standards and data processing principles for all personal data in various fields, such as the government sector and the private sector, as well as the adoption of a unified legislative model of "blanket protection."[7] The so-called unified legislative model refers to the legislative model that unifies and regulates the collection, utilization, and processing of personal data between its government organs and civil subjects (Qi Aimin 2009c, p. 177). Under this legislative model, states are required to formulate a unified personal data protection law and to strictly implement the basic principles of personal data protection. Based on this, some special authorities had to be set up. The EU's unified legislative model has greatly influenced national legislation since then. Objectively speaking, this was not merely because the EU adopted this model, but because the model was consistent with most other legal systems in the world.

The EU's adoption of the unified legislative model is rooted in its profound historical background. On the one hand, the EU is a regional, multilateral, and international organization with a unique characteristic; it requires member states to adopt a unified legislative model for the full protection of its citizens' personal data rights. On the other hand, the EU

7 See *International Comparative Research on Personal Information Protection*. China Financial Publishing House, 2017, p. 68.

had already suffered from the two world wars, so it needed to tighten the protection and controls of personal data. The adoption of a unified legislative model not only provides a unified standard, it also provides effective legal support and a strict authoritative platform through the establishment of a special personal data protection agency with independent authority. It can deal with illegal events such as personal data leakage, protect the personal data security of citizens, reduce the lag and confusion caused by the uncertainty of the application of laws or legal procedures, and can ensure that free data circulates without impediment.

The EU started research on personal data protection quite early, and has a long history of personal data protection through uniform legislation (see Table 18). Back in 1981, the European Parliament adopted the first binding international convention on personal data protection—*the Convention for the Protection of Individuals with Regard to Automatic Processing of Personal Data* (Convention 108), which was the beginning of the EU's uniform legislation. Then, as the European Community developed into the EU, it paid more attention to personal data protection. In 1990, The European Commission began to recognize that personal data protection laws in its fourteen member states restricted personal data circulation and hindered the establishment of the EU's single market. To buffer this conflict, the EU drafted the Data Protection Directive (*Directive 95/46/EC on the protection of individuals with regard to the processing of personal data and on the free movement of such data*), which marked the EU's complete legislative process. In addition, the EU's law on personal data protection contains the *Directive on privacy and electronic communications, Directive 2002/58/EC* and *Directive 2006/24/EC*. Besides which, the *Charter of Fundamental Rights* of *the European Union* was signed and adopted at the 2000 European Council summit, Article 8 of which clearly states that "everyone has the right to personal data protection." Thereafter, the charter was fully incorporated into the EU constitution. As can be seen, The EU has a historical tradition of taking personal data protection seriously.

Table 18. EU Data Protection Legislation

Time	Name	Main Content
1970	*Hessisches Datenschutzgesetz*	This act is the world's first comprehensive data protection legislation, it clarifies the duty of executives to keep personal data confidential and divides the authority and status of local and state administrations in the use of personal data
1973	*The Swedish Data Act*	Requests the establishment of an organization dedicated to the protection of personal data, without the authorization of which no one may process personal data
1977	*The Federal Data Protection Act*	Based on the right to general personality and the right to self-determination of information, the law provides unified protection of personal data. It establishes the basic principles of data protection, the basic contents of personal data rights, the supervisory authority, and the relief system for damages
1978	*The Law No. 78-17 of 6 January 1978 on information technology, files and freedoms*	Provides for the processing of personal data, without prejudice to the rights of individuals with respect to their personality, identity, and private life
1981	*The Convention on the Automated Processing of Personal Data*	The convention provides basic rules for the concept, protection principles, and transnational transmission of personal data, and is the first binding international convention on personal data and privacy protection in the world
1995	*The Data Protection Directive*	Countries are required to adopt a unified legislative model and establish independent data protection agencies to fully protect personal information data. The directive establishes a comprehensive data protection system for personal data protection in the EU, so as to improve the level of personal data protection in the EU as a whole, and remove obstacles to the free flow of personal data among member states

Table 18. Continued

Time	Name	Main Content
2002	*The Privacy and Electronic Communications Directive*	It is prohibited for communications and internet service providers to store or use user data without the consent of the user; when they need to borrow or use user data, they have to inform the user of their intention to process their data, and the user has the right to choose whether or not to agree
2006	*Data Retention Directive*	Public telecommunications service providers, communication service providers, and public communication network service providers are required to retain traffic and location data for a period of time to assist law enforcement agencies in conducting surveys of serious and terrorist crimes
2016	*Directive (EU) 2016/680 of the European Parliament and of the Council of 27 April 2016*	Facilitates and limits personal data use when dealing with criminal offenses committed by public institutions in member states
2018	*The General Data Protection Regulation (GDPR)*	Data collectors are required to collect users' data provided they have clear permission, and users have full title to the data collected, or the right to view personal data and uses, and can withdraw the authorization agreement at any time. When requested by the user, the data collector must delete the relevant data immediately

Source: Based on public information.

The most important legal document for data protection in the EU is the *Data Protection Directive* in 1995. It was the world's first legal system for comprehensive privacy and data protection (which covers almost all sectors and types of data processing) (Zhou Hanhua 2006, p. 26). Article 5 of the Directive stipulates that "the Member States shall regulate more specific legal conditions for personal data processing abiding by this Chapter."

Being a directive, member states were required to enact their own personal data protection laws, which shall include all the elements of the directive (Guo Yu 2012, p. 46). All member states amended their domestic personal data protection laws accordingly (Qi Aimin 2015, p. 57). The guiding principle of the directive is to take into account personal interests protection in data processing without ignoring the free circulation of data.[8] The directive became an international leader in the field of personal data protection by introducing data processing principles and concepts, such as data quality principles and purpose limitation principles. Based on the directive, a unified EU legal framework for personal data protection was established to facilitate cross-border policy dialogue between EU members and established free circulation within the internal market (Korff 2008).

The *Data Protection Directive* of 1995 has a quite informative preface, which has seventy-two paragraphs focused on the legislative purpose and scope of application. The main text that follows consists thirty-four articles in seven chapters.

> In Article 1—object of the directive, it states: "In accordance with this Directive, Member States shall protect the fundamental rights and freedoms of natural persons, and in particular their right to privacy with respect to the processing of personal data." However, it also provides that: "Member States shall neither restrict nor prohibit the free flow of personal data between Member States for reasons connected with the protection afforded under paragraph 1."
>
> In Article 3—scope, it states: "This Directive shall apply to the processing of personal data wholly or partly by automatic means, and to the processing otherwise than by automatic means of personal data which form part of a filing system or are intended to form part of a filing system."

The directive regulates the obligation of data controllers in terms of principles relating to data quality (Article 6), criteria for making data processing legitimate (Article 7), the prohibition of processing for sensitive data (Articles 8, 9), and information to be given to the data subject

8 European Parliament and of the Council, "Directive 95/46/EC of the European Parliament and of the Council of 24 October 1995 on the Protection of Individuals with Regard to the Processing of Personal Data and on the Free Movement of Such Data," *Official Journal* 281, no. 38 (1995): 31–50.

(Articles 10, 11). For example, with regard to the obligation to give notice, Articles 10 and 11 provide that, when processing data, the data processors and controllers are obliged to provide relevant information for the data subject, giving some basic details and facts of the data processing.

Besides the obligations of the data controller, the directive also stipulates the rights of data subjects, including their right to participate, right to access their own data, right to dissent, and right to relief from damages in data processing. To be specific, Article 12[9] provides that data subjects have access to their own data, including the data source, and the purpose of and the place for data processing, which is not subject to a reasonable period of time, to excessive delay or expense. If it is found that the data processing does not comply with the Directive, the data owners have the right to require appropriate alterations and deletions. Article 14 states: "Member States shall grant the data subject the right: [...] to object at any time on compelling legitimate grounds relating to his particular situation to the processing of data relating to him [...] to object [...] to the processing of personal data relating to him which the controller anticipates being processed for the purposes of direct marketing." Article 15 states that "Member States shall grant the right to every person, not subject to a decision which produces legal effects concerning him/her or significantly affects him/her and/or is based on automated data processing intending to evaluate certain

9 Article 12 of the *Data Protection Directive* provides that Member States shall guarantee every data subject the right to obtain from the controller: (a) without constraint at reasonable intervals and without excessive delay or expense: confirmation as to whether or not data relating to him are being processed and information at least as to the purposes of the processing, the categories of data concerned, and the recipients or categories of recipients to whom the data are disclosed, communication to him in an intelligible form of the data undergoing processing and of any available information as to their source, knowledge of the logic involved in any automatic processing of data concerning him at least in the case of the automated decisions referred to in Article 15 (1); (b) as appropriate the rectification, erasure or blocking of data the processing of which does not comply with the provisions of this Directive, in particular because of the incomplete or inaccurate nature of the data and; (c) notification to third parties to whom the data have been disclosed of any rectification, erasure or blocking carried out in compliance with (b), unless this proves impossible or involves a disproportionate effort.

personal aspects relating to him/her." Article 23 states: "Any person who has suffered damages as a result of a wrongful data-processing act or a violation of the domestic law under this Directive shall be entitled to compensate from the data controller."

After taking effect, the directive played a vital role in protecting personal data for a long time. However, because many of the regulatory requirements and the rules of rights and obligations in the directive are not directly applicable,[10] but are transformed and enacted by national legislation according to the directive,[11] member states often adopt different interpretations and choices when transforming directives into domestic law (Liu Yun 2017). The directive did not actually achieve the desired function and objectives of a "unified internal market" and "basic rights protection"(Jiang Ge 2011). To make up for this, the EU issued the *Privacy and Electronic Communications Directive* 2002, which made up for the shortcomings of *the Personal Data Protection Directive* regarding cookies and spam, business information treatment, and confidentiality of information (Li Yuan 2019, p. 45). This directive requires telecommunication providers and internet service providers to take appropriate measures to protect their public users' personal data security.[12] According to this, users of public communication services have the right to privacy in the telecommunications sector and free movement of data, communications equipment, and services; to use personal data for direct marketing purposes; and to regulate the use of small text files and to restrict on the use of records.

In 2006, the EU issued *the Data Retention Directive*, which is primarily a mandatory rule aimed at establishing guidelines for public electronic communication service providers for the processing and retention of their own commercial data so as to ensure that, in the event that national security is endangered by any major criminal case, their clients' personal data can be used to detect criminal activities in a timely manner (Guo Yu 2012, p. 47). The directive requires radio communication enterprises to retain all kinds of data, including IP address, exit time, length of calls, and

10 See Article 27 of the *Personal Data Protection Directive*.

11 See Article 28 of the *Personal Data Protection Directive*.

12 See *International Comparative Research on Personal Information Protection*, China Financial Publishing House, 2017, p. 315.

telephone number, and provides that member states may determine the retention time of such data on their own, but not less than half a year and no more than two years (Li Yuan 2019, p. 46). The directive requires member states to take measures to ensure that the retained data is only used by the judiciary or other governmental bodies with legal authorization. "Data retained by public electronic communication service providers or public communication network service providers shall be submitted to the relevant government organs promptly if necessary" (Hong Hailin 2010, p. 93).

With the development of big data and other information technology, the speed of personal data processing has increased and the means have become diverse; it is thus harder for the directive to deal with personal data protection. In order to better meet these new requirements, the European Parliament adopted the *General Data Protection Regulation* (GDPR) in 2016, which became effective in May 2018. The GDPR was deemed to be the most stringent personal data protection act in history, with its scope of application following the principle of territorial jurisdiction and personal jurisdiction,[13] which means that it not only applies to member states, it is also applicable to non-members when implementing data processing activities in the EU. Compared with the *Personal Data Protection Directive*, the GDPR has adopted provisions on the right to be forgotten (Article 17) and the right to data portability (Article 20), raised the requirements for data subjects' consent (Article 7), expanded the scope of data controllers (Article 27), added data controllers' reporting obligations (Articles 19, 33, and 34), enhanced the regulation of data protection (Article 58), and increased penalties for violations of regulations (Article 83) (Ji Leilei 2017).

The above articles establish strict protection of personality rights associated to personal data. The EU believes that "the importance of personal data protection lies in the protection of fundamental human rights and respect for human dignity" (Lei Wanlu 2018). During the two world wars, people in Europe were subjected to dreadful human rights abuses by Nazi Germany, and they quickly came to recognize the importance of human rights and the protection of personality rights. Therefore, the EU and its

13 Article 3 of the GDPR: Territorial scope, Intersoft Consulting, March 27, 2019, <https://gdpr-info.eu/art-3-gdpr>.

member states tend to give priority to human dignity when making any regulations, defining it as the core value and ethical basis of personal data protection legislation to promote the free circulation of personal data. In the EU, the theory of personality rights is the basic theory underlying the protection of personal data by law, and personal data is the embodiment of general personality interests. Both the *Personal Data Protection Directive* and the GDPR aim to protect human dignity and freedom, and regard personal data protection as a fundamental right that transcends other rights (Schwartz P. and Solove D. J. 2014).

In general, the EU's unified legislative model is characterized by the formulation of a unified personal data protection law that has three features. First, it inclines toward the protection of data rights subjects, as it regards personal data rights as a basic human right which is inherent to the subject and related to human dignity, which is non-economic and non-transferable (Wang Xiuxiu 2017), and is aimed at establishing data rights as a basic right of citizens. Second, it puts the state, which holds public power, in a leading position, formulating unified legal norms and aligning standards for the collection, processing, and use of personal data by the state, enterprises, and individuals. The third is the establishment of a national data protection agency—the European Data Protection Board—which is charged with supervising the data processing activities of enterprises and other organizations, as well as auditing, investigating, punishing, and sanctioning illegal data collection. The EU's unified legislation model has played a positive role in personal data protection, and has also had a profound impact on the legislation of almost all countries in the world. Its main advantages are: first, personal data protection can be clearly defined within each country to the extent that a natural persons' data rights become statutory absolute (Qi Aimin 2009a); second, it can provide uniform legal standards and authoritative, normative, and law-based personal data protection; and third, it can provide sufficient relief and necessary safeguards.

The unified legislative model is suitable for every field, and can protect data rights and safeguard human dignity more effectively than any other model (Qi Aimin c. 2009, p. 79). While it makes data protection more specific and comprehensive, the unified legislative model also has some defects: first, it may hinder the free circulation of personal data and other data, and may be costly to implement (Dane Roland and Elizabeth MacDonald 2004, p. 308); second, there is the insufficient power in the legislation—as unified legislation needs a unified legislature, the phenomenon of "decentralized management" in the legislation may cause setbacks to the introduction of unified personal data protection laws; third, it cannot take into account the particularity of personal data protection in various fields, and it is not easy to adapt to the changes of the legal environment because of its lack of flexibility and diversification, its prominent lag, and its heavy reliance on high technology. However, although there are some inevitable defects in the unified legislative model adopted by the EU, it actually made a profound and lasting influence on the data power legislation for both the Roman and common law legal systems.

India's Legislation for Data Localization

In the digital age, the cross-border flow of personal data has become an important factor in social interaction, economic development, and technological progress. At the same time, the PRISM incident, global data infrastructure attacks, and similar events have highlighted the security risks when personal data crosses a border. In this context, to effectively maintain national security, protect personal privacy, and promote the development of the data industry, many countries have adopted localized legislative models to regulate the storage, use, and flow of data. For example, India has adopted local access control to restrict the cross-border flow of personal data following the principle that data sovereignty is the priority. This legislative model results in closed-door protection of data power to some extent. However, it has hindered the development of domestic digital trade and hampered free data circulation, which had a negative impact on overall economic growth of India.

With rapid economic globalization, world trade exchanges between countries are becoming more and more frequent. Cross-border services such as cloud services, e-commerce, and digital trade have become a hot topic of the era; cross-border data flow has become normal and common, exerting an impact on the world economy and changing trade patterns. According to a study by the Brookings Institution, a famous American think tank, global cross-border data flow has contributed 10.1 percent to global economic growth in the decade from 2009, and in 2014 in particular, its contribution amounted to more than $2.8 trillion (US). This is expected to exceed $11 trillion by 2025 (Zhang Monan 2020). At the same time, global data leakage incidents have been frequent. Serious data leakage makes it more risky to carry out cross-border data flow. This is a common problem for all countries that wish to balance security interests, such as national security and personal privacy protection, with economic value, which is a conflict in cross-border data flow (Huang Daoli and Hu Wenhua 2019). Against such a background, on the one hand, promoting data liberalization and eliminating trade barriers have become a hot topic in international multilateral and bilateral negotiations; while on the other hand, in order to maintain data sovereignty, ensure national security, promote industrial development, and protect personal privacy, some countries have implemented legislation for data localization [14] to regulate the storage, use, and flow of data (Zhang Qianwen 2020), in order to deal with the possible security risks caused by cross-border data transmission (Hu Wenhua and Kong Huafeng 2019).

Legislation for data localization began with the PRISM incident. Through the *Guardian* and the *Washington Post* in June 2013, Edward Snowden, a former employee of Booth Allen Consulting Company, a U.S. Defense contractor, disclosed that the United States National Security Agency and the Federal Bureau of Investigation were conducting a secret surveillance project code named "PRISM," through which the two agencies had direct access to the central servers of nine large US multinational IT companies to tape audio, video, photos, emails, documents, and connection

14 Data localization means that a government requires that the storage and processing of personal data collected in its own country must be carried out in its own country, and it is not allowed to transfer personal data freely abroad. For example, some countries such as Belgium, Denmark, Finland, Germany, Russia, Sweden, and the United Kingdom all require financial data within a certain scope to be stored locally, and some countries, including Australia and the United Kingdom, require health records to be kept within their own territories.

logs; these companies included Apple, Microsoft, PalTalk, Skype, etc. (Greenwald 2013, p. 1). This event caused immense anxiety about foreign surveillance and national security, which led to a significant increase in legislation for data localization in various countries. According to the Information Technology Innovation Fund of the United States, with the exception of Africa where information technology is somewhat underdeveloped, most countries have put in place varying levels of legislation for data localization (Huang Daoli and Hu Wenhua 2019) (see Table 19). Data localization is reflected in different legal compliance requirements, including the prohibition of sending data abroad, the requirement to obtain the consent of the data owner before the data is transmitted across borders, the requirement to keep copies of data in the territory, and the taxation of data output, etc. (Anupam and Uyen 2015, pp. 679–704).

Table 19. Legislation on Data Localization Worldwide

Intensity of Data localization Requirement	Country (Region)
High requirement: explicitly requires data to be stored on domestic servers	India, Brunei, Vietnam, Nigeria, Russia
Implementation requirements: Data transmission requirements under relevant laws are equivalent to data localization	European Union
Partial requirements: the consent of the data owner is required when taking many measures before data cross-border transmission	Belarus, Kazakhstan, Malaysia, the Republic of Korea
Low requirements: restrictions on data cross-border transmission under certain conditions	Argentina, Brazil, Colombia, Peru, Uruguay
Requirements in specific areas: health, telecommunications, finance, and national security	Australia, Canada, New Zealand, Turkey, Venezuela
Unspecified requirements: no legal requirements for data localization	The United States and other countries

Source: Based on public information

Unlike the bottom-up approach of the EU which protects personal data as a fundamental human right, India's legislation is more about keeping things local and protecting personal data under the principle that data sovereignty is the priority. As a typical representative of strong data localization legislation, with the development of the digital economy, India has promulgated a series of important laws and documents in recent years, tending to adopt extensive data localization restrictions. India's data localization legislation for personal data protection was first seen in the *Public Records Act*, introduced in 1993.

> Section 4 of the Act states: "No person shall take or cause to be taken out of India any public records without the prior approval of the Central Government; Provided that no such prior approval shall be required if any public records are taken or sent out of India for any official purpose."

The act expressly requires that IT companies should place part of their infrastructure within the Indian territory and that personal data, government data, and business data stored in such enterprises shall not to be transmitted abroad (see Table 20).

Table 20. Data Protection Legislation of India

Time	Name	Main Content
1993	*Public Records Act*	Provides for the prohibition of public records transmission outside India except for "public purposes"
2000	*Information Technology Act*	Provides that any institution or individual that has not taken reasonable security measures or procedures (RSPPs) in the protection of sensitive personal data or information (SPDI) shall be liable for loss of ill-gotten gains resulting from that negligence.
2005	*Indian Telecommunications Authority (Access Information) Regulations*	Provides that service providers are entitled to be exempted from the provisions of commercially or economically sensitive information if the disclosure of such information is likely to cause unfair profit or loss to them.

Table 20. Continued

Time	Name	Main Content
2011	*Information Technology (Reasonable Security Practices and Procedures and Sensitive Personal Data or Information) Rules*	Restricts the cross-border transmission of sensitive personal data or information to two situations when necessary or with the consent of the data owner
2018	*Draft E-pharmacy Rules*	Provides that data generated through the electronic pharmacy portal shall be maintained in India and not transmitted to or stored outside India in any way.
	Electronic Commerce in India: Draft National Policy Framework	There are extensive data localization requirements for personal data and others. "Key personal data" identified by the Indian government and data generated by e-commerce platforms, social media, and search engines can only be stored in India.
2019	*Personal Data Protection Act*	Internet companies are required to store key personal data collected in India, and should desensitize the data before transferring them abroad for processing for legally permitted purposes only.

Source: Based on public information

At present, the collection, processing, storage, disclosure, and transmission of personal data is mainly regulated by the *Information Technology Act*, which was implemented in 2000. It provides that necessity or the consent of the data owner is a prerequisite for the transmission of sensitive personal data or information abroad. In 2011, the Ministry of Technology and Communications of India issued rules aimed at implementing several provisions of this act,[15] limiting the overseas transmission of sensitive personal

15 In 2011, the Ministry of Technology and Communications of India promulgated the Indian Rules on Information Technology (Reasonable Security Practices and Procedures and Sensitive Personal Data or Information), which detailed and

data or information in two situations: by reason of necessity, or with the consent of the data owner.[16] Under these rules, when transmitting sensitive personal data or information from a corporation or a natural person in India, or from other countries by their representatives, it is necessary to ensure that such corporations or natural persons will be provided with some level of data protection. Such a transmission will only be permitted if it is for the purpose of fulfilling a legal contract between the corporation or natural person and the data provider, or if the data provider agrees to carry out the transmission (Li Jianing 2018).

In December 2019, the most stringent data localization measure in Indian history—*The Personal Data Protection Bill*—was approved by the Indian Federal Cabinet (Hu Wenhua and Kong Huafeng 2019).

> As a whole, the Bill followed the rules of the EU GDPR, and introduced new rights such as the rights to correct and delete, the data portability, the rights to be forgotten and new mechanisms such as the privacy impact assessment, the privacy design and protection, to enhance the level of personal data protection in India. (Hu Wenhua and Kong Huafeng 2019)

Here, personal data is divided into general personal data, sensitive personal data, and key personal data, and different requirements are established for these three types (see Table 21). There are two important specified requirements for data localization. First, sensitive personal data can be transmitted out of India if such data can continue to be stored in India. Second, key personal data can only be processed in India. In addition, this Bill provides that all organizations must obtain the explicit consent of

---

clarified several provisions of *the Information Technology Act of 2000* issued by the Government of India.

16 Information Technology Rules (Reasonable Security Practices and Procedures and Sensitive Personal Data or Information), 2011, Gazette of India. India's Information Technology Act 2000 (No. 21, Act of Parliament, 2008) focuses only on computer abuse, not data security matters. In 2008, the law was amended, with two additional articles—43A and 72A—added for personal data loss and protection matters (Information Technology [Amendment] Act, 2008, No. 10, Act of Parliament, 2009).

the data owner when collecting personal data (Article 11),[17] except when involving national security or handling medical emergencies (Article 12).[18]

Table 21. Special Requirements for Different Types of Personal Data

Classification	Specific Definition	Special Requirement
General personal data	It mainly refers to the data or data related to the natural person that can be identified directly or indirectly after considering any characteristic of the natural person, or after combining with these characteristics.	No person shall process any personal data except for a specific, clear, and lawful purpose. General personal data can be freely transferred to foreign countries without localization storage requirements.

(*continued*)

17 Section 11(1) of *Personal Data Protection Act 2019* states: "Personal data shall not be processed except with the consent of the data owner before the processing of personal data begins."

18 Article 12 of *Personal Data Protection Act 2019* states: "Notwithstanding anything contained in section 11, the personal data may be processed if such processing is necessary—(a) for the performance of any function of the State authorized by law for (i) the provision of any service or benefit to the data principal from the State; or (ii) the issuance of any certification, license or permit for any action or activity of the data principal by the State; (b) under any law for the time being in force made by the Parliament or any State Legislature; or (c) for compliance with any order or judgment of any Court or Tribunal in India; (d) to respond to any medical emergency involving a threat to the life or a severe threat to the health of the data principal or any other individual; (e) to undertake any measure to provide medical treatment or health services to any individual during an epidemic, outbreak of disease or any other threat to public health; or (f) to undertake any measure to ensure safety of, or provide assistance or services to, any individual during any disaster or any breakdown of public order."

Table 21. Continued

Classification	Specific Definition	Special Requirement
Sensitive personal data	It includes financial data, health data, official identifiers, religion, political beliefs, sexual life, biometric identification, genetic data, transgender identity, bisexual identity, caste, tribe, and other data categories defined by the DPA.	Cross-border circulation of sensitive personal data is subject to the conditions of Article 34 (1). Such sensitive personal data shall continue to be stored in India.
Critical personal data	It refers to the personal data notified by the central government, which is regulated by the government.	In principle, it is forbidden to transmit overseas, except when subject to Article 34 (2) in respect of emergency medical treatment or other conditions allowed by the central government

Source: Based on public information.

Among the different branches of law, data localization is particularly important for data protection in banking, health, e-commerce, and some other fields. For example, in April 2018, the Reserve Bank of India issued a circular requiring all payment data to be stored only in India, with October 15, 2018, set as the deadline for companies to fulfill this requirement (Reserve Bank of India 2019). In the field of health, the *Draft E-pharmacy Rules* issued by the Ministry of Health and Family Welfare in 2018 stipulates that data generated through e-pharmacy portals must not be transmitted or stored abroad in any way and shall be kept within India (Mondaq 2018). In the field of e-commerce, the preface to *Electronic Commerce in India: Draft National Policy Framework* clearly states that India will gradually promote data localization and require the establishment of data centers (Alibaba Data Security Research Institute 2019). Besides, the draft stipulated that data generated by social media and e-commerce platforms, as well as what the Indian government considers critical personal data, can only be stored within the territory of India (Huang Daoli and Hu Wenhua 2019).

Although some of the above-mentioned regulations have not been finalized, as far as the published version is concerned the data localization legislation model of India has three characteristics. First, the coverage is expanded from personal data to non-personal data. In addition to providing for the mechanisms of cross-border data flow, the *India Personal Data Protection Bill 2019* also requires that personal data be stored within the country, which includes personal data in the scope of data localization. As a typical representative of the latest legislation and policy trend on data localization, the *Draft National Policy Framework for E-commerce* in India does not deal with personal data particularly, but applies data localization rules uniformly. Predictably, for Indian lawmakers, data localization is as important to personal data as it is to cross-border data flow. Data is not only the regulation object of the former, but is also an important regulation object of the latter. Second, the bill distinguishes between different data types and implements hierarchical control. Although India has established extensive data localization requirements, it does not regulate all types of data in the same way. Instead, it regulates different types of data separately based on factors such as the sensitivity threshold. For example, the *India Personal Data Protection Bill 2019* places personal data into three levels: general personal data, sensitive personal data, and critical personal data. Sensitive personal data includes financial data, health data, official identifiers, sexual life data, sexual orientation data, biometric data, genetic data, transgender identity, gender neutral identity, caste or tribe data, religious or political beliefs data, etc.[19] Although the Bill does not specify the scope of critical personal data, it gives the government the right to define and sets higher requirements for cross-border data flow and data localization, which reflects India's governance logic that the localization of data will lead to the localization of data value (Huang Daoli and Hu Wenhua 2019). Third, there are multiple

19 See the *Personal Data Protection Bill 2019*.

regulatory mechanisms and exemption rules. Due to the wide range of data localization and complex legal relations, India has taken strict regulatory measures based on its national conditions. Even so, India has just set up a supervisory mechanism that does not take the "one size fits all" approach. On the one hand, it utilizes the experience of the European Union and sets up a variety of feasible cross-border data circulation mechanisms, including the standard contract mechanism, the data protection agency approval mechanism, etc. On the other hand, it has formulated some alternative measures for the departure of personal data from the country and has adopted different methods to manage different types of personal data in the case of a cross-border flow, according to the particularity of different industries and fields (Huang Daoli and Hu Wenhua 2019). In addition, there are a number of exemption clauses. For example, the *Personal Data Protection Bill 2019* allows the Government of India to exempt some general personal data from localization requirements. The draft *National Policy Framework for E-commerce in India* defines five types of data that are not required to comply with data localization or cross-border transmission requirements—these include cloud service-related data transmission and intra-business data transmission between companies in different countries (Huang Daoli and Hu Wenhua 2019).

Whereas data localization has become a major legislative trend in the world, India has enacted data localization legislation from the perspective of personal data protection, which aims to solve the problem of the localization of data value. Based on the advantages of scale in the domestic user market, India will accumulate data resources, promote the construction of digital infrastructure and local data centers, and realize the localization of data value through data localization (Huang Daoli and Hu Wenhua 2019). Data localization legislation in India protects the development of information technology and related industries within the country to some extent; however, it can also exclude foreign companies that provide cross-border services to the domestic market. On the other hand, data localization legislation increases compliance costs and weakens the competitiveness of foreign companies. In addition, Indian data localization legislation not only provides basic resources for the development of new technologies in India, it also provides opportunities for the development of a local data center and digital infrastructure service market. According to a research report by Cushman & Wakefield, a global consulting firm, India is expected witness data growth twice as fast as the global average rate by 2020, and the total amount of data may reach up to 230,000 petabytes. It is predicted that if India possesses all of the data, it will be the fifth largest data center market by 2050 (The Economic Times 2018).

It is of strategic value for India to adopt data localization legislation under the principle that data sovereignty is the priority. Strict domestic storage can maintain data sovereignty and data security, protect personal privacy, and promote the development of the data industry, but this measure also has serious drawbacks, such as the mismatching of purpose and means. Specific measures that require cross-border data to be stored locally don't fully guarantee the priority of data sovereignty. This may be called "narrow isolation," which will become an extreme kind of data sovereignty protection that impedes the development of the data industry (Hu Wei 2018), which is already hampering the development of digital trade. Furthermore, restricting the free flow of data may have a negative impact on GDP growth (Shi Yue 2015). A study by the European Centre for International Political Economy estimates that data localization has reduced the GDP of India by 0.80 percent. In addition, with the deepening development of globalization, Indian strict data localization legislation has also attracted wide attention from the international community. And it has been fiercely opposed by European and American countries, which believe that the measure is "protectionism" and "a sign of the backward globalization process."

Comprehensive Legislation Model of Japan

For personal information protection legislation, Japan adopts a comprehensive legislation model, which is a compromise between the decentralized legislation model and the unified legislation model, adopting different norms to regulate the information collected and processed by individuals and administrative organs through separate legislation. This legislation model, with its own characteristics, is compatible with both the European and American models, while providing sufficient protection for Japanese personal information and promoting the development of the digital economy in the country. However, it does bring some problems.

Since the Meiji Restoration, Japan has been implementing a system of local autonomy. Autonomous entities can formulate their own regulations within a certain scope; thus, the personal information protection systems in different parts of the country are different, according to specific local conditions. It is due to the implementation of local autonomy that personal information protection systems were put in place in Japanese local autonomous entities long before any unified national legislation. In 1973, Tokushima City first enacted the *Regulations on the Protection of Personal Information Procured by Computer*. Afterwards, more of the same came out in a variety of local autonomous entities. In 1982, under the positive influence of a report from the Japan Administration Agency, various autonomous entities enacted personal information protection regulations. By April 1999, 72.3 percent of the local autonomous entities had established personal information protection systems, including laws, acts, and regulations (Shinbao Shizo 2016).[20] In 1984, Haruhi City, in Fukuoka Prefecture, took the lead in issuing *Haruhi City Personal Information Protection Regulation*. The next year, Kawasaki City enacted its *Personal Information Protection Regulation*.

20 See Shinbao Shizo, *The Creation and Development of Privacy Rights*. Seimundo Corporation, 2000, pp. 349–50; Zhou Hanhua, ed. 2006. *Research on the Frontier Issues of Personal Information Protection*. Law Press, p. 157.

Table 22. Personal Information Protection Legislation of Japan

Year	Name	Main content
1973	*Tokushima City Regulations on the Protection of Personal Information Processed by Computer*	It regulates the government to respect the privacy rights while processing the personal information.
1988	The *Law on the Protection of Personal Information Processed by Computer in Administrative Organs* (行政機関の保有する個人情報の保護に関する法律)	It mainly stipulates the use of computers by state administrative organs to process personal information.
1997	The *Guidelines on the Protection of Processing Personal Information Through Computer by Private Sectors*	It issues privacy authentication identification (P-ARK authentication) to enterprises with good protection measures.
1999	*Law on Registration Correction of Basic Information of Residents*	In particular, it strengthens the recognition of the necessity to protect personal information for private enterprises, and adds a clause in the annex that "the relevant measures should be improved as soon as possible, in order to protect personal information completely.
2003	*Act on the Protection of Personal Information*（個人情報の保護に関する法律）	They are known as the personal information protection quintuplet laws. The *Act on the Protection of Personal Information* is the basic law, which regulates the collection, processing, and use of personal information. The basic principles of the law apply to both public and non-public sectors.
	Act on the Protection of Personal Information Held by Administrative Organs（行政機関の保有する個人情報の保護に関する法律）	
	Act on the Protection of Personal Information Held by Incorporated Administrative Agencies, etc.（独立行政法人等の保有する個人情報の保護に関する法律）	

(*continued*)

Table 22. Continued

Year	Name	Main content
	Act on Establishing an Supervision Authority for Information Publication and Personal Information Protection	
	Act on Improving the Laws that Involving the Implementation of Act on the Protection of Personal Information Held by Administrative Organs	
2017	*Personal Financial Information Protection Guidelines*	It regulates the use and circulation of personal information in the financial field.
2020	*Amendment to the Act of Personal Information Protection*	In order to meet the demand of technological innovation in the big data era and resolve the potential risks with personal information protection in the future, the amendment involves a substantial number of contents, such as protecting individual rights, promoting the use of information, expanding company responsibility, increasing legal penalties, and strengthening extraterritorial application.

Source: Based on public information.

Compared with the positive legislation trend in local autonomous entities, legislation in this regard has been more conservative and cautious at the national level in Japan. According to the eight principles of data protection established by the Organization for Economic Cooperation and Development, Japan adopted its first legal document on the protection of personal information nationwide in 1988, the *Law on the Protection of Personal Information Processed by Computer in Administrative Organs*. This law regulates the administrative behavior of collecting, processing, and storing personal electronic information, which has three main characteristics. The first is about the scope of application. It applies to personal data processed by national administrative organs. The second is about individual rights. It mainly includes the right to read, the right to request revision, and the right to request re-investigation. The third is about the obligations of administrative organs. The administrative organs should not keep any personal information beyond the necessary limit of the business scope—and they should determine the specific purposes for which the personal information files are kept. Regulations shall also prohibit the use and provision of personal information except for preservation. The administrative organs that store the personal information shall compile personal information files in advance, and keep them somewhere convenient and free for the citizens to read.

However, as stated above, it only regulates the collection, processing, and storage of personal information by administrative organs, which has limited scope. For example, the law does not control the collection and storage of personal information by private enterprises. Moreover, since this law is not complete, its enactment amounts to a preliminary exploration of personal information protection. There are other problems, such as the failure to address personal information leakage.

Because of the strict regulations on personal information protection by administrative organs, various industries in Japan have also formulated industry norms for personal information protection. For example, the Ministry of Trade and Industry of Japan issued the *Guidelines on the Protection of Processing Personal Information by the Private Sector* in 1997, and the Ministry of Post issued the *Guidelines on the Protection of Personal Information in the Telecommunications Industry* in 1998. Whereas the above policy documents are not mandatory, they serve as guidance in various industries.

Subsequently, a number of unacceptable incidents occurred in Japan, such as the leakage and reselling of personal information by enterprises and banks, which made the public realize that the personal information protection system was still incomplete. Consequently, in November 1998, the Japanese government revised the *Basic Guidelines for Promoting the Development of a High Quality Information and Communication Society*. It emphasized the need for further legislative governance while continuing to strengthen government supervision and civil self-regulation in the sphere of personal information protection (Chi Jianxin 2016). In October 2000, the Japanese government formally submitted the *Basic Outlines on the Protection of Personal Information* to the Prime Minister and the Minister of the Cabinet. The Japanese IT General Strategy Department decided to add some specific content on the basis of this outline and submitted it to the National Assembly for deliberation, so as to complete the comprehensive legislation on the personal information protection as soon as possible (Horibe Masao, 2000). In May 2003, the Japanese parliament adopted the *Act on the Protection of Personal Information*, the *Act on the Protection of Personal Information Held by Administrative Organs*, the *Act on the Protection of Personal Information Held by Incorporated Administrative Agencies*, the *Act on Establishing a Supervision Authority for Information Publication and Personal Information Protection*, the *Act on Improving the Laws that Involving the Implementation of Act on the Protection of Personal Information Held by Administrative Organs*, which are known as the personal information protection quintuplet laws. Thus, the legal system for personal information protection in Japan is now formally complete.

Table 23. Brief Introduction to the Japanese Data Rights Law System

The basic law	*Act on the Protection of Personal Information*	Backbone content	The general rule (purpose and basic idea)
			The responsibilities and obligations of national and local public groups
			Measures to protect personal information
		Branch content	Obligations of Personal Information Processors
			Responsibilities of the Personal Information Protection Committee
			Supplementary articles (sphere of application)
			Penalty provisions (liability for violation of law)

Table 23. Continued

Supporting laws and regulations	The administrative organs	*Act on the Protection of Personal Information Held by Administrative Organs*
	Independent administrative legal persons, etc.	*Act on the Protection of Personal Information Held by Incorporated Administrative Agencies, etc.*
	Local public groups, etc.	The regulations of local public groups

Source: Based on public information.

In terms of the form, the legal system of personal information protection in Japan has been constructed by a combination of unification and division, which includes national unified legislation and industry self-regulation (Qi Aimin 2009a). Drawing lessons from international regulatory standards and relevant international norms, a multi-level legal regulation system has been formed, ranging from international law norms to personal information protection laws, government policies, and guidelines. Moreover, government and private industry can also formulate industry self-regulation norms according to the personal information protection law, finally forming a complete legal system of personal information protection. In general, the Japanese personal information protection legislation model is a compromise between the European Union model and the United States model. Japan paid attention to the limitations of the domestic industry self-regulation mechanism and the necessity of legalization. However, it does not blindly cater to the strict regulations of data rights protection in the EU, but instead tries to find a balance between personal information protection and free flow of data (Zhou Hanhua 2006, p. 164). It can be said that Japanese practice fully reflects the advanced model of western developed countries, and is a successful legislative practice in terms of data rights protection.

The new *Act on the Protection of Personal Information*, which came into effect in 2015, lies at the core of the Japanese personal information protection legal system—it is the basic law in that area. The law meets the requirements of the EU's *Data Protection Directive* in form, but it also shows some of the characteristics of the American personal information protection law in essence. In the meantime, it adheres to some original legislative ideas. In terms of content, the law does not directly grant special rights to individual citizens. Instead, it ensures that the legitimate rights and interests of citizens are protected from damage on the premise of recognizing the effective use of personal information (Li Dandan 2015). In terms of structure, the law consists of fifty-nine articles in six chapters and seven articles in the annex. Among them, the first chapter stipulates the purpose and basic idea of the law. The second chapter clarifies the responsibility and obligation of local public organizations and the state. The third chapter regulates the measures of personal information protection. The fourth chapter is about the obligations of personal information processing enterprises. The fifth chapter includes the exceptions to the application of law. The sixth chapter is about implementation rules. It is extremely important for individuals and enterprises to enact the law: On one hand, individuals can take legal action to protect their personal information; on the other hand, enterprises will attach importance to the protection of users' personal information up to the strategic level.

In order to ensure traceability in information circulation, Japan strengthened the unified management of personal information by national regulatory authorities in 2017, and made substantial revisions to the new *Act on the Protection of Personal Information* (Sogabe Masahiro 2017). The first revision added the concept of "sensitive information," which refers to information about political views, religion, union membership, race and ethnicity, as well as place of birth and residence, health care, sex life, criminal record information, etc. (Watanabe Masayuki 2016). The second revision added a new chapter about the Personal Information Protection Committee (Articles 59–74). This chapter mainly provides for the establishment, tasks, and powers of the Personal Information Protection Committee, as well as some other issues, such as the tenure system, identity protection, and the general affairs bureau (Zhang Hong 2020). The third revision added the crime of illegally providing information. The crime refers to the behavior by which legal persons (including senior officers and managers) engage in processing personal information or related databases, and providing or stealing personal information for themselves or a third party to pursue illegitimate interests (including the copying and processing of the information in part or in full). A person who commits such a crime shall be sentenced to imprisonment for up to one year, or a fine up to 500,000 yen.

Compared with the previous version, the new *Act on the Protection of Personal Information* has seven chapters and contains eighty-eight articles. The first chapter describes the general rules. The second chapter stipulates the responsibilities and obligations of the local public organizations and the state. The third chapter stipulates the specific guidelines, national policies, and the assistance of the state and local autonomous organizations in personal information protection. The fourth chapter regulates personal information processing obligations. The fifth chapter is related to the personal information protection committee. The sixth chapter consists of some relevant standards. The seventh chapter is about penalties. It is noteworthy that the new *Act on the Protection of Personal Information* expands and improves the relevant chapters based on the framework of the old law. For example, a section in the fourth chapter stipulates restrictions to providing personal information to a third person abroad (Article 24). The second section regulates the obligations of the anonymous information processing industry (Articles 36 to 39). The third section formulates the supervisory power of the personal information protection committee (Articles 40 to 46). Meanwhile, the fifth chapter enacts provisions about the personal information committee (Hiro Nishimura 2016).

The new *Act on the Protection of Personal Information* contains some expanded and targeted provisions according to specific circumstances. It mainly has the following characteristics. First, it introduces the concept of "personal identification symbol." Including the basic definition of "personal information," Article 2 (1) also adds "personal identification symbol" to the definition of "personal information."[21] As a supplement, paragraph 2 provides

21 According to Article 2 of the *Act on the Protection of Personal Information*: (1) "Personal information" in this Act means information relating to a living individual that falls under any of the following items: those containing a name, date of birth, or other descriptions, etc. (excluding an individual identification code) stated, recorded, or otherwise expressed using voice, movement, or other methods in a document, drawing, or electromagnetic record; (2) An "individual identification code"

two situations that can be considered a "personal identification symbol." The first situation is the conversion of a characteristic part of the individual body into words, numbers, symbols, and other symbols by computer.[22] The second situation is assigning different symbols based on different objects in normal work.[23] Second, it strengthens measures to protect personal information. Article 25 (1) stipulates that,

> [T]he specific time period of the relevant personal information provided to the third party, the name of the third party and other contents must be recorded and kept within a statutory period in accordance with the relevant regulations of the Personal Information Protection Committee, except in special circumstances.[24]

Third, it established the Personal Information Protection Committee and enacted punishment standards for violations. The Personal Information Protection Committee has the power to regulate the processing of all personal information (including all types of personal information specified in Article 2 of the act).

---

in this Act means those prescribed by cabinet order which are any character, letter, number, symbol, or other code falling under any of the following items: (i) those able to identify a specific individual that are a character, letter, number, symbol, or other codes into which a bodily partial feature of the specific individual has been converted in order to be used by computers, (ii) those characters, letters, numbers, symbols, or other codes that are assigned in regard to the use of services provided to an individual, or to the purchase of goods sold to an individual, or which are stated or electromagnetically recorded in a card or other document issued to an individual so as to be able to identify a specific user or purchaser, or recipient of issuance, by having made the said codes differently assigned, or stated, or recoded for the said user or purchaser, or the recipient of issuance.

22 See the *Application Directive of the Act on the Protection of Personal Information*, Article 1(1).

23 See the *Application Directive of the Act on the Protection of Personal Information*, Articles 1(2)–(8), 3, 4.

24 See the *Application Directive of the Act on the Protection of Personal Information*, Article 25 (recording the provision of personal information to a third party, etc.) and Article 26 (confirmation of the acceptance of the provision by a third party).

The new *Act on the Protection of Personal Information* fully reflects the legislative mode of personal information protection in Japan. Article 1 in Chapter I describes the purpose of the legislation as follows,

> This Act aims to protect an individual's rights and interests while considering the utility of personal information including that the proper and effective application of personal information contributes to the creation of new industries and the realization of a vibrant economic society and an enriched quality of life for the people of Japan.

The new *Act on the Protection of Personal Information* is a combination of the United States and the EU model, which achieves a balance between personal information protection and information circulation. The law adopted the feature of both the basic law of the EU model and the general law of the US model (Chi Jianxin 2016). The first three chapters contain the basic rules, mainly concerning the principles of public and non-public organs. The last four contain the general rules, mainly dealing with the compulsory provisions for natural persons, enterprises, and non-public organs. Among them, media and political organizations are exempt from compulsory provisions, but they shall take self-regulation measures (Xie Qing 2006).

The Japanese legislation model mainly implements comprehensive personal information protection in the public and private fields; however, it also enacts special laws in special fields, and encourages civil organizations to develop industrial self-discipline mechanisms. This comprehensive legislation model not only integrated the advantages of the American model and the EU model, it also overcame the defects and deficiencies in the two models. While the comprehensive legislation model fully protects data rights, it also creates some problems. For example, everyone's behavior will involve personal information to a greater or lesser degree. The Japanese model restricts the ways in which citizens may express themselves, thus restraining the development of Japanese society to some extent. Meanwhile, the somewhat confusing standards for individual interests and national interests also lead to difficulty in understanding the limits of regulatory behavior.

China's Approach to Data Right Legislation

There is no doubt that it will be beneficial to learn from the success or failure of laws from other countries, or borrow some laws and systems that have worked. If we examine international data governance rules from a comparative perspective, we will be able to grasp the essence of data legislation and the core of data right law. In other countries, research on data protection has already evolved from a minor interest to a significant field by reason of government attention and social concern. In China, data rights legislation has been discussed from different angles on the basis of a variety of theories, and at different levels. Based on China's national conditions, responding to actual demand is key to the success of data rights legislation.

Practical Significance of Data Rights Legislation

Proper legal systems often promote social development and stand the test of history and reality. Experience shows that advanced systems form the basis and guarantee for economic prosperity and stability—the realities of the contemporary world confirm that effective governance is essential to the competitiveness of a country and the rejuvenation of the Chinese nation. China today is experiencing the most extensive and profound changes in human history, leading toward a digital society, and it is pursuing the most ambitious and unique innovations concerning data rights legislation. The birth of the *Civil Code of the People's Republic of China* marks China's entry into a new era of codes in the realm of legislation. The *Civil Code* not only fully reflects the characteristics of the digital era, dealing with the challenges brought by changes in society, it also makes special institutional arrangements for products of the digital era. If the *French Civil Code of 1804* is the civil code of the steam age, and *the German Civil Code of 1900* is the civil code of the electrical age, then China's *Civil Code* of 2020 is the civil code of the digital age. Unlike most countries in the world, China has not formulated a unified special law for data rights protection. Instead, it has adopted a decentralized legislation model. The legislation system is composed of laws, regulations, rules, and various normative documents, and together they form a multi-level, multi-field, and complex legal system on data rights protection. Codification is a realistic requirement and an inevitable trend of data rights legislation with which to enhance the data rights system.

We should take data rights legislation as the starting point to having China's voice heard in the formulation of international rules in this regard. In the digital age, whoever holds data and controls how data is interpreted will have an upper hand in future competition. President Xi Jinping stressed that to embrace the world and participate in international affairs as a responsible major country China must do a good job in advancing the rule of law. The data rights law is an innovation in the legal field, leading and promoting the globalization of law. This has amplified China's voice and influence in global governance and has contributed China's wisdom to data rights legislation around the world.

We should regard data rights legislation as a commanding height in our efforts to safeguard national data sovereignty—with the progress of data globalization, data sovereignty is confronted with difficult challenges. On the one hand, as different countries adopt different legislative models and strategies for data management and protection, plus factors such as cross-border data flow, inherent features of data processing, and competition for data sovereignty between countries, the ability of various countries to exercise their data sovereignty is generally weak, and their ability to store and control data is also dampened. On the other hand, there is not yet any clear definition of data sovereignty in the international community, which is a lacuna in international law. At the same time, data sovereignty, as a new right of a country, is facing new challenges and threats, which includes data security issues, data hegemonism, data protectionism, data capitalism, and data terrorism (the Key Laboratory of Big Data Strategy 2020, p. 124). Therefore, it is important that we take data rights legislation as the commanding height in our effort to explore ways to uphold data sovereignty.

We should take data rights legislation as a support to enhance data security and personal information protection. We ought to accelerate data rights legislation by establishing data rights law as the superior law, and advance the development of data rights, the data rights system, relevant theoretical research, and the data rights legislation system. This will play a guiding role for the improvement and implementation of digital legal systems such as the *Cybersecurity Law*, the *Data Security Law*, and the *Personal Information Protection Law*.

We should let data rights legislation play a leading role in comprehensively advancing the modernization of data governance. The true symbol of China's rise is the modernization of national governance and a louder voice in the global governance system. Governance technology, with data governance at its core, is a key factor in the modernization of national governance. The modernization of national governance would be impossible without the modernization of data governance. On December 8, 2017, while presiding over the second group study session of the Political Bureau of the CPC Central Committee on the implementation of the national big data strategy, President Xi Jinping stressed that China should strengthen research on international data governance rules, and put forward Chinese solutions. As the largest country in terms of data, China should make full use of its unique advantages in data scale and scenario-based applications; strengthen the role of governance technologies, such as the Internet, big data, artificial intelligence, and blockchain and quantum informatics in national governance modernization; and transform the advantages of the data law system into data governance efficiency. Led by the data rights law, we ought to reinforce the interaction between domestic law and international law, and establish a global data governance system that not only maintains national interests, but also encourages dialogue, competition, and cooperation to comprehensively amplify China's voice in the international data governance system and governance ability.

Model of Data Rights Legislation

Although there has been a global consensus on the protection of personal data, the specific regulations adopted by countries are still quite different. So far, there is no global consensus on the balance of competing interests, personal rights protection, and regulatory frameworks. In general, the

EU model has proven to be more beneficial for personal data protection, while the U.S. model is more conducive to data circulation. Both models have advantages and disadvantages. The main dispute in the personal data protection model is how to strike a balance between promoting the commercial use of data and protecting individual rights.

Governance framework. At present, the Chinese academic circle has reached the consensus that data rights should be protected with dedicated legislation, but there has been no discussion as to which legislation model should be adopted (Yang Ji 2012). Globally, different countries have chosen their legislation models for the protection of data rights based on their own national conditions. Therefore, China should not simply copy any model from another country, but give consideration to the reasonable balance between national interests, economic development, and personal privacy interests. Data rights protection is a complex issue that requires the joint force of ethics and law, including ethics-oriented social norms, an algorithm-based technology system, and a law-based risk prevention system. First, legal regulation. Although the current data rights protection system in China incorporates all levels and types of legal documents these documents are scattered quite extensively, so it is necessary to make data rights legislation more systematic. Second, technology response. The law alone cannot solve all problems, and it is unrealistic to rely solely on legislation. In technological terms, we can use the Internet, big data, cloud computing, blockchain, and other technologies to set up barriers and take data rights protection to a new level. Third, ethical constraints. When new technologies are misused in the absence of ethical constraints, "it is not a blessing for humanity, but a descent into darkness" (Chen Jiang 2019). At present, industrial self-discipline for data rights protection is still in the exploratory stage in China, and lacks ethical constraints. Thus, it is necessary to build a better mechanism for it and improve the function of industrial self-discipline on the basis of legislation.

Areas of governance. At present, China has formed a multi-level and multi-field legal system for data rights protection. In addition to the internet industry, data rights protection is expanding to the traditional fields of finance, transportation, telecommunications, education, health care, etc. In general, the current provisions on data rights protection cover different types of data in various fields, mainly including financial data, children's data, public data, etc. The essence of financial data is special personal information. At present, there is no clear definition of financial data in Chinese legislation, but it is generally believed that financial data is the data collected and used by financial institutions (He Yuan 2020). In legal terms, dedicated legislation on financial data protection is mainly in the form of departmental regulations and national standards, forming a preliminary normative system. For example, in February 2020, the People's Bank of China issued the *Personal Financial Information Protection Technical Specification*, which put forward comprehensive and systematic institutional requirements for the financial data protection obligations of financial institutions. The protection of children's data has become an important topic. The United Nations has vigorously promoted children's data protection, and Western countries have also been strengthening efforts in this area. In China, more and more attention has been paid to children's data protection, which is an important part of the protection of minors. At present, China is actively exploring and improving its system of children's data protection, and has issued special legislation in this field—*Provisions on the Cyber Protection of Children's Personal Information*. With progress made in open government data, the big data industry has become a key area in the implementation of China's big data strategy. To initiate legislation on public data protection, the first question is which legislative model to adopt. Although China has promulgated a series of laws and regulations related to public data protection there is no unified legislation, and the scope of public data can still be blurry when it comes to the collection, sharing, and use of public data by local governments and relevant departments (Wang Yongqi 2019).

Governance principles. Law adjusts social relations and is the organic unity of the codes of conduct and judgment norms. If the law contains only prohibitive or mandatory requirements, the effective implementation is bound to be affected by the incompatibility of incentives (Zhou Hanhua 2018). Both theoretical research and practical development show that if the incentives are not compatible, legislation will be management-oriented, rather than governance-oriented (Zhang Shouwen 2014).[25] Law formulated in this way is difficult to implement (Ding Huang 2002), and it may also lead to a chain of problems, including intermittent law enforcement, poor effectiveness, selective law enforcement, impaired authority, conflict of regulations, and fraud in enforcement (Zhou Xueguang 2008).[26] Despite the different legislation models, whether the US, EU, Indian, or Japanese model, there are actually some common rules to follow. No matter which legislation model is adopted, or how strict the law is, it is only incentive compatibility that will achieve the desired protection effect. With non-compatibility, laws will be difficult to enforce (Edwards 2010).[27] It can even inhibits innovation and, in effect, fail to protect data (Zarsky 2017). Therefore, the key to success does not lie in which legislative model to choose, but in whether the governance principle is reasonable. On the one hand, we must go beyond the simple comparison of the four models to find the differences between them and gain useful experience. On the other hand, it is necessary to summarize the experience of the reforms and the opening up of China, and the general trend of global governance reform to avoid detours (Zhou Hanhua 2015). Only in this way can we

25 Many regulations in the past reflected the idea of management, with too much emphasis on government power and too little attention to the rights of market subjects.

26 Zhou Xueguang analyzed, from the perspective of organizational science, the institutional roots of why policy implementation deviates from the original intention and why grassroots government departments collude to cheat, concluding: the purpose of incentive design in organizations is to induce behaviors conducive to organizational goals. However, improper incentive design will lead to behaviors contrary to organizational goals. In the case of inconsistency between incentives and organizational goals, the stronger the formal incentive mechanism is, the more serious the phenomenon of goal substitution will be, and the stronger the driving force of collusion will be. It is also very convincing to use this theory to analyze the implementation dilemma of some seemingly strict legal provisions in practice.

27 British academics have said that the European Union's *Personal Data Protection Directive* is seen by business organizations as introducing more red tape and bureaucratic requirements than helping companies make better products. Thus, although the directive is very strict, it is only observed on paper rather than in substance.

draw on the strength of others and embark on a path toward digital rule of law with Chinese characteristics.

Suggestions for Data Rights Legislation

Enact unified and dedicated data laws. Due to reasons related to social awareness, the digital industry, science and technology, and legislation planning, China has not yet issued a unified and dedicated law on data rights protection, and the legal norms related to data rights protection are mostly scattered in civil law, criminal law, and other legal documents issued by the national legislature. Meaningful explorations have been carried out for data rights legislation in some regions and industries, promoting the materialization of the abstract legal principles of data rights protection to a certain extent. However, due to the lack of clear guidance from upper-level law, this kind of bottom-up legislative practice has limited effect on the improvement of data rights protection nationwide.

Establish a unified and dedicated data rights protection organization. At present, data governance in China sees regulatory efforts from too many different authorities, each extending its authority to the protection of data within their own scope of responsibilities. Data protection responsibilities are usually performed by industry-specific regulatory departments, for example, in finance, telecommunication, medical care, cyberspace, and other industries. The advantage of such decentralized protection is that it fits the characteristics of each industry better, but in the long run data use and related supervision cannot remain separate for different scenarios, and such decentralized protection may bring even more regulatory bodies into the scene resulting in unclear responsibilities and weak supervision. It is a common practice for all countries to set up specialized data protection agencies that can improve the supervision and implementation of national data protection laws, pushing up the data protection level in the whole country, and establishing a one-stop service system for data subjects for data rights protection. Therefore, in the Chinese data legislation, we can learn from the Federal Trade Commission of the United States, the Data Protection Commission of the European Union, the Personal Information

Protection Commission of Japan, and their counterparts in some other countries, to set up our own single and specialized data protection agency for supervision and regulation, the effective solution of disputes, and the smooth development of the market.

Strengthen judicial relief and establish the class action system. Any infringement on the legitimate interest of a data subject constitutes infringement of data rights. Any infringement requires relief. In order to realize any original right, there must be a remedy. At present, judicial relief is available in the case of improper behavior in public, and there is no provision for the improper collection and use of data through new technology, new businesses, and new models in the context of big data. According to the experience of other countries, the common trend is the combination of strict government law enforcement, industrial self-discipline (under pressure), and a low-intensity litigation mechanism. When data rights are infringed, the data owner can not only appeal to the competent supervision department for administrative enforcement relief, but also choose to seek judicial relief through litigation. In contrast, the judicial relief system in China does not give full play to the important value of data rights. It is suggested that judicial relief be reinforced with regard to data rights infringement in the big data by issuing judicial interpretations. A class action procedure should be established to allow data subjects to become co-plaintiffs and give similar rights protection problems to professional agents so as to further reduce the cost of rights protection while enhancing judicial relief.

Enhance international cooperation and draw on advanced international experience. In a highly integrated world, domestic legislation is inevitably placed in the international environment, and the extraterritorial effect of national law should be coordinated with international law. Many countries are paying more attention to data rights protection, but legal conflicts in this field have also caused problems. Data rights protection is no longer a matter of domestic law; a large amount of data can be collected, stored, and utilized in a country, or even globally, without limitation of time and space. Based on different purposes, different countries have come up with different ways to protect data rights. Therefore, China should strengthen international cooperation and actively participate in the drafting of international conventions. We should establish a law enforcement cooperation mechanism and jointly build a security protection platform. At the same time, we should learn the advanced norms, principles, and laws of relevant international organizations, countries, and regions and establish a legal system that conforms to the demands of the digital economy. If we push forward data rights legislation as fast as possible, and set the tone for the value norms of data in the long-term vis-à-vis global perspectives and future vision, we will be able to master the future course of data legislation. At the same time, if our digital economy is to lead the world, we must provide higher-quality, fairer, and more sustainable institutional guarantees for the data rights of various subjects by providing complete and accurate legal rules.

Bibliography

Alibaba Data Security Research Institute. 2019. "Global Data Cross-Border Flow Policy and China Strategy Research Report." *Security Internal Reference.*

Bennett, Colin, and John Rawls. 1992. *Regulating Privacy: Data Protection and Public Policy in Europe and the United States.* Ithaca: Cornell University Press.

Burkert, Herbert, "Privacy – Data Protection, A German/European Perspective." In *Governance of Global Networks in the Light of Differing Local Values*, edited by Christoph Engel and Kenneth H. Keller, 43–70. Baden-Baden: Nomos Verlagsgesellschaft.

Chander Anupam, and Uyen P. Le. 2015. "Data Nationalism." *Emory Law Journal* 64, 679–704.

Chen Jiang. 2019. "Avoiding Injury with New Technology Requires Ethical and Legal Constraints, Qianjiang Evening News", November 18, 2016.

Chi Jianxin. 2016. "Comparison and Analysis of Personal Information Protection System in Japan and South Korea." *Intelligence Journal*, 12th issue.

Dane Roland, Elizabeth MacDonald. 2004. *Information Technology Law*, Trans. Song Lianbin, Lin Yifei, Lu National, Wuhan: Wuhan University Press.

Ding Huang. 2002. "The Scientific Nature of Policy Making and the Effectiveness of Policy Implementation." *Nanjing Social Science*, 1st issue.

Flaherty, David, 1989. *Protecting Privacy in Surveillance Societies: The Federal Republic of Germany, Sweden, France, Canada, and the United States.* Chapel Hill and London: University of North Carolina Press.

Graham Pearce, and Nicholas Platten. 1998. "Achieving Personal Data Protection in the EU." *Journal of Common Market Studies* 36, 4th issue.

Greenwald, G. June 6, 2013. "US Orders Phone Firm to Hand Over Data on Millions of Calls: Top Secret Court Ruling Demands Ongoing." *The Guardian*.

Guo Yu. 2012. *Legal Protection of Personal Data*. Beijing: Peking University Press.

He Yuan, ed. 2020. *Data Law*. Beijing: Peking University Press.

Hiro Nishimura. 2016. "Japan's Personal Information Protection System and Its Enlightenment for China." *Internet Law Review*, 1st issue.

Hong Hailin. 2010. *Research on Civil Law Protection of Personal Information*. Beijing: Law Press.

Horibe Masao. 2000. "The Current Situation of Personal Information Protection." *Jurist*, No. 119, p. 22.

Hu Wei. 2018. "The Value Orientation of Cross-border Data Flow Legislation and China's Choice." *Social Science*, 4th issue.

Hu Wenhua, and Kong Huafeng. 2019. "Indian Data Localization and Cross-Border Flow Legislation Practice." *Computer Applications and Software*, 8th issue.

Huang Daoli, and Hu Wenhua. 2019. "The Basic Pattern of Legislative Regulation on Global Data Localization and Cross-Border Flow." *Information Security and Communications Privacy*, 9th issue.

Ji Leilei. 2017. "Comparative Study of Legislation Path of Personal Information Protection." *Library Development*, 9th issue.

Jiang Ge. 2011. "On the Modell of a Personal Data Protection Act: A Study Based on the German Experience." *Journal of Northwest University of Political Science and Law*, 2nd issue.

Jiang Po. 2001. "Comparison of International Policies and Laws on Information." *Law Press China*.

Korff, Douwe. 2008. "EC Study on the Implementation of the Data Protection Directive." SSRN, October 24, <http：//ssrn.com/abstract=1287667>.

Lei Wanlu. 2018. "Legislative Protection of Personal Information Right in China – Comparative Analysis of the Latest Development in Personal Information Protection in the United States and the European Union." *Frontiers*, 23th issue.

Li Dandan. 2015. "Measures and Enlightenment of Personal Information Protection in Japan." *People's Forum*, 11th issue.

Li Jianing. 2018. "The Legal Study of Personal Information Protection in India." *Legal and Economy*, 9th issue.

Li Yuan. 2016. "Protection Information Privacy in the Era of Big Data." Ph. D. thesis, Southwest University of Political Science and Law.

Li Yuan. 2019. *Personal Information Protection in the Era of Big Data*. Wuhan: Huazhong University of Science &Technology Press.

Lilian Edwards. 2010. "Coding Privacy" *Chicago-Kent Law Review* 84.

Liu Yun. 2017. "Development Process of and Reform and Innovations in the European Personal Data Protection Law." *Jinan Journal (Philosophy and Social Sciences)*, 2nd issue.

Mondaq. 2018. "Draft Rules for E-Pharmacy under the Drugs and Cosmetic Rules", September 27, <https://www.mondaq.com/india/food-and-drugs-law/740234/draft-rules-for-e-pharmacy-under-the-drugs-and-cosmetic-rules-1945>.

Personal Information Protection Research Group, 2017, *International Comparative Research on Personal Information Protection*. Beijing: China Financial Press.

Privacy Alliance. 1998. "Online Privacy Alliance Will Serve as Vanguard of Industry Efforts to Protect Privacy in Cyberspace", June 22, <http://www.privacyalliance.org/news/06221998/>.

Qi Aimin. 2004. "Comparative Study of Personal Data Protection Legislation in America and Germany – On Value Orientation and Basic Position of Personal Data Protection Legislation in China." *Gansu Shehui Kexue*, 3rd issue.

Qi Aimin. 2005. "Analysis of Information Privacy Legislation in American." *Present Day Law Science*, 2nd Issue.

Qi Aimin. 2009a. "On Uniform Legislation Mode of Personal Information Protection Law." *Journal of Chongqing Technology and Business University (Social Science Edition)*, 4th issue.

Qi Aimin. 2009b. *Research on Information Legislation in China*. Wuhan: Wuhan University Press.

Qi Aimin. 2009c. *Saving the Personality from the Information Society: General Introduction to Personal Information Protection Law*. Beijing: Peking University Press.

Qi Aimin. 2015. *International Comparative Study of Personal Information Protection Law in Big Data Era*. Beijing: Law Press China.

Ren Longlong. 2017. "The Civil Law Protection of Personal Information in the Age of Big Data." Ph. D. thesis, University of Foreign Economics and Trade.

Reserve Bank of India. 2019. "Storage of Payment System Data", June 26, <https://www.rbi.org.in/CommonPerson/english/Scripts/FAQs.aspx?Id=2995>.

Schwartz, Paul, and Daniel Solove. 2014. "Reconciling Personal Information in the United States and EU." *California Law Review* 102, 2nd issue.

Shi Yue. 2015. "Cross-Border Data Flow Management in the Digital Economy." *Information Security and Communication Secrecy*, 10th issue.

Shinbao Shizo, 2000. *The Creation and Development of Privacy Rights*. Seimundo Corporation.

Spinello, Richard A. 1999. *Ethical Aspects of Information Technology*, Trans. Liu Gang, Beijing: Central Compilation and Translation Press.

Sogabe Masahiro. 2017. "Law on the Personal Information and the Media." *Mass Communication Ethics*, No. 695, p. 2.

Tal Z. Zarsky. 2017. "Incompatible: The GDPR in the Age of Big Data." *Seton Hall Law Review* 47.

The Economic Times. 2018. "All about India's Data Localisation Policy", October 21, <https://economictimes.indiatimes.com/tech/ites/all-about-indias-data-localisation-policy/articleshow/66297596.cms>.

The Key Laboratory of Big Data Strategy. 2020. *Sovereignty Blockchain 1.0: Orderly Internet and a Community with a Shared Future for Mankind*. Hangzhou: Zhejiang University Press.

Wang Xiuxiu. 2017. "Economic Analysis and Path Choice of Personal Data Protection Legislation." *Journal of Shanghai Normal University (Philosophy & Social Sciences)*, 3rd issue.

Wang Yongqi. 2019. "Legal Connotation of Public Data and Its Normative Application Path." *Digital Library Forum*, 8th issue.

Xiang Dingyi. 2019. "Comparison and Enlightenment: Research on the Normative Modes of Commercial Utilization of Personal Information in the EU and the US." *Journal of Chongqing University of Posts and Telecommunications (Social Science Edition)*, 4th issue.

Xie Qing. 2006. "The Legal System of Personal Information Protection in Japan and Its Enlightenment." *Politics and Law*, 6th issue.

Yang Ji. 2012. "A Comparative Study on the Legislative Model of Extraterritorial Personal Information Protection – Taking the United States and Germany as an Example." *Library Theory and Practice*, 6th issue.

Zhang Hong. 2020. "Research on Japan's Personal Information Protection Law in the Era of Big Data." *Financial and Economic Law*, 3rd issue.

Zhang Jiaxin. 2019. "An Analysis of Personal Information Security in the Age of Big Data – A Comparison Based on Sino-US-European Systems." *China Market*, 12th issue.

Zhang Li, ed. 2019. *Data Governance and Data Security*. Beijing: Posts & Telecom Press.

Zhang Monan. 2020. "Cross-border Data Flow: Global Situation and the Countermeasures for China." *China Opening Journal*, 2nd issue.

Zhang Qianwen. 2020. "The Legality of Data Localizations in International Investment Treaties and China's Responses." *Research in Law and Business*, 2nd issue.

Zhang Shouwen. 2014. "The Legal Adjustment of the Relationship between Government and Market." *China Legal Science*, 5th issue.

Zhang Xinbao. 2015. "From Privacy to Personal Information: The Theory of Interest Remeasurement and Institutional Arrangement." *China Legal Science*, 3rd issue.

Zhou Hanhua, ed. 2006. *Research on the Frontier Issues of Personal Information Protection*. Beijing: Law Press.

Zhou Hanhua. 2018. "Exploring Incentive Compatibility of Personal Data Governance – Legislation Direction of China's Personal Information Protection Law." *Legal Research*, 2nd issue.

Zhou Xinyue. 2013. "On the American Industrial Self-Discipline Model and Enlightenment to China's Personal Information Protection Legislation Model." *Journal of Business*, 23rd issue.

Zhou Xueguang. 2008. "Collusion Phenomenon among Grassroots Governments – Institutional Logic of a Government's Action." *Sociological Research*, 6th issue.

CONCLUSION

Data Rights Law: Timeliness and Rebalance

The world is in a critical period of major changes unseen in a century. In 1945, mankind used nuclear weapons for the first time and developed the ability to destroy itself. Since then, mankind's ability to exterminate itself has continued to grow, as more threats to the survival of civilizations emerge – from climate change to a disastrous pandemic, from genetic technology to artificial intelligence . . . According to the existential risk theory, the period from our invention of various self-destructive methods to the emergence of global governance allows us to solve challenges in a coordinated and systematic way instead of relying on luck. This constitutes a pivotal stage in history. The current Covid-19 crisis once again prompts us to think more about the position of human beings in the ecosystem and the entire history of biological evolution. The challenge brought by Covid-19 to the world also highlights the conflict between eastern and western cultures. The essence of this conflict lies in different civilizations, or in other words, this conflict is an inevitable product under the background of industrial civilization. Behind the kind of conflict, a question of profound significance that we need to ponder is how mankind is to move toward the future. Our research shows that promoting the construction of a community with a shared future for mankind is the solution, and we will jointly build a global architecture in the digital age with vision and foresight. Central to this, building a new order of digital civilization has become the top priority.

An Examination of Jurisprudence in the Digital Age

From a binary world to a ternary world. Human society is moving from a binary world to a ternary world. In the past, people lived in a world composed of the physical space and the human social space. The order of activities were formed on the basis of interactions and mutual influence between people and things. People were the makers and leaders of the human social order. The development of integrated networking, data, and intelligence has broken through physical time and space and digitally reconstructed it. Digital space has become a new pole of world space. In this new space, data is the breeding ground for everything. The world has turned from a binary structure to a ternary one and the order of human activities are bound to change as the laws of production and life, social organizations, social governance systems, legal systems and other structures, formed and operated based on the original binary world are now bound to face the impact of the development logic of the ternary world. New types of legal relations such as the digital economy, self-driving cars, and gene editing continue to emerge. The existing experience and rules of mankind are encountering disruptive challenges and structural reconstructions, therefore, theoretical research and practical responses are urgently needed. Only by changing the law in accordance with reality can we achieve our governance goals. We should pay close attention to cutting-edge technology and actively respond to challenges, avoid and defuse possible risks, align the law with the requirements of the times, and actively promote the transformation of legal principles, laws, and the rule of law in response to social transformations.

From the hypothesis of natural person to that of data person. Human nature is the logical starting point of law, and law is a concentrated expression of human nature. The legal basis of data rights law lies in human nature, and an expression of the legal rights law system can only be found in human nature. Whereas people are not yet independent from other people and things, they are now dependent on data as well. When data-based production and data-based life become reality, human intelligence and artificial intelligence will merge; natural persons will gradually evolve into data persons, and the image, connotation, and extension of a "person" will profoundly change. In the future, human society is likely to be composed of natural persons, robots, and gene-edited persons, with "data person" as the manifestation of a new facet of human nature in the digital age. What needs to be pointed out is that the status of a data person is a legal issue that has to be faced in the future. The development of biotechnology and intelligent technology is substantially changing what mankind is. Humans are being repaired, transformed, and reorganized. Human-machine complementation, human-machine interaction, human-machine combination, human-machine collaboration, and human-machine integration are trending. The data power and the data relations of the digital age must require legal principles and systems different from what worked in the nineteenth century featured by assembly lines and the twentieth century marked by automation. The traditional legal system, especially the part related to legal subjects, has been facing or is about to face unprecedented challenges. From the perspective of legal evolution, it seems that there is no reason to suspect that the institutional configuration of legal subjects in the future will extend to data persons or a new species in cyberspace. Although these are just assumptions, mankind should probably take precautions and handle this possible major legal issue with caution.

From traditional human rights to digital human rights. Data has become an important strategic resource and a key production factor, covering and keeping records of all aspects of a person's life from cradle to grave, and has become a new carrier and value expression of human rights in the new era. Human rights are undergoing profound digital reshaping. In terms of its attributes, elements, content, or forms, human rights are moving from the physical world to the digital world, and digital human rights have emerged. Digital technology is a double-edged sword which brings not only blessing, but also a crisis. For this reason, it is important and necessary to adapt to the development needs of the digital age, promote the transformation and upgrading of human rights from the physical world to the digital world, and use the power and authority of human rights to strengthen the ethical constraints and legal regulation on the development and application of digital technology. In global governance, China's influence clearly does not match its role as a major country in the world. Amplifying our voice to match the status of a major country as soon as possible, especially in the field of human rights, has become an urgent task. We should seize the opportunity of the digital age, grasp the pulse of the times, instantly start the legal interpretation and the building of a digital human rights system, and use this to guide the theoretical, systematic, and practical innovation for the building of a community with a shared future for mankind. Thus, we will be the one to create and uphold of the future human rights system.

Transformation of Laws in the Digital Age

From possession and exclusivity to sharing and altruism. Whether it is the agricultural era or the industrial era, the exclusive possession of resources is the core of all rules. Yours belongs to you and mine is mine, and this is true for land, mining sites, and all kinds of things. It is precisely because of this exclusivity that human society is often caught in life-or-death competition for resources, causing inequality and a huge waste of social resources. In the digital age, ownership and the right to use will be separate. It can be said that the right to use is more important than ownership and using is better than possessing. The essence is to open your own resources to exchange and connect with others. Data ownership may not be important, but who has the right to use data and what value can be generated is. The data factor market urgently needs a sharing-centered mentality that pursues not ownership but the right to use. The relations of the digital age determine that society is inherently decentralized, flat, and borderless, and its basic spirit is openness, sharing, cooperation, and mutual benefit. These characteristics form the foundation of a people-centered society and also determine that altruism is the core value of this era. Altruism adds to people's willingness to transfer and share data rights, thereby promoting the positive transformation toward more transfer and sharing. When data resources are extremely abundant and can be distributed according to demand, the concept of fair sharing will be deeply rooted in the hearts of the people; digital labor will become what leads to happiness, and altruism will greatly increase. When the altruism hidden in human nature is activated, we may regard the data rights system as the midwife who pushes it out.

From legal empowerment to technological empowerment. Philosophers of the seventeenth and eighteenth centuries designed a sophisticated system, from natural human rights to law-endowed human rights: abandoning certain rights that stem from human nature, and introducing public power and legal constraints to restrict natural rights. A major feature of the modern world is that countries and governments are established and laws and regulations are formulated all on the basis of social contract. This is legal empowerment. As human society continues to evolve toward networking, data, and intelligence, technological empowerment has become a major feature of the digital age. The composition power in society shifts from violence, wealth, knowledge, etc. to technology, and each "technology center" becomes a "power center." Professor Lawrence Lessig of Harvard University even put forward the argument that "code is law" in his book *Code* (1999). With the advent of digital technology, the baton of people's actions has gradually shifted from social factors to technological architecture. Because code sets out all the steps and rules in advance, people can only follow the code's arrangement and follow suit. Since the law of the Internet is determined by code, whoever has the code has the right to define the law. The ever-increasing supply of technology has led to the rise of code and algorithm-based regulation. As Yuval Harari said in *A Brief History of the Future*: "Our law will become a kind of digital rule, which will regulate all human behaviors except for the laws of physics." Codes and laws will go hand-in-hand in the future.

From approaching justice to digital justice. With the continuous breakthroughs in digital technology, disputes grow exponentially in cyberspace, going beyond what traditional trial models and alternative dispute resolution mechanisms can handle. At present, there is an urgent need for online dispute resolution mechanisms, smart courts, etc. to ensure that people's rights in the digital society can be protected. Digital technology provides new possibilities for resolving data-related disputes. It not only diverts cases, streamlines procedures, reduces costs, prevents disputes, and improves dispute resolution procedures, but also helps people get closer to justice than ever before. Ethan Katsh and Orna Rabinovich-Einy first proposed the theory of digital justice in the internet world in *Digital Justice – When Dispute Resolution Meets Internet Technology* (2019), pointing out that the theory of digital justice will gradually replace the traditional theory of justice and become the principle and benchmark of the digital world. The theory of digital justice has an epoch-making significance. It is not just an important milestone in the study of justice theory, but it also provides instructions and codes for the future, understands the future, and is the master of the future. As Lord Briggs said:

> Traditional courts are the result of the industrial age, while online courts are the product of the Internet era; traditional courts will inevitably decline, and online courts will rise. Achieving the goal of establishing online courts is worth the time, money and effort, because online courts will be the most revolutionary and subversive courts in this era and will change the way for courts to produce justice and the way for parties to achieve justice. (Lord Justice Briggs 2017, p. 49)

Great epoch-making inventions have triggered a revolution in the legal world. In the digital age, equality, freedom, democracy, law, order, and justice will all be redefined. The integration of law and technology has become a significant development trend.

The Rule of Law Paradigm in the Digital Age

Data rights law is a solution to the deficit of digital governance. "If there will be a huge social revolution in human society, it will not be a violent revolution to smash the old state apparatus, but a rule of law revolution that regulates the data empire." Law is the most important tool for the governance of a country, and good law is the precedent for good governance. The rule of law is a fundamental means of global governance and the basic guarantee of good global governance. The rule of law, with rules as the procedural criteria, is not only the dominant model of global governance today and what is shared by the whole world, but a yardstick for the development and progress of a civilization. Clear and predictable rule of law is the pursuit, demand, and expectation of all countries in the world. The problem of global governance deficit requires a new solution. Mutual consultation, joint contribution, and sharing are the right way toward a solution to the problem of global digital governance deficit. Data rights legislation is of special significance for maintaining national data sovereignty, firmly grasping the power to make international rules and having one's voice heard in the international community, and promoting the global cyberspace governance which will lay the foundation of the rule of law. Data rights law is an innovation that is based on reality and in line with what would be needed in the future. It will have a positive impact on the development of the digital economy, digital government, digital social governance, and the digital civilization.

The right to share is the core right in the era of a digital civilization. Data rights law is based on a digital rights system established in the framework of an altruistic culture, and is committed to promoting the rule of law in the digital field. The data person hypothesis provides a theoretical basis for an altruistic culture and system. If altruism is established, then it will be possible for the right to share to become a basic human right. This will then reveal the nature of digital rights which will be the basis for the building of a digital rights system and the corresponding legal system, thereby promoting the establishment of a new order of a digital civilization. In this sense, the right to share is a theoretical assumption based on the current human rights system, an essential characteristic of the digital rights system, and the cultural connotation of altruism, providing important support for the digital civilization and a value orientation in the building of a community with a shared future for mankind. As an important tool in the jurisprudence of global governance, the right to share will play a decisive role. Through the theoretical innovation and continuous efforts of mankind, the right to share is expected to become a new milestone in the history of human rights.

Let digital rule of law lead the way forward in the governance of China. Historical experience has shown that advanced systems are the foundation and guarantee of economic prosperity, stability, and security; the reality of the contemporary world confirms that effective governance is the core and foundation of the competitiveness of a country and the rejuvenation of the Chinese nation. The rule of law is the backbone of the country's governance.

"He who establishes good laws in the world shall govern the world; he who establishes good laws in one country shall govern the country." General Secretary Xi Jinping pointed out that to embrace the world and participate in international affairs as a responsible major country, China must do a good job in advancing the rule of law; that the global governance system is in a critical period of adjustment and reform and we must actively participate in the formulation of international rules and be a participant, promoter, and leader in the process of global governance reform. However, for a long time, China has been a weak country in the formulation of international laws, and has even been marginalized by international law in international relations. But today, China is taking a different attitude and displaying a new image, transforming itself from a participant in the international order to a constructive leader in the system. Strengthening data-related legislation is of great significance in building and improving a digital governance system with Chinese characteristics, mustering new driving forces for innovation-driven development, and comprehensively shaping new development advantages. "If Chinese law is to go global, it most likely will start with the law on the digital economy." The Fifth Plenary Session of the 19th CPC Central Committee proposed to create an internationally competitive digital industry cluster. As a major country in the digital economy, China has the responsibility to explore the digital rule of law and lead the way into the future. Against this background, data rights legislation is an innovation, and it is expected to become a major tool to enable the rise of Chinese law and its move toward the center of the world stage. The current international situation is turbulent, with increasing instability and uncertainty. The impact of Covid-19 is widespread and far-reaching; economic globalization has encountered a countercurrent and the world has entered a period full of changes. Unilateralism, protectionism, and hegemony pose threats to world peace and development. In this context, building a community with a shared future for mankind has been proposed exactly when it is appropriate and necessary. Building a community with a shared future for mankind requires advancement in and support from international digital rule of law. It is necessary to establish good law and promote good governance in the international community, give full play to the pivotal role of digital rule of law in the global cyberspace governance, move toward a new realm of the governance of China, and strive to turn the community with a shared future for mankind from a proposal to a reality.

At present, digital rule of law is emerging and data law has become a prominent research topic. No answer can be found in old textbooks, and innovation and breakthroughs are needed. In the post-Covid era, international competition in the digital realm is bound to intensify, and the complexity of the problem is bound to increase exponentially. The Fifth Plenary Session of the 19th CPC Central Committee emphasized that to "accelerate digital development," "unswervingly build a strong country in cyberspace, digital China" and "take scientific and technological self-reliance as a strategic support for national development . . . accelerate the building of a technological power." Compared with this requirement, the construction of the discipline system, academic system, and the discourse system of the digitalized rule of law is only a small step forward. We lack answers to many practical questions, and the unknown is far greater than the known.

In recent years, the Key Laboratory of Big Data Strategy has devoted itself to the theoretical research of digital order, and has successively released its research findings in three series of publications – block data, data rights law, and sovereignty blockchain, collectively called the "digital civilization trilogy." The core is to erect three pillars for the new order of a digital civilization as the three series focus on three core issues in the new order of a digital civilization, and have become stepping stones on the way from an industrial civilization to a digital civilization. Block data addresses the issue of integration. As long as everything is digitalized, integration becomes possible. Data rights law focuses on the topic of sharing. The core of the data rights law is the right to share, which is based on an altruistic culture. Sovereignty blockchain is about goodness. The "goodness" here means "conscience," as in Wang Yangming's philosophy of the mind. If the three value orientations of integration, sharing, and conscience are theoretically established, the cultural obstacles to humans' move toward a digital civilization will be removed.

The biggest international political change in the twenty-first century is the rise of China. The real rise of a country lies in providing a new paradigm of civilization for the world. The famous American jurist Roscoe Pound once proposed that the legal order has two tasks: maintaining the value of the existing civilization and promoting the development of human capabilities. In this sense, digital civilization can be regarded as the digital ethics, digital governance, and digital jurisprudence on which the digital rights law is based, guiding and supporting the value, selection, and functions of the data rights law, and effectively balancing between conflicting interests. It also maintains a digital order that is conducive to data protection and good use of data, and ultimately realizes the protection of digital human rights. In the context of the development of a new scientific and technological revolution and industrial transformation, and the interweaving and coexistence of the industrial civilization and the digital civilization, it is urgent to reflect and evolve my country's digital rights legislation with the times and the balance of interests. Anthony Giddens once called the moment when ontological security is disturbed as the "moment of destiny," for the "moment of destiny" means "saying goodbye to the past, moving into the future, stepping out of the old self, and reshaping the new self." In the journey of fulfilling the great historical mission of maintaining and promoting digital civilization, we hope that the data rights law will be a great achievement.

Postscript

The term "data rights law" was first proposed by Professor Lian Yuming, director of the Key Laboratory of Big Data Strategy, in March 2017, and then was officially recognized and released by China National Committee for Terms in Sciences and Technologies. For this, China has become the first country to put forward the concept of "data rights law" in the world. On June 6, 2017, Guiyang Municipal People's Government signed an agreement with China University of Political Science and Law to jointly establish the Research Base of Key Laboratory of Big Data Strategy. On July 6, 2017, the first research center, that is the Research Center of Data Rights Law in China University of Political Science and Law, received approval for its establishment.

On May 28, 2019, China University of Political Science and Law and the Guiyang Municipal People's Government jointly convened the Inaugural Meeting of Digital China Think Tank Alliance and Symposium on *Data Rights Law 1.0* (simplified Chinese, traditional Chinese, and English versions). Zhao Deming, member of the Standing Committee of the CPC Guizhou Provincial Committee and Secretary of the CPC Guiyang Municipal Committee, attended the meeting and delivered a speech. He commended *Data Rights Law 1.0* as a major theoretical innovation and believed that "data rights law" would certainly have a positive impact on the development of the digital economy, the construction of e-government, the governance of the digital society, and the progress of the digital civilization. Upon its release, *Data Rights Law 1.0* drew worldwide attention. It was covered by more than 170 Chinese and over 200 foreign media agencies in English, French, German, and Spanish, as well as Chinese languages. One foreign media agency commented: "Its release provides a jurisprudential basis for the transformation of human society from the industrial civilization to the digital civilization, and gives us a key to unlock the door of the digital civilization in the future."

On July 28, 2020, China University of Political Science and Law and the Guiyang Municipal People's Government held a news conference to release the *Data Rights Law* publication. The French and German versions of *Data Rights Law 1.0* and the simplified Chinese, traditional Chinese, and English versions of *Data Rights Law 2.0* were released in Beijing and Guiyang in synch. This new title of the data rights law series, the Key Laboratory of Big Data Strategy, not only deepened theoretical research on data rights law, but also marked a major breakthrough in Guiyang's pursuit of theoretical innovations in the field of big data. The greatest innovation and breakthrough of *Data Rights Law 2.0* lies in three points. First, it puts forward the data man hypothesis for the first time. Second, it puts forward three major categories of digital rights: the right to data, the right to share, and data sovereignty. Third, it is a response to President Xi Jinping's important instructions in his congratulatory letter to the 2019 China International Big Data Industry Expo that we should "handle the challenges of big data development properly in the fields of law, security and governance."

For *Data Rights Law 3.0*, we gathered more than 300 legal norms relating to privacy, information, and data published by major countries, regions, and international organizations all over the world to study the prospective topics relevant to data rights legislation in China. We traced the origins of, sorted out, compared, and analyzed the relevant provisions in foreign laws and regulations in this regard and selected the most important and meaningful ones to form the *Translation Collection of Data Rights Law*. By doing this, we aim firstly to advance the development of data rights law in China by learning from and borrowing experience from other countries, and secondly, on the basis of comparison, suggest the data rights rules that are best suited for China's national interests and push Chinese legislation to the world so as to build regional or global data rights norms.

This book is firmly based on discussions, exchanges, and in-depth research efforts organized by the Key Laboratory of Big Data Strategy, and was produced through collective efforts. In the process, the general structure and the core ideas of this book came from Lian Yuming, and a more detailed outline as well as the main points were worked out mainly by Long Rongyuan. Authors include Lian Yuming, Zhu Yinghui, Song

Qing, Wu Jianzhong, Zhang Tao, Long Rongyuan, Song Xixian, Zhang Longxiang, Zou Tao, Chen Wei, Shen Xudong, Yang Zhou, Yang Lu and Xi Jinting, with Long Rongyuan serving as the coordinator. Chen Gang also offered many important forward-looking and guiding ideas for this book. Meaningful and forward-looking inputs also came from Zhao Deming, member of the Standing Committee of the CPC Guizhou Provincial Committee, Secretary of the CPC Guiyang Municipal Committee, and Secretary of the Party Working Committee of Gui'an New District; Chen Yan, Vice Chairman of the Guizhou Provincial CPPCC Committee, Deputy Secretary of the CPC Guiyang Municipal Committee, Mayor of Guiyang, and Deputy Secretary of the Party Working Committee and Director of Management Committee of Gui'an New District; Xu Hao, the then member of the Standing Committee of the CPC Guiyang Municipal Committee and Executive Vice Mayor of Guiyang; and Liu Benli, member of the Standing Committee and Secretary General of the CPC Guiyang Municipal Committee. It can be said that this book is the crystallization of collective wisdom. Special thanks go to the leaders and editors of Social Science Academic Press. Wang Limin, Director of the Press, offered support and organized editors for the publishing of this book with profound insights, unique vision, and great courage. Without their careful planning, conscientious editing work, and excellent design, this book would not have come out as scheduled.

During the research and compilation of this book, we held a number of high-level academic seminars and invited many experts, authoritative scholars, and enterprise elites from the law, science, and practical circles to have multiple rounds of discussions. Among them, Wu Dahua (Guizhou Academy of Social Sciences), Pan Shanbin (Guizhou Minzu University), Sun Zhiyu (Guizhou University), and Shen Xuefeng (Guiyang University) believed that when data becomes a factor of production, laws should also keep up the pace and provide effective and timely legal protection, just like protecting the other factors such as land, labor, capital, and technology. Li Zheng (China University of Political Science and Law), Qu Qingchao (Long Institute), Li Youxing (Zhejiang University), and Su Yu (People's Public Security University of China) pointed out that data rights law is not only about the protection and utilization of data, but also about the fundamental transformation of data rights legislation – from the protection of data interests to the legislation of data rights. The governance technology based on the data rights law will become a new engine for the modernization of governance system and governance capacity. Gu Fugang (Guiyang Municipal Bureau of Big Data Development and Management), Zhao Hong (China University of Political Science and Law), Qin Shuai (People's Public Security of China), Song Qing (Guiyang Innovation-Driven Development Strategy Research Institute), and Wu Yueguan (Guizhou Academy of Social Sciences) believed that if property law is deemed as a legal cornerstone of the industrial civilization, then the data rights law can be deemed as a cornerstone of the digital civilization. Yang Xiaohu (Zhejiang University), Luo Yihong (Guizhou Academy of Social Sciences), Xiao Yu (Guizhou ZhongChuangLian Law Firm), and Zheng Weicheng (Guiyang Big Data Industry Group Co. Ltd.) stated that the key to data rights law is to achieve a balance between the effective protection of data rights and making the best use of data, so as to achieve the purpose of safeguarding public interests and public security while promoting the free flow and sharing of personal data.

The three book series, known as the data civilization trilogy—*Block Data*, *Data Rights Law* and *Sovereignty Blockchain*—by the Key Laboratory of Big Data Strategy are hailed as the three major pillars of the new order of the digital civilization. They have great influence both at home and abroad. Our laws have never been faced with greater challenges like the ones posed by science and technology development today. We should pay close attention to these cutting-edge technologies and actively respond to related challenges, effectively manage possible risks, balance between the development of law and science, and actively promote the reform of laws, the rule of law, and jurisprudence in response to social transformation. We will continue with our work and produce the traditional Chinese, English, French, German, and other versions of this book. We are striving to have our voice heard in the international community and make our contribution to the making of international rules for the governance of the cyber world, where sound legislation is still absent.

In the process of writing this series of books, we have witnessed how legal research in China gradually embraced the digital era. Major law schools have set up dedicated institutions for the research of cyber law, data law, intelligent law, digital rule of law, and future rule of law—these research forces are growing rapidly, with an increasing number of young scholars joining. In addition, countless legal practitioners are making their efforts to this cause through their practices at the forefront. Therefore, it is exactly the right time for this series of monographs to come out. This series aims to present the latest research findings in the theoretical research of data rights law at home and abroad, highlighting and further promoting progress. It is our hope that such efforts will benefit the theoretical exploration and rulemaking in this field. This book start with theoretical exploration, and then puts forward its own ideas on the value orientation, core issues, difficulties, key systems, and legislative models of data rights law. We have tried our best to cover the latest ideas and findings as much as possible, but for sure there may still be omissions and errors. For any possible errors and mistakes, and particularly any regrettable omission of the existing literature, we apologize and welcome comments from all readers.

Key Laboratory of Big Data Strategy
November 15, 2020

APPENDIX I

Interpretations of Internet Information and Data-Related Clauses in the *Civil Code*[1]

Article III: Personal Information Rights

A natural person's personal information is protected by law. Any organization or individual that needs to access other's personal information must do so in accordance with law and guarantee the safety of such information, and may not illegally collect, use, process, or transmit other's personal information, or illegally trade, provide, or publicize such information.

Understanding and Application

According to the *Cyber Security Law*, "personal information" includes all kinds of information recorded in electronic or other forms that can be used independently or in combination with other information to identify a natural person, including but not limited to the natural person's name, date of birth, identification number, biometric personal information, address, and telephone number. According to this article, the concept of personal information should include some basic elements: (1) the subjects are natural persons rather than legal persons or unincorporated organizations; (2) personal information is a kind of information recorded in electronic or other forms; and (3) the information can be used

1 See *Civil Code of the People's Republic of China*. Beijing: China Legal Publishing House, 2020, pp. 82, 96, 304, 321, 344, 553, 560, 562, 564, 567, 681, 682, 684, 685, 706.

independently or in combination with other information to identify a natural person's identity. This is a "bottom-line" provision—besides the common types of personal information listed in the stipulation such as name, date of birth, identification number, biometric personal information, address, and telephone number, all kinds of other information that can be used independently or in combination with other information to identify a natural person shall be regarded as personal information. For instance, with the development of modern information technology, all aspects of personal life can be recorded on the Internet, mobile intelligent terminals, wearable devices, and the like. Location information, behavior data, etc., fall under the category of personal information. Personal information rights are important rights enjoyed by citizens in a modern information society which involve the personality interests of the information subject, and closely relates to other kinds of personal or property interests of the information subject. For this reason, the explicit protection of personal information is of practical significance to guarantee the personal dignity and freedom of citizens, protect them from infringements, and maintain social order.

See also: the *Law on the Protection of Consumer Rights and Interests*, Articles 14, 29, 50; *Cybersecurity Law*, Articles 42 and 76; *Law on Commercial Banks*, Article 29; *Law on Practicing Doctors*, Article 22; *Law on Resident Identity Cards*, Article 19; *Criminal Law*, Article 252 (1); *Interpretation of the Supreme People's Court and the Supreme People's Procuratorate on Several Issues concerning the Application of Law in the Handling of Criminal Cases of Infringing on Citizens' Personal Information.*

Article 127: Protection of Data and Virtual Property in Cyberspace

Where there are laws particularly providing for the protection of data and online virtual assets, such provisions shall be followed.

Understanding and Application

Data can be divided into native data and derivative data. Native data is the kind of data that does not depend on existing rights, whereas derivative data refers to systematic, readable, and valuable data, such as shopping preferences and credit records, which is the result of processing, calculation, and aggregation based on algorithms after native data has been recorded and stored. The data that can be treated as an object of intellectual property rights is derivative data. Network virtual property, which refers to the virtual network itself and the electromagnetic records with property attributes existing on the network, is a category of new digital property that can be measured by current standards. As a new kind of property, network virtual property has different characteristics from existing types of property.

See also: *Cybersecurity Law*, Article 10.

Article 469: Forms of Conclusion of Contracts and Writings

The parties may conclude a contract in writing, orally, or in other forms.

A writing refers to any form that renders the content contained therein capable of being represented in a tangible form, such as a written agreement, letter, telegram, telex, or facsimile.

A data message in any form, such as electronic data interchange and e-mails that renders the content contained therein capable of being represented in a tangible form and accessible for reference and use at any time shall be deemed as a writing.

Understanding and Application

Where the parties did not conclude a contract in a written or verbal form, such an agreement may be inferred from the conduct of both parties, and that both parties intended to conclude a contract. In such circumstances, the people's court may deem the contract concluded in some "other form." (See *Interpretation II of the Supreme People's Court of Several Issues concerning the Application of the Contract Law of the People's Republic of China*, Article 2).

See also: *Civil Code*, Article 135; *Electronic Signature Law*, Article 4; *Arbitration Law*, Article 16.

Article 491: Confirmation Letter and the Time of Contract Conclusion; Order Submission and the Time of Contract Conclusion

Where the parties conclude a contract in the form of a letter, data message, or the like, and a confirmation letter is required to be signed, the contract is formed when the confirmation letter is signed.

Where the information about goods or services published by a party via information network, such as the Internet, conforms to the conditions for an offer, unless otherwise agreed by the parties, a contract is formed at the time when the other party chooses such product or service and successfully submits the order.

Understanding and Application

Where the parties conclude a contract by letter or data message, the contract is formed when the acceptance becomes effective. However, if the parties agree to sign a written confirmation letter, the contract is formed when the confirmation letter is signed, so the time that both parties sign the confirmation letter is the time the contract is concluded, whether in writing or by a data message. According to the characteristics of online transactions, namely the lack of distinct signs of offer and acceptance for a contract signed online, when the information on goods or service is released by one party on an information network such as the Internet, that is considered to be an offer of a network transaction contract, as long as it meets the conditions for an offer. When the other party, the consumer, selects the goods or service and submits the order, that is deemed to be acceptance. A contract is formed when the transaction service interface on the web shows that the order was submitted successfully. Thus, when the interface shows that "order submitted successfully," that is the time when the contract is formed.

See also: *E-Commerce Law*, Article 49; *Auction Law*, Article 52.

Article 512: Rules Regarding the Delivery Time of an Electronic Contract

Where the object of an electronic contract is concluded through the internet or other information network is the delivery of goods, and the goods are to be delivered by express delivery services, the time of delivery is the time of acknowledging receipt of the goods by the recipient. Where the object of the said electronic contract is the provision of services, the time for provision of the service is the time stated in the automatic generated electronic certificate or physical certificate. Where there is no time stated in such a certificate or the time stated therein is inconsistent with the actual time for provision of the service, the actual time for provision of the service shall prevail.

Where the subject matter of the said electronic contract is delivered by online transmission, the time of delivery is the time when the subject matter of the contract enters the specific system designated by the other party and can be searched and identified.

Where the parties to the said electronic contract agree otherwise on the mode and time of delivery of goods or provision of services, such agreement shall be complied with.

Understanding and Application

Three situations determine the delivery time of a network transaction contract: (1) where the subject matter of an online transaction contract is the delivery of commodities by express delivery, the delivery time shall be the time of signature by the consignee. Where the subject matter of a network contract is the provision of services, which have no obvious mark of delivery, the delivery time shall be the time specified in the electronic document or hard-copy document; if the said document specifies no time, or the time specified is not the same as the time for the actual provision of services, the delivery time shall be the time of the actual provision of services; (2) where the subject matter of an electronic contract is to be delivered by means of online transmission, such as in the case of an online consulting service contract, the delivery time shall be the time when the subject matter (e.g., an advisory report) enters the particular system designated by the other party and is capable of being searched for and identified; (3) if the parties to an electronic contract agree otherwise on the method and time of delivery of goods or provision of services, such an agreement shall prevail. For example, if the buyer in an online sales contract claims to receive the goods by express delivery, the delivery time shall be the time when the express delivery service provider delivers those goods to the buyer.

See also: *E-Commerce Law*, Articles 51–7.

Article 1019: Protection of the Rights to Likeness

No organization or individual may infringe upon the other's rights to likeness by vilifying or defacing the image thereof, or through other ways such as falsifying other's image by utilizing information technology. Unless otherwise provided by law, no-one may make, use, or publicize the image of the right holder without the latter's consent.

Without the consent of the person holding the right to likeness, a person holding a right in the works of the image of the former person shall not use or publicize the said image by ways such as publishing, duplicating, distributing, leasing, or exhibiting thereof.

Understanding and Application

Infringement upon any other's rights to likeness is often manifested as vilification and deface. However, not all defamation and deface will be determined as illegal. For instance, if an amusement park changes the faces of tourists into cartoon pictures to make the images amusing, it is not so serious as vilification or defacing and does not constitute an illegal act. This article also provides that no organization or individual may infringe upon any other's rights to likeness by forgery using information technology. At present, artificial intelligence and other information technology can be used to make "deep forgery" of human faces and transplant the portraits arbitrarily, which leads to confusing the real with the false. Actors who forge the portrait of another by using information technology shall be governed by this Article and Book Seven (Tort Liability) of the *Civil Code*. Further, websites that sell "face-changing" software may be held jointly and severally liable for failing to fulfill their corresponding obligations to network users.

See also: *Law on the Protection of Women's Rights and Interests, Article 42*; *Mental Health Law, Article 4*; *Law on the Protection of Heroes and Martyrs, Article 22*; *Regulation on the Prevention and Treatment of HIV/AIDS, Article 39*; *Letter of the Supreme People's Court over Infringements upon the Rights to Likeness in the Appellate Case of Shanghai Science and Technology Newspaper v. Chen Guanyi & Zhu Hong.*

Article 1028: Inaccurate Content of Media Report as an Infringement upon Reputation

Where a person under the civil law has evidence to prove that the content reported by a media, such as a newspaper, a periodical, or an online website, is inaccurate and thus defames his/her reputation, he/she has the right to request the media to take necessary measures, including requiring the publisher to correct and/or delete the content in a timely manner.

Understanding and Application

This Article is connected with Article 1025, Paragraph 2, in Book Four (Personality Rights) of the *Civil Code*. Where the content of a report in a newspaper or journal, on the internet, or with other media are inaccurate and infringes upon the reputation of any other person, the media shall fulfill the obligations of making corrections or deletion in a timely manner. Where the media causes any damage to another person, the media shall assume compensatory liability.

Article 1032: The Right to Privacy and Privacy

A natural person enjoys the right to privacy. No organization or individual may infringe upon the other's right to privacy by prying into, intruding upon, disclosing, or publicizing other's private matters.

Privacy is the undisturbed private life of a natural person and his private space, private activities, and private information that he does not want to be known to others.

Understanding and Application

The right to privacy is part of the right to personality enjoyed by natural persons, which refers to the specific right to personality that a natural person independently controls the tranquility of his/her private life, private space, private activities, private information, and other security interests. His/her private life is personal information which he/she does not wish to be known to and disturbed by others.

Article 1033: Infringements upon the Right to Privacy

Unless otherwise provided by law or expressly consented to by the right holder, no organization or individual shall do the following acts:

(1) intruding upon another person's private life through making phone calls, sending text messages, using instant messaging tools, sending emails and flyers, and the like means;
(2) entering into, taking photographs of, or peeping into other's private spaces, such as the residence or hotel room of another person;

(3) taking photographs of, peeping into, eavesdropping, or disclosing the private activities of another person;
(4) taking photographs of or peeping at the private parts of another person's body;
(5) processing another person's private information; and
(6) infringing upon another person's privacy through other means.

Understanding and Application

As the subject of an obligation to the right to privacy, no organization or individual may conduct the following acts that infringe upon another person's right to privacy, such as private space, private activities, private body parts, private information, and the tranquility of life—(1) invading the tranquility of life of any other by phone calls, SMS, instant messaging tools, emails, leaflets, or any other means. The tranquility of life is the status of a private life enjoyed by natural persons to maintain peace and tranquility, to exclude the illegal intrusion by others, and to satisfy the intangible personal spiritual needs. Invading the tranquility of the private life often refers to harassing phone calls, harassing messages, harassing emails, etc., which constitute an infringement on the right to privacy; (2) entering, photographing, or peeping at any other's residence, hotel room, or any other private space. The private space under the protection of the right to privacy includes concrete private spaces and abstract private spaces. The former refers to personal residence, hotel room, passenger's luggage, schoolbags, etc., while the latter refers specifically to the private space of the mind; (3) photographing, peeping at, eavesdropping on, or disclosing to the public the private activities of any other. Private activities include all the personal activities that are of no concern to public interest, such as daily life, social interactions, marital life, extramarital affairs, and so on. Photographing, recording, peeping at or disclosing to the public these activities shall be determined to be an infringement upon other's private activities; (4) photographing or peeping at any private part of any other's body. Private parts of the body are also a kind of privacy, namely body privacy, which includes genital organs and intimate parts of the body. Photographing or peeping at any private part of any other's body constitutes an infringement of the right to privacy; (5) handling the private information of any other. Private information is the personal private information of a natural person, and the handling of which, such as accessing, deleting, making public, buying, and selling, constitutes a violation of the right to privacy; and (6) infringing upon the right to privacy of another by other means. This is a miscellaneous clause, which means that all the acts that violate private information, private activities, private space, private parts of body, the tranquility of life and the like, constitutes an infringement upon the right to privacy.

See also: *Constitution*, Article 39; *Criminal Procedure Law*, Article 136; *Supervision Law*, Article 24; *Criminal Law*, Article 245; *Counterespionage Law*, Article 32; *Public Security Administration Punishments Law*, Articles 42 and 48; *People's Police Law*, Articles 12 and 22; *Law on the People's Armed Police*, Article 19; *Regulations Concerning Diplomatic Privileges and Immunities*, Article 4; *Regulation on the Administration of Security and Guarding Services*, Article 25; *Interpretation of the Supreme People's Court on the Application of the Civil Procedure Law of the People's Republic of China*, Article 496; *Law on the Protection of Minors*, Articles 39 and 58.

Article 1034: Protection of Personal Information

A natural person's personal information is protected by law.

Personal information is the information recorded electronically or in other ways that can be used by itself, or in combination with other information, to identify a natural person, including the name, date of birth, identification number, biometric information, residential address, telephone number, email address, health information, whereabouts, and the like of the person.

The provisions on the right to privacy or, in the absence of which, the provisions on the protection of personal information, shall be applied to the private personal information.

Understanding and Application

The definition of personal information in the *Civil Code* is almost the same as that in *Cybersecurity Law*, the core content of which can be summarized as "information recorded electronically or in other forms that can identify a specific natural person separately or in combination with other information." According to Article 76 of the *Cybersecurity Law of the People's Republic of China*, personal information means "all kinds of information recorded in electronic or other forms, which can be used independently or in combination with other information to identify a natural person's identity, including but not limited to the natural person's name, date of birth, identification number, biometric personal information, address, and telephone number." From the above definition of personal information, it can be seen that the *Civil Code* and the *Cybersecurity Law* have different expressions on "the information that can identify a natural person." The *Civil Code* particularly emphasizes "various information that can identify a specific natural person," while the *Cybersecurity Law* highlights "all kinds of information to identify a natural person's personal identity." In fact, the personal information of a natural person is not only related to all kinds of information that can identify a natural person, it also includes information unrelated to the identity of a natural person. Considering that the *Civil Code* defines personal information as "various information recorded electronically or in other forms that can identify a specific natural person independently or in combination with other information," we can say the content and scope of personal information protection is broader than that prescribed in the *Cybersecurity Law*. Besides, Article 1 of the *Interpretation of the Supreme People's Court and the Supreme People's Procuratorate on Several Issues concerning the Application of Law in the Handling of Criminal Cases of Infringing on Citizens' Personal Information* provides that "citizens' personal information" as prescribed in Article 253(1) of the *Criminal Law* means all kinds of information recorded in electronic or any other form, which can be used independently or in combination with other information to identify a specific natural person or reflect a specific natural person's activities, including the natural person's name, identification number, contact information, address, account password, property status, and whereabouts—among others. On the basis of the kinds of "personal information" regulated by the *Cybersecurity Law*, Article 1034 of the *Civil Code* adds three examples, that is, "email address, health information, and whereabouts." Emails have a virtual address existing in electronic form rather than an actual address; health information involves the status of an individual's health, human characteristics, genetic information, etc., and whereabouts reflects the location and travels of a specific natural person, such as personal transportation, accommodation information, location, and so on, almost all of which amount to private information. Currently, the legislative scope of the protection for personal information is relatively narrow, and the content of personal privacy is not highlighted. While personal information has the dual attributes of personality rights and property rights, the right to personal privacy information is only a kind of personality right; it is suggested that legislation protecting personal information in China should focus on the protection of a natural person's privacy information. Despite the provision of protecting "private information" within personal information, the *Civil Code* is not a special law for the protection of personal information. This has led to the enactment of the *Personal Information Protection Law* to regulate the rights of claim, the mechanism of relief and protection, and circulation transactions involving non private information of an individual. In this regard, the *Civil Code* provides: "Private information in personal information shall be governed by the provisions on the right to privacy; where there are no provisions, the provisions on the protection of personal information shall apply," which leaves a legislative space in the *Personal Information Protection Law* to further emphasize the protection of personal private information of a natural person.[2] (Wang Chunhui and Cheng Le 2020)

2 Wang Chunhui and Cheng Le. 2020. "Interpretation on 'the Right to Privacy and the Protection of Personal Information' in the *Civil Code*." *Journal of Nanjing University of Posts and Telecommunications (Social Science Edition)*, 3rd issue.

Article 1035: Restrictions on the Processing of Personal Information

The processing of personal information shall be in compliance with the principles of lawfulness, justification, and within a necessary limit, and shall not be excessively processed; meanwhile, the following conditions shall be satisfied:

(1) consent has been obtained from the natural person or his guardian, unless otherwise provided by laws or administrative regulations;
(2) the rules for processing information are publicized;
(3) the purpose, method, and scope of the information processing are clearly indicated; and
(4) it is not in violation of laws or administrative regulations or against the agreement of both parties.

The processing of personal information includes the collection, storage, use, refinement, transmission, provision, disclosure, and the like of the personal information.

Understanding and Application

At present, legislation on the protection of personal information in China follows "the principles of lawfulness, justification, and necessity." These principles first appeared in Article 29 of the *Law on the Protection of Consumer Rights and Interests* (2013 Amendment): "In collecting and using the personal information of consumers, business operators shall adhere to the principles of legality, rationality and necessity, explicitly state the purposes, methods and scope of collection or use of information, and obtain the consent of consumers." Article 41 of the *Cybersecurity Law*, which came into force on June 1, 2017, provides that "to collect and use personal information, network operators shall follow the principles of legality, rightfulness and necessity." The principles of personal information protection in Article 1035 of the *Civil Code* are basically in line with these, which states that "the personal information of a natural person shall be processed under the principles of lawfulness, justification and necessity." However, compared with the *Cybersecurity Law* and the *Law on the Protection of Consumer Rights and Interests*, in which the two verbs "collect" and "use" precede the words "personal information," Article 1035 of the *Civil Code* uses only one verb, "process." As a matter of fact, the principles of "lawfulness, justification and necessity," set in our laws for protecting personal information have not been well implemented. In practice, as long as the information subject accepts the privacy terms provided by the information controller or processor, the principles of "lawfulness, justification and necessity" will be deemed as fulfilled. In addition to the provision that "the personal information of a natural person shall be processed under the principles of lawfulness, justification and necessity," Article 1035 of the *Civil Code* also emphasizes that the personal information of a natural person "shall not be excessively processed" and sets four legal conditions for processing personal information.[3] (Wang Chunhui and Cheng Le 2020)

Article 1036: Exemptions from Liability for Personal Information Processing

When processing personal information, an actor shall not bear civil liability in any of the following situations:

(1) the actor reasonably performs the act to the extent that the natural person or his guardian consents to;
(2) the actor reasonably processes the information disclosed by the natural person himself or the other information that has already been legally

3 Wang Chunhui and Cheng Le. 2020. "Interpretation on 'the Right to Privacy and the Protection of Personal Information' in the *Civil Code*." *Journal of Nanjing University of Posts and Telecommunications (Social Science Edition)*, 3rd issue.

disclosed, unless the said person explicitly refuses or the processing of the information infringes upon a significant interest of the person; and

(3) the actor reasonably performs the other acts to protect the public interest or the lawful rights and interests of the person.

Understanding and Application

This Article sets out three situations where an actor shall not assume any civil liability for personal information processing, the third of which is other acts reasonably conducted for protecting the public interest or the lawful rights and interests of the natural person. On the whole, exemptions from personal information processing liabilities in the *Civil Code* are subject to certain conditions and restrictions: (1) conducting the acts reasonably within the scope consented to by the natural person or his or her guardian. Under this paragraph, the subject of "consent," which provides that adult natural persons and guardians of minors or mentally ill persons shall deal with personal information within the scope consented to by the natural person or his or her guardian and shall not be over processed; (2) reasonably processing the information that a natural person has published on his or her own initiative or other information that has been legally published, except where a natural person has explicitly refused to permit the processing of information that infringes upon his or her major interests. This paragraph has two meanings: first, an actor can process information that a natural person has published on his or her own initiative, or other information that has been legally published, such as the name, telephone number, and email address of the natural person, as published to another person. But the information shall be processed under the principles of lawfulness, justification, and necessity. Second, where the processing of information relating to a natural person infringes upon his or her major interests, the actor shall not process it even if the said information has already been published on the initiatives of the natural person concerned, or the information has already been legally published; (3) Other acts reasonably conducted for protecting the public interest or the lawful rights and interests of a natural person. Here, "public interest" is a kind of interest opposite to "private interest," and it is more appropriate for the *Civil Code* to adopt the expression "public interest." In the internet age, we should limit exemptions from liability in the name of the "public interest" to the maximum extent so as to avoid infringement upon "privacy information" of a natural person. On the issue of exemptions from liability on handling the personal information for the aim of "protecting the public interest," the *Civil Code* sets an optional application between "protecting the public interest" and "protecting the lawful rights and interests of the natural person," and requires that even "for protecting the public interest or the lawful rights and interests of the natural person," the actor shall conduct personal information processing in a reasonable way to be exempted (Wang Chunhui and Cheng Le 2020).[4]

Article 1037: Right to Personal Information Determination

A natural person may retrieve or make copies of his personal information from the information processers in accordance with law. Where the person discovers that the information is incorrect, he has the right to raise an objection and request corrections or other necessary measures to be taken in a timely manner.

Where a natural person discovers that an information processer has violated the provisions of laws or administrative regulations, or breached the agreement between both parties while processing his personal information, he has the right to request the information processor to delete it in a timely manner.

4 Wang Chunhui and Cheng Le. 2020. "Interpretation on 'the Right to Privacy and the Protection of Personal Information' in the *Civil Code*." *Journal of Nanjing University of Posts and Telecommunications (Social Science Edition)*, 3rd issue.

Understanding and Application

The right to erasure and the right to rectification of a natural person for his or her personal information first appeared in the *Cybersecurity Law*. According to the *Cybersecurity Law*, there are two main situations in which citizens have the right to erase their information; one is where an individual finds that a network operator has collected or used his or her personal information in violation of the provisions of any law, administrative regulation, or bilateral agreement; the other is where the specific purpose of collecting the personal information by a network operator has already been achieved, or the period agreed upon by the parties has expired. In both circumstances, the individual has the right to require the operator to delete and stop using his or her personal information. The right of citizens to rectify the errors in information refers to situations where an individual finds that his or her personal information was collected or stored by the network operator and is erroneous, he or she shall be entitled to request the network operator to make supplements or corrections. According to Article 1037 of the *Civil Code*, the subject of personal information has three rights. First, a natural person has the right to retrieve and the right to reproduce his or her personal information from the information processor according to the law. The "information processor" here refers to the network service provider who "collects, stores, uses, processes, transmits, provides and publishes" personal information, and the subject of the personal information enjoys the right to retrieve and the right to reproduce in accordance with the law. Second, upon discovery of any error in the personal information, a natural person has the right to raise an objection and request correction and other necessary measures to be taken in a timely manner. Generally, it is difficult for the subject of personal information to find errors in the course of controlling and processing their personal information by the network operator. It is only by retrieving or reproducing his or her personal information from the information processor, according to operation of the law, that a natural person can discover the errors. This provision of the *Civil Code* makes up for the defects in the *Cybersecurity Law*. Third, upon discovering that an information processor has processed information in violation of the law and administrative regulations or the agreement between the two parties, a natural person has the right to request that it be deleted in a timely manner. Based on this paragraph in the *Civil Code*, the subjects of personal information can exercise their rights to erasure in the following two legal situations: where the information processor has processed the information in violation of the laws and administrative regulations, and where the information processor has processed the information in violation of an agreement between the two parties. The subject of personal information has the right to request the information processor to delete the information in a timely manner once the above two conditions have been fulfilled. Here, special emphasis is placed on "timely," that is, "without delay." Considering that it is difficult for network service providers to know the personal information they control and process is incorrect, it is difficult to "delete" the same. The provisions on the right to rectification and the right to erasure in both the *Civil Code* and *Cybersecurity Law* adopt the rule of "safe harbor" protection; that is, the network service provider shall "correct" or "delete" the personal information after being informed, which reflects the tolerance provided by the *Civil Code* and *Cybersecurity Law* to the network operator or information (data) service provider (Wang Chunhui and Cheng Le 2020).[5]

Article 1038: Security of Personal Information

An information processor shall not disclose or tamper with the personal information he collects and stores, and shall not illegally provide to others the personal information of a natural person without the latter's consent, unless the information, after being processed, cannot be used to identify any specific individual and cannot be restored to its original status.

5 Wang Chunhui and Cheng Le. 2020. "Interpretation on 'the Right to Privacy and the Protection of Personal Information' in the *Civil Code*." *Journal of Nanjing University of Posts and Telecommunications (Social Science Edition)*, 3rd issue.

An information processor shall take technical measures and other necessary measures to ensure the security of the personal information he collects and stores, and prevent the information from being leaked, tampered with, or lost. Where a person's personal information has been or is likely to be leaked, tampered with, or lost, he shall take remedial measures in a timely manner, notify the natural persons concerned in accordance with the regulations, and report to the relevant competent authorities.

Understanding and Application

Article 42 of the *Cybersecurity Law of the People's Republic of China* stipulates: "Network operators shall not divulge, tamper with or damage the personal information collected by them, and shall not provide personal information to any other person without the consent of the persons whose information is collected, except that the information has been processed in a manner that it is impossible to distinguish a specific person and it cannot be retraced. Network operators shall take technical measures and other necessary measures to ensure the security of personal information collected by them, and prevent information leakage, damage and loss. In the event that personal information has been or is likely to be divulged, damaged or lost, the operator shall immediately take remedial measures, and inform users in a timely manner and report it to the competent department according to relevant provisions." Article 1038 of the *Civil Code* almost follows the content of Article 42 of the *Cybersecurity Law*, but the related provision in the *Civil Code* places more emphasis on the processing of "stored" information on the basis of the information collection. Information and data storage services are important for network operators who process information based on the actual control of the information or data. Four requirements have been advanced for network operators and information processors to perform the information security obligations stipulated in the *Civil Code* and the *Cybersecurity Law*. First, an information processor shall not disclose or tamper with any personal information collected or stored thereby. In cases where the personal information collected and stored by the information processor is in accordance with the law and contract, a legal relationship of mandate management will be formed between the information operator and the subject of the personal information; further, an information processor shall not disclose or tamper with any personal information collected or stored without the consent and permission of the personal information subject or data subject. Second, without consent from a natural person, no personal information shall be illegally provided to any other person, excluding information through which the specific individual cannot be identified after processing and which cannot be restored. It is an inviolable red line that information processors are strictly prohibited from disclosing personal information collected and stored by an information processor, or under contract, without the consent of the subject of that personal information. Of course, the de-identification of personal information by means of information technology such as the desensitization of personal information does not lie within the scope of limitations stipulated in this paragraph—for the reason that a specific individual cannot be identified or restored. Third, an information processor shall take technical measures and other necessary measures to ensure the security of the personal information collected and stored thereby, and prevent information leakage, tampering, and loss. From this paragraph, "take technical measures and other necessary measures" refers to two main parts: one is the leakage prevention technology of personal information which takes encryption technology as its core, such as database encryption, database firewalls, and the desensitization of databases; the "other necessary measures," which mainly refer to various systems and mechanisms to prevent information leakage, tampering, and loss, such as the compliance management system of personal information and data, the security audit mechanism of personal information and data, the classification of personal information and data, the backup of important personal information and data, and so on. Four, for any personal information leakage, tampering, or loss that occurs or is likely to occur, remedial measures shall be taken in a timely manner; the natural person shall be notified according to the provisions, and the matter shall be reported to the competent department. Some events of data leakage, tampering, and loss are caused by subjective reasons that relate to the network operator, while others are caused by hackers who steal information, tamper with data, and illegally access the data system of network operators by the use of network technology which results in data destruction and loss. For any personal information leakage, tampering, or loss that occurs, the network operators shall take remedial measures in a timely manner, particularly in the event of any personal information "leakage, tampering, or loss" that results or is likely to result in serious consequences. Such persons shall report the matter to the competent department immediately and cooperate with the investigation of and supervision by the relevant departments. Another article has been added after Article 286 of the *Criminal Law*, Article 286 (1) in *Amendment (IX) to the Criminal Law of the People's Republic of China*, which stipulates that any network service provider who fails to perform their information network security management obligations as prescribed by law or administrative regulation, and refuses to make corrections after being ordered by the regulatory authority to take correction measures shall be investigated for criminal responsibility in the following circumstances: causing the spread of a large amount of illegal information, causing the leakage of users' information with serious consequences, and causing the loss of criminal case evidence with serious consequences (Wang Chunhui and Cheng Le 2020).[6]

See also: *Cybersecurity Law*, Article 42; *Law on Protection of Consumer Rights and Interests*, Article 29; *Regulation on Map Management*, Article 35; *Provisions of the Supreme People's Court on Several Issues concerning the Application of Law in the Trial of Cases involving Civil Disputes over Infringements upon Personal Rights and Interests through Information Networks*, Article 12.

6 Wang Chunhui and Cheng Le. 2020. "Interpretation on 'the Right to Privacy and the Protection of Personal Information' in the *Civil Code*." *Journal of Nanjing University of Posts and Telecommunications (Social Science Edition)*, 3rd issue.

Article 1039: Confidentiality Obligations of State Organs and Their Staff on Personal Information

State organs and the chartered institutions assuming administrative functions, as well as their staff, shall keep confidential the privacy and the personal information of natural persons known to them during the performance of their responsibilities, and shall not disclose or illegally provide it to others.

Understanding and Application

Article 14 of *Several Provisions of the State Council on Online Government Services* stipulates: "Where a government service institution or any of its staff members divulges, sells or illegally offers to any other party the personal information, privacy or trade secret to which it or he has access in the process of performing its or his duties, or fails to perform its or his duties pursuant to the law, neglects its or his duties, abuses its or his power, practices favoritism, or makes falsification, it or he shall be held liable in accordance with the law." Besides the state organs and their staff members, the departments assuming network supervision and administration functions should also include other statutory institutions that assume administrative supervision functions assigned by state supervisory and administration organs to engage in network supervision and administration. State organs and their staff members, as well as institutions and all personnel of these institutions assigned by state organs to engage in network supervision functions, have access to a large amount of personal information, especially the personal privacy information, in the course of fulfilling their duties. This kind of information shall be kept confidential and shall not be disclosed or be illegally provided to others. Whereas personal information has the dual attributes of personality rights and property rights, while the right to personal privacy information is only a kind of personality right, the legislation protecting personal information in China should focus on the protection of a natural person's privacy information—and despite the provision of protecting "private information" within personal information, the *Civil Code* is not a special law for the protection of personal information. This led to the enactment of the *Personal Information Protection Law* to regulate the rights of claimants, mechanisms of relief and protection, and circulation transactions involving non private information of an individual (Wang Chunhui and Cheng Le 2020).[7]

Article 1194: Tort Liability of a Network User or Network Service Provider

Network users and network service providers who, through the network, infringe upon the civil law rights and interests of another person shall bear tort liability, unless otherwise provided by law.

Understanding and Application

Network infringement refers to all kinds of acts infringing upon the civil rights or interests of another person, which is not a specific infringement upon a certain right (interest), nor does it belong to special torts with certain particularities in their constitutive elements, but refers to all infringements that occur in the internet space. The tort that a network user commits as against the civil rights or interests of another person can be divided into the following types: The first is infringing upon personality rights, which is manifested as: (1) infringing upon any other's right to name by misappropriation or counterfeiting; (2) infringing upon the rights to likeness by using the likeness of any likeness rights holder without consent;

7 Wang Chunhui and Cheng Le. 2020. "Interpretation on 'the Right to Privacy and the Protection of Personal Information' in *Civil Code*." *Journal of Nanjing University of Posts and Telecommunications (Social Science Edition)*, 3rd issue.

(3) infringing upon the right of reputation by publishing works that contain insulting or defamatory content about another person; (4) infringing upon the right to privacy by illegally intruding in the computer of another person, illegally intercepting information transmitted by others, publishing personal information relating to other persons without consent, and sending spam communications. The second is infringing upon property interests. It is common to infringe upon property interests online because of the convenience and commercial value of network activities, such as stealing funds from other person's online bank account, infringing upon network virtual property, online game software, and virtual currency and the like. The third is infringing upon intellectual property rights, which is mainly in the form of infringements of copyright and trademarks. Infringing copyright protection means transmitting the work of other persons in digital form without authorization by accessing the persons' database: Infringing trademarks, such as using others' trademarks on a website, deliberately making consumers mistake their website for the trademark owner's website, and applying for or registering a domain name that is the same or similar to a trademark with an established reputation in violation of the principle of good faith. The term "network service provider" has a broad meaning, which includes not only technical service providers, but also content service providers. The former mainly refers to the network subject who provides access and cache services, information storage space, and search and link services, and does not supply information to a network user directly. The latter refers to the network subject that actively offers content to the network user. The content service provider has the same legal status as that of publishers and shall be responsible for the authenticity and legality of the uploaded content, which leads to the assumption of tort liability for providing information, such as fabricating false facts to defame others and publishing and infringing the copyright of films and television works. The general rules of network tort liability include the rules of network users' liability for committing a tort on the website of any other person, and the liability of network service providers for torts committed on their own networks. No matter which one of the above, the principle of fault liability shall be applied, and the network user or network service provider shall assume liability for

committing a tort. The statement "unless otherwise provided by law" in this Article refers to circumstances stipulated in other laws which provide that the net user and network service provider shall assume civil liability for infringing upon the civil rights and interests of any other person. For example, where these kind of torts are specially stipulated in *E-Commerce Law*, *Law on the Protection of Consumer Rights and Interests*, and *Food Safety Law*, the tortious liability of the parties shall be determined in accordance with these special provisions.

See also: *Regulation on the Protection of the Right to Communicate Works to the Public over Information Networks*, Articles 13–17, Articles 20–24; *Provisions of the Supreme People's Court on Several Issues concerning the Application of Law in Hearing Civil Dispute Cases Involving Infringement of the Right of Dissemination on Information Networks*.

Article 1195: Notification Rules of "Safe Harbor" Protection for Network Tort Liability

Where a network user commits a tortious act through using the network service, the right holder is entitled to notify the network service provider to take such necessary measures as deletion, block, or disconnection. The notice shall include the preliminary evidence establishing the tort and the real identity information of the right holder.

After receiving the notice, the network service provider shall timely forward the notice to the relevant network user and take necessary measures based on the preliminary evidence establishing the tort and the type of service complained about.

Where it fails to take necessary measures in time, it shall assume joint and several liability for the aggravated part of the damage with the network user.

The right holder who causes damage to the network user or network service provider due to erroneous notification shall bear tort liability, unless otherwise provided by law.

Understanding and Application

A right holder's right of notice. Where a network user commits a tort through the network services of others, the network service provider shall not assume liability by reason that it cannot bear the obligation to review a large amount of information. The way to handle these kind of infringement disputes is to apply the "notice-take down" procedure; that is, if the right holder believes that his or her own right has been infringed, he or she shall be entitled to notify the network service provider to take necessary measures, such as deleting, blocking, or disconnecting the information published by a network user so as to eliminate the adverse effects. The main purpose of applying this procedure is to conditionally exempt the network service provider from assuming indirect tort liability for the direct torts committed by a network user. The network service provider, after receiving notification from the owner, shall carry out two actions: first, transfer the notification to the relevant network user in a timely manner and, second, immediately take such necessary measures as deletion, block, or disconnection based on the prima facie evidence of the tort and the type of service. A network service provider that fulfills these conditions shall not assume tort liability, while a network service provider who fails to take necessary measures in a timely manner shall be jointly and severally liable for any additional harm caused to the network user. Where a network service provider actively commits a tort, the network service provider shall assume tort liability rather than applying the "notice-take down" procedure to secure exemption from liability. The main content of the notice should include preliminary evidence to prove the infringement and the true identity information of the right holder, without which the notice will be determined invalid. Measures shall be taken to punish a right holder who wrongly exercises the right to notice: if notification by the owner causes a loss to a network user or the network service provider by reason of that erroneous notice, the right holder shall be liable for compensation, unless otherwise provided by law.

Article 1196: Counter-Notification Rules of "Safe Harbor" Protection for Network Tort Liability

After receiving the forwarded notice, the network user may submit a declaration of non-infringement to the network service provider, which shall include the preliminary evidence of non-infringement and the real identity information of the network user.

After receiving the declaration, the network service provider shall forward it to the right holder who issued the notice and inform him that he may file a complaint to the relevant department or file a lawsuit with the people's court. The network service provider shall timely terminate the measures taken where, within a reasonable period of time after the forwarded declaration reaches the right holder, it fails to receive notice that the right holder has filed a complaint or a lawsuit.

Understanding and Application

After the right of notice that necessary measures should be taken on the information published by a network user has been exercised by the right holder and this notice has been sent from the network service provider to the relevant network user, the network user shall have the right of counter-notification, and may submit a statement of non-existence of tort to the network service provider. The statement of counter-notification shall include preliminary evidence to prove the non-existence of tort and the true identity of the network user, without which the counter-notice will be ineffective. If a right holder does not notify the network service provider within a reasonable period that he/she has already complained to a relevant authority or instituted an action in a people's court, the network service provider shall immediately terminate the measures of deletion, block, and disconnection of the information provided by the network user to protect the right of expression of the counter-notification right holder, that is, the network users.

Article 1197: The Joint and Several Liability of the Network Service Provider and Network User

A network service provider who knows or should have known that a network user has infringed upon the civil law rights and interests of another person by using its network services, but fails to take necessary measures, shall assume joint and several liability with the network user.

Understanding and Application

To determine what is "knowing" here is very difficult in practice. Judges should consider various factors in combination and coordination, and in specific cases use a reasonable criterion to make his/her judgment. Generally, there are three principles to followed: First, the criteria should be different for different types of network service providers. Specifically, the criteria for "knowing" should be more stringent with network service providers who provide access and cache services than with those who provide other services. Access service providers are those who connect users to websites and all information, including the infringement information can only be transmitted via an access service provider. However, this transmission is instant and the amount of information transmitted is huge, so it is impossible for the service provider to check all the information. If the criteria are the same for all with insufficient distinction, access service providers may assume heavier liability than they actually should, and normal service provision may be hampered. Second, the criteria should vary according to different protection objects. For copyright, if the infringement is not very obvious, network service providers shall generally not be held accountable for infringement as long as they have not manually tampered the information uploaded by a user. For acts that may constitute the defamation of another person's reputation, improper use of the likeness of another person, or publishing the personal information of another person illegally, it can be difficult to determine whether they are torts without going to trial. Network service providers are not judicial organs, so it is inappropriate to require professional legal knowledge and skills from them to make such judgments or to check every single piece of information uploaded by a network user. Network service providers shall be exempted from liability when the acts are considered not torts from the perspective of an ordinary person. Third, network service providers that provide technical services have no obligation to carry out universal check, so in judicial practice caution should be exerted when trying to determine whether a network service provider "knows" that a network user is infringing upon a civil right or the interests of another person through its network services. If the criteria is too stringent, network service providers would actually have to carry the obligation of a universal review. If this is the case, network service providers would face a much higher operational cost and the development of the network industry on the whole may be hampered.

Article 1226: Medical Institutions' Liability for Violating Patients' Right to Privacy and Confidentiality Obligations for Personal Information

Medical institutions and their medical staff shall keep their patients' private information and personal information confidential. Anyone who divulges the private information or personal information of a patient or discloses his medical records without the patient's consent shall bear tort liability.

Understanding and Application

In order to accurately diagnose a disease, patients often give their doctor private and personal information. The medical history data recorded in this process is private and the personal information belongs to the patient. As for medical institutions and their staff, they shall keep confidential private and personal information, and the medical history data of the patient. If any privacy data and personal information is divulged, or any of the medical history data of a patient is opened to the public without the consent of the patient, the medical institution shall be liable for compensation. In such cases the medical institution shall be assumed to have infringed on the patients' right to privacy and personal information, leaving the institution liable to a claim for personality rights, as stipulated in *Book Four (Personality Rights)* of the *Civil Code*. Article 995 of the *Civil Code* stipulates: "where the personality rights are infringed upon, a victim has the right to request the actor to assume civil liability in accordance with this Code and other laws"; the patient may not only claim compensation based on Article 1226, he/she may also claim other damages from the medical institution. However, compared with the general rules, the Article here is a special provision, and it will be more proper for the victims to claim compensation from the medical situation.

See also: *Civil Code*, Article 995; *Law on Practicing Doctors*, Article 22; *Interpretation of the Supreme People's Court on Problems Regarding the Ascertainment of Compensation Liability for Emotional Damages in Civil Torts*, Article 1.

APPENDIX II

List of Foreign Laws and Regulations Concerning Data Protection

Country / Organization	Law
Argentina	Law for the Protection of Personal Data
Azerbaijan	Law of the Republic of Azerbaijan on Information, Informatization, and the Protection of Information
	Law of the Republic of Azerbaijan on Right to Obtain Information
Ireland	A Practical Guide to Personal Data Breach Notifications under the GDPR
	Data Sharing and Governance Bill
	General Scheme of the Online Safety and Media Regulation Bill
	Data Protection Act 2018
Egypt	Data Protection Law
	مكافحة جرائم تقنية المعلومات
Estonia	Personal Data Protection Act
Angola	Law 22/11 on Personal Data Protection
Austria	Bundesgesetz über den Schutz personenbezogener Daten
	Bundesgesetz vom 18. Oktober 1978 über den Schutz personenbezogener

Country / Organization	Law
Australia	Australian Privacy Principles (PPs) 1988 Privacy Amendment (Public Health Contact Information) Act 2020
	Personally Controlled Electronic Health Records Act
	Notifiable Data Breaches Act
	Privacy Amendment (Privacy Sector) Act
	Customer Data Rights Bill
	Information Security Management Framework
	Privacy Act
Barbados	Computer Misuse Act
Papua New Guinea	Cybercrime Code Act 2016
Bahamas	Data Protection (Privacy of Personal Information) Act
Pakistan	Prevention of Electronic Crimes Bill
Paraguay	Law for the Protection of Personal Data
Brazil	Protection of Software, Intellectual Property Rights of Software Products and Other Relevant Regulations
	Crimes cibernéticos sob a égide da Lei 12.737/2012
	Lei Geral de Proteção de Dados Pessoais
Bulgaria	Personal Data Protection Act
	Access to Public Information Act
	Protection of Classified Information Act
Benin	Loi n° 2017–20 portant code du numérique en République du Bénin
Belgium	Act of 8 December 1992 on the Protection of Privacy in Relation to the Processing of Personal Data
	The Act of 21 March 2018 modifying the act on the installation and use of cameras (Camera Act)
	The Act of 30 July 2018 on the protection of natural persons with regard to the processing of their personal data ("Privacy Act")
Peru	Personal Data Protection Law
Iceland	Act on Data Protection and the Processing of Personal Data

Country / Organization	Law
Botswana	Data Protection Act
Poland	Act on the Protection of Personal Data
Burkina Faso	Law N° 010- 2004/AN Portant Protection des Données à Caractère Personnel
Denmark	Danish Data Protection Act
	Act on Processing of Personal Data
	Act on the Reuse of Public Sector Information
Germany	Second EU Data Protection Adaptation and Implementation Act
	Bundesdatenschutzgesetz
	Hessisches Datenschutzgesetz
	Federal Data Protection Act
	Teleservices Act
	IT Sicherheitsgesetz
Togo	Data Protection Law
Russia	Federal Law on Personal Data (No. 152-FZ)
	the Federal Law On Security of Critical Russian Federation Information Infrastructure
	The Federal Law (No. 149-FZ of July 27, 2006) On Information, Informational Technologies and the Protection of Information
	Federal Law No. 242-FZ, On the Introduction of Amendments to Certain Legislative Acts of the Russian Federation with regard to the Clarification of the Procedure for the Processing of Personal Data in Data Telecommunications Networks
	The Federal Law (No. 184 of 27.12.2002) on Technical Regulation
	Федеральный закон от 01.05.2019 n 90-ФЗ "О внесении изменений в Федеральный закон "О связи" и Федеральный закон" Об информации, информационных технологиях и о защите информации
	Федеральный закон от 21 июля 2014 г N 242 ФЗ О внесении изменений в отдельные за
	Доктрины информационной безопасности
	Russia's New "Bloggers Law"

Country / Organization	Law
France	Proposition de loi visant à lutter contre les contenus haineux sur internet
	la loi n° 2004-801 du 6 août 2004 relative à la protection des personnes physiques à l'égard des traitements de données à caractère personnel transpose
	Personal Data Protection Act
	LOI n° 2016–1321 du 7 octobre 2016 pour une République numérique
	Act NO. 78–17 of 6 January 1978 on Data Processing, Data Files and Individual Liberties
	LOI n° 2019-759 du 24 juillet 2019 portant création d'une taxe sur les services numériques et modification de la trajectoire de baisse de l'impôt sur les sociétés
The Philippines	Data Privacy Act
African Union	Personal Data Protection Guidelines for Africa
	African Union Convention on Cyber Security and Personal Data Protection
Finland	Data Protection Act
	Personal Data Protection Act
Colombia	Personal Data Protection law 2012 (Law 1581/2012)
Grenada	Electronic Transaction Act
Czech Republic	Personal Data Protection Act
	Personal Data Processing Act
Republic of Korea	Act on Promotion of Utilization of Information and Communication Network and Data Protection
	Personal Information Protection Act
	공공기관 개인정보 보호법
	Regulations on Establishing Information System Security and Protecting Personal Information Privacy
	로봇기본법안
	Act on the Protection, Use, etc., of Location Information

Country / Organization	Law
	정보보호산업의 진흥에 관한 법률
	정보보호산업의진흥에관한법률
	Credit Information Use and Protection Act
	Act on the Development of Cloud Computing and Protection of its Users
	Act on Promotion of Information and Communications Network Utilization and Information Protection
	Intelligent Robots Development and Distribution Promotion Act
The Netherlands	Wet op de inlichtingen en veiligheidsdiensten
	Data Protection Act
Canada	Digital Charter Implementation Act, 2020
	Deposit Insurance Corporation Deposit Insurance Information Regulations
	Electronic Application and Provision of Information (GST/HST) Regulations
	Electronic Documents and Electronic Information Regulations
	High Risk Child Sex Offender Database Act
	Personal Information Protection and Electronic Documents Act
	Broadcast Information Regulations
	Maritime Liability and Information Return Regulations
	Access to Information Regulations
	Security of Canada Information Sharing Act
	Input Tax Credit Information (GST/HST) Regulations
	Digital Chapter
	Digital Privacy Act
	Security of Information Act
	Access to Information Act
	Credit Notes and Debit Memo Information (GST/HST) Regulations
	Credit Information (Insurance Company) Regulations
	Privacy Act
	Hazardous Materials Information Review Act

Country / Organization	Law
Zimbabwe	Cybersecurity and Data Protection Bill
	The Access to Information and Protection of Privacy Act
Organization for Economic Co-operation and Development	Principles and Guidelines for Access to Research Data from Public Funding
	Recommendation of the Council concerning Guidelines Governing the Protection of Privacy and Trans-border Flows of Personal Data
	Declaration on Trans-border Data Flows
	OECD Guidelines on the Protection of Privacy and Trans-border Flows of Personal Data
Qatar	Law No. 13 of 2016 Concerning Privacy and Protection of Personal Data
Croatia	Personal Data Protection Act
Kenya	Kenya Data Protection Bill
	Data Protection Act
Latvia	Personal Data Protection Law
Laos	Law on Electronic Data Protection
Lithuania	Law on the Legal Protection of Personal Data
	Guidelines Concerning Computerized Personal Data Files
Liechtenstein	Datenshutzgesetz (DSG)
United States of America	Personal Data Protection and Privacy Principles
	Guidelines for the Regulation of Computerized Personal Data Files
	Act Concerning Use of Nominal Data in Computer Processing
	Data Privacy, Ethics and Protection: Guidance Note on Big Data for Achievement of the 2030 Agenda
Luxembourg	Specific Provision for the Protection of Persons with Regard to the Processing of Personal Data in the Electronic Communications Act
	Act of 1 August 2018 on the Organisation of the National Data Protection Commission and the General Data Protection Framework
	Law No. 677/2001 on the Protection of Individuals with regard to the Processing of Personal Data and Free Movement of Such Data
	The Law of 2 August 2002 on the Protection of Persons with Regard to the Processing of Personal Data

Country / Organization	Law
Romania	Law No. 102/2005 on the Setting Up, Organisation and Functioning of the National Supervisory Authority for Personal Data Processing
	Data Protection Act
Malta	Data Protection Act
Malaysia	Personal Data Protection Act
Mauritius	Cybersecurity Act of 2012
	Data Protection Act
United States of America	Secure and Trusted Communications Networks Act
	Children's Online Privacy Protection Act
	Insurance Data Security Model Law
	Protecting Data at the Border Act
	Clarifying Lawful Overseas Use of Data Act ("Cloud" Act)
	Telephone Robocall Abuse Criminal Enforcement and Deterrence Act
	Telephone Consumer Protection Act
	Cable Communications Policy Act
	Computer Matching and Privacy Protection Act
	Telecommunication Act
	ESign Act
	Electronic Communications Privacy Act
	The Electronic Freedom of Information Act (Amendment)
	Pallone-Thune Traced (Pallone-Thune Telephone Robocall Abuse Criminal Enforcement and Deterrence)
	Countering Foreign 5 Propaganda and Disinformation Act
	Personal Data Privacy and Security Act
	Secure Public Networks Act
	Fair Credit Reporting Act
	Critical Infrastructure Information Act
	A Grand Bargain On Data Privacy Legislation For America

Country / Organization	Law
	Safe Harbor Privacy Principles
	Restoring Internet Freedom Order Draft
	Genetic Information Nondiscrimination Act
	Computer Fraud and Abuse Act
	California Consumer Privacy Act
	Computer Security Enhancement Act (Amendment)
	Drivers Privacy Protection Act
	California Consumer Privacy Act Regulation
	California Privacy Rights Act
	Family Educational Rights and Privacy Act
	Health Insurance Portability and Accountability Act
	Financial Services Modernization Act (Gramm-Leach-Bliley Act)
	Right to Financial Privacy Act
	Open Government Data Act
	Open Government Directive
	Broadband Data Act
	The Fair Credit Reporting Act
	Federal Information Security Management Act
	Federal Information Security Amendment Act
	Video Privacy Protection Act
	Facial Recognition Technology Warrant Act
	Biometric Information Privacy Act Illinois
	Data Security and Breach Notification Act
	Data Breach Prevention and Compensation Act of 2018
	Digital Global Access Policy Act of 2019
	Framework for Improving Critical Infrastructure Cybersecurity
	Promoting United States Wireless Leadership Act
	The Foreign Intelligence Surveillance Act (Amendment)

Country / Organization	Law
	Executive Order on Strengthening the Cybersecurity
	Cyber Security Enhancement Act
	Network Security Framework
	Cyber Vulnerability Remediation Act
	Cybersecurity Information Sharing Act
	Cyber Vulnerability Disclosure Reporting Act
	Cyber Intelligence Sharing and Protection Act
	Network Neutrality Act
	Equitable Data Collection and Disclosure on COVID 19 Act
	Security and Privacy Controls for Information Systems and Organizations
	Freedom of Information Act
	Video Privacy Protection Act
	Self-discipline Norms for Effective Protection of Privacy
	Active Cyber Defense Certainty Act
	USA Freedom Act
	Blocking the Property of Certain Persons Engaging in Significant Malicious Cyber-Enabled Activities
Morocco	Law No. 09–08 relating to protection of individuals with regard to the processing of personal data
Mexico	The Ley Federal de Protección de Datos Personales en Posesión de los Prticulares (Federal Law on the Protection of Personal Data Possessed by Private Persons)
South Africa	Proclamation No. R21 of 2020 on the Commencement of Certain Sections of the Protection of Personal Information Act
	Protection of Personal Information Act of 2018
	Protection of Personal Information Act of 2013
	Consumer Protection Act
	Promotion of Access to Information Act
	Act Relating to Personal Data Registers

Country / Organization	Law
Southern African Development Community	Model Data Protection Act
Nigeria	Personal Data Act of 2000
	Nigeria Data Protection Regulation (NDPR)
Norway	Lov om behandling av personopplysninger (personopplysningsloven) Lov data of 2018
	Personal Data Regulations
	Act Relating to the Processing of Personal Data
European Union	Guidelines for Extraterritorial Application of GDPR
	Guidelines for the Protection of Personal Data in the Internet of Vehicles
	Council Framework Decision 2005 222 JHA of 24 February 2005 on attacks against information systems
	Directive on Copyright in the Digital Singles Market
	Telecom Industry Personal Data Processing and Privacy Protection Directive
	Electronic Communication Data Protection Directive
	EU e-Evidence Regulation
	Framework for Free Flow of Non-Personal Data
	Regulation on the Free Flow of Non-personal Data
	EDPS Guidelines on Assessing the Proportionality of Measures that Limit the Fundamental Rights to Privacy and to the Protection of Personal Data
	Guidelines on Personal Data Breach Notification under Regulation 2016/679
	EU Stronger Protection, New Opportunities – Commission Guidance on the Direct Application of the General Data Protection Regulation
	Guidelines 2/2020 on Articles 46 (2) (a) and 46 (3) (b) of Regulation 2016/679 for Transfers of Personal Data between EEA and Non-EEA Public Authorities and Bodies

Country / Organization	Law
	Guidelines on the Right to be Forgotten in Search Engine Cases under GDPR
	Directive 2006_24_EC on the Retention of Data Generated or Processed in Connection
	2002/58/EC (Directive on Privacy and Electronic Communications) Concerning the Processing of Personal Data and the Protection of Privacy in the Electronic Communications Sector
	Convention for the Protection of Individuals with Regard to Automatic Processing of Personal Data
	Recommendation 1/99 on Invisible and Automatic Processing of Personal Data on the Internet Performed by Software and Hardware
	Regulation (EC) No. 460_2004 of European Network and Information Security Agency
	Guidelines on the Processing of Personal Data through Video Equipment
	Regulations Regarding the Protection of Individuals Related to the Processing of Personal Data by the European Community and Organizations and the Free Flow of Such Data
	Guidelines for the Protection of Individuals with Regard to the Collections and processing on the Information Highway
	Guidance on Automated Individual Decision-making and Profiling for the Purposes of Regulation
	General Principles for the Protection of Privacy on the Internet
	Convention on Cybercrime
	Council Directive 2008_114_EC European Critical Infrastructures
	Draft Report with Recommendations to the Commission on Civil Law Rules on Robotics
	The Charter of Fundamental Rights of the European Union
	Guidance on Cross-Border International Data Transfer
	Proposal for a regulation of the European Parliament and of the Council on the European data governance (Data Governance Act)

Country / Organization	Law
	Directive 2006/24/EC of the European Parliament and of the Council of 15 March 2006 on the Retention of Data Generated or Processed in Connection with the Provision of Publicly Available Electronic Communications Services of Public Communication Networks and Amending Directive
	Directive 95/46/EC on Data Protection
	Guidelines on the Concepts of "Controller" and "Processor" under the GDPR
	Guidelines for Application of Data Protection by Design and Default
	Guidelines for the Protection of Individuals with Regard to the Collection and Processing of Personal Data on Information Highways
	The General Data Protection Regulation (GDPR)
	Guidelines on Consent under Regulation
	Guidelines on Transparency under Regulation
	Proposal for a Regulation on Privacy and Electronic Communications
	The First Annual Review of the Functioning of the EU–US Privacy Shield
	Guidelines on the Targeting of Social Media Users
	Mobile applications in support of contact tracing for Covid-19
	Data Protection Directive (EU) 2016/680 for Police and Criminal Justice Authorities
	EU Coordinated Risk Assessment of the Cybersecurity of 5G Networks
Council of Europe	Convention for the Protection of Individuals with regard to Automatic Processing of Personal Data
	Directive 2002/58/EC of the European Parliament and of the Council of 12 July 2002 concerning the processing of personal data and the protection of privacy in the electronic communications sector

Country / Organization	Law
European Parliament	EU data protection in police and judicial cooperation matters: Rights of suspects and defendants under attack by law enforcement demands
	Network and Information Security Directive
EU-US	Safe Harbor Agreement Framework
	The EU-US Privacy Shield Framework Principles
Portugal	Lei no. 58/2019 – Lei de execução do RGPD
Japan	電子計算機処理に係るデータ保護管理規程
	電子行政オープンデータ戦略
	独立行政法人等の保有する個人情報の保護に関する法律
	高度情報通信ネットワーク社会形成基本法
	個人情報の保護に関する法律
	官民データ活用推進基本法
	個人情報保護基本法制に関する大綱
	行政機関の保有する個人情報の保護に関する法律
	不正アクセス行為の禁止等に関する法律
	犯罪捜査のための通信傍受に関する法律
	サイバーセキュリティ基本法
	Act on the Protection of Personal Information Held by Administrative Organs
	行政機関の保有する個人情報の保護に関する法律
	高度情報通信社会に向けた基本方針
	行政機関の保有する個人情報の保護に関する法律
Swiss	Federal Act on Data Protection
Sweden	Personal Data Act Amendment
	Data Act
Senegal	Personal Data Act
	Loi n°2008–12 sur la protection des données à caractère personnel
	The Processing of Personal Data Law
	Policy Framework for the Responsible Use of Face Recognition Technology

Country / Organization	Law
Cyprus	Law 2015 (I) of 2018 Providing for the Protection of Natural Persons with regard to the Processing of Personal Data and for the Free Movement of Such Data
Slovakia	Performances and Phonograms Treaty
	Act 18/2017 on Personal Data Protection and Amendment and Supplementing Certain Acts
	Act on Protection of Personal Data in Information System
Slovenia	Personal Data Protection Act
Thailand	The Personal Data Protection Act
	Official Information Act
	Thailand Cybersecurity Act
Tunisia	Data Protection Act
Turkmenistan	The Law of Turkmenistan No. 519-V 'On Information about Private Life and its Protection
Uganda	Data Protection and Privacy Bill
	Data Protection and Privacy Act
Ukraine	Ukraine Cybersecurity Cooperation Act of 2017
Uzbekistan	Personal Data Law
Spain	Ley Orgánica 3/2018, de 5 de Diciembre, de Protección de Datos Personales y Garantía de los Derechos Digitales
	Cookie Usage Guidelines
ECOWAS	Supplementary Act A/SA.1/01/10 on Personal Data Protection
Greece	Protection of Personal Data and Measures for the Implementation of the GDPR (Law 4624/2019)

Country / Organization	Law
Singapore	Report on Public Consultation on the Draft Cybersecurity Bill
	Trusted Data Sharing Framework
	Identity Information Protection Guidelines
	Guide on Developing a Data Protection Management Program
	Guide to Data Protection Impact Assessments
	Model Data Protection Code For The Private Sector
	Cybersecurity Strategy
	Personal Data Protection Act, PDPA
	Cybersecurity Law
	Cybersecurity Code of Practice for Critical Information Infrastructure
New Zealand	Privacy Act
	The Algorithm Charter for Aotearoa New Zealand
Hungary	Law on the Protection of Personal Data and the Disclosure of Data of Public Interest
	Act on Informational Self-Determination and Freedom of Information
Asia-Pacific Economic Cooperation	APEC Privacy Framework
	APEC Cross Border Privacy Rules
Israel	The Privacy Protection Law
Italy	Personal Data Protection Code
	Decreto-Legge 21 settembre 2019, n. 105

Country / Organization	Law
India	The Information Technology (Reasonable Security Practices and Procedures and Sensitive Personal Data or Information) Rules
	Non-Personal Data Governance Framework
	White Paper on Data Protection in India
	Information Technology Act
	Right to Information Act of 2005
	Freedom of Information Act of 2002
	Personal Data Protection Bill (Draft)
	Regulations on the Administration of Credit Information Companies 2005
Indonesia	Personal Data Protection Bill (Draft)
	Electronic System and Transaction Operation Government Regulation 82/2012
	Law No. 11 of 2008 on Electronic information and transactions
United Kingdom	Freedom of Information Act of 2000
	Data Protection Act of 2018
	Code of Practice for Protecting Children's Online Privacy
	Electronic Communication Act
	The Data Protection (Designated Codes of Practice) (No. 2) Order
	Security of Network and Information Systems
	The United Kingdom's Official Secrets Act
	Computer Misuse Act
	ICO GDPR Guidance Data Protection Impact Assessments (Draft)
	Electronic Signatures Regulations
	Lawful Basis for Processing Special Category Data
	Communications Data Acquisition Regulations
	Guide to the General Data Protection Regulation
	Data Protection Act
Vietnam	Cyber Security Law

Country / Organization	Law
Iran	Personal Data Protection and Safeguarding Draft Act
Zambia	Electronic Communications and Transactions Act
	Information and Communication Technologies Act
Chile	Law for the Protection of Private Life

Index